Lecture Notes in Computer Science 4856

Commenced Publication in 1973
Founding and Former Series Editors:
Gerhard Goos, Juris Hartmanis, and Jan van Leeuwen

T0223193

Feng Bao   San Ling   Tatsuaki Okamoto
Huaxiong Wang   Chaoping Xing (Eds.)

Cryptology and Network Security

6th International Conference, CANS 2007
Singapore, December 8-10, 2007
Proceedings

 Springer

Volume Editors

Feng Bao
Institute for Infocomm Research
Singapore
E-mail: baofeng@i2r.a-star.edu.sg

San Ling
Nanyang Technological University
Singapore
E-mail: lingsan@ntu.edu.sg

Tatsuaki Okamoto
NTT Laboratories
Japan
E-mail: okamoto.tatsuaki@lab.ntt.co.jp

Huaxiong Wang
Nanyang Technological University
Singapore
E-mail: hxwang@ntu.edu.sg

Chaoping Xing
Nanyang Technological University
Singapore
E-mail: matxcp@nus.edu.sg

Library of Congress Control Number: 2007939802

CR Subject Classification (1998): E.3, D.4.6, F.2.1, C.2, J.1, K.4.4, K.6.5

LNCS Sublibrary: SL 4 – Security and Cryptology

ISSN   0302-9743
ISBN-10   3-540-76968-4 Springer Berlin Heidelberg New York
ISBN-13   978-3-540-76968-2 Springer Berlin Heidelberg New York

Springer is a part of Springer Science+Business Media

springer.com

© Springer-Verlag Berlin Heidelberg 2007
Printed in Germany

Typesetting: Camera-ready by author, data conversion by Scientific Publishing Services, Chennai, India
Printed on acid-free paper   SPIN: 12196395   06/3180   5 4 3 2 1 0

Preface

The sixth International Conference on Cryptology and Network Security (CANS 2007) was held at the Grand Plaza Park Hotel, Singapore, 8–10 December 2007. The conference was sponsored by *Nanyang Technological University* and the *Lee Foundation*, Singapore.

The goal of CANS is to promote research on all aspects of cryptology and network security, as well as to build a bridge between research on cryptography and network security. The first International Conference on Cryptology and Network Security was held in Taipei, Taiwan, in 2001. The second one was held in San Francisco, California, USA, on September 26–28, 2002, the third in Miami, Florida, USA, on September 24–26, 2003, the fourth in Xiamen, Fujian, China, on December 14–16, 2005 and the fifth in Suzhou, Jiangsu, China, on December 8–10, 2006.

The program committee accepted 17 papers from 68 submissions. The reviewing process took nine weeks, each paper was carefully evaluated by at least three members of the program committee. We appreciate the hard work of the members of the program committee and the external referees who gave many hours of their valuable time.

In addition to the contributed papers, there were six invited talks:

- Artur Ekert: *Quantum Cryptography*
- Christian Kurtsiefer: *Aspects of Practical Quantum Key Distribution Schemes*
- Keith Martin: *A Bird's-Eye View of Recent Research in Secret Sharing*
- Mitsuru Matsui: *The State-of-the-Art Software Optimization of Block Ciphers and Hash Functions*
- Josef Pieprzyk: *Analysis of Modern Stream Ciphers*
- David Pointcheval: *Adaptive Security for Password-Based Authenticated Key Exchange in the Universal-Composability Framework.*

We would like to thank all the people involved in organising this conference. In particular, we would like to thank the organising committee for their time and efforts, and Krystian Matusiewicz for his help with LaTeX.

December 2007

Feng Bao
San Ling
Tatsuaki Okamoto
Huaxiong Wang
Chaoping Xing

6th International Conference on Cryptology and Network Security (CANS 2007)

Sponsored by

Nanyang Technological University, Singapore
Lee Foundation, Singapore

CANS Steering Committee

Yvo Desmedt	University College London, UK
Matt Franklin	UC, David, USA
Yi Mu	University of Wollongong, Australia
David Pointcheval	CNRS and ENS, France
Huaxiong Wang	Nanyang Technological University, Singapore

General Chairs

San Ling	Nanyang Technological University, Singapore
Chaoping Xing	National University of Singapore, Singapore

Program Chairs

Feng Bao	Institute for Infocomm Research, Singapore
Tatsuaki Okamoto	NTT Labs, Japan

Program Committee

Michel Abdalla	École Normale Supérieure, France
Colin Boyd	QUT, Australia
Mike Burmester	Florida State University, USA
Hao Chen	Fudan University, China
Liqun Chen	HP Bristol Labs, UK
Robert Deng	SMU, Singapore
Alex Dent	Royal Holloway, UK
Eiichiro Fujisaki	NTT Labs, Japan
Jun Furukawa	NEC, Japan
David Galindo	École Normale Supérieure, France
Aline Gouget	Gemalto, France
Amir Herzberg	Bar Ilan University, Israel

Atsuo Inomata   JST, Japan
Akinori Kawachi   Titech, Japan
Angelos Keromytis   Columbia University
Aggelos Kiayias   University of Connecticut, USA
Hiroaki Kikuchi   Tokai University, Japan
Eike Kiltz   CWI, Netherlands
Kwangjo Kim   Info. and Comm. University, Korea
Arjen Lenstra   EPFL, Switzerland
Peng Chor Leong   NTU, Singapore
Javier Lopez   University of Malaga, Spain
Mitsuru Matsui   Mitsubishi Electric, Japan
Yi Mu   University of Wollongong, Australia
Joern Mueller-Quade   University of Karlsruhe, Germany
Antonio Nicolosi   NYU & Stanford University, USA
Kenny Paterson   Royal Holloway, UK
Olivier Pereira   UCL, Belgium
Giuseppe Persiano   Università di Salerno, Italy
Josef Pieprzyk   Macquarie University, Australia
C. Pandu Rangan   IIT, India
Frederic Rousseau   EADS, France
Rei Safavi-Naini   University of Calgary, Canada
Berry Schoenmakers   TU Eindhoven, Netherlands
Jorge Villar   Universitat Politècnica de Catalunya, Spain
Xiaoyun Wang   Shandong University, China
Duncan Wong   City University of Hong Kong, China
Sung-Ming Yen   National Central University, Taiwan
Yiqun Lisa Yin   Security Consultant, USA
Yunlei Zhao   Fudan University, China
Jianying Zhou   I^{2}R, Singapore

Organising Committee

Huaxiong Wang   Nanyang Technological University, Singapore
Eiji Okamoto   Tsukuba, Japan
Guat Tin Goh   Nanyang Technological University, Singapore
Hwee Jin Soh   Nanyang Technological University, Singapore
Sen How Chia   Nanyang Technological University, Singapore

External Referees

Frederik Armknecht	Scott Contini	Eiichiro Fujisaki
Sébastien Canard	Cunsheng Ding	Steven Galbraith
Kai Yuen Cheong	Gerardo Fernandez	Clemente Galdi
Benoit Chevallier-Mames	Pierre-Alain Fouque	Paul Hoffman

Table of Contents

Signatures

Network Security

Secure Keyword Search and Private Information Retrieval

Public Key Encryption

Intrusion Detection

Email Security

Denial of Service Attacks

Authentication

Mutative Identity-Based Signatures or Dynamic Credentials Without Random Oracles

Fuchun Guo[1], Yi Mu[2,*], and Zhide Chen[1,**]

[1] Key Lab of Network Security and Cryptology
School of Mathematics and Computer Science
Fujian Normal University, Fuzhou, China
fuchunguo1982@gmail.com,
zhidechen@fjnu.edu.cn
[2] Centre for Computer and Information Security Research
School of Computer Science and Software Engineering
University of Wollongong, Wollongong NSW 2522, Australia
ymu@uow.edu.au

Abstract. We introduce a new identity-based signature scheme that possesses the feature of mutability in terms of its mutable signer identity. We name this new signature scheme *Mutative Identity-Based Signature* (MIBS). The merit of this proposed scheme lies in the novel property on protection of private information such as birthdate, social security number, credit card number, etc. that have to be employed as part of a user identity served as a public key. In MIBS, we allow all these private information to serve as a user identity, while only one of these information (along with the user name, as non-secret part of a user identity) is revealed to the verifier. For example, when using a signature to a legitimate merchant, only the credit card number and the user name are revealed without leaking other private information. This signature scheme is naturally associated with a *dynamic* credential system, where a signature accommodates the feature of a secret credential. We provide a security model and then prove its security based on the q-Strong Diffie-Hellman (q-SDH) problem and the Computational Diffie-Hellman (CDH) problem in the standard model.

Keywords: ID-based Signature, Mutative Identity.

1 Introduction

In 1984, Shamir [11] first introduced the idea of Identity-Based (or ID-based) Signature (IBS), aimed to create a signature on a message where any user can verify the signature using the signer's public information such as email address, ID numbers or telephone numbers instead of a conventional public key in order to simply the certificate management. Since Boneh and Franklin [2] introduced the first ID-Based Encryption (IBE) from pairings in 2001, several novel IBS

---

* This project was partially supported by the UoW Near Miss grant.
** Partially supported by Science and Technology of Fujian Province (2006F5036).

F. Bao et al. (Eds.): CANS 2007, LNCS 4856, pp. 1–14, 2007.

schemes have been proposed (e.g., in the random oracle model [6,9,5] and in the standard model [10]).

An ID-based system requires a constant identity of a user. This identity must be fixed as the unique public key. We are motivated by the following scenario.

A normal identity such as a user name or an email address is not sufficient to identify a user. For instance, two users could have the exactly same name. Because of this, a compound identity accommodating multiple information about a user identity such as name, birthdate, tax number, driver's licence number, credit card number, etc. is used. However, some information in this compound identity are private to some parties but non-private to some others. For example, a client can provide his name along with his credit card number to a legitimate merchant, while his birthdate should not be revealed.

A clumsy solution to the privacy of compound identity is to allow the private key generator to create a number of private keys for a user. Each private key is associated with a piece of the compound identity, i.e., the public key is composed of a general identity (e.g. a user's name) and an extra identity (e.g. a credit card number). A signature is created in terms of the piece of identity that can be revealed to the verifier. This approach is obviously problematic due to difficulty in key management.

Motivated by the above scenario, in this paper, we present a new notion of IBS: *Mutative Identity-Based Signature* (MIBS). In MIBS, a public key (the compound identity) is composed of the basic public information (non-private identity) and extra information (private identities). A compound identity maps a single private signing key. When a signature is formed, the signer can choose which piece of the compound identity should be revealed to the verifier. Our scheme can be considered as a private credential scheme with dynamic and selective private contents. In this scenario, The private key generator can be considered as a credential issuer. A credential can be *dynamically* generated (signed) by the private key holder. Furthermore, our scheme can also be applied to multi-identity-based access control. That is, a user has a number of identities that form an unique compound identity. An identity in the compound identity is associated with a key for accessing an entity.

We provide a security model and then prove its security based on the n-Strong Diffie-Hellman (n-SDH, known as q-SDH) problem and the Computational Diffie-Hellman (CDH) problem in the standard model.

Road Map: In Section 2, we provide the definitions of MIBS, including the security model and the complexity assumption. In Section 3, we review the accumulator technique from Nguyen's construction. In Section 4, we propose our MIBS scheme and its security proof against chosen message attacks. In Section 5, we give some discussions. We conclude our paper in Section 6.

2   Definition

A Mutative Identity-Based Signature (MIBS) can be described as the following algorithms:

Setup: This algorithm is run by the Private Key Generator (PKG). On input a security parameter 1^k, it outputs master public parameters $params$ and master secret key. The PKG publishes $params$ and keeps the master secret key.

KeyGen: This algorithm is run by the PKG. On input $params$, the master secret key and a compound identity $U = \langle ID, A_1, A_2, \cdots, A_t \rangle$ $(1 \le t \le n)$, it outputs the signing key d_u of U, where ID is the basic non-private information and A_i are private information.

Sign: This algorithm is run by the signer. On input the signing key d_U, a compound identity U, a verification identity $V_u = \langle ID, A_i \rangle$, a message M and $params$, it outputs the verification key v_k (only the verification identity V_u exposes to the verifier) and the signature σ, where $A_i \in \langle A_1, A_2, \cdots, A_t \rangle$ is decided by the original signer.

Verify: This algorithm is run by any verifier. On input the signature (M, v_k, σ) and $params$, it outputs **accept** if the signature is valid on M for verification identity V_u; otherwise outputs **reject**.

2.1   Security Model

Mutative Identity-Based Signature (MIBS) is unforgeable against the chosen message attack, denoted by UF-MIBS-CMA, where the game between a challenger and an adversary is described as follows:

Setup: The challenger runs the algorithm Setup of the MIBS scheme and gives the master public $paramas$ to the adversary.

Queries: The adversary adaptively makes a number of different queries to the challenger. Each query can be one of the following.

- Signing Key Queries. The adversary makes queries on the signing key of $U = \langle ID, A_1, A_2, \cdots, A_t \rangle$. The challenger responds by running the algorithm KenGen and forwarding the signing key d_u to the adversary.
- Signature Queries. The adversary makes queries on the signature of (U, V_u, M) of compound identity $U = \langle ID, A_1, A_2, \cdots, A_t \rangle$, where $V_u = \langle ID, A_i \rangle$. The challenger responds by first running algorithm KeyGen to generate the signing key d_u and then running the algorithm Sign to obtain a signature σ, which is forwarded to the adversary.

Forgery: The adversary outputs a signature (M^*, v_k^*, σ^*) of compound identity U^* and verification identity V_u^*. The adversary succeeds if the following hold true:

- σ^* is a valid signature on M^* for verification identity V_u^*;
- No signing key query on U^*. No signature query on (U^*, V_u', M^*) for any V_u'.

The advantage of an adversary in the above game is defined as

$$Adv_{\mathcal{A}} = \Pr[\mathcal{A} \; succeeds]$$

Definition 1. *An adversary $\mathcal{A}$ is said to be an (ϵ, t, q_k, q_s)-forger of a MIBS if $\mathcal{A}$ has at least ϵ advantage in the above game, runs in time at most t and makes at most q_k and q_s queries on the signing key and the signature. A MIBS scheme is said to be (ϵ, t, q_k, q_s)-secure if no (ϵ, t, q_k, q_s)-forger exists.*

2.2   Bilinear Pairing

Let $\mathbb{G}$ and $\mathbb{G}_T$ be two cyclic groups of prime order p. Let g be a generator of $\mathbb{G}$. A map $e : \mathbb{G} \times \mathbb{G} \to \mathbb{G}_T$ is called a bilinear pairing (map) if this map satisfies the following properties:

- Bilinear: for all $u, v \in \mathbb{G}$ and $a, b \in \mathbb{Z}_p$, we have $e(u^a, v^b) = e(u, v)^{ab}$;
- Non-degeneracy: $e(g, g) \neq 1$. In other words, if g be a generator of $\mathbb{G}$, then $e(g, g)$ generates $\mathbb{G}_T$;
- Computability: There is an efficient algorithm to compute $e(u, v)$ for all $u, v \in \mathbb{G}$.

2.3   Complexity Assumption

The security of our MIBS scheme will be reduced to the hardness of n-Strong Diffie-Hellman (n-SDH) problem and the Computational Diffie-Hellman (CDH) problem in the group in which the signature is constructed. So, We briefly review the definition of the n-SDH problem and the CDH problem [7,10]:

Definition 2. *Let $\mathbb{G}$ be the group defined as above with a generator g and elements $g^s, g^{s^2}, \cdots, g^{s^n} \in \mathbb{G}$ where s is selected uniformly at random from $\mathbb{Z}_p$, the n-SDH problem in $\mathbb{G}$ is to compute $\langle c, g^{1/c+s} \rangle$ for any $c \in \mathbb{Z}_p/\{-s\}$.*

Definition 3. *We say that the (ϵ_A, t_A) n-SDH assumption holds in the group of $\mathbb{G}$ if there is no algorithm running in time t_A at most can solve the n-SDH problem in $\mathbb{G}$ with the probability at least ϵ_A.*

Definition 4. *Let $\mathbb{G}$ be the group defined as above with a generator g and elements $g^a, g^b \in \mathbb{G}$ where a, b are selected uniformly at random from $\mathbb{Z}_p$, the CDH problem in $\mathbb{G}$ is to compute g^{ab}.*

Definition 5. *We say that the (ϵ, t)-CDH assumption holds in the group of $\mathbb{G}$ if there is no algorithm running in time t at most can solve the CDH problem in $\mathbb{G}$ with the probability at least ϵ.*

3   Accumulator Overview

The idea of accumulator was first introduced by Benaloh and de Mare [1] and further developed in [3]. Basically, an accumulator scheme is an algorithm where we can combine a large set of elements into one short one. For a given element, if it was included into the accumulator, then there must be a corresponding witness; otherwise it is impossible to find such a witness. Camenisch and Lysyanskaya introduced dynamic accumulators [4], which allow us to dynamically delete and add elements from/into the original set. Recently, Nguyen [8] presented a dynamic accumulator scheme from bilinear pairings and used it to construct an ID-based ring signature. Accumulators is a useful technique that has a number of applications.

3.1 Definition

A secure accumulator $f : X \times Y \to X$ for a family inputs $\{y_i\}$ is a function with the following properties:

- Efficient evaluation: On input $(u, y_i) \in X \times Y$, outputs a value $v \in X$, where X is an accumulator domain for the function f and Y is the domain whose elements are to be accumulated;
- Quasi-commutative: $f(f(u, y_1), y_2) = f(f(u, y_2), y_1)$, i.e. the communication is independent of the order of y_i for all accumulated elements;
- Witnesses: Let $v \in X$ and $x \in X$. A value $w \in X$ is called a witness for x in v under f if $f(w, x) = v$;
- Security(Collision Resistant): Let $\mathbf{A} = f(u, Y^*)$ be the accumulator of $Y^* = \{y_i\}$. It is hard for all adversaries to forge an accumulator value $y' \notin Y^*$ and a witness w' such that $\mathbf{A} = f(w', y')$.

3.2 Accumulator from Bilinear Pairing

We make use of Nguyen's accumulator scheme from Bilinear Pairing [8] defined as follows: Let $T = (g, g^s, g^{s^2}, \cdots, g^{s^n})$ be the tuple of elements from $\mathbb{G}$ and $u = g^z$ for some known z randomly from $\mathbb{Z}_p$. The secure accumulator based on the number of elements in T is defined as:

$$f(u, y_i) = u^{y_i+s} = g^{z(y_i+s)}$$

which satisfies the requirements of a secure accumulator.

- Efficient evaluation: For $u \in \mathbb{G}$ and $Y^* = \{y_1, y_2, \cdots, y_t\} \in \mathbb{Z}_p \setminus \{-s\}$, where n elements in Y^* at most, the accumulator value is

$$f(u, Y^*) = g^{z(y_1+s)(y_2+s)\cdots(y_t+s)}$$

can be computed in time polynomial in t from T, z and $\{y_1, y_2, \cdots, y_t\}$ without the knowledge of the auxiliary information s.
- Quasi-commutative:

$$f(f(u, y_1), y_2) = g^{z(y_1+s)(y_2+s)} = f(f(u, y_2), y_1).$$

- Witness: The witness for y_t in $f(u, Y^*)$ are two elements $W_0, W_1 \in \mathbb{G}$, where

$$W_0 = g^{z(y_1+s)(y_2+s)\cdots(y_{t-1}+s)}, \quad W_1 = g^{zs(y_1+s)(y_2+s)\cdots(y_{t-1}+s)}$$

which can be verified by

$$e\left(\mathrm{W}_0, g^s\right) = e\left(g^{z(y_1+s)(y_2+s)\cdots(y_{t-1}+s)}, g^s\right) = e\left(\mathrm{W}_1, g\right)$$

$$\mathrm{A} = (\mathrm{W}_0)^{y_t}\mathrm{W}_1 = g^{z(y_1+s)(y_2+s)\cdots(y_t+s)}.$$

– Security (Collision Resistant): It holds according to the following theorem.

Theorem 1. *The accumulator is Collision Resistant if the n-SDH assumption holds, where n is the upper bound on the number of elements to be accumulated by the accumulator.*

Proof. [8].   □

4   The MIBS Scheme

4.1   Construction

Let $e : \mathbb{G} \times \mathbb{G} \to \mathbb{G}_T$ be the bilinear map, $\mathbb{G}, \mathbb{G}_T$ be two cyclic groups of order p and g be the corresponding generator in $\mathbb{G}$. We set $z \equiv 1$ of the accumulator scheme in our MIBS scheme.

Setup: The system parameters are generated as follow: Select two secrets $\alpha, \beta \in \mathbb{Z}_p$ at random, choose g, g_2, u_0, m_0 randomly from $\mathbb{G}$, and set the value $g_1 = g^\alpha, k_i = g^{\beta^i}$ for all $i \in \{1, 2, \cdots, n\}$. Choose one vector $\boldsymbol{u} = (u_i)$ of length n_u and one vector $\boldsymbol{m} = (m_i)$ of length n_m, where $u_i, m_i \in \mathbb{G}$. A collision-resistant hash functions $H : \{0, 1\}^* \to \{0, 1\}^{n_u}$. The master public *params* and the master secret key are

$$params = (g, g_1, g_2, k_1, k_2, \cdots, k_q, u_0, \boldsymbol{u}, m_0, \boldsymbol{m}, H), \quad \text{secret key} = \alpha, \beta.$$

KeyGen: To generate a signing key for $U = \langle ID, A_1, A_2, \cdots, A_n \rangle$, where all $A_i \in \mathbb{Z}_p$, PKG does the following:

– Compute the accumulator value $\mathbf{A}_U = g^{(A_1+\beta)(A_2+\beta)\cdots(A_n+\beta)} \in \mathbb{G}$;
– Compute the hash value $h_U = H(ID, \mathbf{A}_U) \in \{0, 1\}^{n_u}$;
– Let $h_U[i]$ be the ith bit of h_U. Define $\mathcal{H}_U \subset \{1, 2, \cdots, n_u\}$, the set of indices, such that $h_U[i] = 1$. Pick a random r and outputs d_U, where

$$d_U = (d_1, d_2) = \left(g_2^\alpha (u_0 \prod_{i \in \mathcal{H}_U} u_i)^r, g^r\right)$$

Note that there are two ways for the PKG to compute the accumulator: using g, A_i and the master secret key β and using g, A_i and all k_i in the master *params* without the master secret key β. However, the computational cost of the second way is higher.

Sign: To generate a signature σ on $M \in \{0, 1\}^{n_m}$ of identity $\langle ID, A_i \rangle$ with d_U, the signer does the following:

- Compute the two witnesses

$$\mathbf{W}_0 = g^{(A_1+\beta)\cdots(A_{i-1}+\beta)(A_{i+1}+\beta)\cdots(A_n+\beta)},$$

$$\mathbf{W}_1 = g^{\beta(A_1+\beta)\cdots(A_{i-1}+\beta)(A_{i+1}+\beta)\cdots(A_n+\beta)},$$

from U and $k_1, k_2, \cdots, k_n$.
- Output the verification key

$$v_k = \Big(\langle ID, A_i\rangle, \mathbf{W}_1, \mathbf{W}_2\Big) \equiv (\langle ID, A_i\rangle, \sigma_1, \sigma_2).$$

- Let $M[j]$ be the jth bit of M. Define $\mathcal{M} \subset \{1, 2, \cdots, n_m\}$, the set of indices, such that $M[j] = 1$. Pick a random s and outputs the signature:

$$\sigma_{A_i} = \Big(g_2^{\alpha}(u_0 \prod_{i\in\mathcal{H}_U} u_i)^r (m_0 \prod_{j\in\mathcal{M}} m_j)^s, g^r, g^s\Big) \equiv (\sigma_3, \sigma_4, \sigma_5).$$

Verify: Let $(v_k, \sigma_{A_i}) = (\sigma_1, \sigma_2, \sigma_3, \sigma_4, \sigma_5)$ be a valid signature for $(\langle ID, A_i\rangle, M)$. A verifier does the following:

- Check if the following equation holds:

$$e(\sigma_1, k_1) = e(\sigma_2, g).$$

- Compute $\mathbf{A}_U = \sigma_1^{A_i}\sigma_2$ and its hash value $h_U = H(ID, \mathbf{A}_U)$.
- Accept the signature σ if the following equation holds

$$e\Big(\sigma_3, g\Big) = e\Big(g_2, g_1\Big) \cdot e\Big(u_0 \prod_{i\in\mathcal{H}_U} u_i, \sigma_4\Big) \cdot e\Big(m_0 \prod_{j\in\mathcal{M}} m_j, \sigma_5\Big).$$

Correctness

$$\begin{aligned}
e(\sigma_1, k_1) &= e\Big(g^{(A_1+\beta)\cdots(A_{i-1}+\beta)(A_{i+1}+\beta)\cdots(A_n+\beta)}, g^{\beta}\Big) \\
&= e\Big(g^{\beta(A_1+\beta)\cdots(A_{i-1}+\beta)(A_{i+1}+\beta)\cdots(A_n+\beta)}, g\Big) \\
&= e(\sigma_2, g).
\end{aligned}$$

$$\begin{aligned}
e(\sigma_3, g) &= e\Big(g_2^{\alpha}(u_0 \prod_{i\in\mathcal{H}_U} u_i)^r (m_0 \prod_{j\in\mathcal{M}} m_j)^s, g\Big) \\
&= e\Big(g_2^{\alpha}, g\Big) e\Big((u_0 \prod_{i\in\mathcal{H}_U} u_i)^r, g\Big) e\Big((m_0 \prod_{j\in\mathcal{M}} m_j)^s, g\Big) \\
&= e\Big(g_2, g_1\Big) e\Big(u_0 \prod_{i\in\mathcal{H}_U} u_i, \sigma_4\Big) e\Big(m_0 \prod_{j\in\mathcal{M}} m_j, \sigma_5\Big).
\end{aligned}$$

4.2   Analysis

In both Waters identity-based encryption scheme [12] and Paterson and Schuldt identity-based signature scheme [10], the identity space is $\{0,1\}^{n_u}$ for a fixed n_u and can be extended to an arbitrary string using a collision-resistant hash function such that a hash value can only represent an "identity," where the extension can achieve the same level of security.

In our MIBS scheme, the verification key is the triple $(V_u, \mathbf{W}_0, \mathbf{W}_1)$ and the signer, knowing the full compound identity, can change the verifying key in terms of the actual application. The extra information in a compound identity is hidden in the witness, while the verifier can only know one of $\{A_i\}$. However, the final accumulated value for a compound identity is the same, i.e. the final "public key" of $H(ID, \mathbf{A}_U)$ is constant in each signing. So, when the security of accumulator holds and collision-resistant hash function holds, the hash value of $H(ID, \mathbf{A}_U)$ represents the "identity" of $U = \langle ID, A_1, A_2, \cdots, A_t \rangle$. I.e. All adversaries cannot find $U' \neq U$ and $U' = \langle ID', A_1', A_2', \cdots, A_t' \rangle$ such that $H(ID, \mathbf{A}_U) = H(ID', \mathbf{A}_{U'})$.

According to the definition of the security model and our construction, we know that the success of forging a valid signature on V_u^* by the adversary actually is on $H(ID^*, \mathbf{A}_U^*)$ of U^* that cannot be queried. So, with the same idea of both Waters and Paterson-Schuldt, we can only prove the security in the identity space of $\{0,1\}^{n_u}$, i.e., we define that the adversary is successful in forging a valid signature of an identity $H(ID^*, \mathbf{A}_U^*)$ even if it knows nothing about the actually identity in $H(ID^*, \mathbf{A}_U^*)$. The interaction between a challenger and an adversary are described as follows:

Setup: The challenger runs the algorithm Setup of the MIBS scheme and gives the master public *paramas* to the adversary.

Queries: The adversary adaptively makes a number of different queries to the challenger. Each query can be one of the following.

- Signing Key Queries. The adversary makes an query on a bit string of $h_U = \{0,1\}^{n_u}$. The challenger responds by running the algorithm KenGen and forwarding the signing key d_u to the adversary. Note that, the challenger can just run the last step of algorithm KeyGen.
- Signature Queries. The adversary makes query on the signature of (h_U, M). The challenger responds by first running algorithm KeyGen to generate the signing key d_u and then running the algorithm Sign to obtain a signature σ without $\mathbf{W}_0, \mathbf{W}_1$, which is forwarded to the adversary.

Forgery: The adversary outputs a signature (M^*, h_U^*, σ^*) of string h_U^*. The adversary succeeds if the following hold true:

- σ^* is a valid signature on M^* for h_U^*;
- No signing key query on h_U^* and no signature query on (h_U^*, M^*).

4.3   Security

Theorem 2. *The security of the accumulator algorithm where $z \equiv 1$ in our MIBS scheme construction holds if the n-SDH assumption holds. I.e., the accumulator algorithm is (ϵ_A, t_A) secure, assuming that the (ϵ_A, t'_A) n-SDH assumption holds, where $t'_A = t_A + \zeta + n\eta + \theta$ and ζ is the time in re-arranging the polynomial, η is the average time in computing B_i (refer to the proof) and θ is the time in an exponential computation.*

Proof. Let $T = (g, g^s, g^{s^2}, \cdots, g^{s^n})$ be the challenge tuple that $\mathcal{B}$ receives and let $\mathbf{A}_U$ be the accumulator of the t elements $U = \{A_1, A_2, \cdots, A_t\}$ $(1 \leq t \leq n)$ in this tuple. Suppose an adversary $\mathcal{A}$ can find an element $A \notin U$ and its valid witness $\mathbf{W}_0, \mathbf{W}_1$ in $\mathbf{A}_U$ such that $e(\mathbf{W}_0, k_1) = e(\mathbf{W}_1, g)$, then we have:

$$\mathbf{A}_U = g^{(s+A_1)(s+A_2)\cdots(s+A_t)} = \mathbf{W}_0^A \mathbf{W}_1 = \mathbf{W}_0^{A+s}$$

and

$$\mathbf{W}_0 = g^{\frac{(s+A_1)(s+A_2)\cdots(s+A_t)}{s+A}}.$$

Since $A \notin \{A_1, A_2, \cdots, A_t\}$, there exist $c_0, c_1, \cdots, c_{t-1} \in \mathbb{Z}_p$ where $c_0 \neq 0$, such that

$$(s+A_1)(s+A_2)\cdots(s+A_t) = (s+A)^t + c_{t-1}(s+A)^{t-1} + \cdots + c_1(s+A)^1 + c_0.$$

With $A, U, \mathbf{A}_U, \mathbf{W}_0, \mathbf{W}_1$ and T, $\mathcal{B}$ then outputs $g^{1/(s+A)}$ as follows:

- Compute $c_0, c_1, \cdots, c_t$ satisfying the above equation;
- Compute $B_i = g^{\frac{c_i(s+A)^i}{s+A}} = g^{c_i(s+A)^{i-1}}$ from T and A for all $i \neq 0$;
- Output $A, g^{1/(s+A)}$, since

$$\left(\frac{\mathbf{W}_0}{B_1 B_2 \cdots B_t}\right)^{\frac{1}{c_0}} = \left(\frac{g^{\frac{(s+A_1)(s+A_2)\cdots(s+A_t)}{s+A}}}{g^{\frac{c_t(s+A)^t}{s+A}} \cdots g^{\frac{c_1(s+A)^1}{s+A}}}\right)^{\frac{1}{c_0}}$$

$$= \left(\frac{g^{\frac{c_t(s+A)^t + c_{t-1}(s+A)^{t-1} + \cdots + c_1(s+A)^1 + c_0}{s+A}}}{g^{\frac{c_t(s+A)^t}{s+A}} \cdots g^{\frac{c_1(s+A)^1}{s+A}}}\right)^{\frac{1}{c_0}}$$

$$= \left(g^{\frac{c_0}{s+A}}\right)^{\frac{1}{c_0}} = g^{\frac{1}{s+A}}.$$

$\square$

Theorem 3. *When the security of the accumulator based on n-SDH assumption holds, the Mutative Identity-Based Signature scheme is (ϵ, t, q_k, q_s)-secure, assuming that the (ϵ', t')-CDH assumption holds in $\mathbb{G}$:*

$$\epsilon' = \frac{\epsilon}{16(q_k + q_s)q_s(n_u + 1)(n_m + 1)},$$

$$t' = t + O\Big((q_k n_u + q_s(n_u + n_m))\rho + (q_k + q_s)\tau\Big),$$

and ρ, τ are the time for a multiplication and an exponentiation in $\mathbb{G}$, respectively.

Proof. The proof is given in Appendix.

5   Discussions

5.1   Witness-Indistinguishability of Private Identities

In MIBS, the verification of a signature requires the clear ID and one of private ID's; that is, when the verification identity for signature σ is $V_U = \langle ID, A_1 \rangle$ of compound identity $U = \langle ID, A_1, A_2, \cdots, A_n \rangle$, the other privacy identities $A_2, A_3, \cdots, A_n$ are hidden in the witness $\mathbf{W}_0, \mathbf{W}_1$. Since the space of $\{A_i\}$ is rather small, the private ID's could be subject to knowledgeable guess attacks. Given the witness $\mathbf{W}_0, \mathbf{W}_1$, any verifier can guess a set of extra privacy identities $A_2', A_3', \cdots, A_n'$ and compute the guess witness $\mathbf{W}_0'$ (any one can compute the witness), if $\mathbf{W}_0' = \mathbf{W}_0$, the verifier (attacker) asserts that all privacy identities hidden in witness $\mathbf{W}_0, \mathbf{W}_1$ has been found out.

We propose the following scheme to repair the problem. In the key generation phase, the signer and the PKG arrange a random value ω, set as a piece of privacy identity embedded in the compound identity. Because the secret ω is only a random value, it is infeasible for an attacker to verify whether a guess $\mathbf{W}_0'$ is true or not. Accordingly, the signing key for signer is now the double d_{ID} and ω.

5.2   Using Multiple Private Identities for Verification

In our construction, one of privacy identities is employed for a verification. It is easy to extend our scheme to a multiple-private-identity case, where a verification identity $V_u = \langle ID, \mathcal{A}_I \rangle$ and $\mathcal{A}_I$ is a subset of $\langle A_1, A_2, \cdots, A_n \rangle$.

The change required to make is minimal. Without losing generality, consider two private identities as an example. Let us set $V_u = \langle ID, A_1, A_2 \rangle$. The tuple of v_k is now $V_u, \mathbf{W}_0, \mathbf{W}_1, \mathbf{W}_2$:

$$\mathbf{W}_0 = g^{(A_3+\beta)(A_4+\beta)\cdots(A_n+\beta)}$$
$$\mathbf{W}_1 = g^{\beta(A_3+\beta)(A_4+\beta)\cdots(A_n+\beta)}$$
$$\mathbf{W}_2 = g^{\beta^2(A_3+\beta)(A_4+\beta)\cdots(A_n+\beta)}$$

where $\mathbf{W}_2$ can be computed from $g, g^{\beta}, \cdots, g^{\beta^n}$ and $A_3, A_4, \cdots, A_n$, similarly to $\mathbf{W}_0, \mathbf{W}_1$. The accumulator $\mathbf{A}_U = g^{(A_1+\beta)(A_2+\beta)\cdots(A_n+\beta)}$ can be computed from $A_1, A_2, \mathbf{W}_0, \mathbf{W}_1, \mathbf{W}_2$.

6   Conclusion

In this paper, we presented a novel Mutative Identity-Based Signature scheme, where the signer identity can be mutable. The feature of mutability can protect the signer's higher bound of privacy when a compound identity is used as the public key. We provided the definition and security model of MIBS and then reduced its security to the n-SDH problem and the CDH problem based on Paterson and Schuldt's IBS scheme.

Acknowledgement. The authors would like to thank the anonymous reviewers of CANS 2007 for their helpful comments on this work.

References

1. Benaloh, J., de Mare, M.: One-way accumulators: a decentralized al ternative to digital signatures. In: Helleseth, T. (ed.) EUROCRYPT 1993. LNCS, vol. 765, pp. 274–285. Springer, Heidelberg (1994)
2. Boneh, D., Franklin, M.: Identity-Based Encryption from the Weil Pairing. In: Kilian, J. (ed.) CRYPTO 2001. LNCS, vol. 2139, pp. 213–229. Springer, Heidelberg (2001)
3. Baric, N., Pfitzmann, B.: Collision-free accumulators and fail-stop signature schemes without trees. In: Fumy, W. (ed.) EUROCRYPT 1997. LNCS, vol. 1233, pp. 480–494. Springer, Heidelberg (1997)
4. Camenisch, J., Lysyanskaya, A.: Dynamic accumulators and applications to efficient revocation of anonymous credentials. In: Yung, M. (ed.) CRYPTO 2002. LNCS, vol. 2442, pp. 61–76. Springer, Heidelberg (2002)
5. Cha, J., Cheon, J.: An Identity-Based Signature from Gap Diffie-Hellman Groups. In: Desmedt, Y.G. (ed.) PKC 2003. LNCS, vol. 2567, pp. 18–30. Springer, Heidelberg (2002)
6. Hess, F.: Efficient Identity Based Signature Schemes Based on Pairings. In: Nyberg, K., Heys, H.M. (eds.) SAC 2002. LNCS, vol. 2595, pp. 310–324. Springer, Heidelberg (2003)
7. Mitsunari, S., Sakai, R., Kasahara, M.: A new traitor tracing. IEICE Trans. E85-A(2), 481–484 (2002)
8. Nguyen, L.: Accumulators from Bilinear Pairings and Applications. In: Menezes, A.J. (ed.) CT-RSA 2005. LNCS, vol. 3376, pp. 275–292. Springer, Heidelberg (2005)
9. Paterson, K.G.: ID-based signatures from pairings on elliptic curves, http://eprint.iacr.org/2002/004
10. Paterson, K.G., Schuldt, J.C.N.: Efficient identity-based signatures secure in the standard model. In: Batten, L.M., Safavi-Naini, R. (eds.) ACISP 2006. LNCS, vol. 4058, pp. 207–222. Springer, Heidelberg (2006)
11. Shamir, A.: Identity-based cryptosystems and signature schemes. In: Blakely, G.R., Chaum, D. (eds.) CRYPTO 1984. LNCS, vol. 196, pp. 47–53. Springer, Heidelberg (1985)
12. Waters, B.: Efficient Identity-Based Encryption without Random Oracles. In: Cramer, R.J.F. (ed.) EUROCRYPT 2005. LNCS, vol. 3494, pp. 114–127. Springer, Heidelberg (2005)

Appendix

Proof of Theorem 3. Suppose there exists a (t, q_k, q_s, ϵ)-adversary $\mathcal{A}$ against our scheme, we construct an algorithm $\mathcal{B}$ that solves the CDH problem. Our approach is actually the same as that in [10]. Algorithm $\mathcal{B}$ is given as input a random tuple (g, g^a, g^b). $\mathcal{B}$'s goal is to output g^{ab}. $\mathcal{B}$ works by interacting with $\mathcal{A}$ as follows:

Setup: To generate the master public *params* $= (g, g_1, g_2, u', \boldsymbol{u}, m', \boldsymbol{m})$, $\mathcal{B}$ sets l_u, l_m be two integers with $0 \leq l_u, l_m \leq p$ and randomly chooses two integers $0 \leq k_u \leq n_u$ and $0 \leq k_m \leq n_m$, such that $l_i(n_i + 1) < p, i = u, m$. $\mathcal{B}$ then randomly chooses two integers $x' \in \mathbb{Z}_{l_u}$, $y' \in \mathbb{Z}_{l_m}$ and two vectors $X = (x_i), Y = (y_j)$ of length n_u, n_m with x_i, y_j randomly from $\mathbb{Z}_{l_u}, \mathbb{Z}_{l_m}$ for all i, j, respectively. $\mathcal{B}$

chooses two tuple of $\gamma_i', \Gamma_i = (\gamma_i^j), i = 1, 2$ (same as before) vectors except that all of $\gamma_i^j \in \mathbb{Z}_p$. Now, $\mathcal{B}$ defines the master public *params* as:

$$
\begin{array}{ll}
g_1 = g^a & g_2 = g^b \\
u' = g_2^{-l_u k_u + x'} g^{\gamma_1'} & u_i = g_2^{x_i} g^{\gamma_1^i} \\
m' = g_2^{-l_m k_m + y'} g^{\gamma_2'} & m_j = g_2^{y_j} g^{\gamma_2^i}
\end{array}
$$

Let

$$
F(h_U) = x' + \sum_{i \in \mathcal{H}_U} x_i - l_u k_u, \; J(h_U) = \gamma_1' + \sum_{i \in \mathcal{H}_U} \gamma_1^i
$$

$$
K(M) = y' + \sum_{j \in \mathcal{M}} y_j - l_m k_m, \; L(M) = \gamma_2' + \sum_{j \in \mathcal{M}} \gamma_2^j
$$

We have the following equations hold

$$
u' \prod_{i \in \mathcal{H}_U} u_i = g_2^{F(h_U)} g^{J(h_U)}, m' \prod_{j \in \mathcal{M}} m_j = g_2^{K(M)} g^{L(M)}
$$

Then, $\mathcal{B}$ sends the master public *params* to $\mathcal{A}$.

Queries

- $\mathcal{A}$ makes signing key queries. To generate a signing key query on $h_U = \{0, 1\}^{n_u}$, if $F(h_U) = 0 \mod l_u$, abort. Otherwise, $\mathcal{B}$ chooses a random r_u and sets the signing key to be:

$$
d_{h_U} = (d_1, d_2) = (g_1^{-\frac{J(h_U)}{F(h_U)}} (g_2^{F(h_U)} g^{J(h_U)})^{r_u}, g_1^{\frac{-1}{F(h_U)}} g^{r_u}).
$$

Let $\widetilde{r_u} = r_u - \frac{a}{F(h_U)}$, we have

$$
\begin{aligned}
d_1 &= g_2^a (u' \prod_{i \in \mathcal{H}_U} u_i)^{\widetilde{r_u}} \\
&= g_2^a (g_2^{F(h_U)} g^{J(h_U)})^{r_u - \frac{a}{F(h_U)}} \\
&= g_2^a \cdot g_2^{F(h_U) r_u} g_2^{-a} g^{J(h_U) r_u} g^{-\frac{J(h_U) a}{F(h_U)}} \\
&= g_1^{-\frac{J(h_U)}{F(h_U)}} (g_2^{F(h_U)} g^{J(h_U)})^{r_u}
\end{aligned}
$$

$$
d_2 = g_1^{\frac{-1}{F(h_U)}} g^{r_u} = g^{\frac{-a}{F(h_U)}} g^{r_u} = g^{r_u - \frac{a}{F(h_U)}} = g^{\widetilde{r_u}}
$$

So, d_{h_U} is a valid signing key for h_U. $\mathcal{B}$ gives it to the adversary.

Remark: Actually, $\mathcal{B}$ aborts only for $F(h_U) = 0 \mod p$. In order to use the result of [10], we will force $\mathcal{B}$ to abort whenever $F(h_U) = 0 \mod l_u$.

- $\mathcal{A}$ makes signature queries. To generate a signature query on (h_U, M). If $F(h_U) = 0 \mod l_u$ and $K(M) = 0 \mod l_m$, abort. Otherwise, $\mathcal{B}$ computes the signatures as follows:

- If $F(h_U) \neq 0 \bmod l_u$, compute the signing key which is the same as signing key query and then creates the signature on M using the algorithm Sign.
- If $F(h_U) = 0 \bmod l_u$ and $K(M) \neq 0 \bmod l_m$, $\mathcal{B}$ picks random r_u, r_m and sets the signature as:

$$\sigma = (\sigma_3, \sigma_4, \sigma_5)$$
$$= (g_1^{-\frac{L(M)}{K(M)}}(g_2^{K(M)}g^{L(M)})^{r_m}(g_2^{F(h_U)}g^{J(h_U)})^{r_u}, g^{r_u}, g_1^{-\frac{1}{K(M)}}g^{r_m})).$$

Let $\widetilde{r_m} = r_m - \frac{a}{K(M)}$, we have

$$\sigma_3 = g_2^a (u' \prod_{i \in \mathcal{H}_U} u_i)^{r_u} (m' \prod_{j \in \mathcal{M}} m_j)^{\widetilde{r_m}}$$
$$= g_2^a (g_2^{F(h_U)} g^{J(h_U)})^{r_u} (g_2^{K(M)} g^{L(M)})^{\widetilde{r_m}}$$
$$= g_2^a (g_2^{F(h_U)} g^{J(h_U)})^{r_u} (g_2^{K(M)} g^{L(M)})^{r_m - \frac{a}{K(M)}}$$
$$= g_2^a (g_2^{F(h_U)} g^{J(h_U)})^{r_u} \cdot g_2^{r_m K(M)} g_2^{-a} g^{r_m L(M)} g^{\frac{-aL(M)}{K(M)}}$$
$$= g_1^{-\frac{L(M)}{K(M)}} (g_2^{K(M)} g^{L(M)})^{r_m} (g_2^{F(h_U)} g^{J(h_U)})^{r_u}$$

$$\sigma_5 = g_1^{-\frac{1}{K(M)}} g^{r_m} = g^{\frac{-a}{K(M)} + r_m} = g^{\widetilde{r_m}}$$

So, σ is a valid signature of (h_U, M). $\mathcal{B}$ gives it the adversary.

Forgery: The adversary outputs a valid forgery signature σ^* on (h_U^*, M^*). If $F(h_U^*) \neq 0 \bmod p$ or $K(M^*) \neq 0 \bmod p$, abort. Otherwise, let the forgery signature be

$$\sigma^* = (\sigma_3^*, \sigma_4^*, \sigma_5^*) = (g_2^\alpha (u' \prod_{i \in \mathcal{H}_U^*} u_i)^{r_u} (m' \prod_{j \in \mathcal{M}^*} m_j)^{r_m}, g^{r_u}, g^{r_m}).$$

$\mathcal{B}$ computes and outputs

$$\frac{\sigma_3^*}{(\sigma_4^*)^{J(h_U^*)}(\sigma_5^*)^{L(M^*)}} = \frac{g_2^\alpha (u' \prod_{i \in \mathcal{H}_U^*} u_i)^{r_u} (m' \prod_{j \in \mathcal{M}^*} m_j)^{r_m}}{g^{r_u J(h_U^*)} g^{r_m L(\mathcal{M}^*)}}$$
$$= \frac{g_2^\alpha (g^{J(h_U^*)})^{r_u} (g^{L(M^*)})^{r_m}}{g^{r_u J(h_U^*)} g^{r_m L(\mathcal{M}^*)}}$$
$$= g_2^a$$
$$= g^{ab}$$

Which is the solution to the given CDH problem.

This completes the description of the simulation. It remains to analyze the probability of $\mathcal{B}$ for not aborting. We divide the queries into two groups, one is for the queries involving h_U^* and the other is for the queries that does not involve h_U^*. The simulation for not aborting includes the following two cases.

- $h_U = h_U^*$: the queries can only be (h_U^*, M). Then, the probability for not aborting is greater than q_s in signature queries.
- $h_U \neq h_U^*$: the queries can be (h_U) and (h_U, M). Then, the probability for not aborting is greater than that of $q_k + q_s$ in the signing key queries.

Define the following events A_i, A^*, B_j, B^* as

$$A_i : F(h_{U_i}) \neq 0 \bmod l_u, \quad A^* : F(h_U^*) = 0 \bmod p$$
$$B_j : K(M_j) \neq 0 \bmod l_m, \quad B^* : K(M^*) = 0 \bmod p$$

So, for both cases, the lower bound on the probability of $\mathcal{B}$ for not aborting is that

$$\Pr\left[\neg abort\right] \geq \Pr\left[\bigwedge_{i=1}^{q_u} A_i \wedge A^* \bigwedge_{j=1}^{q_m} B_j \wedge B^*\right]$$

where $q_u = q_k + q_s$ and $q_m = q_s$.

The proof is based on Paterson and Schudlt's scheme [10]. We omit the probability analysis and present the result directly. Let $l_u = 2(q_k + q_s)$ and $l_m = 2q_s$ as in the simulation, it gives

$$\Pr\left[\bigwedge_{i=1}^{q_u} A_i \wedge A^*\right] \geq \frac{1}{4(q_k + q_s)(n_u + 1)}, \quad \Pr\left[\bigwedge_{j=1}^{q_m} B_j \wedge B^*\right] \geq \frac{1}{4q_s(n_m + 1)}.$$

Because $(\bigwedge_{i=1}^{q_u} A_i \wedge A^*)$ and $(\bigwedge_{j=1}^{q_m} B_j \wedge B^*)$ are independent, we have

$$
\begin{aligned}
\Pr[\neg abort] &\geq \Pr\left[\bigwedge_{i=1}^{q_u} A_i \wedge A^* \bigwedge_{j=1}^{q_m} B_j \wedge B^*\right] \\
&\geq \Pr\left[\bigwedge_{i=1}^{q_u} A_i \wedge A^*\right] \Pr\left[\bigwedge_{j=1}^{q_m} B_j \wedge B^*\right] \\
&\geq \frac{1}{4(q_k + q_s)(n_u + 1)} \cdot \frac{1}{4q_s(n_m + 1)} \\
&= \frac{1}{16(q_k + q_s)q_s(n_u + 1)(n_m + 1)}.
\end{aligned}
$$

If the simulation does not abort, $\mathcal{A}$ will create a valid forgery with probability at least ϵ. The algorithm $\mathcal{B}$ can then compute g^{ab} from the forgery as shown above. Since the time complexity of the $\mathcal{B}$ includes $O(n_u)$ and $O(n_u + n_m)$ multiplication and $O(1)$ exponentiations in signing key query and signature query, the time complexity of $\mathcal{B}$ is $t + O\Big((q_k n_u + q_s(n_u + n_m))\rho + (q_k + q_s)\tau\Big)$, where ρ, τ are the time for a multiplication and an exponentiation in $\mathbb{G}$, respectively. Thus, the theorem follows. □

A Generic Construction for
Universally-Convertible Undeniable Signatures

Xinyi Huang, Yi Mu, Willy Susilo, and Wei Wu

Centre for Computer and Information Security Research
School of Computer Science & Software Engineering
University of Wollongong, Australia
{xh068,ymu,wsusilo,wei}@uow.edu.au

Abstract. Undeniable signatures are classic digital signatures which are
not universally verifiable and can only be verified with the help of the
signer. Its extended version, convertible undeniable signatures, equips
the signer with the additional ability to make his undeniable signatures
universally verifiable whenever required. A selectively-convertible undeniable signature scheme allows the signer to convert a single signature
into a universally verifiable signature by releasing a selective proof in a
later time, while "universally-convertible" refers to the case where the
signer has the additional ability to generate a universal proof which
can finally convert *all* his undeniable signatures into universally verifiable signatures. In this paper, we propose a *generic* construction for
universally-convertible undeniable signatures. Our construction is based
on three building blocks: a strongly unforgeable classic signature scheme,
a selectively-convertible undeniable signature scheme and a collision-
resistant hash function. Formal proofs guarantee that our construction
has a tight security reduction to the underlying security assumptions. As
one of the applications of our generic construction, one can obtain the
first provable secure universally-convertible undeniable signature scheme
in the standard model.

Keywords: Undeniable Signature, Universally-Convertible, Generic
Construction, Provable Security.

1 Introduction

Universal verifiability is one of the most important properties in classic digital signatures. This property allows everybody to check the correctness of a
signature. However, for some personally or commercially sensitive applications,
universal verifiability is not required or even undesirable during certain periods.
Therefore, the concept of undeniable signature was introduced by Chaum and
van Antwerpen in Cypto'89 [6].

Undeniable signatures are like classic digital signatures, with the only difference that they are not universally verifiable. Instead, the validity or invalidity
of an undeniable signature can only be verified via the Confirmation/Disavowal

F. Bao et al. (Eds.): CANS 2007, LNCS 4856, pp. 15–33, 2007.

protocol with the help of the signer. Undeniable signatures have found various applications in cryptography such as in licensing software [6], electronic cash [43], electronic voting and auctions. The first undeniable signature was proposed by Chaum and van Antwerpen [6] and it was further improved by Chaum in [7]. However, the unforgeability of the FDH (Full Domain Hash) variant of Chaum's scheme remains as an open problem and was recently proven formally in the random oracle model [41]. There have been a wide range of research covering a variety of different schemes for undeniable signatures in the literature [4,3,9,11,14,15,16,17,20,24,29,30,31,33,34,36,48,47,49,50].

The concept of convertible undeniable signatures was introduced by Boyar, Chaum, Damgård and Pedersen [4], where the convertibility refers to the ability of the signer to convert one or more his undeniable signatures into universally verifiable. "Convert" in the undeniable signatures has two types: **Selectively-Convert** and **Universally-Convert**. A selectively-convertible undeniable signature scheme allows the signer to convert an undeniable signature into a universally verifiable signature by releasing a **Selective Proof** in a later time. Then, one can check the validity of this signature using the selective proof and signer's public key. However, the validity of other undeniable signatures remains unknown and can only be verified via the confirmation/disavowal protocol with the help of the signer. Universally convertible refers that the signer has the additional ability to generate a universal proof which can finally convert *all* his undeniable signatures into universally verifiable signatures. Thus, one can check the validity of any undeniable signature without requiring any help from the signer.

1.1 Previous Works

The first convertible undeniable signature scheme proposed in [4] has been broken by Michels, Petersen and Horster [34] who proposed a repaired version with heuristic security. In Eurocrypt'96, Damgård and Pedersen [9] proposed two convertible undeniable signature schemes, in which forging signatures is provably equivalent to forging El Gamal signature. An efficient convertible undeniable signature based on Schnorr signature was proposed by Michels and Stadler in [35]. The new scheme can be used as a basis of an efficient extension to threshold signature. Other constructions in RSA systems were also introduced. The first RSA based (convertible) undeniable signature was proposed by Gennaro, Rabin and Krawczyk in CRYPTO'97 [16], which was later improved by Miyazaki [33]. Very recently, Kurosawa and Takagi [26] proposed a new approach for constructing selectively-convertible undeniable signature schemes, and presented two schemes based on RSA related assumptions. Furthermore, Kurosawa and Takagi's second scheme is the first selectively-convertible scheme whose security can be proven without random oracles. Based on the computation of characters, Monnerat and Vaudenay proposed a novel construction of undeniable signature which offers the advantage of having an arbitrarily short signature (depending on the required security level) [36]. Monnerat and Vaudenay also generalized and optimized their scheme in [37] and [38], respectively, and claimed that their scheme proposed in [37] can achieve the selective convertibility, without providing a formal security proof to support this claim. Laguillaumie and Vergnaud proposed a new (time-selective) convertible undeniable signature scheme from pairing [31] which a short signature length. Very recently, Huang *et al.* [18] presented a short convertible undeniable proxy signature from pairings. The first construction of identity based selectively-convertible undeniable signature was proposed by Libert and Quisquater. Fig. 1 summarizes the known convertible undeniable signatures.

Scheme	Selectively-Convert	Universally-Convert
Boyar-Chaum-Damgård-Pedersen's [4]	✓	✓
Damgård-Pedersen's [9]	✓	✓
Michels-Petersen-Horster's [34]	✓	✓
Michels-Stadler's [35]	✓	✓
Gennaro-Rabin-Krawczyk's [17]	✓	✓
Miyazaki's [33]	✓	✓
Libert and Quisquater's (ID-based) [29]	✓	
Monnerat-Vaudenay's [37]	✓	
Laguillaumie-Vergnaud's [31]	✓	✓
Kurosawa-Takagi's [26]	✓	
Huang *et al.*'s [18]	✓	✓

Fig. 1. Convertible Undeniable Signature Schemes in the Literature

There are two main challenges in the construction of universally-convertible undeniable signatures. The first one is how to generate the universal proof which can convert all undeniable signatures to be universally verifiable. As shown in the above table, some of the convertible undeniable signatures are not universally-convertible, and only selectively-convertible. It seems that "selectively-convertible" is *relatively easier* to achieve. Very recently, Kurosawa and Takagi showed the first example of selectively-convertible undeniable signature scheme [26], which is provably secure in the standard model. However, there is no universally-convertible undeniable signatures which is provably secure in the standard model. Therefore, it is worthwhile to find an efficient way to construct a universally-convertible undeniable signature scheme.

The other challenge is how to ensure the security of the universally-convertible undeniable signatures. From information theory aspect, a universal proof contains much more information than a selective proof, which might help the adversary to break the scheme. For example, Boyar-Chaum-Damgård-Pedersen's scheme [4] is unforgeable when the universal proof of their scheme is not published. However, it turns out to be insecure after the signer releases the universal proof. An adversary can generate a valid signature for any message after obtaining the universal proof. We can see there are several constructions of universally-convertible undeniable signatures with formal security analysis in the literature. However, most of them only consider the security of the basic undeniable signatures. That is, universal proofs of those schemes are not given to the adversaries, which might weaken their security claims.

1.2   Our Contributions

In this paper, we propose a *generic* construction for universally-convertible undeniable signatures which is based on the following three building blocks: (1) A strongly existentially unforgeable classic signature scheme, (2) A selectively-convertible undeniable signature scheme and (3) A collision-resistant hash function.

We provide a formal proof to show that our construction is strongly unforgeable against the adversary who even has the knowledge of the universal proof of our construction, assuming that the underlying classic signature scheme is strongly unforgeable and the hash function is collision resistant. We also prove that the resulting signatures of our construction are invisible if the underlying classic signature scheme is strongly unforgeable and the selectively-convertible undeniable signature scheme is invisible as well.

As one of the applications of our generic construction, we can obtain the *first* universally-convertible undeniable signature scheme in the *standard* model when certain building blocks are used. In addition, one can also fix and improve some known convertible undeniable signature schemes by applying our generic construction. We believe that the generic construction proposed in this paper is a useful tool for constructing other variants of undeniable signatures with universal convertibility, such as designated confirmer signatures, directed signatures and etc.

Organizations of the Paper
In the next section, we will review some preliminaries required throughout the paper. The outlines and security models of (universally) convertible undeniable signature are proposed in Section 3. In Section 4, we describe our generic construction of the universally-convertible undeniable signatures and its security analysis. Finally, Section 6 concludes this paper.

2   Preliminaries

2.1   Outline of Classic Signatures

A classic signature scheme **Classic-Signature** consists of the following algorithms:

CS-Setup: Given the system security number ℓ, this algorithm outputs the parameter $CS\text{-}Params$ which is shared by all the users in the system.

CS-KeyGen: Given the system parameters $CS\text{-}Params$, this algorithm outputs a public-secret key pair (PK_{CS}, SK_{CS}).

CS-Sign: Given a secret key SK_{CS}, $CS\text{-}Params$ and a message M to be signed, this algorithm outputs a publicly verifiable signature σ_{CS}.

CS-Verify: Given a message-signature pair (M, σ_{CS}), a public key PK_{CS} and $CS\text{-}Params$, this algorithm will check whether (M, σ_{CS}) is valid under the public key PK_{CS}. If it is, outputs Acc. Otherwise, Rej.

2.2 Strong Unforgeability of Classic Signatures

The strong existential unforgeability of **Classic-Signature** under an adaptive chosen-message attack is defined using the game in Fig. 2:

Setup: The challenger runs **CS-Setup** and **CS-KeyGen**. It gives the forger $\mathcal{F}_{CS}$ the resulting public key PK_{CS} and the parameters $CS\text{-}Params$. The challenger keeps the private key SK_{CS} for itself.

CS-Sign Queries: The forger $\mathcal{F}_{CS}$ can issue signature queries $\{M_1, M_2, \cdots, M_{q_S}\}$. To each message M_i, the challenger responds by running **CS-Sign** to generate a valid signature σ_{CS}^i and sending it to $\mathcal{F}_{CS}$ as the answer. These queries might be asked adaptively such that each message M_i may depend on the previously message-signature pairs $\{(M_1, \sigma_{CS}^1), (M_2, \sigma_{CS}^2), \cdots, (M_{i-1}, \sigma_{CS}^{i-1})\}$.

Output: Finally $\mathcal{F}_{CS}$ outputs a pair (M^*, σ_{CS}^*). The forger $\mathcal{F}_{CS}$ wins the game if
1. $Acc \leftarrow$ **CS-Verify**$(M^*, \sigma_{CS}^*, PK_{CS}, CS-Params)$ and
2. $(M^*, \sigma_{CS}^*) \notin \{(M_1, \sigma_{CS}^1), (M_2, \sigma_{CS}^2), \cdots, (M_{q_S}, \sigma_{CS}^{q_S})\}$.

Fig. 2. Strong Unforgeability of **Classic-Signature**

We define the advantage of an adversary $\mathcal{F}_{CS}$ in attacking the classic signature scheme **Classic-Signature** as the probability that $\mathcal{F}_{CS}$ wins the game in Fig. 2, taken over the random bits of the challenger and the adversary.

Definition 1. *A classic signature scheme* **Classic-Signature** *is* (t, q_S, ϵ)*-strongly existentially unforgeable under an adaptive chosen-message attack if no t-time forger* $\mathcal{F}_{CS}$ *making at most* q_S *signature queries has advantage at least* ϵ *in the game in Fig. 2.*

Remark: The adversary can also have access to the random oracles if necessary. It is also the same for the remaining security definitions.

Please refer to [12,2,45,46,27] for how to obtain a strongly existentially unforgeable classic signature scheme.

2.3 Collision-Resistant Hashing

Let $\mathcal{H} = \{H_k\}$ be a keyed hash family of functions $H_k : \{0,1\}^* \rightarrow \{0,1\}^n$ indexed by $k \in \mathcal{K}$. We say that algorithm $\mathcal{A}$ has advantage ϵ in breaking the collision-resistant of function $\mathcal{H}$ if:

$$\Pr[\mathcal{F}(k) = (m_0, m_1) : m_0 \neq m_1, H_k(m_0) = H_k(m_1)] \geq \epsilon,$$

where the probability is over the random choice of $k \in \mathcal{K}$ and the random bits of $\mathcal{A}$.

Definition 2. *A hash family* $\mathcal{H}$ *is* (t, ϵ)*-collision-resistant if no t-time adversary has advantage at least* ϵ *in breaking the collision-resistance of* $\mathcal{H}$.

3   Definitions of Undeniable Signatures

In this section, we will describe the definitions of the universally-convertible undeniable signatures and selectively undeniable signatures, which are denoted by **UC-Undeniable-Signature** and **SC-Undeniable-Signature** respectively.

3.1   Outline of Universally-Convertible Undeniable Signatures

A universally-convertible undeniable signature scheme **UC-Undeniable-Signature** consists of the following algorithms:

UC-US-Setup: Given the system security number ℓ, this algorithm outputs the parameter $UC\text{-}US\text{-}Params$ which is shared by all the users in the system.

US-KeyGen: Given the system parameters $UC\text{-}US\text{-}Params$, this algorithm outputs a public-secret key pair (PK_{UC}, SK_{UC}).

UC-US-Sign: Given a secret key SK_{UC}, $UC\text{-}US\text{-}Params$ and a message M to be signed, this algorithm outputs an undeniable signature σ_{UC} such that the validity of the pair (M, σ) is not publicly verifiable.

UC-US-Verify: Given a message-signature pair (M, σ_{UC}), the signer's public-secret key (PK_{UC}, SK_{UC}) and $UC\text{-}US\text{-}Params$, this algorithm will check whether (M, σ_{UC}) is a qualified pair. If it is not a qualified one, a symbol $\perp$ will be returned. Otherwise, it will further check its validity using the secret key SK_{UC}. If it is, outputs $Valid$. Otherwise, $Invalid$.

UC-US-Confirmation: A protocol between the signer and verifier such that given a message-signature pair (M, σ_{UC}), a public key PK_{UC} and $UC\text{-}US\text{-}Params$, this protocol allows the signer to convince the verifier that the given message-signature pair is valid, with the knowledge of the corresponding secret key SK_{UC}.

UC-US-Disavowal: A protocol between the signer and verifier such that given a message-signature pair (M, σ_{UC}), a public key PK_{UC} and $UC\text{-}US\text{-}Params$, this protocol allows the signer to convince the verifier that the given message-signature pair is invalid, with the knowledge of the corresponding secret key SK_{UC}.

UC-US-SConvert: Given a qualified message-signature pair (M, σ_{UC}), the signer's public-secret key (PK_{UC}, SK_{UC}) and $UC\text{-}US\text{-}Params$, this algorithm outputs a selective proof **SelectiveProof**$\{M, \sigma_{UC}, PK_{UC}\}$.

UC-US-SVerify: Given a message-signature pair (M, σ_{UC}), a pubic key PK_{UC}, **SelectiveProof**$\{M, \sigma_{UC}, PK_{UC}\}$ and $UC\text{-}US\text{-}Params$, this algorithm will check whether (M, σ_{UC}) is valid under the public key PK_{UC}. If it is, outputs Acc. Otherwise, Rej.

UC-US-UConvert: Given the signer's public-secret key (PK_{UC}, SK_{UC}) and $UC\text{-}US\text{-}Params$, this algorithm outputs a universal proof **UniversalProof**$\{PK_{UC}\}$.

UC-US-UVerify: Given *any* message-signature pair (M, σ_{UC}), a public key PK_{UC}, **UniversalProof**$\{PK_{UC}\}$ and $UC\text{-}US\text{-}Params$, this algorithm will check whether (M, σ_{UC}) is valid under the public key PK_{UC}. If it is, outputs Acc. Otherwise, Rej.

The above algorithms should satisfy the following three properties:

1. **Completeness and Soundness:** the **UC-US-Confirmation** and **UC-US-Disavowal** protocols and all the verify algorithms are complete and sound, where completeness means that valid (invalid) signatures can always proven to be valid (invalid), and soundness means that no valid (invalid) signature can proven to be invalid (valid).
2. **Non-Transferable:** a verifier participating in an execution of the **UC-US-Confirmation** and **UC-US-Disavowal** protocols does not obtain information that could be used to convince a third party about the validity/invalidity of a signature.
3. **Impersonation:** only the signer can execute the **UC-US-Confirmation** and **UC-US-Disavowal** protocols. Anyone else who does not have the knowledge of the secret key can not impersonate the signer to carry out these protocols.

3.2   Strong Unforgeability of UC-Undeniable-Signature

The strong existential unforgeability of **UC-Undeniable-Signature** under an adaptive chosen message attack is defined using the game which is similar in Fig. 2. The difference is that the forger is allowed to have the knowledge of the universal proof, which will help the forger to verify the validity of any message-signature pair. In addition, The forger can also obtain some selective proofs of certain message-signature pairs chosen by himself. It is formally defined using the game described in Fig. 3.

We define the advantage of an adversary $\mathcal{F}_{US}$ in attacking **UC-Undeniable-Signature** as the probability that $\mathcal{F}_{US}$ wins the above game, taken over the random bits of the challenger and the adversary.

Setup: The challenger runs **UC-US-Setup** and **UC-US-KeyGen**. It gives the forger $\mathcal{F}_{US}$ the resulting public key PK_{UC} and the parameters $UC\text{-}US\text{-}Params$. The challenger also generates the universal proof **UniversalProof**$\{PK_{UC}\}$ and sends it $\mathcal{F}_{US}$ as well.

US-Sign Queries: The forger $\mathcal{F}_{US}$ can adaptively issue up to q_S signature queries $\{M_1, M_2, \cdots, M_{q_S}\}$. To each message M_i, the challenger responds by running **UC-US-Sign** to generate a valid signature σ_{UC}^i and sending it to $\mathcal{F}_{CS}$ as the answer.

Selective-Conversion Queries: The forger $\mathcal{F}_{US}$ can issue up to q_{SC} selective-conversion queries $\{(M_1, \sigma_{UC}^1), (M_2, \sigma_{UC}^2), \cdots, (M_{q_{SC}}, \sigma_{UC}^{q_{SC}})\}$ which are adaptively chosen by himself. To each pair (M_i, σ_{UC}^i),

    1. If it is a qualified message-signature pair, then the challenger responds by generating a valid **SelectiveProof**$\{M_i, \sigma_{UC}^i, PK_{SC}\}$ and sending it to $\mathcal{F}_{US}$ as the answer.

    2. Otherwise, the symbol $\perp$ is returned which means (M_i, σ_{UC}^i) is not a qualified message-signature pair.

Output: Finally $\mathcal{F}_{US}$ outputs a pair (M^*, σ_{UC}^*). The forger $\mathcal{F}_{US}$ wins the game if

    1. $Valid \leftarrow$ **UC-US-Verify**$(M^*, \sigma_{UC}^*, PK_{UC}, UC\text{-}US\text{-}Params)$ and

    2. $(M^*, \sigma^*) \notin \{(M_1, \sigma_{UC}^1), (M_2, \sigma_{UC}^2), \cdots, (M_{q_S}, \sigma_{UC}^{q_S})\}$.

Fig. 3. Strong Unforgeability of **UC-Undeniable-Signature**

Definition 3. *A   universally-convertible   undeniable   signature   scheme* **UC-Undeniable-Signature** *is* $(t, q_S, q_{SC}, \epsilon)$-*strongly existentially unforgeable under an adaptive chosen-message attack if no t-time forger* $\mathcal{F}_{US}$ *making at most* q_S *signature queries,* q_{SC} *selective-conversion queries and has advantage at least* ϵ *in the game in Fig. 3.*

3.3   Invisibility of UC-Undeniable-Signature

Roughly speaking, the invisibility property requires that a valid message-signature pair is indistinguishable from other qualified pairs, without the help of the signer. It will be defined using the similar game in the Fig. 3. The only difference is that the signer's universal proof is not returned to the distinguisher.

Setup: The challenger runs **UC-US-Setup** and **UC-US-KeyGen**. It gives the distinguisher $\mathcal{D}$ the resulting public key PK_{UC} and the parameters UC-US-$Params$. The challenger keeps the private key SK_{UC} to itself.

Phase 1: In this phase, $\mathcal{D}$ can adaptively issue the following queries :

  US-Sign Queries and **Selective-Conversion Queries**: The challenger responds the same as defined in Fig. 3.

  Verify Queries: The distinguisher $\mathcal{D}$ can issue up to q_V verify queries $\{(M_1, \sigma_{UC}^1), (M_2, \sigma_{UC}^2), \cdots, (M_{q_V}, \sigma_{UC}^{q_V})\}$ where (M_i, σ_{UC}^i) can either be the message-signature pair returned as the answer to one of **US-Sign Queries**, or adaptively chosen by the distinguisher himself. To each message-signature pair (M_i, σ_{UC}^i), the challenger responds by first running the **UC-US-Verify** algorithm. If it is not a qualified message-signature pair, the symbol $\perp$ is returned. Otherwise, the challenger then responds based on whether a passive attack or an active/concurrent attack is mounted.

  1. Active/Concurrent attack: The challenger executes the **UC-US-Confirmation** (**UC-US-Disavowal**) protocol with adversary (acting as a cheating verifier) if the verification result is $Valid$ ($Invalid$).
  2. Passive attack: The challenger returns a transcript of **UC-US-Confirmation** protocol if the verification result is $Valid$. Otherwise, a transcript of **UC-US-Disavowal** protocol is returned.

Challenge: At the end of Phase 1, $\mathcal{D}$ will choose a message M^* with the restriction that M^* has not been issued as one of the **US-Sign** queries. The challenger responds by selecting a random coin $\gamma \in \{0, 1\}$. If $\gamma = 1$, the challenger runs the algorithm **UC-US-Sign** to generate a valid universally-convertible undeniable signature σ_{UC}^* of message M^*. Otherwise, σ_{UC}^* is randomly chosen such that (M^*, σ^*) is a qualified message-signature pair. In both cases, σ_{UC}^* is returned to $\mathcal{D}$ as the challenging signature.

Phase 2: In this phase, $\mathcal{D}$ can adaptively issue **US-Sign Queries**, **Selective-Conversion Queries** and **Verify Queries** with the restrictions that:

  1. If **UC-US-Sign** is a deterministic algorithm, M^* cannot be issued as one of the **US-Sign Queries**.
  2. (M^*, σ_{UC}^*) can not be issued as one of the **Verify Queries** or **Selective-Conversion Queries**.

  The challenger will respond these queries as it does in Phase 1.

Output: Finally $\mathcal{D}$ outputs its guess γ'. The distinguisher $\mathcal{D}$ wins the game if $\gamma = \gamma'$.

Fig. 4. Invisibility of **UC-Undeniable-Signature**

It is formally defined in Fig. 4. The success probability that $\mathcal{D}$ outputs a correct guess is defined as $Succ_{\mathcal{D}}$. We define the advantage of an distinguisher $\mathcal{D}$ in attacking **UC-Undeniable-Signature** as $|Succ_{\mathcal{D}} - \frac{1}{2}|$, taken over the random bits of the challenger and the adversary.

Definition 4. *A universally-convertible undeniable signature scheme* **UC-Undeniable-Signature** *is* $(t, q_S, q_{SC}, q_V, \epsilon)$-*invisible under an adaptive chosen-message attack if no t-time distinguisher $\mathcal{D}$ making at most q_S signature queries, q_{SC} selective-conversion queries, q_V verify queries and has advantage at least ϵ in the game defined in Fig. 4.*

3.4 Definitions of Selectively-Convertible Undeniable Signatures

A selectively-convertible undeniable signature scheme **SC-Undeniable-Signature** consists of 8 algorithms: **SC-US-Setup, SC-US-KeyGen, SC-US-Sign, SC-US-Verify, SC-US-Confirmation, SC-US-Disavowal, SC-US-SConvert** and **SC-US-SVerify**. All these algorithms are basically similar to the corresponding ones in **UC-Undeniable-Signature** defined in Section 3.1, the only difference is that we add "**SC**" to distinguish it from the latter. Therefore, the system's parameters in **SC-Undeniable-Signature** is denoted by $SC\text{-}US\text{-}Params$, user's public-secret key pair is (PK_{SC}, SK_{SC}), a selectively-convertible undeniable signature is denoted by (M, σ_{SC}) and etc..

   SC-Undeniable-Signature should also satisfy the three properties: Completeness and Soundness, Non-Transferable and Impersonation which are the same as defined in Section 3.1. The security notions Strongly Unforgeable and Invisibility can be defined similarly with some minor difference. Here, we only give the definition of the invisibility in **SC-Undeniable-Signature**.

Definition 5. *A selectively-convertible undeniable signature scheme* **SC-Undeniable-Signature** *is* $(t, q_S, q_{SC}, q_V, \epsilon)$-*invisible under an adaptive chosen-message distinguisher if no t-time distinguisher $\mathcal{D}$ making at most q_S signature queries, q_{SC} selective-conversion queries, q_V verify queries and has advantage at least ϵ.*

4 A Generic Construction of UC-Undeniable-Signature

In this section, we will describe our generic construction of the universally-convertible undeniable signature scheme **UC-Undeniable-Signature**. Our construction is based on the following three building blocks: a classic signature scheme **Classic-Signature** which is strongly unforgeable as defined in Definition 1, a hash function which is collision-resistant as defined in Definition 2 and a selectively undeniable signature scheme **SC-Undeniable-Signature** which is invisible as defined in Definition 5. Each algorithm of our generic construction is described as below:

UC-US-Setup: Given the system security number ℓ, this algorithm generates the system parameter $UC\text{-}US\text{-}Params = \{CS\text{-}Params, SC\text{-}US\text{-}Params,$

$H_k\}$, where $CS\text{-}Params$ is the parameters in the classic signature scheme **Classic-Signature** which is the output of **CS-Setup**(ℓ), $SC\text{-}US\text{-}Params$ is the parameters in the selectively-convertible undeniable signature scheme **SC-Undeniable-Signature** which is the output of **SC-US-Setup**(ℓ) and H_k is a random function in the collision-resistant keyed hash family $\mathcal{H}$.

UC-US-KeyGen: Each signer of a universally-convertible undeniable signature has two public-secret key pairs: (PK_{CS}, SK_{CS}) and (PK_{SC}, SK_{SC}) where

1. (PK_{CS}, SK_{CS}) is the public-secret key pair in the classic signature scheme **Classic-Signature** which is generated by the algorithm **CS-KeyGen**.

2. (PK_{SC}, SK_{SC}) is the public-secret key pair in the selective undeniable signature scheme **SC-Undeniable-Signature** which is generated by the algorithm **SC-US-KeyGen**.

The public key PK_{UC} is set as (PK_{CS}, PK_{SC}) and the secret key SK_{UC} is set as (SK_{CS}, SK_{SC}).

UC-US-Sign: The universally-convertible undeniable signature of the message M is $\sigma_{UC} = (\sigma_{SC}, \sigma_{CS})$ where

1. σ_{SC} is a selectively-convertible undeniable signature on the message M which is generated by the algorithm **SC-US-USign**:
$$\sigma_{SC} \leftarrow \textbf{SC-US-USign}(M, SK_{SC}, SC\text{-}US\text{-}Params).$$

2. σ_{CS} is a classic signature on the message $H_k(M\|\sigma_{SC}\|Undeniable)$ which is generated by the algorithm **CS-Sign**:
$$\sigma_{CS} \leftarrow \textbf{CS-Sign}(H_k(M\|\sigma_{SC}\|Undeniable), SK_{CS}, CS\text{-}Params)^1.$$
Here, the world $Undeniable$ indicates that this signature is generated in the scenario of undeniable signature.

UC-US-Verify: Given a message-signature pair $(M, \sigma_{SC}, \sigma_{CS})$, this algorithm first checks whether σ_{CS} is a valid classic signature on $H_k(M\|\sigma_{SC}\|Undeniable)$.

1. If $Rej\leftarrow\textbf{CS-Verify}(H_k(M\|\sigma_{SC}\|Undeniable), \sigma_{CS}, PK_{CS}, CS\text{-}Params)$, then $(M, \sigma_{SC}, \sigma_{CS})$ is regarded as a non-qualified pair and the symbol $\perp$ is output.

   Here the definition of the "qualified pair" is different from the previous one. In most undeniable signature schemes, it refers to the message-signature pairs where the signature could be any element in the signature space. In this sense, the invisibility of the proposed construction is a little weaker than the traditional one, since we require that σ_{CS} must be a valid signature.

2. Otherwise, it further runs the algorithm **SC-US-Verify**$(M, \sigma_{SC}, SK_{SC},$ $SC\text{-}US\text{-}Params)$ and forwards its output.

---

[1] We note that σ_{CS} is *not* a classic (or, publicly verifiable) signature on the message M. Instead, it is a signature on the string "$\xi = M\|\sigma_{SC}\|Undeniable$". Since $\|$ denotes the concatenation of the bit strings, ξ corresponds to many different pairs (M^i, σ_{SC}^i) provided that $\xi = M^i\|\sigma_{SC}^i\|Undeniable$. Therefore, given the signature σ_{CS}, one cannot decide if the signer has actually signed the message M. In the proof of Theorem 1, we also discuss how to remove the message from the input of the hash function.

UC-US-Confirmation: Given a message-signature pair $(M, \sigma_{SC}, \sigma_{CS})$, the verifier first runs the algorithm **CS-Verify**$(H_k(M\|\sigma_{SC}\|Undeniable), \sigma_{CS}$, $PK_{CS}, CS-Params)$.

1. If it outputs Rej, nothing is to be carried out between the verifier and the signer.
2. Otherwise, the verifier will execute the **SC-US-Confirmation** protocol with the signer.

UC-US-Disavowal: Given a message-signature pair $(M, \sigma_{SC}, \sigma_{CS})$, the verifier first runs the algorithm **CS-Verify**$(H_k(M\| \sigma_{SC}\|Undeniable), \sigma_{CS}, PK_{CS}$, $CS-Params)$.

1. If it outputs Rej, nothing is to be carried out between the verifier and signer.
2. Otherwise, the verifier will execute the **SC-US-Disavowal** protocol with the signer.

UC-US-SConvert: Given a pair $(M, \sigma_{SC}, \sigma_{CS})$, it runs the algorithm **CS-Verify** $(H_k(M\|\sigma_{SC}\|Undeniable), \sigma_{CS}, PK_{CS}, CS-Params)$.

1. If it outputs Rej, the symbol $\perp$ is output, which means $(M, \sigma_{SC}, \sigma_{CS})$ is not a qualified pair.
2. Otherwise, it runs the algorithm **SC-US-SConvert**$(M, \sigma_{SC}, PK_{SC}$, $SK_{SC}, SC-US-Params)$ to generate **SelectiveProof**$\{M, \sigma_{SC}, PK_{SC}\}$.

UC-US-SVerify: Given a pair $(M, \sigma_{SC}, \sigma_{CS})$, and its selective proof **SelectiveProof**$\{M, \sigma_{SC}, PK_{SC}\}$, this algorithm outputs Acc if
$Acc \leftarrow$ **CS-Verify**$(H_k(M\|\sigma_{SC}\|Undeniable), \sigma_{CS}, PK_{CS}, CS-Params)$ and
$Acc \leftarrow$ **SC-US-SVerify**$(M, \sigma_{SC},$ **SelectiveProof**$\{M, \sigma_{SC}, PK_{SC}\}, PK_{SC}$, $SC-US-Params)$.

Otherwise, outputs Rej.

UC-US-UConvert: This algorithm outputs SK_{SC} as the universal proof **Universal**$\{PK_{SC}\}$.

UC-US-UVerify: Given a pair $(M, \sigma_{SC}, \sigma_{CS})$, and the universal proof SK_{SC}, this algorithm outputs Acc if

$$Acc \leftarrow \textbf{CS-Verify}(H_k(M\|\sigma_{SC}\|Undeniable), \sigma_{CS}, PK_{CS}, CS-Params) \text{ and}$$

$$Acc \leftarrow \textbf{SC-US-Verify}(M, \sigma_{SC}, SK_{SC}, SC-US-Params).$$

Otherwise, outputs Rej.

5 Security Analysis

In this section, we will give a security analysis of our generic construction. Our generic construction will directly satisfy the properties: **Completeness and Soundness**, **Non-Transferable** and **Impersonation** if the underlying building blocks satisfy those properties as well. Due to the page limitation, we will skip the analysis of those properties and focus on the the unforgeability and invisibility of our construction.

5.1   Strong Unforgeability of Our Generic Construction

Theorem 1. *Our proposed universally-convertible undeniable signature scheme* **UC-Undeniable-Signature** *is* $(t, q_S, q_{SC}, \epsilon)$-*strongly existentially unforgeable assuming the underlying classic signature scheme* **Classic-Signature** *is* $(t, q_S, \epsilon/2)$-*strongly existentially unforgeable and* $\mathcal{H}$ *is* $(t, \epsilon/2)$-*collision-resistant.*

Proof. Suppose there is a forger $\mathcal{F}_{US}$ that $(t, q_S, q_{SC}, \epsilon)$ breaks strong unforgeability of our generic construction proposed in Section 4, then we will show there exists an algorithm $\mathcal{A}$ who can either $(t, q_S, \epsilon/2)$-break the strong unforgeability of the underlying **Classic-Signature** or $(t, \epsilon/2)$-break the collision-resistance of $\mathcal{H}$. Our proof will use the similar techniques in [2].

As defined in Fig 3, $\mathcal{F}_{US}$ can obtain the target public key (PK_{CS}, PK_{SC}), the parameters $(CS\text{-}Params, SC\text{-}US\text{-}Params, H_k)$ and the universal proof SK_{SC}.

$\mathcal{F}_{US}$ can adaptively choose message M_i and is given corresponding signature $(M_i, \sigma_{SC}^i, \sigma_{CS}^i)$. Let $\mathbb{S} = \{(M_i, \sigma_{SC}^i, \sigma_{CS}^i)\}$ be the set of message-signature pairs generated during the **US-Sign** queries. In our construction, the selective proof of a message-signature pair is generated by using SK_{SC} which has been already sent to $\mathcal{F}_{US}$. Therefore, $\mathcal{F}_{US}$ himself can generate the selective proof of any message-signature pair and does not need to issue the **Selective-Conversion Queries** any more. After all the queries, $\mathcal{F}_{US}$ will output a forgery $(M^*, \sigma_{SC}^*, \sigma_{CS}^*) \notin \mathbb{S}$. This forgery must fall into one of the following two types:

Type I: For $\forall (M_i, \sigma_{SC}^i, \sigma_{CS}^i) \in \mathbb{S}$, $(H_k(M_i \| \sigma_{SC}^i \| Undeniable), \sigma_{CS}^i) \neq (H_k(M^* \| \sigma_{SC}^* \| Undeniable), \sigma_{CS}^*)$.

Type II: There exists at least one tuple $(M_i, \sigma_{SC}^i, \sigma_{CS}^i) \in \mathbb{S}$ such that $(H_k(M_i \| \sigma_{SC}^i \| Undeniable), \sigma_{CS}^i) = (H_k(M^* \| \sigma_{SC}^* \| Undeniable), \sigma_{CS}^*)$.

We will show later that the Type I forgery can be used to break the strong unforgeability of the underlying classic signature scheme **Classic-Signature** and Type II forgery can be used to find a collision of $\mathcal{H}$. The simulation will be different due to different forgeries considered. At the beginning, the algorithm $\mathcal{A}$ will flip a *coin* in $\{1, 2\}$. If *coin* $= 1$, $\mathcal{A}$ will guess that Type I forgery will be the output of $\mathcal{F}_{US}$. Otherwise, Type II forgery will be produced.

Type I: Suppose $\mathcal{F}_{US}$ is a Type I forger who can $(t, q_S, q_{SC}, \epsilon)$-break strong unforgeability of our generic construction. We will construct an algorithm $\mathcal{A}$ that can (t, q_S, ϵ)-break the strong unforgeability of the underlying **Classic-Signature**. At the beginning, $\mathcal{A}$ is given a public key PK_{CS} and the parameter $CS\text{-}Params$. $\mathcal{A}$ will answer $\mathcal{F}_{US}$'s queries as described below:

Setup: $\mathcal{A}$ generates $SC\text{-}US\text{-}Params$ by running the algorithm **SC-US-Setup**(ℓ). Then, it runs the algorithm **SC-US-KeyGen** to generate the public-secret key pair (PK_{SC}, SK_{SC}). It also chooses a random hash function H_k in the collision-resistant keyed hash family $\mathcal{H}$. At last, $\mathcal{A}$ returns $(PK_{CS}, PK_{SC}, SK_{SC})$, $CS\text{-}Params$, $SC\text{-}US\text{-}Params$ and H_k to $\mathcal{F}_{US}$.

US-Sign Queries: For a sign query M_i from $\mathcal{F}_{US}$, $\mathcal{A}$ responds as followings:
1. $\mathcal{A}$ first runs the algorithm **SC-US-Sign** using the secret key SK_{SC} to generate σ_{SC}^i.

2. $\mathcal{A}$ then sets $H_k(M_i\|\sigma_{SC}^i\|Undeniable)$ as his own **CS-Sign** query. As the model defined in Fig 2, a valid signature σ_{CS}^i will be returned to $\mathcal{A}$.

At last, $\mathcal{A}$ will return $(\sigma_{SC}^i, \sigma_{CS}^i)$ as the answer.

Selective-Conversion Queries: As we have explained earlier, $\mathcal{F}_{US}$ does not need to issue these queries since the knowledge SK_{SC} enables him to generate the selective proof of our generic construction.

After all the queries, $\mathcal{F}_{US}$ will output a Type I forgery $(M^*, \sigma_{SC}^*, \sigma_{CS}^*) \notin \mathbb{S}$ such that $(H_k(M^*\| \sigma_{SC}^*\|Undeniable), \sigma_{CS}^*) \neq (H_k(M_i\|\sigma_{SC}^i\|Undeniable), \sigma_{CS}^i)$ for $\forall(M_i, \sigma_{SC}^i, \sigma_{CS}^i) \in \mathbb{S}$.

With probability at least ϵ, it is a valid message-signature pair of our proposed construction. Thus, $Acc \leftarrow$ **CS-Verify**$(H_k(M^*\|\sigma_{SC}^*\|Undeniable), \sigma_{CS}^*, PK_{CS},$ $CS-Params)$. Note that the pair $(H_k(M^*\| \sigma_{SC}^*\| Undeniable), \sigma_{CS}^*)$ is not generated during $\mathcal{A}$'s **CS-Sign Queries**. Thus, $(H_k(M^*\| \sigma_{SC}^*\|Undeniable), \sigma_{CS}^*)$ is a valid forgery of the underlying **Classic-Signature** as defined in Fig 2.

Type II: Suppose $\mathcal{F}_{US}$ is a Type II forger who can $(t, q_S, q_{SC}, \epsilon)$-break strong unforgeability of our generic construction. We will construct an algorithm $\mathcal{A}$ that can (t, ϵ)-break the collision-resistance of $\mathcal{H}$. Algorithm $\mathcal{A}$ is given a random key $k \in \mathcal{K}$. Its goal is to output a pair of messages (m_1, m_2) such that $m_1 \neq m_2$ and $H_k(m_1) = H_k(m_2)$. $\mathcal{A}$ will answer $\mathcal{F}_{US}$'s queries as described below:

Setup: $\mathcal{A}$ generates $CS-Params, SC-US-Params, (PK_{SC}, SK_{SC})$ and $(PK_{CS},$ $SK_{CS})$ by running the corresponding algorithms defined in Section 4. It then returns $(PK_{SC}, PK_{CS}, SK_{SC}, CS-Params, SC-US-Params, H_k)$ to $\mathcal{F}_{US}$. $\mathcal{A}$ keeps SK_{CS} as secret to himself.

US-Sign Queries: To each sign query, $\mathcal{A}$ runs the algorithm **UC-US-Sign** using the secret keys SK_{SC} and SK_{CS}.

After all the queries, $\mathcal{F}_{US}$ will output a Type II forgery $(M^*, \sigma_{SC}^*, \sigma_{CS}^*) \notin \mathbb{S}$ and there exists at least one tuple $(M_i, \sigma_{SC}^i, \sigma_{CS}^i) \in \mathbb{S}$ such that $(H_k(M_i\|\sigma_{SC}^i\| Undeniable), \sigma_{CS}^i) = (H_k(M^*\| \sigma_{SC}^*\|Undeniable), \sigma_{CS}^*)$. Thus, $(M_i, \sigma_{SC}^i) \neq (M^*, \sigma_{SC}^*)$ due to the requirement that $(M^*, \sigma_{SC}^*, \sigma_{CS}^*) \notin \mathbb{S}$. As the assumption in [2], we require that any selectively undeniable signature σ_{SC} has a unique encoding. Therefore, $\mathcal{A}$ successfully find the collision $(M_i\|\sigma_{SC}^i\|Undeniable, M^*\|\sigma_{SC}^*\| Undeniable)$ of $\mathcal{H}^2$.

In summary, we have showed how to use $\mathcal{F}_{US}$ to find a new message-signature pair of the underlying classic signature scheme **Classic-Signature** or a collision of $\mathcal{H}$.   □

---

[2] This explains why σ_{CS} must be a classic signature on $H_k(M\|\sigma_{SC}\|Undeniable)$. If we remove the message M from the input of hash function H_k, then the unforgeability of our construction relies on a stronger assumption: Given the signing key of the **SC-Undeniable-Signature** scheme, it is impossible for an adversary to find two different messages which share the same selectively convertible undeniable signature. There is no evidence shows that all **SC-Undeniable-Signature** schemes satisfy this requirement.

Remark: As one can see from the above analysis, the unforgeability of the proposed construction does not rely on the unforgeability of the underlying undeniable signature scheme. This is due to the fact the signer could publish his secret key of the **SC-Undeniable-Signature** as the universal proof.

5.2   Invisibility of Our Generic Construction

Theorem 2. *Our proposed universally-convertible undeniable signature scheme* **UC-Undeniable-Signature** *is* $(t, q_S, q_{SC}, q_V, \epsilon)$-*invisible assuming the underlying classic signature scheme* **Classic-Signature** *is* (t, q_S, ϵ')-*strongly existentially unforgeable and the selectively-convertible undeniable signature scheme* **SC-Undeniable-Signature** *is* $(t, q_S, q_{SC}, q_V, \epsilon \cdot (1 - \epsilon')^{q_V + q_{SC}})$-*invisible.*

Proof. Suppose there is a distinguisher $\mathcal{D}_{UC}$ that $(t, q_S, q_{SC}, q_V, \epsilon)$-breaks the invisibility of our generic construction proposed in Section 4, then we will show there exists an algorithm $\mathcal{D}_{SC}$ who can $(t, q_{SC}, q_{SC}, q_V, (1 - \epsilon')^{q_V + q_{SC}})$-break the invisibility of **SC-Undeniable-Signature** if **Classic-Signature** is (t, q_S, ϵ')-strongly existentially unforgeable.

At the beginning, $\mathcal{D}_{SC}$ receives the public key PK_{SC} and SC-US-$Params$ of **SC-Undeniable-Signature**. $\mathcal{D}_{SC}$ will answer $\mathcal{D}_{UC}$'s queries as described below:

Setup: $\mathcal{D}_{SC}$ generates CS-$Params$ by running the algorithm **CS-Setup**(ℓ). Then, he runs the algorithm **CS-KeyGen** to obtain the key pair (PK_{CS}, SK_{CS}). He also chooses a random hash function $H_k \in \mathcal{H}$. At last, $\mathcal{D}_{SC}$ returns $(PK_{CS}, PK_{SC}, CS$-$Params, SC$-US-$Params, H_k)$ to $\mathcal{D}_{UC}$.

US-Sign Queries: For a sign query M_i from $\mathcal{D}_{UC}$, $\mathcal{D}_{SC}$ responds as following:
  1. $\mathcal{D}_{SC}$ first issues M_i as one of the **US-Sign Queries** to his own challenger and obtains the selectively-convertible undeniable signature σ_{SC}^i.
  2. $\mathcal{D}_{SC}$ generates the signature σ_{CS}^i for $H_k(M_i \| \sigma_{SC}^i \| Undeniable)$ by running the algorithm **CS-Sign** with the knowledge SK_{CS}.

At last, $\mathcal{D}_{SC}$ returns $(\sigma_{SC}^i, \sigma_{UC}^i)$ to $\mathcal{D}_{UC}$ as the answer.

Selective-Conversion Queries: For a selective-conversion query $(M_i, \sigma_{SC}^i, \sigma_{CS}^i)$, $\mathcal{D}_{SC}$ firstly runs the algorithm **CS-Verify**$(H_k(M_i \| \sigma_{SC}^i \| Undeniable),$ $\sigma_{CS}^i, PK_{CS}, CS-Params)$.
  1. If it outputs Rej, the symbol $\perp$ is returned which means $(M_i, \sigma_{SC}^i, \sigma_{CS}^i)$ is not a qualified pair.
  2. Otherwise, $\mathcal{D}_{SC}$ sets (M_i, σ_{SC}^i) as his own selective-conversion query and issues it to his challenger. $\mathcal{D}_{SC}$ will obtain **SelectiveProof**$\{M_i, \sigma_{SC}^i, PK_{SC}\}$ from its own challenger. Then, he returns it to $\mathcal{D}_{UC}$ as the answer.

Verify Queries: For each verify query $(M_i, \sigma_{SC}^i, \sigma_{CS}^i)$, $\mathcal{D}_{SC}$ firstly runs the algorithm **CS-Verify** $(H_k(M_i \| \sigma_{SC}^i \| Undeniable), \sigma_{CS}^i, PK_{CS}, CS-Params)$. If it outputs Rej, the symbol $\perp$ is returned which means $(M_i, \sigma_{SC}^i, \sigma_{CS}^i)$ is not a qualified pair. Otherwise, $\mathcal{D}_{SC}$ will respond as following:
  1. For an active/concurrent attack, $\mathcal{D}_{SC}$ must execute the Confirmation (Disavowal) protocol with $\mathcal{D}_{UC}$. It will act as the middle-man in the sense that $\mathcal{D}_{SC}$ will forward each $\mathcal{D}_{UC}$'s query in the protocol as his own query and return each response from his challenger to $\mathcal{D}_{UC}$.

2. For a passive attack, $\mathcal{D}_{SC}$ will issue (M_i, σ_{SC}^i) as one of his **Verify Queries** to his challenger. $\mathcal{D}_{SC}$ will obtain a transcript of the Confirmation/Disavowal protocol. Then, he returns that transcript to $\mathcal{D}_{UC}$.

Challenging: At the end of Phase 1, $\mathcal{D}_{UC}$ will output a challenging message M^*. $\mathcal{D}_{SC}$ will forward M^* as his own challenging message and obtain the challenging signature σ_{SC}^*. Then, $\mathcal{D}_{SC}$ runs the algorithm **CS-Sign** with SK_{CS} and generates the signature σ_{CS}^*. At last, $\mathcal{D}_{SC}$ returns the challenging signature $(\sigma_{SC}^*, \sigma_{CS}^*)$ to $\mathcal{D}_{UC}$.

Phase 2: $\mathcal{D}_{UC}$ can continue to issue queries as defined in Fig. 4 and $\mathcal{D}_{SC}$ can answer these queries as described previously. In addition, There might be some special queries $(M^*, \sigma_{SC}^*, \sigma_{CS}^\dagger)$ during Phase 2. In these queries, the first two parts M^* and σ_{SC}^* are the same as those in the challenging signature, but $\sigma_{CS}^\dagger \neq \sigma_{CS}^*$. We say these queries are special since $\mathcal{D}_{UC}$ is allowed to issue these queries as one of the **Verify Queries** or **Selective-Conversion Queries**, but $\mathcal{D}_{UC}$ is not allowed to issue (M^*, σ_{SC}^*) as his own query. So, $\mathcal{D}_{SC}$ can not use his own challenger to respond these queries. For each special query, $\mathcal{D}_{SC}$ will act as described below. When $(M^*, \sigma_{SC}^*, \sigma_{CS}^\dagger)$ is issued by $\mathcal{D}_{UC}$, $\mathcal{D}_{SC}$ firstly runs the algorithm **CS-Verify**$(H_k(M^* \| \sigma_{SC}^* \| Undeniable)$, $\sigma_{CS}^\dagger, PK_{CS}, CS-Params)$.

1. It outputs Rej, the symbol $\perp$ is returned because $(M^*, \sigma_{SC}^*, \sigma_{CS}^\dagger)$ is not a qualified pair.
2. Otherwise, it outputs Acc and $\mathcal{D}_{SC}$ will abort. However, if the algorithm **CS-Verify** outputs Acc, then $\sigma_{CS}^\dagger$ and σ_{CS}^* will be two different valid signatures of the same message $H_k(M^* \| \sigma_{SC}^* \| Undeniable)$. Due to the strong unforgeability of **Classic-Signature**, the probability that $\mathcal{D}_{UC}$ can find out the new pair $(H_k(M^* \| \sigma_{SC}^* \| Undeniable), \sigma_{CS}^\dagger)$ is at most ϵ'.

If $\mathcal{D}_{SC}$ does not abort during the simulation, then $\mathcal{D}_{UC}$ will output his guess γ' which is correct with advantage ϵ. $\mathcal{D}_{SC}$ will forward γ' as his own guess. It is obvious that if $(M^*, \sigma_{SC}^*, \sigma_{CS}^*)$ is a valid message-signature pair of our generic scheme, then (M^*, σ_{SC}^*) will be valid of **SC-Undeniable-Signature** as well. Thus, If $\mathcal{D}_{SC}$ does not abort during the simulation, $\mathcal{D}_{SC}$ can also output a correct guess with the same advantage ϵ. We now go to compute the probability that $\mathcal{D}_{SC}$ does not abort during the simulation. If the underlying **Classic-Signature** is (t, q_S, ϵ')-strong unforgeable, then $\mathcal{D}_{SC}$ could abort with probability at most ϵ' for each verify query or selective-conversion query. Therefore, the probability that $\mathcal{D}_{SC}$ does not abort during the simulation is at least $(1-\epsilon')^{q_V + q_{SC}}$. Thus, the advantage that $\mathcal{D}_{SC}$ can break the invisibility of the underlying **SC-Undeniable-Signature** scheme with advantage at least $\epsilon \cdot (1 - \epsilon')^{q_V + q_{SC}}$ which contradicts the assumption that **SC-Undeniable-Signature** is $(t, q_S, q_{SC}, q_V, \epsilon \cdot (1 - \epsilon')^{q_V + q_{SC}})$-invisible. $\qquad \square$

5.3   Applications

A direct application of our generic construction is the first provably secure universally-convertible undeniable signature scheme in the standard model. It can be constructed by a strongly existentially unforgeable **Classic-Signature** in the standard model (e.g. BB's scheme [1]) and an invisible selectively-convertible undeniable signature scheme **SC-Undeniable-Signature** [26] in the standard model. In addition, we can fix Boyar-Chaum-Damgård-Pedersen's scheme [4] by applying a strongly unforgeable **Classic-Signature**. We also believe that the ideas in our generic construction can be used for other variants of undeniable signatures with universal convertibility, such as designated confirmer signatures [5], directed signatures [28] and etc. Due to the page limitation, we cannot show the details to these constructions.

6   Conclusion

We introduced a generic construction for universally-convertible undeniable signatures. Our construction uses a strongly existentially unforgeable classic signature scheme, an invisible selectively undeniable signature scheme and a collision-resistant hash function as the building blocks. The security of the proposed construction is formally analyzed, which is tightly related to the security of underlying build blocks. When applying this construction to certain specific schemes, we can obtain some useful results. One of these applications is the first universally-convertible undeniable signature scheme in the standard model.

References

1. Boneh, D., Boyen, X.: Short Signatures without Random Oracles. In: Cachin, C., Camenisch, J.L. (eds.) EUROCRYPT 2004. LNCS, vol. 3027, pp. 382–400. Springer, Heidelberg (2004)
2. Boneh, D., Shen, E., Waters, B.: Strongly Unforgeable Signatures based on Computational Diffie-Hellman. In: Yung, M., Dodis, Y., Kiayias, A., Malkin, T.G. (eds.) PKC 2006. LNCS, vol. 3958, pp. 229–240. Springer, Heidelberg (2006)
3. Biehl, I., Paulus, S., Takagi, T.: Efficient Undeniable Signature Schemes Based on Ideal Arithmetic in Quadratic Orders. In: Designs, Codes and Cryptography, vol. 31(2), pp. 99–123. Springer, Netherlands (2004)
4. Boyar, J., Chaum, D., Damgård, I.B., Pedersen, T.P.: Convertible Undeniable Signatures. In: Menezes, A.J., Vanstone, S.A. (eds.) CRYPTO 1990. LNCS, vol. 537, pp. 189–205. Springer, Heidelberg (1991)
5. Chaum, D.: Designated Confirmer Signatures. In: De Santis, A. (ed.) EUROCRYPT 1994. LNCS, vol. 950, pp. 86–91. Springer, Heidelberg (1995)
6. Chaum, D., van Antwerpen, H.: Undeniable Signatures. In: Brassard, G. (ed.) CRYPTO 1989. LNCS, vol. 435, pp. 212–216. Springer, Heidelberg (1990)
7. Chaum, D.: Zero-Knowledge Undeniable Signatures (Extended Abstract). In: Damgård, I.B. (ed.) EUROCRYPT 1990. LNCS, vol. 473, pp. 458–464. Springer, Heidelberg (1991)
8. Diffie, W., Hellman, M.: New directions in cryptography. IEEE IT 22, 644–654 (1976)
9. Damgård, I.B., Pedersen, T.P.: New Convertible Undeniable Signature Schemes. In: Maurer, U.M. (ed.) EUROCRYPT 1996. LNCS, vol. 1070, pp. 372–386. Springer, Heidelberg (1996)

10. Desmedt, Y., Yung, M.: Weaknesses of Undeniable Signature Schemes (Extended Abstract). In: Davies, D.W. (ed.) EUROCRYPT 1991. LNCS, vol. 547, pp. 205–220. Springer, Heidelberg (1991)
11. Fujioka, A., Okamotoa, T., Ohta, K.: Interactive Bi-Proof Systems and Undeniable Signature Schemes. In: Davies, D.W. (ed.) EUROCRYPT 1991. LNCS, vol. 547, pp. 243–256. Springer, Heidelberg (1991)
12. Goldreich, O.: Foundations of Cryptography, Basic Applications, vol. II. Cambridge University Press, Cambridge (2004)
13. Goldwasser, S., Micali, S., Rivest, R.: A Digital signature scheme secure against adaptively chosen message attacks. SIAM Journal on Computing 17(2), 281–308 (1988)
14. Galbraith, S.D., Mao, W., Paterson, K.G.: RSA-Based Undeniable Signatures for General Moduli. In: Preneel, B. (ed.) CT-RSA 2002. LNCS, vol. 2271, pp. 200–217. Springer, Heidelberg (2002)
15. Galbraith, S.D., Mao, W.: Invisibility and Anonymity of Undeniable and Confirmer Signatures. In: Joye, M. (ed.) CT-RSA 2003. LNCS, vol. 2612, pp. 80–97. Springer, Heidelberg (2003)
16. Gennaro, R., Krawczyk, H., Rabin, T.: RSA-Based Undeniable Signatures. In: Kaliski Jr., B.S. (ed.) CRYPTO 1997. LNCS, vol. 1294, pp. 132–149. Springer, Heidelberg (1997)
17. Gennaro, R., Rabin, T., Krawczyk, H.: RSA-Based Undeniable Signatures. Journal of Cryptology 13(4), 397–416 (2000)
18. Huang, X., Mu, Y., Susilo, W., Wu, W.: Provably Secure Pairing-based Convertible Undeniable Signature with Short Signature Length. In: Pairing 2007. LNCS, vol. 4575, pp. 367–391. Springer, Heidelberg (2007)
19. Jakobsson, M., Sako, K., Impagliazzo, R.: Designated Verifier Proofs and Their Applications. In: Maurer, U.M. (ed.) EUROCRYPT 1996. LNCS, vol. 1070, pp. 143–154. Springer, Heidelberg (1996)
20. Jongkook, L., Shiryong, R., Jeungseop, K., Keeyoung, Y.: A New Undeniable Signature Scheme Using Smart Cards. In: Honary, B. (ed.) Cryptography and Coding. LNCS, vol. 2260, pp. 387–394. Springer, Heidelberg (2001)
21. Jakobsson, M.: Blackmailing Using Undeniable Signatures. In: De Santis, A. (ed.) EUROCRYPT 1994. LNCS, vol. 950, pp. 425–427. Springer, Heidelberg (1995)
22. Furukawa, J., Kurosawa, K., Imai, H.: An Efficient Compiler from Σ-Protocol to 2-Move Deniable Zero-Knowledge. In: Bugliesi, M., Preneel, B., Sassone, V., Wegener, I. (eds.) ICALP 2006. LNCS, vol. 4052, pp. 46–57. Springer, Heidelberg (2006)
23. Kudla, C., Paterson, K.G.: Non-interactive Designated Verifier Proofs and Undeniable Signatures. In: Smart, N.P. (ed.) Cryptography and Coding. LNCS, vol. 3796, pp. 136–154. Springer, Heidelberg (2005)
24. Kim, S., Won, D.: Threshold Entrusted Undeniable Signature. In: Park, C.-s., Chee, S. (eds.) ICISC 2004. LNCS, vol. 3506, pp. 195–203. Springer, Heidelberg (2005)
25. Kurosawa, K., Heng, S-H.: 3-Move Undeniable Signature Scheme. In: Fuhr, N., Lalmas, M., Malik, S., Szlávik, Z. (eds.) INEX 2004. LNCS, vol. 3493, pp. 181–197. Springer, Heidelberg (2005)
26. Kurosawa, K., Takagi, T.: New Approach for Selectively Convertible Undeniable Signature Schemes. In: Lai, X., Chen, K. (eds.) ASIACRYPT 2006. LNCS, vol. 4284, pp. 428–443. Springer, Heidelberg (2006)
27. Huang, Q., Wong, D.S., Zhao, Y.: Generic Transformation to Strongly Unforgeable Signatures. ACNS 2007, Available online
http://eprint.iacr.org/2006/346

28. Laguillaumie, F., Paillier, P., Vergnaud, D.: Universally Convertible Directed Signatures. In: Roy, B. (ed.) ASIACRYPT 2005. LNCS, vol. 3788, pp. 682–701. Springer, Heidelberg (2005)
29. Libert, B., Quisquater, J.-J.: Identity Based Undeniable Signatures. In: Okamoto, T. (ed.) CT-RSA 2004. LNCS, vol. 2964, pp. 112–125. Springer, Heidelberg (2004)
30. Lyuu, Y.-D., Wu, M.-L.: Convertible Group Undeniable Signatures. In: Lee, P.J., Lim, C.H. (eds.) ICISC 2002. LNCS, vol. 2587, pp. 48–61. Springer, Heidelberg (2003)
31. Laguillaumie, F., Vergnaud, D.: Time-Selective Convertible Undeniable Signatures. In: Menezes, A.J. (ed.) CT-RSA 2005. LNCS, vol. 3376, pp. 154–171. Springer, Heidelberg (2005)
32. Laguillaumie, F., Vergnaud, D.: Short Undeniable Signatures Without Random Oracles: The Missing Link. In: Maitra, S., Madhavan, C.E.V., Venkatesan, R. (eds.) INDOCRYPT 2005. LNCS, vol. 3797, pp. 283–296. Springer, Heidelberg (2005)
33. Miyazaki, T.: An Improved Scheme of the Gennaro-Krawczyk-Rabin Undeniable Signature System Based on RSA. In: Won, D. (ed.) ICISC 2000. LNCS, vol. 2015, pp. 135–149. Springer, Heidelberg (2001)
34. Michels, M., Petersen, H., Horster, P.: Breaking and Repairing a Convertible Undeniable Signature Scheme. In: Third ACM Conference on Computer and Communications Security, pp. 148–152. ACM Press, New York (1996)
35. Michels, M., Stadler, M.: Efficient Convertible Undeniable Signature Schemes. In: SAC 1997. The 4th International Workshop on Selected Areas in Cryptography, pp. 231–244 (1997)
36. Monnerat, J., Vaudenay, S.: Undeniable Signatures Based on Characters: How to Sign with One Bit. In: Bao, F., Deng, R., Zhou, J. (eds.) PKC 2004. LNCS, vol. 2947, pp. 69–85. Springer, Heidelberg (2004)
37. Monnerat, J., Vaudenay, S.: Generic Homomorphic Undeniable Signatures. In: Lee, P.J. (ed.) ASIACRYPT 2004. LNCS, vol. 3329, pp. 354–371. Springer, Heidelberg (2004)
38. Monnerat, J., Vaudenay, S.: Optimization of the MOVA Undeniable Signature Scheme. In: Dawson, E., Vaudenay, S. (eds.) Mycrypt 2005. LNCS, vol. 3715, pp. 196–209. Springer, Heidelberg (2005)
39. Monnerat, J., Vaudenay, S.: Short 2-Move Undeniable Signatures. In: Nguyen, P.Q. (ed.) VIETCRYPT 2006. LNCS, vol. 4341, pp. 19–36. Springer, Heidelberg (2006)
40. National Institute of Standards and Technology (NIST). Digital Signature Standard (DSS). Federal Information Processing Standards Publication 186-2 (January 2000)
41. Ogata, W., Kurosawa, K., Heng, S.-H.: The Security of the FDH Variant of Chaum's Undeniable Signature Scheme. In: Vaudenay, S. (ed.) PKC 2005. LNCS, vol. 3386, pp. 328–345. Springer, Heidelberg (2005)
42. Okamoto, T., Pointcheval, D.: The Gap-Problems: A New Class of Problems for the Security of Cryptographic Schemes. In: Kim, K.-c. (ed.) PKC 2001. LNCS, vol. 1992, pp. 104–118. Springer, Heidelberg (2001)
43. Pointcheval, D.: Self-Scrambling Anonymizers. In: Frankel, Y. (ed.) FC 2000. LNCS, vol. 1962, pp. 259–275. Springer, Heidelberg (2001)
44. Pointcheval, D., Stern, J.: Security arguments for digital signatures and blind signatures. Journal of Cryptology 13(3), 361–396 (2000)
45. Steinfeld, R., Pieprzyk, J., Wang, H.: How to Strengthen Any Weakly Unforgeable Signature into a Strongly Unforgeable Signature. In: Abe, M. (ed.) CT-RSA 2007. LNCS, vol. 4377, pp. 357–371. Springer, Heidelberg (2006)

46. Teranishi, I., Oyama, T., Ogata, W.: General Conversion for Obtaining Strongly Existentially Unforgeable Signatures. In: Barua, R., Lange, T. (eds.) INDOCRYPT 2006. LNCS, vol. 4329, pp. 191–205. Springer, Heidelberg (2006)

47. Wang, G.: An Attack on Not-interactive Designated Verifier Proofs for Undeniable Signatures, Available online http://eprint.iacr.org/2003/243

48. Wang, G., Qing, S., Wang, M., Zhou, Z.: Threshold Undeniable RSA Signature Scheme. In: Qing, S., Okamoto, T., Zhou, J. (eds.) ICICS 2001. LNCS, vol. 2229, pp. 221–232. Springer, Heidelberg (2001)

49. Wang, G., Zhou, J., Deng, R.H.: On the Security of the Lee-Hwang Group-Oriented Undeniable Signature schemes. In: Katsikas, S.K., Lopez, J., Pernul, G. (eds.) TrustBus 2004. LNCS, vol. 3184, pp. 289–298. Springer, Heidelberg (2004), Available online http://eprint.iacr.org/2002/150

50. Zhang, F., Safavi-Naini, R., Susilo, W.: Attack on Han et al.'s ID-based Confirmer (Undeniable) Signature at ACM-EC 2003, Avalibale online http://eprint.iacr.org/2003/129

51. Zhang, F., Safavi-Naini, R., Susilo, W.: An Efficient Signature Scheme from Bilinear Pairings and Its Application. In: Bao, F., Deng, R., Zhou, J. (eds.) PKC 2004. LNCS, vol. 2947, pp. 277–290. Springer, Heidelberg (2004)

Fast Digital Signature Algorithm Based on Subgraph Isomorphism

Loránd Szőllősi[1], Tamás Marosits[1], Gábor Fehér[1], and András Recski[2],*

[1] Dept. of Telecommunications and Media Informatics, Budapest University of
Technology and Economics
[2] Dept. of Computer Science and Information Theory, Budapest University of
Technology and Economics

Abstract. A major drawback of nearly all currently existing digital
signature schemes is their computational requirements. Fast algorithms
exist for PCs or hardware accelerated smart cards, but not for low-end
embedded devices which are found in e.g. sensor networks. Such algorithms are also necessary for introduction of inexpensive signature creation devices to the civil sphere. Our purpose is to analyze a class of
problems that are based on graph theoretic problems instead of modular
arithmetics, and to provide very fast signature creation for embedded
systems at the cost of somewhat longer signatures.

1 Introduction

1.1 Digital Signature, One-Time Signature; Research Goals

From the beginning of network development, there has been a great need for an
algorithm to provide the transmission of "genuineness" of messages. Digital signatures [1,2] warrant three properties: authenticity, integrity and non-repudiation.
A digital signature scheme always relies on a parametric hard problem, usually
but not exclusively based on modular arithmetics. The two parameters of the
problem are the *user's private key* (which authenticates the user) and the *message hash* (which depends on the message via a cryptographically strong hash
function). The user ought to be the only one who should be able to calculate the
signature (solve the given instance of the problem) in reasonable time, while - in
the case of asymmetric signature schemes - any person should be able to *verify*
the signature using the signer's *public key*. Since the public key of the user first
has to be circulated amongst the users of the system, we usually have a *Certificate Authority* (CA) [3] that associates personal identification information with
public keys. To do this, the CA also uses asymmetric signatures: it signs the
public key and id of the user, therefore issues a *certificate*. As long as the public

* The authors wish to thank the High Speed Networks Laboratory and the Hungarian
National Research Fund (Grant Number OTKA 67651) for continuous support of
our research.

F. Bao et al. (Eds.): CANS 2007, LNCS 4856, pp. 34–46, 2007.
© Springer-Verlag Berlin Heidelberg 2007

key of the CA is known to all users and it is trusted, a new user can enter the system without first exchanging keys with all the existing users.

A common weak point of currently existing digital signature schemes is their speed. RSA and DSA are exceptionally slow when implemented on embedded microprocessors, therefore an additional hardware accelerator has to be included, increasing system cost. Albeit schemes like SFLASH [4,5] exist that have limited computational requirements, this is still in the order of thousands of modular multiplications per signature. Furthermore, according to a yet unpublished article referred by Ecrypt Newsletter [6], SFLASH, amongst other C*-schemes, is fully broken. One of our goals in the research was to decrease the time of the signature creation to a similar order as hash calculations.

Our other goal was purely theoretic: to estimate how well a signature algorithm based on graph theory can perform. This is a much less researched field in cryptography than modular arithmetics, but also offers problems that are much simpler to calculate. A simple example is subgraph isomorphism [7] or subgraph matching: given a graph H and a pattern graph G, find the latter in the former in a way that an edge in H exists between two given vertices if there is an edge between the corresponding two vertices in G. Most of the hard graph problems, however, are hard to parameterize by both the message *and* the user key, because reusing such a problem multiple times might leak out enough information to reconstruct the private key. The solution is to use *One-Time Signatures* (OT-Ses), which are digital signature systems that can only sign exactly one message with a user's private key. To sign multiple messages, multiple keys have to be constructed.

The relation between digital signatures and one-time signatures has been studied by Merkle [8], who constructed a tree for signing bits of a message. We will use a similar concept, as shown in Section 3 but sign actual keys instead of message bits. We do so to decrease the signature length and supply an infinite sequence of user keys instead of a sequence with pre-specified length.

1.2 Legal Considerations

Since we are going to sign latter user keys with former ones of the same user (and not of the CA), the legal basis of such signatures should also be investigated. In the European Union, any document that is signed by a person should be considered de jure legitimate [9]. Therefore, according to the current directive, users are able to issue their own certificates on further keys (although they certainly cannot assign a different personal identification information to it). In the United States of America, Uniform Electronic Transactions Act (UETA, [10]) states that the legal consequences of a document may not be denied solely because it is in electronic form. Furthermore, Electronic Signatures in Global and National Commerce Act (E-SIGN [11], in effect since the 1st of October, 2000) contains some exceptions that prevent the use of electronic signatures in some areas; according to these two acts, extension of OTS-based signature schemes to digital signature schemes are legally achievable in both continents.

2   A Graph-Based One-Time Signature Algorithm

As described in Section 1.1, subgraph isomorphism (or as sometimes called, subgraph matching) is the hard problem of finding a subgraph in a large graph that is isomorphic to a pattern graph. Not only is this problem NP-hard [12,7] in general (and NP-complete when considered as a decision problem), it is also well studied for the purpose of pattern recognition and graph transformations, yet no effective solution has been found. An other possible problems for reliable signature creation would be Levin's graph coloration [13,14], which is DistNP-hard [12] (meaning that random instances tend to be hard to solve, not only specific instances); or a simplified version of that problem, the graph 3-coloration, which is NP-hard and studied by [15].

In order to create hard to solve instances of graph and subgraph isomorphism one needs to avoid some special, easy to solve graph types. These include graph with many different degrees and graphs with low genus. Further studies of when to consider an instance hard can be found in [16,17,18,19]. It should be noted, that the hardness of this problem mainly relies in choosing proper graphs; but a graph can be checked before applying for a certificate. Problem size versus attack hardness was extensively studied by Shuichi Ichikawa and Shoji Yamamoto [20]; hardware (custom FPGA-based logic) and software-based (Pentium III/600MHz) solutions were compared. These results confirm the expected exponential growth as problem size increases, and (with regression of measured data) shows that a graph of 81 or more vertices cannot be mapped faster than in 100000 years with a software-based solution (for the same defense against custom hardware-based attacks, 264 nodes are required, 256 nodes provide security for more than 70000 years with current technology and fits in a byte per node; although actual implementation of such a hardware is unlikely due to the high number of gates to be used).

The formal protocol of IzoSign OTS is as follows:

Key Generation

1. User generates a random graph G with n vertices having a constant degree δ.
2. G is tested for being an easy to match pattern for the subgraph isomorphism (as described in the beginning of Section 2). If it is such an instance, then restart the algorithm.
3. Extend G randomly to $2n$ vertices, add edges randomly, keeping the graph uniform degree.
4. Permute the nodes of the extended graph. The permuted graph will be called H; the mapping of the nodes of G to H will be called $D(.)$.

- **Public key:** G, H (see 1 for a simplified example)
- **Private key:** $D(.)$ (see 2 for a simplified example)

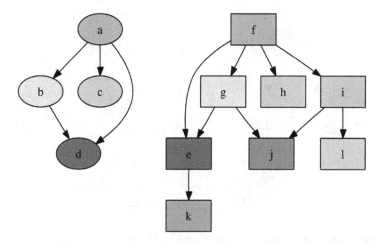

Fig. 1. Public key: G (round nodes) and H (rectangular nodes) graphs of IzoSign

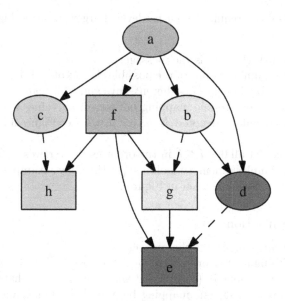

Fig. 2. Private key: mapping (dashed) between the nodes of G (round) and H (rectangular)

Signature Generation

Signature generation can be performed once per key as this is a one-time signature algorithm. To extend it to a digital signature algorithm, see Section 3. We assume that the users of the system have agreed upon a secure hash algorithm (denoted as $h(.)$) that maps messages to an integer between 0 and $\binom{n}{k} - 1$, where

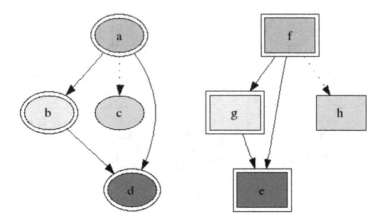

Fig. 3. Signature generation: subgraph chosen by the hash function in G (round) and corresponding nodes in H (rectangular)

$k \leq \binom{n}{k}$ specifies the required security level. Larger k means higher level but longer signatures.

1. Calculate $h(m)$ where m is the message.
2. Interpret this number as one of the possible choices of k of the n vertices of G. Since this can be done in $\binom{n}{k}$ different ways and $h(m)$ can have $\binom{n}{k}$ different values, this is a one-to-one mapping between hash values and choices. The chosen vertices will be denoted as v_i, $0 < i \leq k$ (see Figure 3 for a simplified example).
3. Present $D(v_i)$ for all $0 < i \leq k$ in the order as the vertices of G are indexed. This step is simply k memory lookups. (In the above example, for the nodes a, b, d, output f, g, e as seen in Figure 2).

Signature Verification

1. Calculate $h(m)$ where m is the message.
2. Interpret this number as one of the possible choices of k of the n vertices of G. Since this can be done in $\binom{n}{k}$ different ways and $h(m)$ can have $\binom{n}{k}$ different values, this is a one-to-one mapping between hash values and choices. The chosen vertices will be denoted as v_i, $0 < i \leq k$.
3. Check whether the subgraph of H specified by $D(v_i)$ is exactly the same as the subgraph of G specified by v_i. Since the vertices $D(v_i)$ in H will appear in the order as v_i appear in G, this is merely a memory compare operation of the restricted adjacency matrices.

Security of the Algorithm

Security analysis of the IzoSign OTS protocol is a relatively easy task, as it relies on a problem researched widely for the purpose of pattern recognition. Simple

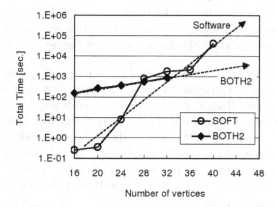

Fig. 4. Speed comparison of software-based and custom logic hardware-based (BOOT2) subgraph isomorphism algorithms (image from [20])

cases of the problem are known [16,17,18,19] and can be avoided at the time of graph generation; for general graphs, both the fastest algorithms and custom logics are exponential in the number of nodes. In particular, one should avoid graph generation algorithms that produce graphs with fixed genus (especially planar graphs), bounded valence, or graphs with adjacency matrices that have bounded eigenvalue multiplicity. Trivially testable necessary criterion for each of these properties exist. If all of them are tested and proven not to hold for a given graph, then this graph can be used as a key, because with high probability we can conclude that no currently known algorithm is able to break it in reasonable time.

According to the available literature, the following graph classes are "easy" for the algorithm:

- k-*connected partial k-trees:* having an algorithm in the order of $\mathcal{O}(n^{k+2})$ (that is, polynomial in n but exponential in k) [21];
- *partial k-trees of bounded degree:* also having an algorithm in the order of $\mathcal{O}(n^k)$ [22]. Either $k \sim n$, when this limit becomes exponential; or the k-tree has a linear number of edges (explained below), which is impossible using the graph generation specified in Section 2.
- *trees:* a subproblem of the above two cases, which is easy to match, but also easy to detect; furthermore, a tree of n nodes will have exactly $n-1$ edges, whereas the algorithm described generates graphs with quadratic edge count;
- *two-connected outerplanar graphs:* these graphs can be matched in cubic time[23], but outerplanar graphs are also planar and as such theycan be recognized in linear time [24]. These graphs can also be avoided if the number of edges is high (see below);
- *two-connected series-parallel graphs:* [25], series-parallel graphs are also outerplanar and therefore avoided;
- k-*connected partial k-paths:* [21,26], these graphs are a subset of k-connected partial k-trees with very low edge count, and are therefore avoided;

- *strongly regular graphs:* are easy for isomorphism [27,28] (albeit not yet shown to be polynomial for subgraph isomorphism), these graphs are avoided if the criteria of strong regularity is checked for when the key graph is generated.

We have seen that, by avoiding two cases of problems (namely partial k-trees and outerplanar graphs), we can avoid all currently known easy cases of the problem. It should be noted here that, albeit the problem itself is very well analyzed, there is no warranty that a research dated later than this paper will not find other simple classes of this problem. As long as these classes do not cover the whole set of key graphs, however, this will only break a given subset of keys and will only need minor patches to the algorithm. We will now prove that the simple cases are either avoided or are not that simple (i. e., polynomial) at all.

Partial k-trees of n nodes have $kn - \frac{k^2}{2} - \frac{k}{2} \leq kn$ edges [29], while every vertex of our key graph has a degree of $\frac{n}{2}$, thus it has an edge count in the order of n^2. Therefore, if our graph is a partial k-tree, then $k \sim n$. This results in an execution time of $\mathcal{O}(n^n)$, which is asymptotically worse than testing all the possible permutations.

Outerplanar graphs are planar. Planarity, first of all, can be checked in linear time [24]. One should also notice that the planarity criteria $e \leq 3n - 6$ for $n \geq 3$ leads to an edge count that is linear in the number of vertices. Our key graph, however, has quadratic edge count, therefore, for all practical values of n, it cannot be a planar graph.

We still need to specify the parameters of the graph. Extrapolating the research results of [20] with exponential fitting (see Figure 4), we choose $n = 256$ and $k = 128$ as key size of the algorithm. With these choices the matching of one resulting graph pattern is expected to require 70000 years to break using data-dependent custom logic circuits. This specifies H as a graph of 512 vertices.

Properties of the Algorithm

As shown above, this is a very fast algorithm for both signature and verification. *Fine-tuning* of the security level is possible both at key generation *and at signature creation time.* One might choose to present a longer signature for documents that require more confidence. With the parameters described above, vertex index can be stored on 9 bits. With these choices, the signature size will be 1152 bits; the public key is 130816 bits or 16 KB (if the adjacency matrix is stored), while the private key is 2304 bits (by simply storing the index of mapped vertices). These values are summarized in Figure 6.

Creating distributed signatures is feasible with the naive algorithm of dividing the knowledge of $D(.)$ between multiple users. A more sophisticated algorithm would be to have one distinct mapping $D_u(.)$ for each user and specify $D = D_1 \circ D_2 \circ ... \circ D_U$, where U is the count of users. This requires all the users to participate in the signature creation. Extending this algorithm is one of our current research directions.

All the above described properties will be preserved when IzoSign is converted into a digital signature scheme.

3   Extending IzoSign to a Digital Signature Scheme

As presented in Section 1, Merkle tree scheme can be used to transform an OTS into a digital signature scheme. We use a modified version of this scheme, where we store (and thus sign) keys in the vertices rather than message bits. It is important to notice that we still use public key signatures in the tree as opposed to the original Merkle tree.

We first define the user's private key as a graph, as in IzoSign (Section 2), and a pseudorandom sequence of permutations and extensions of this graph. We assume that this pseudorandom sequence can only be calculated by the user (i.e., it is a strong pseudorandom generator). We shall build a tree of this sequence; each node of this tree will be used for exactly one signature creation over either a message or a *self-certificate*.

A self-certificate can be thought of as a message saying "the messages signed with the private key whose public key is included should be considered signed by the owner of this key". It is mathematically a signed hash of a list of public keys. This way, by consuming only one key, a user can produce arbitrary many valid (OTS) keypairs. In order to make these keypairs easy to calculate on the fly, they shall be the elements of a random access pseudorandom sequence. Clearly, earlier elements of this sequence are used to sign further elements. Public elements are the public keys in the tree and the certificates; while private elements are private keys and the pseudorandom number generator. The number of elements signed in each round plays an important role as the list of keys (that are signed) should also be transmitted with the signature; and, as we will see, they will be transmitted with the signature of the message.

First, the CA issues $2z$ keys for the user. It does so by signing the hash of these keys (concatenated into one message, which also includes personal identification information) with one of its own keys. Then the user uses the first z keys to sign messages, while the remaining z keys will be used later to sign key lists of another $2z$ elements. We graphically represent the latter by connecting the given key to the $2z$ keys that it signs (Figure 5). This results in a tree of keys, with the root node being the key of the CA. We define the order of nodes as the breadth-first search. Whenever the user wants to sign a message, he first searches for the first unused key that can be used to sign a message. In order to have this signature accepted, he has to present

1. the signature;
2. all the public keys on the path from the root node to this node;
3. the signatures of the public key lists that contain the above nodes; and
4. to be able to verify the signatures, all the remaining public keys in the above key lists.

One might notice that, although a considerably large block is to be signed, constructing this block only requires memory reads, evaluation of the pseudorandom function and hash calculations. All these operations are very fast when compared to modular arithmetic calculations. After testing several criteria on G

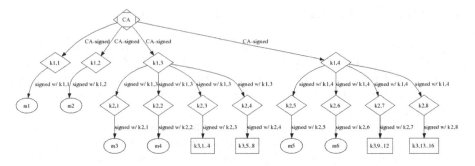

Fig. 5. Modified Merkle scheme

(before creating the first signature), only fast and memory-efficient operations are performed on the signature creation device. Therefore, this signature scheme is more useful in situations where computing performance and power consuption are more restricted than either available bandwidth or transmission time. It should also be noted that signature length is not constant, it grows over time. The first z signatures can be transmitted in $\sim k \log n$ bytes, while the further nodes will require $\sim kz \log n \log i$ bytes (where i is the count of signatures already consumed).

Another interesting property is that the signature security level (and thus the signature size) can be fine-tuned at the time of signature creation. One might choose a different k value for each message; larger k values provide more confidence while smaller values allow for shorter signatures. With the choices presented in Section 2 (that is, $n = 256$ and $k = 128$), and setting $z = 10$, the public key of the algorithm will be around 320 KB (a list of $2z$ IzoSign keys plus one signature on the hash), and the first 10 signatures will only require 1152 bits, while the next 100 require about 320 KB (for transmitting the second key block and its signature), and the next 1000 will need 640 KB. With one key, more than 111000 signatures are possible that are shorter than 1.2 MB. One should also note that, since all subtrees and signatures are generated on-the-fly, the memory requirements on the signer does not exceed the memory requirements for two IzoSign signatures. This adds up to 2.3 KB RAM and 576 bytes of ROM (see summary in Figure 6) plus the requirements of the hash function. All the memory-intensive calculations are done on the verification side, which does not require as secure computations as the signature creation and thus can be performed on a conventional PC.

4   Cached Subkeys Protocol

When two parties exchange messages regulary, it is quite impractical to send everything described above along each message. These messages will share some common parts as the whole path from the root node to the actual node (see Figure 5) are parts of the signature. The first note one should take that parts

Performance of algorithms	One-Time Signature	Digital Signature	Cached Subkeys	RSA
Public key	16KB	320KB	16KB	1-4KB
Private key	2304 bits	<300 bytes	<300 bytes	1-4KB
Initialization	-	-	320KB - 1.2MB	-
Signature	1152 bits	320KB - 1.2MB	~34KB	1-4KB
Signature creation	~1μs	~1ms (incl. transmission)	~20μs	~1-3s
Signature verification	~1μs	~1ms (incl. transmission)	~20μs	~1-3s

Fig. 6. Comparison of presented algorithms and RSA (on embedded devices)

already sent should not be sent again; instead, they should be cached on the other side. This, however, would not predict any decrease of the signature size if one communicates with multiple parties.

A naive algorithm would be to use distinct keys for each partner. This would increase the total number of keys in the system quadratically in the number of users. If, however, self-generated keys are used, then these keys are not necessarily known by the Certificate Authority, and thus will not put additional load on the system. So we will build two types of modified Merkle trees (see Figure 5): the first type have a root node signed by the CA, sign their own keys and the root key of the trees of the second type; while each second type tree will be used for signing messages for a given communicating partner. Each user has one first type tree, and will build one second type tree for each other party before sending messages to him. Since trees are traversed breadth-first while generating signatures, using one node in a second type tree also means that every node with a smaller index ("to the left or above" in Figure 5) are already transmitted. Therefore, these nodes should not be transmitted again. One either transmits these as required, or transmits key blocks ahead to avoid the variance of message size.

The non-common parts require $\sim kz \log n$ bytes, independent of the number of already consumed signatures, while the pre-transmitted blocks require space for $1/z$ graph and one signature. With the parameters above, this adds up to $\sim$ 34KB per message plus an initialization of 320KB to 1.2MB as seen in Figure 6, the latter required only once per communicating partner.

5   Conclusions

We presented a simple one-time signature scheme, and an application of a modified Merkle scheme to convert it into a digital signature scheme. The scheme is based on the hard problem of subgraph isomorphism, and is as hard as that problem. The main property of this scheme is that it generates signatures very fast (fast enough to make the hash calculation the bottleneck instead of actual signatures), in the expense of logarithmically growing signature sizes. In practical network use, the expected amount of data to be transmitted for each signature converges to a constant. There are two practical areas where this algorithm might be found useful: signature generation in sensor networks and inexpensive signature generation devices for everyday use.

In sensor networks, the central node might request a signature on a set of measurements that would generate an alert (we only sign important messages, as signing all of the measurements is usually uneconomical because of bandwidth requirements and key exposure). However, most currently existing algorithms are slow on embedded devices to generate signatures in real-time, at the request of the central node. With an IzoSign-based digital signature scheme, virtually any low-end hardware device can be equipped with the signature creation capability.

The everyday use of signature creation devices is mainly limited by their price. Decreasing the cost of signature creation devices by a factor of 10 would be necessary to make them competitive in the areas of micro- and macropayment and ticket vendor systems. In these areas, both the customer and the service provider are interested in non-repudiable signatures, and its not unlikely that a service provider would provide temporarily signature creation devices to the customers free of charge (i.e., costs included in the service fee) if prices of these devices would drop significantly.

Both the OTS and the digital signature scheme have fine-tunable parameters; some of them can be decided at signature creation time, thus allowing shorter signatures for transactions with lower requirements while maintaining the possibility of creating very strong signatures when needed.

References

1. Schneier, B.: Applied Cryptography: Protocols, Algorithms, and Source Code in C. John Wiley & Sons, Inc., New York (1993)
2. Rivest, R.L., Shamir, A., Adelman, L.M.: A method for obtaining digital signatures and public-key cryptosystems. Technical Report MIT/LCS/TM-82 (1977)
3. Cooper, D., Santesson, S., Farrell, S., Boeyen, S., Housley, R., Polk, W.: Internet x.509 public key infrastructure certificate and certificate revocation list (crl) profile (internet-draft) (2006),
   http://www.ietf.org/internet-drafts/draft-ietf-pkix-rfc3280bis-06.txt
4. Courtois, N.T., Goubin, L., Patarin, J.: Sflashv3, a fast asymmetric signature scheme. Cryptology ePrint Archive, Report 2003/211 (2003),
   http://eprint.iacr.org/
5. Gilbert, H., Minier, M.: Cryptanalysis of sflash. In: Knudsen, L.R. (ed.) EUROCRYPT 2002. LNCS, vol. 2332, Springer, Heidelberg (2002)
6. Dubois, V., Fouque, P.A., Shamir, A., Stern, J.: Breaking sflash,
   http://www.ecrypt.eu.org/webnews/webnews1206.htm#sflash

7. Cormen, T.H., Leiserson, C.E., Rivest, R.L.: Introduction to Algorithms. MIT Press, Cambridge, MA (1990)
8. Merkle, R.C.: A certified digital signature. In: Proceedings on Advances in Cryptology (1989)
9. European Parliament and Council: Directive 1999/93/ec on a community framework for electronic signatures (1999),
   http://europa.eu.int/ISPO/legal/en/ecommerc/digsig.html
   http://www.legi-internet.ro/diresignature.htm
10. U.S. House of Representative: Uniform electronic transactions act (UETA),
    http://www4.law.cornell.edu/uscode/15/7001.html
11. U.S. House of Representative: Electronic signatures in global and national commerce act (e-sign) (2000),
    http://frwebgate.access.gpo.gov/cgi-bin/getdoc.cgi?dbname=106_cong_
    public_laws&docid=:publ229.106.pdf
12. Aaronson, S.: (Complexity zoo),
    http://qwiki.caltech.edu/wiki/Complexity_Zoo
13. Venkatesan, R., Levin, L.: Random instances of a graph coloring problem are hard. In: Proceedings of the Twentieth Annual ACM Symposium on Theory of computing, ACM Press, New York (1988)
14. Levin, L.A., Venkatesan, R.: An average case NP-complete graph problem. Computer Science (2001)
15. Xu, S., Zhu, H., Zhang, G.: Digital signature schemes based on graph isomorphism and graph 3-colorability problems In: Proceedings of CrypTEC 1999
16. Filotti, I.S., Mayer, J.N.: A polynomial time algorithm for determining isomorphism of graphs of fixed genus. In: Proceedings of the Twelfth Annual ACM Symposium on Theory of Computing (1980)
17. Miller, G.: Isomorphism testing for graphs of bounded genus. In: Proceedings of the Twelfth Annual ACM Symposium on Theory of Computing (1980)
18. Luks, E.M.: Isomorphism of graphs of bounded valence can be tested in polynomial time. In: Proceedings of 21st IEEE FOCS Symp. (1980)
19. Babai, L., Grigoryev, D.Y., Mount, D.M.: Isomorphism of graphs with bounded eigenvalue multiplicity. In: Proceedings of the Fourteenth Annual ACM Symposium on Theory of Computing (1982)
20. Ichikawa, S., Yamamoto, S.: Data dependent circuit for subgraph isomorphism problem. In: Proceedings of 12th Int'l Conf. on Field Programmable Logic and Applications (2002)
21. Dessmark, A., Lingas, A., Proskurowski, A.: Faster algorithms for subgraph isomorphism of k-connected partial k-trees. In: European Symposium on Algorithms (1996)
22. Gupta, A., Nishimura, N.: The complexity of subgraph isomorphism for classes of partial k-trees. tcs 164 (1996)
23. Lingas, A.: Subgraph isomorphism for biconnected outerplanar graphs in cubic time. Theor. Comput. Sci. 63(3) (1989)
24. Hopcroft, J., Tarjan, R.: Efficient planarity testing. J. ACM 21(4), 549–568 (1974)
25. Lingas, A., Syslo, M.M.: A polynomial-time algorithm for subgraph isomorphism of two-connected series-parallel graphs. In: Lepistö, T., Salomaa, A. (eds.) Automata, Languages and Programming. LNCS, vol. 317, Springer, Heidelberg (1988)

26. Gupta, A., Nishimura, N.: Characterizing the complexity of subgraph isomorphism for graphs of bounded path-width. In: Puech, C., Reischuk, R. (eds.) STACS 1996. LNCS, vol. 1046, Springer, Heidelberg (1996)
27. Babai, L.: Automorphism groups, isomorphism reconstruction. In: Graham, R., Grötschel, M., Asz, L.L. (eds.) Handbook of Combinatorics, Elsevier Science, Amsterdam (1995)
28. Spielman, D.A.: Faster isomorphism testing of strongly regular graphs. In: STOC 1996: Proceedings of the twenty-eighth annual ACM symposium on Theory of computing, ACM Press, New York (1996)
29. Biedl, T.: Graph-Theoretic Algorithms. University of Waterloo (2004), http://www.student.cs.uwaterloo.ca/~cs762/Notes/lecture9.ps

Efficient ID-Based Digital Signatures
with Message Recovery

Raylin Tso[1], Chunxiang Gu[2], Takeshi Okamoto[1,†], and Eiji Okamoto[1,‡]

[1] Department of Risk Engineering
Graduate School of Systems and Information Engineering
University of Tsukuba, Japan
{raylin, †ken, ‡okamoto}@risk.tsukuba.ac.jp
[2] Network Engineering Department, Information Engineering University
Zhengzhou P.R. China
gcxiang5209@yahoo.com.cn

Abstract. A digital signature with message recovery is a signature that the message itself is not required to be transmitted together with the signature. Comparing with other (non-short) digital signatures, it has the advantage of small data size of communication. This kind of signature schemes have been widely investigated a decade ago, but, no ID-based message recovery signature is proposed until 2005 by Zhang et al. Since, up to the present, no method can be used to shorten ID-based signatures directly, ID-based message recovery signatures are regarded as a useful method to shorten ID-based signatures, in contrast to proposing a short signature scheme. In this paper, two new ID-based signature schemes with message recovery are proposed. The first one can deal with messages of fixed length and the second one can deal with messages of arbitrary length. Similar to Zhang et al.'s schemes, our schemes shows the idea of shortening ID-based signatures. However, our schemes are more efficient than Zhang et al.'s schemes. In addition, after comparing with Boneh et al.'s short signature (which is not ID-based), we find that although the communication cost is still a little larger than that of a short signature, the computational cost of our scheme is less than that of Boneh et al.'s short signature in the verification phase and our schemes surpass a short signature scheme in the concept of ID-based property. Under the hardness of k-BDHI problem, our schemes are proven secure in the random oracle model.

Keywords: ID-based signature, k-BDHI problem, message recovery, pairing, short signature.

1 Introduction

A digital signature scheme with message recovery [1,9] is a signature scheme that the original message of the signature is not required to be transmitted together with the signature. The message is embed in a signature and can be recovered

F. Bao et al. (Eds.): CANS 2007, LNCS 4856, pp. 47–59, 2007.

according to the verification/message-recovery process. It is different from an authenticated encryption scheme [12,13] or a signcryption scheme [2,22] in the sense that, in message recovery schemes, the embed messages can be recovered by anyone without any secret information. The purpose of this kind of signatures is to minimize the total length of the original message and the appended signature. Signature schemes with message recovery are useful for an organization where bandwidth is one of the main concerns. For example, on wireless devices such as PDAs, cell phones, RFID chips and sensors, battery life is the main limitation. Communicating even one bit of data uses significantly more power than executing one 32-bit instruction [3]. Reducing the number of bits to communicate saves power and is important to increase battery life.

It is also useful for the applications in which small messages should be signed. For example, small messages including time, date and identifiers are signed in certified email services and time stamping services. For instance of signing a postcard, it is also desirable to minimize the total length of the original message and the appended signature.

Related Works: It is obvious that an RSA signature [18] can be used with message recovery since it is unique in the sense that the signature and encryption functions are inverse to each other. But, for small size messages, it yields much larger signatures. For example, to sign a 100-bit message, the signature will be the size of 1024-bit. In 1993, Nyberg and Ruepple [15] proposed the first digital signature with message recovery based on the discrete logarithm problem (DL problem). Schemes based on the DL problem produce relatively small signatures when they are implemented over a finite group over elliptic curve. For example, a 320-bit signature is enough for a 100-bit message. Accordingly, DL problem based signature schemes with message recovery (as well as their variants) are appropriate for signing small messages and have been extensively investigated in the literatures (e.g., [1,14,15,16,20]).

The concept of identity-based (ID-based) cryptosystem was firstly introduced by Shamir [19] in 1984 which can simplify key management procedures of traditional certificate-based cryptography. Following this pioneering work, many ID-based cryptosystems have been proposed [4,6,8,10,21]. But, no ID-based signature scheme with message recovery was proposed until the scheme proposed by Zhang et al. [21] in 2005.

In [21], Zhang et al. proposed two schemes: an ID-based message recovery signature scheme for messages of fixed length, and an ID-based partial message recovery signature scheme for messages of arbitrary length. Their schemes not only showed message recovery signatures in an ID-based scenario but also solved the drawbacks of previous proposed schemes. That is, previous proposed signature schemes with message recovery can only deal with messages of fixed length and it is unclear how to extend them when the message exceeds some given size. In addition, since no method can be found to shorten ID-based signatures up to the present, Zhang et al. 's idea gives a new direction to shorten ID-based signatures in contrast to proposing a short signature scheme [7].

Our Contribution: Following Zhang et al. 's idea, this paper is supported by the motivation, namely how to shorten ID-based signatures *efficiently*, in construct to proposing a short signature scheme. The main contribution of this paper is to propose two ID-based signature schemes with message recovery which are more efficient than Zhang et al. 's schemes. Similar to their schemes, our second scheme is a variation of our first scheme in order to deal with messages of arbitrary length. In addition, comparing with Zhang et al. 's schemes, our schemes improve the computation cost by *one scalar multiplication* in the signing phase and almost *one pairing computation* in the verify/message-recovery phase. Our idea is inspired from Barreto et al.'s ID-based signature scheme [4] in the benefits that our schemes inherit the efficiency (ie., computation cost) of their scheme on one side and also reduce the communication cost comparing with [4] on the other side. Based on the hardness assumption of the Bilinear Diffie-Hellman Inverse (BDHI) problem [23], we will prove the security of the proposed scheme in the random oracle model.

The rest of this paper is organized as follows. in Section 2, we recall some preliminary works which will be used throughout this paper. In Section 3 and Section 4, we present our new scheme, its variation and the efficiency comparisons with other schemes. In Section 5, we give a concrete proof of our scheme in the random oracle model. Finally, we conclude this paper in Section 6.

2 Preliminaries

2.1 Bilinear Pairings and the Related Computational Assumption

Let $(G_1, +)$ and $(G_2, \cdot)$ be two cyclic groups of the same prime order q. $\hat{e} : G_1 \times G_1 \rightarrow G_2$ be a map which satisfies the following properties:

1. Bilinear: $\forall P, Q \in G_1, \forall \alpha, \beta \in Z_q, \hat{e}(\alpha P, \beta Q) = \hat{e}(P, Q)^{\alpha\beta}$,
2. Non-degenerate: If P is a generator of G_1, then $\hat{e}(P, P)$ is a generator of G_2,
3. Computable: There is an efficient algorithm to compute $\hat{e}(P, Q)$ for any $P, Q \in G_1$.

Such an bilinear map is called an *admissible bilinear pairing* [6]. The Weil pairings and the Tate pairings of elliptic curves can be used to construct efficient admissible bilinear pairings.

We review a complexity problem related to bilinear pairings: the Bilinear Diffie-Hellman Inverse (BDHI) problem [23]. Let P be a generator of G_1, and $a \in Z_q^*$.

- **k-BDHI problem:** given $(P, aP, a^2P, ...a^kP) \in (G_1^*)^{k+1}$, output $\hat{e}(P, P)^{a^{-1}}$. An algorithm $\mathcal{A}$ solves k-BDHI problem with the probability ε if

$$Pr[\mathcal{A}(P, aP, a^2P, ...a^kP) = \hat{e}(P, P)^{a^{-1}}] \geq \varepsilon,$$

where the probability is over the random choice of generator $P \in G_1^*$, the random choice of $a \in Z_q^*$ and random coins consumed by $\mathcal{A}$.

Definition 1. We say the hardness assumption of k-BDHI problem is (t, ϵ)-secure if there is no such algorithm $\mathcal{A}$ with at least ϵ advantage in solving the above problem within time t.

2.2 Scheme Model

An ID-based message recovery signature scheme is defined by four algorithms:

- **Setup:** A deterministic algorithm which takes as input a security parameter λ, outputs the Key generation Center KGC's private key, S_{KGC}, and public key, P_{pub}, together with the system parameters, *para*.
- **Extract:** A probabilistic algorithm which takes as input an identity, ID_i, of a user, outputs the user's private key, S_{ID_i}.
- **Sign:** A probabilistic algorithm which takes as input a signer's private key S_{ID} and a message m, outputs a signature σ.
- **Verify:** A deterministic algorithm which takes as input the sender's identity, ID, and the signature, σ, outputs 1 if σ is a valid signature. In this case, the original message can be recovered successfully. Otherwise, outputs 0.

2.3 Security Definition

For digital signatures, the widely accepted notion of security was defined by Goldwasser et al. in [11] as *existential forgery against adaptive chosen-message attack* (EF-ACMA). It's ID-based variation is defined via the following game. This game is executed between a challenger $\mathcal{C}$ and an adaptively chosen message adversary $\mathcal{A}$.

- The challenger $\mathcal{C}$ runs the setup algorithm to generate the system's parameters and sends them to the adversary $\mathcal{A}$.
- The adversary $\mathcal{A}$ performs a series of queries to the following oracles:
  - **Key extraction oracle $\mathcal{EX}$:** For each key extraction query on an identity ID, returns a private key corresponding to the identity.
  - **Signing oracle $\mathcal{OS}$:** For each signing query on a message and a signer's identity ID, produces a signature on the message using the private key corresponding to the identity.
- $\mathcal{A}$ outputs a triple (ID^*, M^*, σ^*) made of an identity ID^*.

We say $\mathcal{A}$ wins the game if the private key corresponding to the identity ID^* was never extracted, and a message-signature pair (M^*, σ^*) such that (M^*, ID^*) was not submitted to the signing oracle.

Definition 2. An ID-based digital signature scheme is said to be secure against EF-ACMA and identity attacks if no probabilistic polynomial time (PPT) adversary has a non-negligible advantage in the above game.

2.4 Notations

The following notations will be used throughout this paper:

- $a||b$: a concatenation of two strings a and b,.
- $\oplus$: X-OR computation in the binary system.

- $[x]_{10}$: the decimal notation of $x \in \{0,1\}^*$.
- $[y]_2$: the binary notation of $y \in Z$.
- $_{l_2}|\beta|$: the first l_2 bits of β from the left side.
- $|\beta|_{l_1}$: the first l_1 bits of β from the right side.
- G_1, G_2: two cyclic groups of the same order q, $|q| = l_1 + l_2$.
- $\hat{e} : G_1 \times G_1 \rightarrow G_2$: the admissible bilinear pairing.
- μ: the value of $\hat{e}(P, P)$.
- $H : \{0,1\}^* \rightarrow Z_q^*$: a cryptographic one-way hash function.
- $H_1 : \{0,1\}^* \rightarrow \{0,1\}^{l_1+l_2}$: a cryptographic one-way hash function.
- $F_1 : \{0,1\}^{l_1} \rightarrow \{0,1\}^{l_2}$: a cryptographic one-way hash function.
- $F_2 : \{0,1\}^{l_2} \rightarrow \{0,1\}^{l_1}$: a cryptographic one-way hash function.

3   Proposed Schemes

In this section, we present our first ID-based message recovery signature scheme with the restriction that it can deal with only messages of some fixed length (ie., $m \in \{0,1\}^{l_1}$ for some fixed integer l_1).

- **Setup:** On input a security parameter $\lambda \in N$, the algorithm outputs a random number $s \in Z_q^*$ as KGC's private key and sets $P_{pub} = sP$ as KGC's public key. The system parameters made public are

$$para = \{G_1, G_2, \hat{e}, q, P, P_{pub}, \mu, H, H_1, F_1, F_2, l_1, l_2\}.$$

- **Extract:** On input a user's identity $ID_i \in \{0,1\}^*$, KGC computes the user's private key $S_{ID_i} = (H(ID_i) + s)^{-1}P$. The user's ID-based public key P_{ID_i} is $(H(ID_i) + s)P$. From the view of a verifier, this can be computed as $H(ID_i)P + P_{pub}$.
- **Sign:** To sign a message $m \in \{0,1\}^{l_1}$, a signer A with private key S_{ID_A} does the following steps:
  (1) pick a random number $r_1 \in Z_q^*$, compute μ^{r_1} and $\alpha = H_1(ID_A, \mu^{r_1}) \in \{0,1\}^{l_1+l_2}$, where ID_A is a binary string representing the signer's identity,
  (2) compute $\beta = F_1(m)||(F_2(F_1(m)) \oplus m)$ and $r_2 = [\alpha \oplus \beta]_{10}$,
  (3) compute $U = (r_1 + r_2)S_{ID_A}$.
  The signature σ on m is (r_2, U).
- **Verify:** Given the signature σ and ID_A, a verifier does the following steps:
  (1) compute $\tilde{\alpha} = H_1(ID_A, \hat{e}(U, P_{ID_A})\mu^{-r_2})$,
  (2) compute $\tilde{\beta} = [r_2]_2 \oplus \tilde{\alpha}$,
  (3) recover the message $\tilde{m} = |\tilde{\beta}|_{l_1} \oplus F_2(_{l_2}|\tilde{\beta}|)$,
  (4) output 1 and accept σ as a valid signature of the message $\tilde{m}(= m)$ if and only if $_{l_2}|\tilde{\beta}| = F_1(\tilde{m})$.

Correctness: The correctness of this scheme can be proved as follows:

$$\hat{e}(U, P_{ID_A})\mu^{-r_2}$$
$$= \hat{e}((r_1 + r_2)S_{ID_A}, P_{ID_A})\hat{e}(P, P)^{-r_2}$$
$$= \hat{e}(S_{ID_A}, P_{ID_A})^{(r_1+r_2)}\hat{e}(P, P)^{-r_2}$$
$$= \hat{e}((H(ID_A) + s)^{-1}P, (H(ID_A) + s)P)^{r_1+r_2}$$
$$\hat{e}(P, P)^{-r_2}$$
$$= \hat{e}(P, P)^{r_1+r_2}\hat{e}(P, P)^{-r_2}$$
$$= \hat{e}(P, P)^{r_1} = \mu^{r_1}.$$

If σ is a valid signature, then $H_1(ID_A, \mu^{r_1}) = \alpha$ and

$$F_1(m)\|(F_2(F_1(m)) \oplus m) = \beta = [r_2]_2 \oplus \alpha.$$

Hence, we obtain

$$|\beta|_{l_1} \oplus F_2(l_2|\beta|)$$
$$= (F_2(F_1(m)) \oplus m) \oplus F_2(F_1(m))$$
$$= m.$$

Finally, the integrity of m is justified if $l_2|\beta| = F_1(m)$. $\qquad\square$

3.1   Variation (A Partial Message Recovery Scheme for Long Messages)

In this section, we simply modify the previous scheme so that the modified scheme can be used for messages of arbitrarily length (i.e., $m \in \{0, 1\}^*$).

- **Setup:** The same as the previous scheme.
- **Extract:** The same as the previous scheme.
- **Sign:** To sign a message $m \in \{0, 1\}^*$, A does the following steps:
  (1) divide m into $m_2\|m_1$ with $|m_1| = l_1$,
  (2) pick a random number $r_1 \in Z_q^*$, compute μ^{r_1} and $\alpha = H_1(ID_A, m_2, \mu^{r_1})$,
  (3) compute $\beta = F_1(m_1)\|(F_2(F_1(m_1)) \oplus m_1)$ and $r_2 = [\alpha \oplus \beta]_{10}$,
  (4) compute $U = (r_1 + r_2)S_{ID_A}$.
  The signature σ on m is (r_2, U) and the partial message m_2 is sent together with σ.
- **Verify:** Given the signature σ, the partial message m_2 and ID_A:
  (1) compute $\tilde{\alpha} = H_1(ID_A, m_2, \hat{e}(U, P_{ID_A})\mu^{-r_2})$,
  (2) compute $\tilde{\beta} = [r_2]_2 \oplus \tilde{\alpha}$,
  (3) recover $\tilde{m}_1 = |\tilde{\beta}|_{l_1} \oplus F_2(l_2|\tilde{\beta}|)$,
  (4) output 1 and accept σ if and only if $l_2|\tilde{\beta}| = F_1(\tilde{m}_1)$, otherwise, output 0 and abort the next step,
  (5) recover $m = m_2\|\tilde{m}_1$.

Correctness: The correctness of the scheme is straightforward according to that of the previous scheme.

Table 1. Performance Evaluation

	ID-based	Total Length	Sign	Verify
Scheme 1*	Y	$\lvert q \rvert + \lvert G_1 \rvert$	$1Exp. + 1EC$	$1\hat{e} + 1Exp. + 1EC$
Scheme 2†	Y	$\lvert m \rvert - l_1 + \lvert q \rvert + \lvert G_1 \rvert$	$1Exp. + 1EC$	$1\hat{e} + 1Exp. + 1EC$
BLMQ[4]	Y	$\lvert m \rvert + \lvert q \rvert + \lvert G_1 \rvert$	$1Exp. + 1EC$	$1\hat{e} + 1Exp. + 1EC$
BLS[7]	No	$\lvert m \rvert + \lvert G_1 \rvert$	$1EC + 1\mathcal{H}$	$2\hat{e} + 1EC + 1\mathcal{H}$
ZSM[21] 1*	Y	$\lvert q \rvert + \lvert G_1 \rvert$	$1Exp. + 2EC$	$2\hat{e} + 1Exp + 1\mathcal{H}.$
ZSM[21] 2†	Y	$\lvert m \rvert - k_2 + \lvert q \rvert + \lvert G_1 \rvert$	$1Exp. + 2EC$	$2\hat{e} + 1Exp. + 1\mathcal{H}$

* Available for messages of fixed length only.
† $k_2 = l_1 = 91$.

4   Performance Comparison

Denote our scheme and the modified scheme by Scheme 1 and Scheme 2, respectively. In this section, we compare our schemes with [7], [4] and [21] in total length of "$\lvert signature \rvert + \lvert message \rvert$" and the computation cost required by a signer and a verifier, respectively. The scheme in [7] is a short signature scheme with efficient communication and computation cost. The scheme in [4] is an efficient ID-based signature scheme which our schemes are based on, and the schemes in [21] are the first ID-based message recovery signature schemes proposed by Zhang et al.

In Table 1, we denote by $\hat{e}$ a computation of the pairing, EC an ordinary scalar multiplication in G_1, and $Exp.$ an exponential operation in G_2. In addition, the hash functions used by our schemes and the scheme of BLMQ[4] are generic and efficient so the computation cost can be neglected. On the contrary, Boneh et al. [7] and Zhang et al. [21] 's schemes depend on a special hash function called "MaptoPoint", which is still probabilistic and usually not efficient enough to be neglected. The computation of a "MaptoPoint" hash is denoted by $\mathcal{H}$ in Table 1.

To compare at approximately the same security as a standard 1024-bit RSA signature, q should be a 170-bit prime and G_1 be a group where each element of G_1 is 171-bit if we use any of the families of curves described in [7]. In addition, $l_1 = k_2 = 91$ according to [21] in order to obtain a 2^{-80} probability of the verification condition holding for an attempted forgery generated by an adversary.

The total length of the signature produced by our scheme I is $\lvert r_2 + U \rvert = \lvert q \rvert + \lvert G_1 \rvert$. This signature can be used to sign and recover a message m with $\lvert m \rvert = l_1 = 91$ bits. The total length required in our scheme II is $\lvert m_2 + r_2 + U \rvert = \lvert m \rvert - l_1 + \lvert q \rvert + \lvert G_1 \rvert$. Scheme II can be used to sign a message m of arbitrary length. The communication cost (ie., the total length) required in our schemes and ZSM[21] are the same. But, our schemes improves the computational cost by $1EC$ in the signing phase and almost $1\hat{e}$ in the verify/recovery phase.

To compare with Boneh et al. 's short signature scheme [7] which has the least data size of a signature, we see from these results that the total length in our schemes is about $\lvert q \rvert - l_1 = 79$-bit larger then that of [7]. But, our schemes happens to be faster than [7] at verification and exceed [7] in the aspect of ID-based propoerty.

To compare with the scheme in [4], we have the same computation cost but different communication cost. Actually, our schemes are faster than all known pairing-based IBS methods according to [4] since our schemes inherit the efficiency of [4] but surpass [4] in the aspect of total length (i.e., $|message|$ + $|signature|$).

5   Security Proof

Since the two schemes are essentially the same and can be proved in a similar way, we give a concrete security proof of the basic scheme in this section only. We will show that the proposed scheme is secure against EF-ACMA and identity attacks in the random oracle model, assuming the hardness of k-BDHI problem (see Definition 1).

We assume through this paper that the k-BDHI problem is intractable, which means that there is no polynomial time algorithm to solve k-BDHI problem with non-negligible probability.

Theorem 1. In the random oracle model, let $\mathcal{A}_0$ be a polynomial-time adversary whose input only consists of public data, and can succeed in existential forgery on our scheme (IDMR) with un-negligible probability. We denote respectively by n_0, n_1 and n_s the number of queries that $\mathcal{A}_0$ can ask to the random oracle $H(.)$, $H_1(.)$ and the singing oracle $Sign(.)$. Then we show how to construct another adversary $\mathcal{A}_1$ who can solve the $(n_0 + 1)$-BDHI problem with un-negligible probability.

Proof: Without any loss of generality, we may assume that for any ID, $\mathcal{A}_0$ queries $H(.)$ with ID before ID is used as (part of) an input of any query to $Extract(.)$ and $Sign(.)$.

$\mathcal{A}_1$ is given input parameters of pairing $(q, G_1, G_2, \hat{e})$ and a random instance $(P, aP, a^2P, ..., a^{n_0}P, a^{n_0+1}P)$ of the (n_0+1)-BDHI problem, where P is random in G_1^* and a is a random number in Z_q^*. $\mathcal{A}_1$ simulates the challenger and interacts with $\mathcal{A}_0$ as follows:

1. $\mathcal{A}_1$ randomly chooses different $h_0, h_1, ...h_{n_0-1} \in Z_q^*$, and computes $f(x) = \prod_{i=1}^{n_0-1}(x+h_i) = \sum_{i=0}^{n_0-1} c_i x^i$.
2. $\mathcal{A}_1$ computes $Q = \sum_{i=0}^{n_0-1} c_i a^i P = f(a)P$, $aQ = \sum_{i=0}^{n_0-1} c_i a^{i+1}P$, and $Q' = \sum_{i=1}^{n_0-1} c_i a^{i-1}P$. In the (unlikely) situation where $Q = 1_{G_1}$, there exists an $h_i = -a$, hence, $\mathcal{A}_1$ can solve the (n_0+1)-BDHI problem directly and abort.
3. $\mathcal{A}_1$ computes $f_i(x) = f(x)/(x+h_i) = \sum_{j=0}^{n_0-2} d_j x^j$. Obviously, $(a+h_i)^{-1}Q = (a + h_i)^{-1}f(a)P = f_i(a)P = \sum_{j=0}^{n_0-2} d_j a^j P$ for $1 \le i \le n_0$.
4. $\mathcal{A}_1$ randomly chooses an index t with $1 \le t \le n_0$, sets $v = 0$.
5. $\mathcal{A}_1$ sets the system parameters $para = (G_1, G_2, q, \hat{e}, Q, P_{pub}, \mu, H, H_1, F_1, F_2, l_1, l_2)$, where $P_{pub} = aQ - h_0Q$ and $\mu = \hat{e}(Q, Q)$. H, H_1, F_1 and F_2 are random oracles controlled by $\mathcal{A}_1$.

6. $\mathcal{A}_1$ runs $\mathcal{A}_0$ by giving $\mathcal{A}_0$ the system parameters *para*. During the execution, $\mathcal{A}_1$ emulates $\mathcal{A}_0$'s oracles as follows:

   - $H(.)$: $\mathcal{A}_1$ maintains a H-List, initially empty. For a query ID, if ID already appears on the H-List in a tuple (ID, l, D), $\mathcal{A}_1$ responds with l. Otherwise, sets $v \leftarrow v + 1$ and $ID_v \leftarrow ID$. Then, if $v = t$, $\mathcal{A}_1$ sets $l_v \leftarrow h_0$, $D_v \leftarrow \perp$; otherwise, $\mathcal{A}_1$ selects a random ϑ with $n_0 \geq \vartheta > 0$ which has not been chosen and sets $l_v \leftarrow h_\vartheta + h_0$, $D_v \leftarrow (a + h_\vartheta)^{-1}Q$. In both case, adds the tuple (ID_v, l_v, D_v) to H-List and responds with l_v.

   - $H_1(.)$: If $\mathcal{A}_0$ makes a query (ID, μ^r) to random oracle $H_1(.)$, $\mathcal{A}_1$ checks if $H_1(ID, \mu^r)$ is defined. If not, it picks a random $\alpha \in \{0, 1\}^{l_1 + l_2}$, and sets $H_1(ID, \mu^r) \leftarrow \alpha$. $\mathcal{A}_1$ returns α to $\mathcal{A}_0$ and records (ID, μ^r, α) to the H_1-List.

   - $F_1(.)$ and $F_2(.)$ queries: $\mathcal{A}_0$ can also query the random oracle $F_1(.)$ and $F_2(.)$ at any time. $\mathcal{A}_1$ simulates the oracles $F_1(.)$ and $F_2(.)$ in a same similar to that of the $H_1(.)$ oracle, keeping an F_1-List and F_2-List of tuples, respectively.

   - *Extract*$(.)$: For input ID_i, $\mathcal{A}_1$ searches in H-List for (ID_i, l_i, D_i). If $D_i = \perp$ then $\mathcal{A}_1$ aborts. Otherwise, $\mathcal{A}_1$ responds with D_i.

   - *Sign*$(.)$: For input ID_i and message m, If $i \neq t$, $\mathcal{A}_1$ uses D_i as the private key to sign on m. Otherwise, $\mathcal{A}_1$ simulates ID_t's signature as following:

     - Pick randomly $U \in G_1$, $r_2 \in Z$ with $|r_2| \leq |q|$.
     - Compute $\delta = \mu^{-r_2} \cdot \hat{e}(U, aQ)$, in the unlikely situation where $\delta = 1$, we discard the results and restart the simulation.
     - Compute $\alpha = r_2 \oplus F_1(m) \| (F_2(F_1(m)) \oplus m)$. Record $F_1(m)$ and $F_2(m)$ to the corresponding list if necessary (ie., if m has not been queried to $F_1(.)$ and $F_2(.)$).
     - Check the H_1-List and restart the simulation if $\alpha = H_1(x)$ already exists for some x while $x \neq (ID_i, \delta)$. Otherwise, set $\alpha = H_1(ID_i, \delta)$ and record (α, ID_i, δ) to the H_1-List.
     - returns (r_2, U).

7. $\mathcal{A}_1$ keeps interacting with $\mathcal{A}_0$ until $\mathcal{A}_0$ halts or aborts. If $\mathcal{A}_0$ outputs a forgery (ID_i, m, r_2, U), and $i = t$, $\mathcal{A}_1$ can get a forgery corresponding to identity ID_t (whose secret key is $a^{-1}Q$). Using the "General" Forking Lemma [5], by replays of Step 6 with the same random tape but different choices of $H_1(.)$, $\mathcal{A}_1$ can get another valid forgery (ID_i^*, r_2^*, U^*) such that $r_2^* \neq r_2$ while $ID_i = ID_i^*$ and $\mu^{-r_2} \cdot \hat{e}(U, aQ) = \mu^{-r_2^*} \cdot \hat{e}(U^*, aQ)$. This part will be discussed later.

8. $\mathcal{A}_1$ can computes $a^{-1}Q$ as follows:

$$a^{-1}Q = (r_2 - r_2^*)^{-1}(U - U^*).$$

9. $\mathcal{A}_1$ computes $\hat{e}(Q, a^{-1}Q) = \hat{e}(Q, Q)^{a^{-1}}$. Then, $\mathcal{A}_1$ computes and outputs

$$\hat{e}(P, P)^{a^{-1}} = \hat{e}(Q, Q)^{a^{-1}} / \hat{e}(Q', Q + c_0 P))^{c_0^{-2}}$$

as the solution to the given instance of $(n_1 + 1)$-BDHI problem.

This completes the description of $\mathcal{A}_1$.

The proof in step 7 uses the forking technique which involves running the attacker $\mathcal{A}_0$ for solving our scheme twice, answering its l^*-th $H_1(.)$ query differently in the two runs to obtain two distinct solutions (r_2, U) and (r_2^*, U^*) such that $\mu^{-r_2} \cdot \hat{e}(U, aQ) = \mu^{-r_2^*} \cdot \hat{e}(U^*, aQ)$, from which the solution $a^{-1}Q = (r2 - r_2^*)^{-1}(U - U^*)$ can be found.

Since our scheme is not a generic signature scheme, the original Forking Lemma defined in [17] can not be applied in this proof. Another solution is to use the General Forking Lemma recently proposed by M. Bellare and G. Neven in [5]. For completeness, we give the details of the forking technique used in this proof in the appendix. □

6   Conclusion

This paper presents two efficient ID-based signature schemes with message recovery. Our schemes are more efficient than the previous schemes proposed by Zhang et al. The scheme we proposed in this paper can be regarded as an improvement of Barreto el al. 's signature scheme [4] since our scheme not only inherits the efficiency of their scheme but also reduce the total length of a message and the corresponding signature comparing to [4]. We showed in this paper a new idea to efficiently shorten ID-based signatures in contrast to proposing a short signature scheme directly.

References

1. Abe, M., Okamoto, T.: A signature scheme with message recovery as secure as discrete logarithm. In: Lam, K.-Y., Okamoto, E., Xing, C. (eds.) ASIACRYPT 1999. LNCS, vol. 1716, pp. 378–389. Springer, Heidelberg (1999)
2. Bao, F., Deng, R.H.: A signcryption scheme with signature directly verifiable by public key. In: Imai, H., Zheng, Y. (eds.) PKC 1998. LNCS, vol. 1431, pp. 55–59. Springer, Heidelberg (1998)
3. Barr, K., Asanovic, K.: Energy aware lossless data compression. In: MobiSys 2003. Proceedings of the ACM Conference on Mobile Systems, Applications, and Services (2003)
4. Barreto, P.S.L.M., Libert, B., McCullagh, N., Quisquater, J.: Efficient and provably-secure identity-based signatures and signcryption from bilinear maps. In: Atkinson, C., Bunse, C., Gross, H.-G., Peper, C. (eds.) ASIACRYPT 2005. LNCS, vol. 3778, pp. 515–532. Springer, Heidelberg (2005)
5. Bellare, M., Neven, G.: Multi-signatures in the plain public-key model and a general forking lemma. In: Proceedins of the 13th ACM Confetence on Computer and Communication Security, pp. 390–398 (2006)
6. Boneh, D., Franklin, M.: Identity-based encryption from the Weil pairing. In: Kilian, J. (ed.) CRYPTO 2001. LNCS, vol. 2139, pp. 213–229. Springer, Heidelberg (2001)
7. Boneh, D., Lynn, B., Shacham, H.: Short signatures from the weil pairing. In: Boyd, C. (ed.) ASIACRYPT 2001. LNCS, vol. 2248, pp. 514–533. Springer, Heidelberg (2001)

8. Boyen, X.: Multipurpose identity-based signcryption: a Swiss army knife for identity-based cryptography. In: Boneh, D. (ed.) CRYPTO 2003. LNCS, vol. 2729, pp. 382–398. Springer, Heidelberg (2003)
9. Chen, K.: Signature with message recovery. Electronics Leters 34(20), 1934 (1998)
10. Chen, L., Lee, J.M.: Improved identity-based signcryption. In: Vaudenay, S. (ed.) PKC 2005. LNCS, vol. 3386, pp. 362–379. Springer, Heidelberg (2005)
11. Goldwasser, S., Micali, S., Rivest, R.L.: A digital signature scheme secure against adaptive chosen-message attacks. SIAM Journal of Computing 17(2), 281–308 (1988)
12. Horster, P., Michels, M., Petersen, H.: Authenticated encyprtion scheme with low communication costs. Electronics Letters 30(15), 1212–1213 (1994)
13. Lee, W.-B., Chang, C.-C.: Publicly verifiable authenticated encryption. Electronics Letters 31(19), 1656–1657 (1995)
14. Miyaji, A.: A message recovery signature scheme equivalent to DSA over elliptic curves. In: Kim, K.-c., Matsumoto, T. (eds.) ASIACRYPT 1996. LNCS, vol. 1163, pp. 1–14. Springer, Heidelberg (1996)
15. Nyberg, K., Tuepple, R.A.: A new signature scheme based on the DSA giving message recovery. In: Proceedings of the 1st ACM conference on communication and computer security, pp. 58–61 (1993)
16. Nyberg, K., Ruepple, R.A.: Message recovery for signature schemes based on the discrete logarithm problem. In: De Santis, A. (ed.) EUROCRYPT 1994. LNCS, vol. 950, pp. 182–193. Springer, Heidelberg (1995)
17. Pointcheval, D., Stern, J.: Security arguments for digital signatures and blind signatures. Journal of Cryptology 13(3), 361–396 (2000)
18. Rivest, R.L., Shamir, A., Adleman, L.: A method for obtaining digital signatures and public key cryptosystems. Communications of the ACM 21, 120–126 (1978)
19. Shamir, A.: Identity-based cryptosystems and signature schemes. In: Blakely, G.R., Chaum, D. (eds.) CRYPTO 1984. LNCS, vol. 196, pp. 47–53. Springer, Heidelberg (1985)
20. Yeun, C.Y.: Digital signature with message recovery and authenticated encryption (signcryption)- a comparison. In: Walker, M. (ed.) Cryptography and Coding. LNCS, vol. 1746, pp. 307–312. Springer, Heidelberg (1999)
21. Zhang, F., Susilo, W., Mu, Y.: Identity-based partial message recovery signatures (or How to shorten ID-based signatures). In: Patrick, A.S., Yung, M. (eds.) FC 2005. LNCS, vol. 3570, pp. 45–56. Springer, Heidelberg (2005)
22. Zheng, Y.: Digital signcryption or how to achieve cost (signature & encryption $\ll$ cost (signature) + cost (encryption). In: Kaliski Jr., B.S. (ed.) CRYPTO 1997. LNCS, vol. 1294, pp. 165–179. Springer, Heidelberg (1997)
23. Boneh, D., Boyen, X.: Efficient Selective ID Secure Identity Based Encryption without Random Oracles. In: Cachin, C., Camenisch, J.L. (eds.) EUROCRYPT 2004. LNCS, vol. 3027, pp. 223–238. Springer, Heidelberg (2004)

Appendix

The Forking Technique

Let Θ, Ω be the random tapes given to the simulator $\mathcal{A}_1$ and the adversary $\mathcal{A}_0$, respectively, such that $\mathcal{A}_0$ outputs a forged signature. Notice that the success probability of $\mathcal{A}_0$ is taken over the space defined by Θ, Ω and the random oracles.

At the first run, the simulator $\mathcal{A}_1$ acts exactly the same as that described at the beginning of this proof. At the end of this run, $\mathcal{A}_0$ outputs a successful forgery (ID_i, m, r_2, U).

Note: In our scheme, the method of computing α is equivalent to querying $(ID_i, \mu^{-r_2} \cdot \hat{e}(U, aQ))$ to $H_1(.)$ Due to the ideal randomness of $H_1(.)$, with probability at least $1 - 2^{-(l_1 + l_2)}$, there exists a $H_1(.)$ query on input $(ID_i, \mu^{-r_2} \cdot \hat{e}(U, aQ))$ if (r_2, U) is a successful forgery. Assume this query occurs at the l^*-th $H_1(.)$ query.

At the second run, with the same random tapes Θ, Ω given to the simulator $\mathcal{A}_1$ and the adversary $\mathcal{A}_0$, this run is almost the same as the first run except the simulation of the $H_1(.)$ oracle. This time, for any j-th $H_1(.)$ query with $j < l^*$, $\mathcal{A}_1$ responds to $\mathcal{A}_0$ with the same value as that at the first run. However, for any j-th $H_1(.)$ query with $j \geq i^*$, $\mathcal{A}_1$ picks a random number $\alpha_j \in \{0,1\}^{l_1 + l_2}$ and responds with α_j. Finally, at the end of the second run, $\mathcal{B}$ outputs its forgery (ID_i^*, r_2^*, U^*) on a message m^*.

Remember that $\mathcal{A}_0$ can query at most n_1 times to the $H_1(.)$ query. For $l \in \{1, \cdots, n_1\}$, we call a run of $\mathcal{A}_0$ l-successful if $\mathcal{A}_0$ succeeds and $l^* = l$. Note that if both runs of $\mathcal{A}_0$ are l-successful for some l with regard to the $H_1(.)$ query, then, since the view of $\mathcal{A}_0$ in both runs is the same up to the l-th $H_1(.)$ response, ID_i, δ (here δ equals to μ^{r_1} and is in the input of the l-th $H_1(.)$ query in the first run) must be equal to ID_i^*, δ^*. This implies that $r_1 = r_1^*$ in both runs. In addition, due to the ideal randomness of $F_1(.)$ and $F_2(.)$, when $ID_i = ID_i^*$, $r_1 = r_1^*$ and $\alpha_1 = H_1(ID_i, \delta) \neq H_1'(ID_i^*, \delta^*) = \alpha^*$, the probability of $r_2 = r_2^*$ is negligible (which is equal to $1/2^{l_1 + l_2}$). $r_2 \neq r_2^*$ implies $U \neq U^*$ since $r_1 = r_1^*$. Consequently, from this forking technique, the $(n_0 + 1)$-BDHI problem can be solved.

It remains to estimate the probability of the event $\mathcal{S}^*$ that both runs of $\mathcal{A}_0$ are l-successful with regard to the $H_1(.)$ query for some $l \in \{1, \cdots, n_1\}$. To do this, we split $\mathcal{S}^*$ into n_1 distinct subevents $\mathcal{S}_i^*$ according the value of l and bound each one. For each l, let Γ_l denote the outcome space for the random variable $X_l = (\Theta, \Omega, \alpha_1, \cdots, \alpha_{l-1})$ consisting of the view of $\mathcal{A}_0$ up to the l-th query to $H_1(.)$, and let Υ_i denote the outcome space for the independent random variable $Y_i = (\alpha_l, \cdots, \alpha_{n_1})$ consisting of the view of $\mathcal{A}_0$ after the l-th query to H_1. We need the following lemma.

Lemma 1. (The Splitting Lemma): [17] Let $\mathcal{S} \subset \Gamma \times \Upsilon$ such that $Pr[(X,Y) \in \mathcal{S}] \geq \varepsilon$. For any $\lambda < \varepsilon$, define

$$\varphi = \left\{ (X,Y) \in \Gamma \times \Upsilon \mid \Pr_{Y' \in \Upsilon}[(X,Y') \in \mathcal{S}] \geq \varepsilon - \lambda \right\},$$

then the following statements hold:

(i) $Pr[\varphi] \geq \lambda$.
(ii) $\forall (X,Y) \in \varphi$, $\Pr_{Y' \in \Upsilon}[(X,Y') \in \mathcal{S}] \geq \varepsilon - \lambda$.

Define $\mathcal{S}_l$ be the event that a run of $\mathcal{A}_0$ is l-successful. Then, $\mathcal{S}_l$ is a subset of $\Gamma_l \times \Upsilon_l$ with probability $p_l \overset{\Delta}{=} \Pr[(X_l, Y_l) \in \mathcal{S}_l]$. Applying the Splitting Lemma and set $\lambda \leftarrow p_l/2$, we know that there exists a subevent φ_l of $\mathcal{S}_l$ such that $\Pr[(X_l, Y_l) \in \varphi_l] \geq p_l/2$ (according to (i)), and for each $(X, Y) \in \varphi_l$, the probability that $(X, Y') \in \mathcal{S}_l$ over a random choice of Y' in φ_l is also at least $p_l/2$ (according to (ii)). Therefore, the probability that the outcome (X, Y) of the first run of $\mathcal{A}_0$ in our algorithm is in φ_l is at least $p_l/2$, and, for each of those outcomes, the probability over the random choice of $Y' = (\alpha'_l, \cdots, \alpha'_{n_1})$ that the second run outcome (X, Y') is in $\mathcal{S}_l$ is at least $p_l - p_l/2 = p_l/2$. Since α'_l is uniformly chosen in $\{0,1\}^{l_1+l_2}$, with probability $1/2^{l_1+l_2}$ it will collide with α_l. Consequently, we have that $(X, Y) \in \varphi_l$, $(X, Y') \in \mathcal{S}_l$ and $\alpha_l \neq \alpha'_l$ with probability at least $p_l/2 \cdot (p_l/2 - 1/2^{l_1+l_2})$ which implies that both runs are l-successful and $\alpha_l \neq \alpha'_l$. That is, the event $\mathcal{S}_l^*$ occurs.

Since p_l is the probability that a run of $\mathcal{A}_0$ is l-successful, define $Adv_{\mathcal{A}_0}^{IDMR}$ be the probability of event that $\mathcal{A}_0$ can break the unforgeability of our scheme. We have

$$Adv_{\mathcal{A}_0}^{IDMA} = \Sigma_{l=1}^{n_1} p_l \quad \text{and}$$

$$
\begin{aligned}
Pr[\mathcal{S}^*] &= \Sigma_{l=1}^{n_1} Pr[\mathcal{S}_l^*] = \Sigma_{l=1}^{n_1} p_l/2 \cdot (p_l/2 - 1/2^{l_1+l_2}) = \Sigma_{l=1}^{n_1} (p_l^2/4 - p_l/2^{l_1+l_2+1}) \\
&\geq 1/(4n_1) \cdot (\Sigma_{l=1}^{n_1} p_l)^2 - \Sigma_{l=1}^{n_1} p_l/2^{l_1+l_2+1} \\
&= 1/(4n_1) \cdot (Adv_{\mathcal{A}_0}^{IDMR})^2 - Adv_{\mathcal{A}_0}^{IDMR}/2^{l_1+l_1+1}.
\end{aligned}
$$

$Pr[\mathcal{S}^*]$ is the success probability on $\mathcal{A}_1$ to solve (n_0+1)-BDHI problem when $i = t$ in step 7. The inequality above comes from the Cauchy-Schwartz inequality. Since t is random chosen from $\{1, \cdots, n_0\}$, $\mathcal{A}_1$ solves (n_0+1)-BDHI problem with probability $Pr[\mathcal{S}^*]/n_0$. This ends the proof.   □

Achieving Mobility and Anonymity in IP-Based Networks

Rungrat Wiangsripanawan[1], Willy Susilo[1], and Rei Safavi-Naini[2]

[1] Centre for Computer and Information Security Research (CCISR)
School of Computer Science and Software Engineering
University of Wollongong, Australia
rw26@uow.edu.au, wsusilo@uow.edu.au
[2] University of Calgory, Canada
rei@cpsc.ucalgary.ca

Abstract. Mobility and anonymity are two essential properties desirable in IP-based networks. In this paper, we aim to address the issue on how to achieve mobility and anonymity concurrently. At a glance, these two properties seem to be contradictory. This is partly due to the fact that there exists *no* single definition that clearly defines these notions. We approach this problem by firstly define these properties formally and address the problem of achieving these properties at the same time. Then, we proceed with a concrete construction based on an existing IP-based network, which is Tor. Without losing generality, our method can be applied to any other existing network, such as Morphmix or Tarzan. We highlight the difficulty of achieving mobility and anonymity concurrently although it seems trivial to merge these two properties altogether. Finally, we evaluate our proposed construction based on the definition that we have developed. Our work can be seen as the *first* attempt towards formalizing the notions of mobility, anonymity and location privacy.

Keywords: mobility, anonymity, location privacy, IP networks, Tor, Mobile IP.

1 Introduction

Consider a situation where a businessman is on his holiday. Firstly, he does not want his location to be traced by his company when he is accessing the Internet. Considering the nature of the businessman, he wants to have *mobility*. That means during his movement, he wants to have a continuous connection to the Internet. This requirement implies that if he is downloading streaming contents on a train, for example, the process should continue even if the train has enforced network movements. Furthermore, he wants his anonymity to be ensured during his trip. For instance, from time to time, the businessman would like to check the status of the stock market, etc. and he wants his identity to be protected. In this scenario, we have seen that mobility and anonymity is often desirable *at the same time*. Additionally, location privacy is an additional feature that people would like to have since the support from the Internet has made this

F. Bao et al. (Eds.): CANS 2007, LNCS 4856, pp. 60–79, 2007.

possible. Unfortunately, as we shall show in the next section, these requirements are contradictory to each other as adding mobility to an anonymous network system means that location privacy is lost.

Our Contributions. In this paper, we aim to address how to achieve mobility and anonymity in IP based networks *concurrently.* Additionally, we would like to provide the notion of location privacy to the users in this setting. To date, the existing works do not define precisely what they meant by anonymity and location privacy. Therefore, we firstly define these notions formally. Then, we proceed with a concrete system that will provide mobility and anonymity *at the same time.* We start our design by using the existing systems (i.e. combining Mobile IP with Tor), but unfortunately we will show that a trivial merge between the existing systems will not result in a desirable system. We note that essentially Mobile IP provides mobility and Tor provides anonymity, but a combination between these two will *not* be sufficient to achieve what is required in our scenario. We also propose our new design that can achieve the desirable system as stated in the motivating scenario. Finally, we also show that our design satisfies all the formal definitions that we put forth in the beginning.

1.1 Related Works

To date, there are many works in the literature that have been proposed to provide anonymity. This includes the works on low latency networks (e.g. Tor [20], Morphmix [15] and Tarzan [9]) to name a few. Furthermore, several works have also been proposed to provide mobility [22,17,11,14]. As mobility always leaks the location of the host, some works have been proposed to address this issue by adding location privacy to the existing mobility systems [8,4].

Flying Freedom [7] seems to be the only system to date that provides mobility, anonymity and location privacy at the same time. Nevertheless, this network is built on top of the architecture of the Freedom Network [10], that is no longer available[1,2] and the network itself has ceased.

Therefore, the seek for a system that provides mobility, location privacy and anonymity at the same time remains an interesting research question. A combination of the two different systems, where each system provides either mobility or anonymity, seems to be the candidate to provide the solution to this problem. Unfortunately, an inherent problem that will occur is the location privacy problem. Enhancing the system with the existing location privacy mechanisms also results in a lengthy communication path, which will lead to a very ineffective system. We will elaborate this issue in a later section. We note that we are not interested in building a new system from scratch. Instead, we will use available architectures as our building blocks.

2 Towards Formalizing Mobility and Anonymity Notions

In this section, we aim to clarify the notions of mobility and anonymity by firstly presenting their definition in a high level, and proceed with a formal definition to capture these notions.

2.1   Mobility

Roughly speaking, mobility is the ability of moving from one location to another. In the context of IP-based networks, we are interested to equip applications with the ability to move from one network to another. This definition is closely related, but different, to the concept of *roaming*. In the roaming situation, a mobile host obtains the Internet access via other networks. In the contrary, IP mobility allows the mobile host to move from one IP network to another IP network whilst enjoying to receive the upper layers' services as if the mobile host is a fixed host. In other words, the movement is *transparent* to the upper layers. That implies that the user will not be aware that the network's point of attachment has changed. More specifically, the TCP sessions should not be reset and the mobile host should always be addressed by its home network's address.

To achieve mobility in IP-based networks, essentially there are two mechanisms. The first one is to establish a special route through out the communication path between the mobile host and its correspondent node (recipient). Nevertheless, this approach is not scalable since the special route is always required throughout the entire communication path whenever the host changes its location. The second approach is to assign specific nodes that are responsible to maintain the mobile host's location. Tunneling mechanism is employed to forward packets destined to the mobile host that is away, which are "channeled" via these specific nodes.

Essentially, there are two categories in the mobility management schemes [21], namely one that handles *micromobility*, such as GSM networks, and the other that handles *macromobility*. Micromobility protocol focuses on mobility of the mobile host within a small region (usually within the same subnet). Macromobility protocol is more focussed on a broader term, that is the mobility across the regions. The examples of the latter approach include Mobile IPv4 [17] and Mobile IPv6 [11].

Mobility vs. Location Privacy
We observe that adding mobility to the IP-based networks will have an impact of losing the *location privacy*. The term *location privacy* refers to the case where one would like to conceal his location from anyone else. The need of mobility will enforce the need of the node attachment to *monitor* the location of the mobile host during its movement or the need of the specific route. The node attachment is the node that will ensure the connectivity of the mobile host to the IP networks, or in other words, it will provide the necessary upper layers' services to the mobile host. Therefore, the location of the mobile host is always exposed to the node attachment. Also, if messages exchanged on the communication path between the mobile host and its correspondent node are not carefully protected, an observer (one who can "listen" to the communication by observing the packets travelling through the wire) can obtain the location information either from the content of the messages or the messages' headers. Moreover, a system that allows the mobile host to update its location with its recipients directly for the sake of performance exposes the mobile host's location further.

In the following, we will firstly define the entities involved in the system. After observing what happens in the real environment, we are ready to define the system formally.

Entities. There are three entities involved in the IP-based mobility system: the mobile host, its communication partner and the node attachment. The mobile host entity is represented by its initial IP address that is provided from its home network eg. from the home network's DHCP server. We should stress that the location of the mobile host is *not* an entity rather than the mobile host's attribute, which is an IP address provided by each network it visits. The role of being the sender or the receiver in the communication path depends entirely on the message direction in the path. To illustrate, we refer the mobile host to be the sender and its partner is the receiver when a message is sent from the mobile host to its partner.

Mobile Host Movement to a Different Network. When the mobile host moves to a different network, it will firstly obtain a new location in the new network e.g. from the DHCP server of the new network. Then, it will establish a communication channel from this new location to its partner. This can be done either by creating a channel directly to the partner or a channel through the node of attachment. The aim of the adversary is to learn the mobile host's location. We consider the *adversaries* to be all the other *untrusted* entities in the path. They can simply be an observer that can only wiretap the connection or the nodes that help forwarding packets in the path, such as the node attachment. Therefore, we divide an adversary in the IP-based location privacy into three types: an observer, a mobile host's communication partner, and a node or nodes on the communication path. We note that from the adversaries' point of view, the node attachment is *not* directly related to the ongoing communication between the sender and the receiver during a communication session. Therefore, in the following communication model, we consider the simplest view of the channel by employing a single sender and receiver available in the system.

Model of the Communication Channel. In the following, we assume that the communication will employ a traditional point-to-point model. That is, there is a single host that sends its package via a public untrusted network, and the recipient is sitting at the other end of the network, which refer to the mobile host and its communication partner in the above scenario. As explained above, in the following definition, we shall omit the node attachment as an entity in the environment.

We consider there exists an observer (or an "adversary") who can observe the communication in the network. We assume that the mobile node has obtained its new location from the provided system such as by DHCP [6]. For a more elaborate treatment of this model, we refer the reader to [23], where we carefully analyzed the case that involves the node attachment itself. Note that in this definition we consider the direction when the mobile host is a receiver.

Intuitively, the notion of location privacy is defined as follows. Given a transcript of a message sent by a sender to a receiver in two possible locations of the receiver, the task of the adversary is to correctly guess where the location of the receiver is. Formally, we will define location privacy using the following interaction between an adversary $\mathcal{A}$ and a challenger $\mathcal{C}$. The adversary is given an access to the PacketReq^{LP} oracle, that is, given a message m, a receiver's location $\mathcal{L}$ and a pair of sender-receiver, the oracle is to output the correct transcript of the communication, Ω, that represents a message m sent by the sender to the receiver in the location $\mathcal{L}$. The oracle PacketReq^{LP} represents the capability of the observer (or the adversary) to request a message from a sender of his choice to be sent to a receiver that located in $\mathcal{L}$. Note that in this model the adversary can passively listen to the communication in the channel. The formal definition is as follows.

Location Privacy Interaction: Let $\mathcal{C}$ be the challenger and $\mathcal{A}$ be the adversary who would like to break the location privacy.

1. *Initialization.* Let $k \in \mathsf{N}$ be the security parameter. $\mathcal{C}$ is invoked with all the condition and information known in the communication channel. The information is provided to $\mathcal{C}$ by $\mathcal{A}$. In particular, the pair of sender $\mathcal{S}$ and receiver $\mathcal{R}$ is provided to $\mathcal{C}$ together with some possible locations $\{\mathcal{L}_1, \mathcal{L}_2, \cdots, \mathcal{L}_\ell\} \in \mathcal{L}$ which represent $\mathcal{R}$'s position (note that $\mathcal{L}$ is $\mathcal{R}$'s attribute).

2. *Attacking Phase*
   (a) $\mathcal{A}$ can make the PacketReq^{LP} queries as defined as follows.
       – PacketReq^{LP}. $\mathcal{A}$ can provide a message m_i and select a location $\mathcal{L}_i$ and query the PacketReq^{LP} oracle to obtain a transcript $\Omega(m_i, \mathcal{S}, \mathcal{R}, \mathcal{L}_i)$ to denote a message m_i sent by $\mathcal{S}$ to $\mathcal{R}$, which is currently located at $\mathcal{L}_i$.
       These queries can be invoked for at most $q_{PR_\mathcal{L}}$ times.
   (b) $\mathcal{A}$ outputs two distinct locations $(\mathcal{L}_0, \mathcal{L}_1)$ and a target message $m^* \in \mathcal{M}$ where $\mathcal{M}$ is a set of messages that have been queried before. In return, $\mathcal{C}$ outputs a transcript $\Omega(m^*, \mathcal{S}, \mathcal{R}, \mathcal{L}_i)$ where i is obtained from a coin toss.
   (c) $\mathcal{A}$ can execute PacketReq^{LP} queries for any message $m_j \neq m^*$ for any location in $\mathcal{L}$.

3. *Output Phase.* $\mathcal{A}$ outputs his guess i, where $\mathcal{L}_i$ is the location of the receiver who produces $\Omega(m^*, \mathcal{S}, \mathcal{R}, \mathcal{L}_i)$.

The success probability of the adversary in attacking location privacy is defined by $Succ_{\mathcal{A}}^{PR_\mathcal{L}} = \frac{1}{2} + \epsilon$.

Definition 1. *A system is said to provide* location privacy *if there is no polynomial time algorithm $\mathcal{A}$ that has a non-negligible probability in the* **Location Privacy Interaction** *defined above.*

2.2   Anonymity

In the Internet, anonymity can be classified into two types: *data anonymity* and *connection anonymity* [5]. The term *data anonymity* refers to the identification of information that can be extracted from the data exchanged in a particular application. The term *connection anonymity* refers to the identities of sender and receiver during data transfer.

The ultimate goal of anonymous communication systems is to ensure that an adversary gains no information about the communication that is happening in the communication channel [12]. However, this system is unrealistic in a public network as in the Internet. It is therefore considered adequate if the system satisfies some properties of the anonymous communication system, that include the inability of the adversary to identify the sender or the receiver. We will describe this possibility formally in the following paragraph.

Assuming the same communication channel model as in location privacy is used, the main intention of the sender is to ensure that her identity is not revealed to the observer (*privacy* of the sender). Additionally, the main intention of the receiver is also to ensure that his identity will not be disclosed (*privacy* of the receiver). From the observer's point of view, his task is considered to be "successful", if he can observe the communication channel and figure out who the sender and/or the receiver is (*adversarial goal*). If the observer cannot be successful in this particular task, then we say that the network ensures *anonymity* in the system.

Based on this setting, we further divide the notion of anonymity into three different properties: i) sender anonymity, ii) receiver anonymity, and iii) unlinkability. A system that satisfies these three properties is said to be an *anonymous system* [19].

Oracles. Let the oracle $\mathsf{PacketReq}^{\mathsf{SA}}$, the oracle $\mathsf{PacketReq}^{\mathsf{RA}}$ and the oracle $\mathsf{PacketReq}^{\mathsf{UL}}$ represent the capability of the adversary to request a message sent by a particular sender of his choice to a receiver in the sender anonymity, receiver anonymity and unlinkability games, respectively. This is to represent the ability of the adversary to wiretap the communication channel and to select the messages learnt from the channel.

Sender Anonymity. This property ensures that the observer (or the adversary) cannot identify who the sender is, given a stream of packages traveling through the communication channel. Intuitively, the task of the adversary is to guess who the sender is, given a transcript that could be produced by two different senders. Formally, this property is defined using the following interaction between an adversary $\mathcal{A}$ and a challenger $\mathcal{C}$. The adversary is given an access to the $\mathsf{PacketReq}^{\mathsf{SA}}$ oracle that behaves as follows: given a message m, a particular sender and a receiver, the oracle will return a correct transcript Ω that represents a transcript of a message m that is sent by the sender to the receiver.

Sender Anonymity Interaction: Let $\mathcal{C}$ be the challenger and $\mathcal{A}$ be the adversary who would like to break the sender anonymity.

1. *Initialization.* Let $k \in \mathsf{N}$ be the security parameter. $\mathcal{C}$ is invoked with all the condition and information known in the communication channel. The information is provided to $\mathcal{C}$ by $\mathcal{A}$. In particular, the set of senders $\{\mathcal{S}_1, \mathcal{S}_2, \cdots, \mathcal{S}_\ell\} \in \mathcal{S}$ is provided to $\mathcal{C}$ together with a receiver $\mathcal{R}$.

2. *Attacking Phase*
   (a) $\mathcal{A}$ can make the PacketReq^{SA} queries as defined as follows.
      - PacketReq^{SA}. $\mathcal{A}$ can provide a message m_i and select a sender $\mathcal{S}_j \in \mathcal{S}$ and query PacketReq^{SA} oracle to obtain a transcript $\Omega(m_i, \mathcal{S}_j, \mathcal{R})$ that represents a message m_i sent by $\mathcal{S}_j$ to $\mathcal{R}$.
      These queries can be invoked for at most q_{PR_S} times.
   (b) $\mathcal{A}$ outputs $(\mathcal{S}_0, \mathcal{S}_1)$ and a target message $m^* \in \mathcal{M}$ where $\mathcal{M}$ is a set of messages that have been queried before. In return, $\mathcal{C}$ outputs a transcript $\Omega(m^*, \mathcal{S}_i, \mathcal{R})$ where i is obtained from a coin toss.
   (c) $\mathcal{A}$ can execute PacketReq^{SA} queries for any message $m_j \neq m^*$ for any sender in $\mathcal{S}$.
3. *Output Phase.* $\mathcal{A}$ outputs his guess i, where $\mathcal{S}_i$ is the sender who produces $\Omega(m^*, \mathcal{S}_i, R)$.

The success probability of the adversary in attacking the sender anonymity is defined by $Succ_{\mathcal{A}}^{PR_S} = \frac{1}{2} + \epsilon$.

Definition 2. *A system is said to provide* sender anonymity *if there is no polynomial time algorithm $\mathcal{A}$ that has a non-negligible probability in the* **Interaction Sender Anonymity** *defined above.*

Receiver Anonymity. This property ensures that the observer (or the adversary) cannot identify who the receiver is, given a stream of packages traveling through the communication channel. Intuitively, the task of the adversary is to correctly guess whom the sender has sent her message to, given two possible receivers. Formally, this property is defined using the following interaction between an adversary $\mathcal{A}$ and a challenger $\mathcal{C}$. The adversary is given an access to the oracle PacketReq^{RA} that accepts a message m, a particular receiver and a sender, to output the correct transcript Ω that represents a transcript of a message m that is sent by the sender to the receiver. The formal definition follows.

Receiver Anonymity Interaction: Let $\mathcal{C}$ be the challenger and $\mathcal{A}$ be the adversary who would like to break the receiver anonymity.

1. *Initialization.* Let $k \in \mathbb{N}$ be the security parameter. $\mathcal{C}$ is invoked with all the condition and information known in the communication channel. The information is provided to $\mathcal{C}$ by $\mathcal{A}$. In particular, the set of receivers $\{\mathcal{R}_1, \mathcal{R}_2, \cdots, \mathcal{R}_\ell\} \in \mathcal{R}$ is provided to $\mathcal{A}$ together with a sender $\mathcal{S}$.
2. *Attacking Phase*
   (a) $\mathcal{A}$ can make the PacketReq^{RA} queries as defined as follows.
      - PacketReq^{RA}. $\mathcal{A}$ can provide a message m_i and select a receiver $\mathcal{R}_j \in \mathcal{R}$ and query the PacketReq^{RA} oracle to obtain a transcript $\Omega(m_i, \mathcal{S}, \mathcal{R}_j)$ that represents a message m_i sent by $\mathcal{S}$ to $\mathcal{R}_j$.
      These queries can be invoked for at most q_{PR_R} times.
   (b) $\mathcal{A}$ outputs $(\mathcal{R}_0, \mathcal{R}_1)$ and a target message $m^* \notin \mathcal{M}$ where $\mathcal{M}$ is a set of messages that have been queried before. In return, $\mathcal{C}$ outputs a transcript $\Omega(m^*, \mathcal{S}, \mathcal{R}_j)$ where i is obtained from a coin toss.

(c) $\mathcal{A}$ can execute $\mathsf{PacketReq}^{\mathsf{RA}}$ queries for any message $m_j \neq m^*$ for any receiver in $\mathcal{R}$.

3. *Output Phase.* $\mathcal{A}$ outputs his guess i, where $\mathcal{R}_i$ is the receiver whom receives $\Omega(m^*, \mathcal{S}, \mathcal{R}_i)$, sent by $\mathcal{S}$ in this transcript.

The success probability of the adversary in attacking the receiver anonymity is defined by $Succ_{\mathcal{A}}^{PR_{\mathcal{R}}} = \frac{1}{2} + \epsilon$.

Definition 3. *A system is said to provide* receiver anonymity *if there is no polynomial time algorithm $\mathcal{A}$ that has a non-negligible probability in the* **Interaction Receiver Anonymity** *defined above.*

Unlinkability. This property ensures that the observer (or the adversary) cannot link two different transcripts whether they are coming from the same sender or not. Intuitively, the task of the adversary is to guess whether two transcripts are related to each other (i.e. they come from the same sender, or the same receiver). Formally, this property is defined using the following interaction between an adversary $\mathcal{A}$ and a challenger $\mathcal{C}$. We note that in our definition, we assume that there exists a single receiver $\mathcal{R}$. However, without losing generality, our definition can be trivially modified to include multiple receivers, but this setting has been captured by our model. The adversary is given an access to the oracle $\mathsf{PacketReq}^{\mathsf{UL}}$ that accepts a message m, a sender and a receiver, to output a transcript Ω representing a transcript of a message m that is sent by the sender to the receiver.

Unlinkability Interaction: Let $\mathcal{C}$ be the challenger and $\mathcal{A}$ be the adversary who would like to break the unlinkability.

1. *Initialization.* Let $k \in \mathsf{N}$ be the security parameter. $\mathcal{C}$ is invoked with all the condition and information known in the communication channel. The information is provided to $\mathcal{C}$ by $\mathcal{A}$. In particular, the set of senders $\{\mathcal{S}_1, \mathcal{S}_2, \cdots, \mathcal{S}_\ell\} \in \mathcal{S}$ is provided to $\mathcal{A}$ together with a receiver $\mathcal{R}$.
2. *Attacking Phase*
   (a) $\mathcal{A}$ can make the $\mathsf{PacketReq}^{\mathsf{UL}}$ queries as defined as follows.
      – $\mathsf{PacketReq}^{\mathsf{UL}}$. $\mathcal{A}$ can provide a message m_i and select a sender $\mathcal{S}_j \in \mathcal{S}$ and query the $\mathsf{PacketReq}^{\mathsf{UL}}$ oracle to obtain a transcript $\Omega(m_i, \mathcal{S}_j, \mathcal{R})$ that represents a message m_i sent by $\mathcal{S}_j$ to $\mathcal{R}$.
      These queries can be invoked for at most q_{PR_S} times.
   (b) $\mathcal{C}$ outputs $\mathcal{S}_j$, a transcript $\Omega_1(m_1^*, \mathcal{S}_j, \mathcal{R})$, $\Omega_2(m_2^*, \mathcal{S}_k, \mathcal{R})$, and two target messages $m_1^*, m_2^* \notin \mathcal{M}, m_1^* \neq m_2^*$ where $\mathcal{M}$ is a set of messages that have been queried before and i is obtained from a coin toss. In this output, $j = k$ if the output of the coin toss is 1, and $j \neq k$ otherwise.
   (c) $\mathcal{A}$ can execute $\mathsf{PacketReq}^{\mathsf{UL}}$ queries for any message $m_j \neq \{m_1^*, m_2^*\}$ for any sender in $\mathcal{S}$.
3. *Output Phase.* $\mathcal{A}$ outputs his guess $0/1$ to indicate whether Ω_1 and Ω_2 have been produced by the same sender $\mathcal{S}_j$ or not.

The success probability of the adversary in attacking the unlinkability is defined by $Succ_{\mathcal{A}}^{ULs} = \frac{1}{2} + \epsilon$.

Definition 4. *A system is said to provide* unlinkability *if there is no polynomial time algorithm* $\mathcal{A}$ *that has a non-negligible probability in the* **Unlinkability Interaction** *defined above.*

Definition 5. *A communication channel is said to be* anonymous *if it satisfies sender anonymity, receiver anonymity and unlinkability.*

Definition 6. *A communication channel is said to provide* mobility *and* anonymity *if it provides mobility to its mobile hosts, is anonymous and ensures location privacy.*

3   Review on Existing Infrastructure That Provides Mobility and Anonymity

3.1   Mobile IP

Mobile IP protocol was designed to provide mobility to the IP-based networks. There are two versions of Mobile IP, namely Mobile IP version 4 (MIPv4) and Mobile IP version 6 (MIPv6). MIPv4 has been designed to work on top of the IPv4 network, and MIPv6 is designed for the IPv6 network. Nonetheless, the fundamental concept is essentially the same.

Mobility in Mobile IP protocol is provided via the use of two IP addresses, namely a home address (HoA) and a care-of address. A home address is an IP address of a mobile node when the mobile node resides in its original network. The home address is used for identification purpose. A care-of address is an IP address used by the mobile node when it is away at the visiting network. This IP address is used for identifying the location of the mobile node. The communication between these two addresses is assisted by two other entities, namely a home agent and a foreign agent[1]. When the mobile node is away from its home network, firstly it obtains its care-of address from one of the following possibilities: 1) the visiting network's foreign agent (in the MIPv4 setting); 2) the stateless configuration [11] in MIPV6; or 3) the DHCP mechanism in both MIPv4 and MIPv6 settings. Then, the mobile node registers the newly-obtained care-of address to its home agent. When there are packets destined to the mobile node's home address, then the home agent will forward these packets to the mobile node's care-of address. To avoid an ingress filtering problem at the foreign agents, the Mobile IP protocol employs a reverse tunneling mechanism [16] that allows the mobile node to send packets to its corresponding node via its home agent. When route optimization is deployed, the mobile node is allowed to update its care-of address directly to its correspondent node. It is clear that Mobile IP does *not* provide location privacy protection against the observer when there is no encryption in the tunneling packets. In addition, the location is also revealed

---

[1] We note that there exists no foreign agent in MIPv6.

to the corresponding node in case of route optimization. Moreover, the home agent also needs to monitor the location of the Mobile IP user.

3.2   Tor - A Low Latency Network

Tor [20] is the second-generation of Onion Routing [18]. Tor is a distributed system that provides anonymous connections to low-latency applications, such as web browsing, secure shell and instant messaging. Similar to Onion Routing, the architecture of Tor is based on the Chaum [3] mix network model, but Tor relay node does not perform any mixing operations (i.e. batching, reordering or delaying packets). Tor is an anonymous system. Intuitively, sender anonymity, receiver anonymity and unlinkability provided by Tor are guaranteed due to the use of Tor servers (will be defined later in this section) that will act as the anonymizers in the network.

Entities in A Tor Network. There are three main entities in a Tor connection, which are 1) a Tor client, 2) a Tor-enabled application server[2], and 3) a group of Tor servers. When a user (or a sender, respectively) would like to establish a Tor connection to access any Tor-enabled application servers, the user is required to install a Tor client software. Then, the user's host has become one of the Tor clients in the network. The Tor client is responsible for fetching directories (of all Tor servers), establishing circuits[3] and handling connections from the user's application. The user would like to access the services provided by one of the application servers. This particular application server is known to be the *recipient* of the Tor connection. In order to allow the Tor client to reach the application server, there are several relay nodes that will be involved to establish the connection. These relay nodes are known as the Tor servers. The first node (i.e. a Tor server) in this connection is also known as the *entry node*, whilst the last node is known as the *exit node*. Currently, according to the Tor specification, the size of each circuit is set to involve 3 Tor servers.

How Tor Works. Firstly, a Tor client selects a number of Tor servers as members of the Tor circuit. Circuits in Tor are established preemptively. When an anonymous connection is required, the Tor client can simply select one of the already-established circuits. In contrast to the Onion routing that restricts one circuit per one TCP stream, Tor allows many TCP streams to share a single circuit. When the Tor client would like to send some data (e.g. when a user uses his browser to connect to a website), the streams of packets are divided into *fixed-size cells* and these cells are sent to the selected circuit. During the transmission, these packets are wrapped in a *layer-by-layer* fashion using session keys derived from pre-negotiated common keys. The intended purpose of this mechanism is to allow a Tor server, which will unwrap the packets, *only* to know merely its predecessor and successor nodes. There is no mixing process involved.

---

[2] A Tor-enabled application server is an application server that can function within a Tor network.

[3] Tor system calls a path as a *circuit*.

The incoming cells to any Tor nodes are simply placed into queues, processed and sent out in the first come first served fashion.

Circuit Establishment in Tor. Tor establishes and extends its circuit hop by hop until it reaches the length of the circuit. Normal Tor circuit's length is 3 hops, which comprises the entry node, the second Tor server nodes and the exit node. Suppose Alice wants to use Tor to anonymize her communication, then the description of how a circuit is established can be outlined as follows. Firstly, Alice's Tor client picks three nodes as its Tor entry node, its second node and its exit node, respectively. Without losing generality, let us assume that Alice picks Tor_A, Tor_B and Tor_{Exit} for a circuit path $Alice \rightarrow Tor_A \rightarrow Tor_B \rightarrow Tor_{Exit}$. To establish an onion encryption within the circuit, the Tor client and each of the Tor servers in the circuit must be equipped with a shared key. Tor uses Diffie-Hellman key exchange to accomplish this purpose. In every hop-connection, there is a circuit id used to represent a connection between any two consecutive nodes and this circuit id is known only between these two consecutive nodes. Due to page limitation, we refer the readers to [23] for more details on Tor circuits, commands and diagram.

4   Anonymous Communication with Mobility in IP-Based Networks

For clarity, we reiterate the ultimate goal in our scenario. Consider the situation where Bob, who is the CEO of the company ABC, is having his holiday break and he would like to make an anonymous communication for example downloading a streaming content, such as movies or video clips. In addition to being anonymous, Bob would like to have a continuous session during his trip on a train. Furthermore, he does not want his location to be revealed. We would like to provide a solution to this problem to satisfy Bob's requirements.

In summary, there are essentially three main properties required in this scenario, namely mobility, anonymity and location privacy.

Bob would like to receive a continuous session during his trip on a train. This requires *mobility* to be provided in an IP network. By allowing mobility, Bob will be given a continuous connection to the Internet application regardless his location. Bob's mobile node has to change from one network connection to another, but this movement (or also known as a *hands-off*) needs to be transparent to Bob.

Bob would also like to access the Internet applications anonymously. Bob does not want anyone to find out which services he has used. In short, Bob would like to achieve sender anonymity, recipient anonymity and unlinkability. Firstly, Bob does not want anyone to know that he is the sender of the message requesting the Internet service (sender anonymity). Secondly, he also does not want anyone to know to whom he is sending the message to (or which website Bob is currently browsing - and hence, recipient anonymity). Finally, he does not want anyone to be able to identify whom he is communicating to.

As described earlier, mobility implies exposing the location privacy. This means that Bob's location will need to be acquired by the system to allow the continuous session. Nonetheless, this will defeat Bob's requirement as he is having his holiday. Therefore, the final property that Bob would like to achieve is location privacy. As mentioned earlier, these three requirements seem to be contradictory.

In this section, we will describe how to achieve anonymity and mobility concurrently using the existing networks. We incorporate the existing IP-based networks that can provide us with anonymity or mobility, and we adjust the system so that it can satisfy our needs. We choose Mobile IP as our base system that will provide mobility. Furthermore, we also choose Tor as our building block for our anonymous system because of its rapid usage growth and availability.

Intuitively, by combining Mobile IP and Tor, we could achieve all the properties that we would like to obtain. Unfortunately, as we shall show in the next section, a trivial combination of these two systems will not provide us with a complete and good solution In particular, the new system will suffer from the location privacy feature. Then, we also present our enhancement to Tor to provide a better system. The new system represents a "better" network in terms of latency. Finally, we add the location privacy system to our hybrid system to fully satisfy our requirements.

4.1 Architecture MA1. Achieving Mobility and Anonymity Via Trivial Combination of Mobile IP and Tor

Without losing generality, we discuss our design and implementation using Mobile IP and Tor as our building blocks. Mobile IP is chosen to represent an IP network that is equipped with mobility, whilst Tor is chosen due to its low latency anonymity feature. Mobile IP works in network layer (layer 3) while Tor works in transport layer (layer 4).

Basic Setting. The scenario that we would like to consider is as follows. A user participates in a Mobile IP network. The user also installs a Tor client software

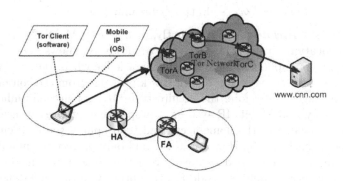

Fig. 1. An Illustration when a Mobile IP node would like to have a Tor connection

in his mobile node, and hence, the user is a Tor client in the Tor network. This scenario is illustrated in Figure 1.

To illustrate our idea, we start by providing a mechanism of how the system works when the mobile node is in its home network.

Phase 1. The mobile node resides in its network. In this phase, we start the scenario with the situation where the mobile node resides in its home network and the mobile node would like to make an anonymous communication to the remote destination (for example http://www.cnn.com). This situation is analogous to a static IP network that incorporates a Tor network. Suppose that a mobile node user, Alice, would like to browse the network anonymously. She starts her Internet browser by pointing its URL to http://www.cnn.com, and her Tor client will firstly selects a circuit to be used to route this particular Tor application. Without losing generality, suppose the Tor client picks a circuit $c1$ that consists of Tor_A, Tor_B and Tor_C as an entry node, the middle node and the exit node, respectively. The communication path between Alice and the HTTP server appears as $Alice \rightarrow Tor_A \rightarrow Tor_B \rightarrow Tor_C \rightarrow$ http://www.cnn.com. Alice's IP address is used by Tor_A as her identity. In this case, it is her home network's address.

Phase 2. The mobile node is away. When Alice moves to a different network (i.e. a foreign network) outside her home network, then her mobile node is away. In a typical Mobile IP scenario, the mobile node is required to report its new point of attachment, namely its care-of address, to its home agent via the registration process. This activity is assisted by the foreign agent in the foreign network in Mobile IPv4. After this process is completed, all the IP connections destined to this mobile node will be redirected to its home agent and the home agent is responsible to forward the packets to the mobile node's current location. This movement is transparent to Tor, since Tor works in the transport layer (layer 4). Hence, the communication path is $MN \rightarrow FA \rightarrow HA \rightarrow Tor_A \rightarrow Tor_B \rightarrow Tor_C \rightarrow$ http://www.cnn.com. When route optimization is deployed, the mobile node is also required to update its location directly to its correspondent node (CN), which is Tor_A in this case. Hence, the communication path is $MN \rightarrow FA \rightarrow Tor_A \rightarrow Tor_B \rightarrow Tor_C \rightarrow$ http://www.cnn.com.

The Drawbacks of Architecture MA1. Firstly, we note that Mobile IP networks do not provide location privacy [13]. The home agent always knows the mobile node whereabout, a correspondent node has this knowledge when route optimization is deployed, and an observer can obtain this knowledge from the content of un-protected messages. Therefore, the architecture MA1 intrinsically inherits this problem. In a typical Mobile IP system, a proposed solution is to use forward and reverse tunneling to the home agent and then applies the ESP encryption in the inner IP packets [13]. However, this could only protect the mobile node's location from an observer. It does not prevent the home agent this knowledge. An idea that comes to mind is to add location privacy to the underlying Mobile IP, using techniques like adding a set of location proxies [8]. Nevertheless, this results in an extremely long communication path between the mobile node and its recipient, in particular when the length of the proxy nodes are quite long. To justify this argument, let us refer to the communication path. Let LP_i denote a location proxy node i. The whole communication path consists of the following entities: $MN \rightarrow FA \rightarrow LP_1 \rightarrow ... \rightarrow LP_n \rightarrow HA \rightarrow Tor_A \rightarrow Tor_B \rightarrow Tor_C \rightarrow$ http://www.cnn.com Furthermore, in this communication path, the benefit given by the low latency network, such as Tor, will be overridden by the lengthy and unnecessary communication path resulted by the location-privacy-enabled mobile IP networks.

Providing location privacy when deploying route optimization remains as an open question in Mobile IP protocol [13]. It seems odd to use the set of location proxy's technique, i.e. $MN \rightarrow FA \rightarrow LP_1 \rightarrow ... \rightarrow LP_n \rightarrow$ http://www.cnn.com to achieve this goal. Particularly, when route optimization is proposed to increase the system performance by allowing a direct connection between the mobile node and the correspondent node instead of tunneling through the home agent. However, the combined system benefits the Mobile IP route optimization some degrees of location privacy. That is, the mobile node's location is transparent to the Tor application's recipient (the CNN server in the above example). Nevertheless, a new problem arises. The mobile node's location is always exposed to the Tor entry node. Unlike the home agent that can be trusted to some extent, Tor nodes are not designed be trusted. Using two sets of proxies and combining them together at the Tor entry node instead of the home agent, as in a typical Mobile IP scenario, also results in the same problem, even though the path is one hop shorter.

In summary, by trivially combining a location-privacy-enabled mobility system and anonymity system seems to be insufficient to achieve mobility and anonymity concurrently. In a typical Mobile IP system scenario, when a high level of location privacy is required, this combination appears as two mix networks that are "glued" together. The first mix network aims at providing location privacy and mobility, whilst the second mix network deals with anonymity. These networks are combined by the point of attachment entity, such as the home agent. In a route optimization system scenario, the combined system seems to provide more location privacy as the mobile node's location is transparent to the Tor application's correspondent node. It instead shifts the problem to the Tor entry node and the seemingly available solution also results in a long communication path.

4.2 Architecture MA2. Adding Mobility to Tor

Essentially, Tor does not support mobility. When there is a change of the client's point of attachment during a Tor connection, all connections in circuits from the Tor client to its application's recipient will be required to be reset. Our architecture MA1 attempted to solve this problem by combining Mobile IP with Tor at the mobile node to add Tor's ability to provide mobility. Unfortunately, as we have shown earlier, the location privacy problem, which is an inherent problem in Mobile IP networks, will occur in the resulting architecture. Adding the location privacy to the underlying mobile IP networks will result in a different

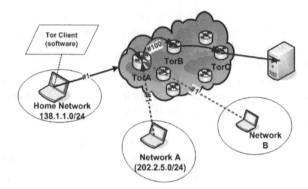

Fig. 2. Illustration of Mobile Node's Movement with a Single Entry Node

problem. Therefore, in this section, we are interested in taking a totally different approach, i.e. by adding the mobility capabilities to Tor instead of relying on another type of network, like Mobile IP. We will limit ourselves to the scenario where we are interested in and then describe the technique that we used to design and implement the mobility for Tor networks.

Limited Scenario: Client-only Mobility. We are interested to add mobility to the client in the Tor networks. As inspired by our scenario mentioned earlier, the recipient (for example http://www.cnn.com) can stay the same during the duration of the movement, but we allow the client to move from one network to another. The mobile node will always initiate the communication. Furthermore, without losing generality, we assume that the recipient, a low-latency application server, is always a fixed host.

Design Strategy 1. Maintaining TCP connection of the Exit Node. A Tor client does not have a direct connection to its recipient. The Tor client requires a series of nodes between itself and the application server, namely the Tor servers. We further note that Tor generates its circuit hop-by-hop. To illustrate this idea, let us consider the following Tor circuit that consists of four Tor connections:

- The first hop is between the Tor client and the Tor entry node
- The second hop is between the entry node and the middle node.
- The third hop is between the middle node and the exit node.
- The fourth hop is between the exit node and the recipient.

Each connection has its own underlying TCP connection. From the recipient's point of view, its "sender" is the exit node. Therefore, if a TCP connection between the exit node and the recipient can be maintained during the mobile node (i.e. the Tor client) movement, then we can preserve the sender-recipient indirect connection. That is, the change of the mobile node's point of attachment is transparent to its applications server. Therefore, our main aim is to maintain this particular TCP connection in the circuit during the mobile node movement.

Design Strategy 2. Modification to The First-Hop Tor Connection. By investigating the Tor circuit, we can observe that the mobile node's movement has a direct implication to the first hop of the established circuit. We note that this first hop is the TCP connection between the mobile node and the entry node. The movement of the mobile node will result in the change of the mobile node's IP address. This change will imply the failure of the first-hop TCP connection. Furthermore, since this TCP connection implies the whole Tor connection, the failure of the first hop will eventually stop the whole Tor circuit.

In order to ensure that the Tor circuit is still established, the Tor servers must provide a mechanism to allow the first-hop Tor connection to stay alive even though its underlying TCP connection is turned down and changed to the new point of attachment. For simplicity, we apply the known technique used in the TCP/IP network to allow the mobile node to acquire its new IP address during its movement, for example, DHCP [6], and to change the point of attachment by using the hands-off mechanism such as the one used in Mobile IP [17]. We do not aim to improve this technique as this is out of the scope of this paper. We illustrate our idea in Figure 2. We note that in this design, in contrast to the previous design, we modified the Tor server and client to handle mobility without relying on mobility entities of other existing mechanisms (eg. Mobile IP's home agent).

The Detail of The Design. Now, we discuss the situation when the mobile node moves to a new network from the above scenario. Once the mobile node obtains a new IP address from the new network, it sends an *additional* Tor-command cell, namely the *Resume* command cell, to the Tor entry node to request the Tor entry node to update its IP address with the newly acquired IP address. The cell must be encrypted with the common key between the Tor entry node and the mobile node. Tor servers need to be modified to allow a waiting period before closing its connection while its communicating partner is unavailable. This allows the whole circuit to stay alive when the mobile node moves.

To guarantee the authenticity of the Tor entry node, we employ a keyed hash function with a random number. The Tor entry node stores the up-to-date IP address of the mobile node as its sender address. We note that the initial IP address of the mobile node can be the home address of the mobile node when the system is just initialized. We also note that each Tor server must allow a longer waiting time period when the host or network unavailability is detected.

The *Resume* command cell consists of the command *Resume*, the circuit id, an encrypted value of the new IP address, the old IP address, a random number and the hash value of the old IP address and the random value. Due to page limitation, we refer the readers to [23] for more details.

Existing Drawbacks: Location Privacy. As in other mobility systems, our system also exposes the mobile node's location to the Tor entry node. Therefore, the problem of location privacy seems to be *inherent* whenever mobility is added to the network. The solution like the set of proxies is not appropriate as previously described in MA1.One could propose that the Tor entry node must be a trusted node. However, this is very unlikely to happen. Tor network itself does not require the Tor entry node to be a trusted node. Also, if the circuit ID has not changed and the IP-packets between the mobile node at different locations and the Tor entry node are not encrypted, then the observer can trace the movement of the mobile node from the unchanged circuit ID and hence can obtain its location. Therefore, a further extension is required to satisfy the requirement of location privacy.

4.3 Architecture MA3. Enhancing Mobility-Equipped Tor with Location Privacy

The main problem with the architecture MA2 is the exposure of the mobile node's location to the Tor entry node, so that the movement of the mobile node will be traceable. In this section, we present a further enhancement to this design, by forcing the mobile node (i.e. the Tor client) to change its circuit every time it moves to a new network. By this enforcement, it will ensure that the Tor entry node will always be different. The restriction is that all other circuits must have the same exit node in order to ensure that the TCP connection between the exit node and the server can continue functioning. Fortunately, the circuits are established *a priori*. This mechanism will allow the mobile node to establish the circuits prior to its movement and hence, the swapping between one circuit to another will not cost too much delay. An additional data must be inserted into the cell's component to allow the exit node to concatenate the connection to the server between the old and the new circuit. The detail of this design and implementation is as follows.

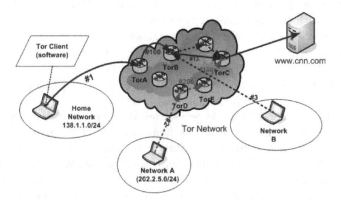

Fig. 3. Illustration of Mobile Node's Movement to achieve Location Privacy

Initialization. Prior to the network activity (and network movement), the mobile node (i.e. the Tor client) must establish several circuits that use the *same* exit node and store them in its circuit pool. These circuits are inactive when they are not in use.

Mobile Node Movements. When the mobile node moves to a new network, it will firstly acquire a new IP address. Then, it selects a new circuit from the available circuit pool. As the circuit has been established *a priori* with the mobile node's initial IP address, it also needs to be updated with the new IP address that has just been acquired. Then, we employ the same mechanism as used in Architecture MA2. That is, the mobile node sends a *Resume* command to the Tor entry node. However, this time it is the Tor entry node of the new circuit.

Then, the mobile node sends a relay cell to the exit node through the new circuit's connection aiming at switching the circuit. The relay cell consists of the following components: a command to notify the exit node to switch the circuit (*ResumeCon*) and a connection identifier that the mobile node uses to notify the exit node of the same destination (*CID*). Once the exit node receives the relay cell, it decrypts the packet (*aka* onion layer). Then, it executes the command by searching its database for the circuit that is currently used with the connection to the server using *CID*, i.e. the old circuit. Finally, it deactivates the old circuit (by removing *CID* from the old circuit's record) and activates the new circuit with the connection to the application server. Note that we name the relay cell's circuit as the new circuit. Due to page limitation, we refer the readers to [23] for more details and diagrams.

Analysis. It is clear that the Tor entry node cannot trace the location of the mobile node. This is due to the fact that the circuit ID and the Tor entry node are always changed when the mobile node moves to a new network. Hence, there is no need to encrypt the circuit ID between the mobile node and the Tor entry node to provide location privacy against the observer. Moreover, even though the exit node can obtain a list of its previous nodes of all circuits belonging to the connection from the mobile node to the application server, it does not have enough information to trace the movement of the mobile node, since there is more than a hop that connects the exit node to the mobile node. We note that by allowing the number of hops in a circuit to vary, we can achieve a better and efficient location privacy protection as it is harder for the adversary to predict even the size of the circuit.

The assumption put in place in Tor networks includes the following. On one extreme, we note that the collusion of all nodes is not permitted, or else the anonymity properties, i.e. sender anonymity, receiver anonymity and unlinkability cannot be provided. On the other extreme, we also note that Tor does not require that all Tor nodes must be trusted either. We note that these two assumptions are indeed valid in practice.

Theorem 1. *Our design* MA3 *provides mobility, anonymity and location privacy according to our definition in Section 2.*

Justification. The mobility of our design MA3 is provided by the inherent Tor networks. For the anonymity, we should consider the three properties, namely sender anonymity, receiver anonymity and unlinkability. In the following, we briefly show that the security of our design can be reduced to the security of Tor.

Sender Anonymity. Consider the following game between $\mathcal{A}$ and $\mathcal{C}$. Assume that $\mathcal{A}$ is an attacker that can break the sender anonymity interaction in our design. In this setting, we set $\mathcal{C}$ as an observer to a Tor network in the real world. Firstly, $\mathcal{C}$ provides all the required Tor parameters to $\mathcal{A}$ and a set of senders $\{\mathcal{S}_1, \mathcal{S}_2, \cdots, \mathcal{S}_n\} \in \mathcal{S}$. The attacking phase can be done by $\mathcal{A}$ by querying $\mathcal{C}$ for any particular sender $\mathcal{S}_j \in \mathcal{S}$ for a particular message $m_j \in \mathcal{M}$. To answer this query, $\mathcal{C}$ can invoke the real world that contains the Tor networks and obtain the real transcript from the Tor networks. The transcript will be provided to $\mathcal{A}$ and hence, the simulation runs completely. The view of the simulated environment is identical to the real world, and hence, the simulation is perfect. Finally, $\mathcal{A}$ outputs two senders $\mathcal{S}_0, \mathcal{S}_1$ of his choice and a target message m^* that has not been queried before and $\mathcal{C}$ provides a transcript Ω_i for a coin toss $i \in \{0, 1\}$. Then, $\mathcal{A}$ can output the choice of i that $\mathcal{C}$ selected. Note that this output means that $\mathcal{A}$ has successfully break the underlying sender anonymity of the Tor network in the real world, and hence we obtain contradiction.

Receiver Anonymity and Unlinkability. Receiver anonymity and unlinkability can be done in similar fashion as above. The underlying idea is to show if there exists an adversary $\mathcal{A}$ who can break the interaction, then this adversary will also break the underlying Tor networks. Therefore, the contradiction is obtained.

Location Privacy. When we consider the mobile node as the receiver of the communication, location privacy interaction is similar to the receiver anonymity, except the location of the receivers can vary. The attacker will not be able to break the location privacy interaction since the circuit for each different location will also be different. If the attacker can break the location privacy interaction in our design, it means that the attacker is capable to observe the whole structure of the Tor networks, and hence, the adversary is in fact a global adversary. The fact that a global adversary does not exist means that our design is secure against location privacy.

5   Conclusion and Further Works

In this paper, we presented a mechanism to achieve mobility and anonymity in IP-based networks concurrently. We started the paper by firstly defining the required properties, that include mobility, anonymity and location privacy. We noted that adding mobility to an IP-based network will imply losing location privacy. We presented a concrete design and implementation based on the existing IP-based network to achieve both mobility and anonymity at the same time. We note that our work in this paper can be considered as the first step towards formalizing mobility, anonymity and location privacy. In our future work, we will consider the location attribute in our design and therefore we can achieve a more robust model. Therefore, our future work will be able to capture a more powerful adversary and a broader scenario.

References

1. Freedom Network, http://www.freedom.net/
2. Onion Router History, http://www.onion-router.net/history.html
3. Chaum, D.: Untraceable Electronic Mail, Return Address, and Digital Pseudonyms. Comm. of ACM 24(2), 84–88 (1981)
4. Choi, S., Kim, K., Kim, B.: Practical Solution for Location Privacy in Mobile IPv6. In: Chae, K.-J., Yung, M. (eds.) Information Security Applications. LNCS, vol. 2908, pp. 69–83. Springer, Heidelberg (2004)
5. Diaz, C., Seys, S., Claessens, J., Preneel, B.: Towards Measuring Anonymity. In: Dingledine, R., Syverson, P.F. (eds.) PET 2002. LNCS, vol. 2482, Springer, Heidelberg (2003)
6. Droms, R.: Dynamic Host Configuration Protocol, RFC 2131 (1997)
7. Escudero-Pascual, A., Hdenfalk, M., Heselius, P.: Flying Freedom: Location Privacy in Mobile Internetworking. In: INET2001, CD-proceedings. (2001)
8. Fasbender, A., Kesdogan, D., Kubitz, O.: Analysis of Security and Privacy in Mobile IP. In: 4th International Conference on Telecommunication Systems Modeling and Analysis (1996)
9. Freedman, M.J., Morris, R.: Tarzan: A Peer-to-Peer Anonymizing Network Layer. In: CCS 2002, USA (2002)
10. Goldberg, I.: A Pseudonymous Communications Infrastructure for the Internet. PhD thesis, UC Berkeley (2000)
11. Johnson, D., Perkins, C., Arkko, J.: IP Mobility Support for IPv6, RFC 3775 (2004)
12. Jones, A.: Anonymous Communication on the Internet (September 2004), http://www10.cs.rose-hulman.edu/Papers/Jones.pdf
13. Koodi, R.: IP Address Location Privacy and Mobile IPv6: Problem Statement RFC 4882 (May 2007)
14. Koponen, T., Gurtov, A., Nikander, P.: Application Mobility with HIP. In: Proc. ICT 2005 (2005)
15. Marc Rennhard, B.P.: Practical Anonymity for the Masses with Morphmix. In: Juels, A. (ed.) FC 2004. LNCS, vol. 3110, Springer, Heidelberg (2004)
16. Montenegro, G.: Reverse Tunneling for Mobile IP, RFC 2344 (May 1998)
17. Perkins, C.: IP Mobility Support for IPv4, RFC 3344 (2002)
18. Reed, M., Syverson, P., Goldschlag, D.: Anonymous Connections and Onion Routing. IEEE Journal on Selected Areas in Communications 16(4), 482–494 (1998)
19. Reiter, M., Rubin, A.: Crowds: Anonymity for Web Transactions. ACM Trans. Inf. Syst. Secur. 1(1), 66–92 (1998)
20. Roger Dingledine, P.S., Mathewson, N.: Tor: The Second-Generation Onion Router. In: Proc. of the 13th USENIX Security Symposium (2004)
21. Salkintzis, A.K. (ed.): Mobile Internet: enabling technologies and services. CRC Press, Boca Raton (2004)
22. Valko, A.G.: Cellular IP: a new approach to Internet host mobility. SIGCOMM Comput. Commun. Rev. 29(1), 50–65 (1999)
23. Wiangsripanawan, R., Susilo, W., Safavi-Naini, R.: Achieving Mobility and Anonymity in IP Based Networks (full version). Available upon request from the first author

Perfectly Secure Message Transmission in Directed Networks Tolerating Threshold and Non Threshold Adversary[*]

Arpita Patra[1], Bhavani Shankar[2], Ashish Choudhary[1,**], K. Srinathan[2], and C. Pandu Rangan[1,***]

[1] Dept of Computer Science and Engineering
IIT Madras, Chennai India 600036
arpita@cse.iitm.ernet.in, ashishc@cse.iitm.ernet.in, rangan@iitm.ernet.in
[2] Center for Security, Theory and Algorithmic Research
International Institute of Information Technology
Hyderabad India 500032
shankar@research.iiit.ac.in, srinathan@iiit.ac.in

Abstract. In this paper we study *Perfectly Secure Message Transmission* (PSMT) between a sender **S** and a receiver **R**, connected in a directed synchronous network through multiple parallel edges (called wires), each of which are directed from **S** to **R** or vice-versa. The unreliability of the network is modeled by a Byzantine adversary with infinite computing power. We investigate the problem with two different adversarial settings: (i) threshold and (ii) non-threshold. In [1], the authors have characterized PSMT against a t-active threshold adversary in directed networks[1]. However, their PSMT protocol was exponential both in terms of number of phases[2] and communication complexity. In addition, they also presented a polynomial phase PSMT protocol with $n' = max(3t-u+1, 2t+1)$ wires from **S** to **R**. In this paper, we significantly improve the exponential phase protocol and present an elegant and efficient three phase PSMT protocol with polynomial communication complexity (and computational complexity) with $n = \max(3t - 2u + 1, 2t + 1)$ wires from **S** to **R**. Also with $n' = \max(3t - u + 1, 2t + 1)$ wires from **S** to **R**, we are able to further improve the communication complexity of our three phase PSMT protocol. Our second contribution in this paper is

---

[*] A brief version of this paper appeared in [7] which permits full expanded version to appear elsewhere.

[**] Work Supported by Project No. CSE/05-06/076/DITX/CPAN on Protocols for Secure Communication and Computation Sponsored by Department of Information Technology, Government of India.

[***] Work Supported by Project No. CSE/05-06/076/DITX/CPAN on Protocols for Secure Communication and Computation Sponsored by Department of Information Technology, Government of India.

[1] The authors have proved the necessity and sufficiency of at least $max(3t - 2u + 1, 2t+1)$ wires from **S** to **R** for any PSMT protocol, where u is the number of wires from **R** to **S** and t is the total number of wires corrupted by a threshold adversary.
[2] A phase is a send from **S** to **R** or **R** to **S**.

F. Bao et al. (Eds.): CANS 2007, LNCS 4856, pp. 80–101, 2007.
© Springer-Verlag Berlin Heidelberg 2007

the first ever characterization for any two phase PSMT protocol.Finally, we also characterize PSMT protocol in directed networks tolerating non-threshold adversary. In [3], the authors have given the characterization for PSMT against non-threshold adversary. However, in their characterization, they have only considered the paths from **S** to **R**, excluding the feedback paths (i.e paths from **R** to **S**) and hence their characterization holds good only for single phase protocols. We characterize multiphase PSMT considering feedback paths.

Keywords: Reliable and Secure Communication, Information Theoretic Security, Communication Efficiency, Directed Networks.

1   Introduction

In the problem of *perfectly reliable message transmission* (PRMT), a sender **S** is connected to **R** in an unreliable network by some vertex disjoint paths called wires; **S** wishes to send a message m chosen from a finite field $\mathbb{F}$ reliably to **R**, in a guaranteed manner, in spite of the presence of several kinds of faults in the network. The problem of *perfectly secure message transmission* (PSMT) has an additional constraint that the adversary should get no information about m. The faults in the network is modeled by an *adversary* who controls the wires in the network in a variety of ways and the adversary has unbounded computing power. Security against such an adversary is called *information theoretic security*.

There are various network settings, fault models and computational models in which PRMT and PSMT problem has been studied extensively in the past [4,1,10,8,5]. The quality of any PRMT and PSMT protocol is measured by the following parameters: the number of wires n between **S** and **R**, the number of phases r required to send m, the total number of field elements b that are communicated during the execution of the protocol, (also known as communication complexity) and the amount of computation done by **S** and **R**.

PRMT and PSMT problem found its origin from unconditionally secure multiparty computation. If **S** and **R** are connected directly via a private and authenticated link which is generally assumed in generic secure multiparty protocols, reliable and secure communication is trivially guaranteed. However, in reality, it is not economical to directly connect every two players in the network. Therefore such a complete network can only be virtually realized by simulating the missing links using PRMT and PSMT protocols as primitives.

In this paper, we use digraph to capture the underlying communication network. We stress that in practice not every communication channel admits bidirectional communication (for instance, a base-station may communicate to even a far-off hand-held device but the other way round is not possible) and hence the digraph model is practically well-motivated.

1.1   Previous Work

PRMT and PSMT in directed networks tolerating *threshold adversary* was first studied by Desmedt et.al. in [1] (An earlier version of this paper appeared in [2]), where it is shown that for the existence of any PSMT protocol, there should be at least $n = \max\{3t - 2u + 1, 2t + 1\}$ wires from **S** to **R** (which is termed as the *top band*), where u denotes the number of wires from **R** to **S** (which is termed as bottom band) and t denotes the total number of wires that can be under the control of adversary. Also the wires in the *top band* and *bottom band* should be disjoint. However to prove the sufficiency, the authors in [1] have provided a PSMT protocol which securely sends a single field element in $\frac{n!}{(n-u)!}$ phases which is exponential. Further they have shown that if there exists $n' = \max\{3t - u + 1, 2t + 1\}$ wires from **S** to **R**, then one can securely send a single field element in polynomial number of phases (polynomial in n).

PSMT in directed networks tolerating *non-threshold* adversary was studied by Desmedt *et.al.* in [3]. However, their characterization does not consider the paths from **R** to **S**. Specifically they have characterized PSMT for single phase in directed networks in the absence of feed-back paths from **R** to **S**.

1.2   Our Contribution and Outline of the Paper

In this paper, we significantly improve the existing results for PSMT in directed networks, both for threshold and non threshold adversary.

1. We present a three phase PSMT protocol securely sending a message with polynomial communication complexity with $n = \max(3t - 2u + 1, 2t + 1)$ wires from **S** to **R**. Our protocol performs polynomial time computation. This is a significant improvement over the exponential phase PSMT protocol proposed in [1].

2. We also show how communication complexity of our PSMT can be further reduced down when $n' = \max\{3t - u + 1, 2t + 1\}$ wires are available from **S** to **R**. Also the communication complexity of our improved protocol is significantly smaller than that of polynomial phase PSMT protocol working under the same constraints and presented in [1].

3. We prove the necessary and sufficient condition for the existence of any two phase PSMT protocol between **S** and **R** in a directed network tolerating a threshold adversary. To our knowledge, this is the first ever characterization of two phase PSMT protocol in such networks.

4. We characterize PSMT in directed networks tolerating non-threshold adversary considering feed-back paths from **R** to **S**. Our characterization shows that in many practical scenarios PSMT is possible but the existing characterization [3] has restricted applicability.

Since, in this paper, we deal with both threshold and non-threshold adversary, for easy understanding, we divide the paper into two halves. The first half deals with threshold adversary while the second half deals with non-threshold adversary. In the next section, we describe the network model used for dealing with threshold adversary. We also briefly describe Reed-Solomon codes and their properties. In section 3 we design a three phase polynomial time (and polynomial communication complexity) PSMT protocol even with $n = \max\{3t - 2u + 1, 2t + 1\}$ wires from **S** to **R**. In section 4 we show that if there are $n' = \max\{3t - u + 1, 2t + 1\}$

wires from **S** to **R**, then the communication complexity of our three phase PSMT protocol is reduced further. In section 5, we characterize *two phase* PSMT protocols in the presence of a threshold adversary. The characterization for PSMT tolerating *non-threshold adversary* is provided in section 6. The papers ends with a brief conclusion and directions for further research.

2   Network Model for Threshold Adversary

The network model used for dealing with threshold adversary is same as used in [1]. **S** and **R** are part of a directed synchronous network, modeled as a directed graph. There exists n vertex disjoint paths called wires, directed from **S** to **R** (which is termed as *top band*) and u vertex disjoint paths from **R** to **S** (which is termed as *bottom band*). The wires in the *top band* and *bottom band* are disjoint from each other. An active adversary having unbounded computing power can corrupt any t of these $u + n$ wires. Any value which is transmitted over all the wires is said to be "broadcast". Any value which is broadcast over at least $2t + 1$ wires may always be correctly obtained at the receiving end by taking a majority value among the values received. For designing protocols against a threshold adversary, we use Reed-Solomon codes. We now briefly recall the definition of Reed-Solomon codes and their properties from [6].

Definition 1. *Let $\mathbb{F}$ be a finite field and $\alpha_1, \alpha_2, \ldots \alpha_n$ be a collection of distinct elements of $\mathbb{F}$. Given $k \leq n \leq |\mathbb{F}|$, and a block $\mathbf{B} = [m_0\ m_1\ \ldots\ m_{k-1}]$ the encoding function for the Reed-Solomon code $RS(n, k)$ is defined as $[p_{\mathbf{B}}(\alpha_1)\ p_{\mathbf{B}}(\alpha_2)\ \ldots\ p_{\mathbf{B}}(\alpha_n)]$ where $p_{\mathbf{B}}(x)$ is the polynomial $\sum_{i=0}^{k-1} m_i x^i$.*

The error correcting and detecting capability of Reed-Solomon codes is given by the following theorem:

Theorem 1 ([6]). *Reed-Solomon codes can correct up to c Byzantine errors and simultaneously detect d more Byzantine errors if the difference between the number of points received (which is same as the length of the codeword) and the degree of the polynomial used for encoding is greater than $2c + d$.*

3   A Three Phase PSMT Protocol

Here we design a three phase polynomial time PSMT protocol called **Protocol I** where $n = \max\{3t - 2u + 1, 2t + 1\}$. We first explain **Protocol I** for $0 < u < \lfloor \frac{t}{2} \rfloor$. For $0 < u < \lfloor \frac{t}{2} \rfloor$, $n = 3t - 2u + 1$. The wires in the *top band* are denoted by $f_i, 1 \leq i \leq n$ while the wires in the *bottom band* are denoted by $b_j, 1 \leq j \leq u$. Let m denote the secret message which **S** wants to send to **R**.

We first briefly explain the principle behind **Protocol I**. In **Protocol I**, **S** hides m in the constant term of a bivariate polynomial $Q(x, y)$ of degree t in both x and y. In order to receive m correctly, **R** should be able to recover $Q(x, y)$ correctly. For this, **S** provides **R** with enough information through the *top band* to recover $Q(x, y)$. At the same time, **S** makes sure that adversary is not able to recover $Q(x, y)$ using this information. **R** may not directly use the information received during the first phase because some portion of the information may be corrupted. Using the information sent by **S** during the first phase, **R** tries to locate the identity of as many faulty wires as he can. Towards this, he construct a *conflict graph* which is explained in the protocol. The *conflict graph* has certain nice properties which are explained in the proof of correctness of the protocol. **R** then sends this *conflict graph* to **S** through the *bottom band*. Now there are two possible cases. If **S** receives this *conflict graph* correctly through at least one wire, then at the end of third phase, **R** will be able to identify "some specific" faulty wires in the *top band*, over which it has received wrong information during the first phase. The information received over the remaining wires in the *top band*, will be correct, from which **R** will be able to recover $Q(x, y)$. On the other hand, if **S** does not receives *conflict graph* correctly even through one wire in the *bottom band*, then **R** will come to know about this at the end of third phase, In this case, **R** will come to know an upper bound on the number of faults that occurred during the first phase. Once **R** knows this bound, he will be able to recover $Q(x, y)$ by applying error correcting algorithm to the information received during the first phase. Thus in both cases, **R** will be able to recover $Q(x, y)$ at the end of third phase. We now prove the correctness of the protocol.

Theorem 2. *In **Protocol I**, any adversary $\mathcal{A}$ who controls at most t wires (including top and bottom band) does not get any information about m.*

Proof: Without loss of generality, suppose $\mathcal{A}$ controls $f_1, f_2, \ldots f_t$ (the first t wires in the *top band*). So $\mathcal{A}$ knows $Q(x, 1), Q(x, 2), \ldots, Q(x, t)$ and using these $\mathcal{A}$ can form $t(t + 1)$ independent equations in the coefficients of $Q(x, y)$. $\mathcal{A}$ will also know t values on each of the polynomials $Q(x, t+1), Q(x, t+2), \ldots, Q(x, n)$, each of which are of degree t and hence $\mathcal{A}$ will fall short of one value for each of these polynomials to interpolate them. Moreover out of these $t+1$ $Q(x, i)$'s, only one is linearly independent from $Q(x, 1), Q(x, 2), \ldots, Q(x, t)$ which are already known to $\mathcal{A}$. So through the t points on the polynomials $Q(x, t + 1), Q(x, t + 2), \ldots, Q(x, n)$, $\mathcal{A}$ can form only t additional independent equations in the coefficients of $Q(x, y)$. Hence the total number of independent equations in the coefficients of $Q(x, y)$ that $\mathcal{A}$ can form is $t(t + 1) + t = t^2 + 2t$ and this is one less than the actual number of coefficients in $Q(x, y)$. Hence, the constant term of $Q(x, y)$ (i.e., m) is information theoretically secure.

On the other hand if $\mathcal{A}$ controls at least one wire in the *bottom band*, then during **Phase II** $\mathcal{A}$ will also know the information corresponding to the *conflict graph*. However, this information will not give $\mathcal{A}$ any extra information about $Q(x, y)$ because if the four tuple $(i, j, Q'(j, i), v'_{ij})$ corresponds to an edge in the *conflict graph*, then it indicates that $\mathcal{A}$ has corrupted either f_i or f_j or both (no two honest wires can conflict each other). If f_j is corrupted then $\mathcal{A}$ already knows the actual value of $Q(j, i)$ which it has changed to v'_{ij}. If f_i is corrupted, then $\mathcal{A}$ already knows $Q(x, i)$ and hence its value at $x = j$; i.e., v_{ij}. Thus $\mathcal{A}$ does not get any extra information to interpolate $Q(x, y)$ and retrieve m.   □

Theorem 3. *In* **Protocol I**, *if during* **Phase II**, S *correctly receives the original conflict graph through at least one wire in the bottom band, then at the end of* **Phase III**, R *will always be able to identify all the wires* f_i *over it has received faulty* $Q(x, i)$ *during* **Phase I**.

Proof: Suppose that over some wire $f_i, 1 \leq i \leq n$, the polynomial $Q(x, i)$ had been changed to some other polynomial $Q'(x, i)$ during **Phase I**. Since $Q(x, i)$ and $Q'(x, i)$ are both of degree t in x, they can be same in at most t values of x. Moreover the adversary who can control at most t wires in the *top band* can change the value of $Q(x, i)$ sent over those t wires to corresponding values of $Q'(x, i)$. So R can get incorrect $Q'(x, i)$ over f_i and correspondingly $2t$ matching values over $2t$ wires. However, since $n \geq 2t + 1$ and the value of original polynomial $Q(x, i)$ is sent at n different points, there will be at least one wire say f_j, which will not be under the control of adversary and will deliver the actual value of $Q(x, i)$ at $x = j$ to R. This value will not lie on $Q'(x, i)$ and hence f_i and f_j will conflict each other and hence in the *conflict graph*, there will be an arc from f_i to f_j. If S receives the *conflict graph* correctly through at least one wire in the *bottom band*, then after S performs the local verification, S will identify that the polynomial $Q(x, i)$ had been changed over f_i and reliably sends this information to R by broadcasting it over all the n wires. ☐

Theorem 4. *In* **Protocol I**, R *will always be able to correctly recover the message* m *after* **Phase III**.

Proof: During **Phase I**, S sends a Reed-Solomon codeword of length n for each of the polynomials $Q(x, i), 1 \leq i \leq n$. From Theorem 1, by putting $d = 0$, the maximum number of errors c that R can correct in the received codeword by using Reed-Solomon decoding is given by $(3t - 2u + 1) - (t) - 1 \geq 2c$ implying $c \leq (t - u)$. Hence, if R some how comes to know that the number of Byzantine errors that took place during **Phase I** is at most $t - u$, then R will be able to recover each of the n $Q(x, i)$'s by applying Reed-Solomon decoding algorithm.

Suppose that more than $t - u$ Byzantine errors took place during **Phase I**. This implies that in the *bottom band* at most $u - 1$ errors can occur. Hence S will receive the *conflict graph* correctly through at least one wire. Hence from Theorem 3, at the end of **Phase III**, R will come to know the identity of all faulty $Q(x, i)$'s received during **Phase I**. R will neglect all these faulty $Q(x, i)$'s and considers only the remaining $Q(x, i)$'s. R will thus have at least $t + 1$ correct $Q(x, i)$'s using which it will interpolate $Q(x, y)$ and recovers m.

On the other hand suppose that at most $t - u$ Byzantine errors took place during **Phase I**. So the adversary might control the entire *bottom band*. Hence, during **Phase II**, when R sends the list X corresponding to the *conflict graph* to S through the *bottom band*, the adversary might change the list X to some arbitrary list X' and forward it to S. In the worst case, the adversary might forward u different *conflict graphs* to S. During **Phase III**, S will find the fault list corresponding to each of the received *conflict graphs* and broadcasts *conflict graph - fault list* pairs to R through all the $n \geq 2t + 1$ wires. However, when R receives these *conflict graph - fault list* pairs, it will not find the list X which it

Protocol I: $n = \max\{3t - 2u + 1, 2t + 1\}$

Phase I: S to R

• **S** selects a bivariate polynomial $Q(x,y) = \sum_{i=0}^{t} \sum_{j=0}^{t} r_{ij} x^i y^j$, where r_{ij}'s are randomly chosen from $\mathbb{F}$ which are independent of m ($\mathbb{F}$ is sufficiently large) such that $r_{00} = Q(0,0)$ is the secret message m.

• **S** evaluates $Q(x,y)$ at $y = 1, 2, \ldots, n$ ($1, 2, \ldots, n$ are public parameters). Each $Q(x,i)$ is a polynomial in x of degree t. **S** sends over wire $f_i, 1 \leq i \leq n$ the polynomial $Q(x,i)$ and the value of the polynomials $Q(x,j), 1 \leq j \leq n$ at $x = i$, denoted by v_{ji}. Note that the n tuple $[v_{j1} v_{j2} \ldots v_{jn}]$, $1 \leq j \leq n$ corresponds to the Reed-Solomon codeword of the polynomial $Q(x,j)$, $1 \leq j \leq n$.

Phase II: R to S

• **R** receives over wire $f_i, 1 \leq i \leq n$, the polynomial $Q'(x,i)$ and the values $v'_{ji}, 1 \leq j \leq n$. The received codeword $[v'_{j1} v'_{j2} \ldots v'_{jn}]$ can differ from the actual codeword $[v_{j1} v_{j2} \ldots v_{jn}]$ in at most t locations.

• **R** creates a directed graph $H = (\mathcal{W}, E)$, called *conflict graph* such that $\mathcal{W} = \{f_1, f_2, \ldots, f_n\}$ and $(f_i, f_j) \in E$ if $Q'(j,i) \neq v'_{ij}, 1 \leq i,j \leq n$. Thus there exists an arc from vertex f_i to vertex f_j in H if the value of the received polynomial $Q'(x,i)$ at $x = j$ does not match the corresponding received value v'_{ij}. This implies that either f_i or f_j or both are corrupted. Corresponding to each edge $(f_i, f_j) \in H$, **R** adds a four tuple $(i, j, Q'(j,i), v'_{ij})$ to a list X. **R** finally sends the list X to **S** through all the wires in the *bottom band*.

Phase III from S to R

S receives u lists through the *bottom band*, among which l are distinct, where $1 \leq l \leq u$. Let these lists be denoted by $L_1, L_2, \ldots, L_l$. For each such list distinct list $L_k, 1 \leq k \leq l$, **S** does the following:

• **S** creates a fault list denoted by $L_{k_{fault}}$ which is initialized to $\emptyset$. For each four tuple $(i'', j'', Q''(j'', i''), v''_{i''j''})$ present in the list L_k, **S** locally checks $Q''(j'', i'') \stackrel{?}{=} Q(j'', i'')$ and $v_{i''j''} \stackrel{?}{=} v''_{i''j''}$. Depending upon the outcome of the test, **S** concludes that during **Phase I**, either **R** had received incorrect $Q(x,i'')$ through wire $f_{i''}$ or incorrect value of the polynomial $Q(x,i'')$ at $x = j''$ through wire $f_{j''}$ (or both) and hence accordingly add $f_{i''}$ or $f_{j''}$ (or both) to $L_{k_{fault}}$.

After performing the above steps for each distinct list $L_k, 1 \leq k \leq l$, **S** broadcasts to **R** the pairs $(L_k, L_{k_{fault}})$ over all n wires.

Message Recovery by R

Since $n \geq 2t + 1$, by taking majority, **R** will correctly receive the pairs $(L_k, L_{k_{fault}})$. **R** then checks for the original *conflict list* X which it had sent during **Phase II**.

• If the list X is present in the received pairs $(L_k, L_{k_{fault}})$, then **R** does the following: Let the received pair corresponding to the sent list X be $(L_z, L_{z_{fault}})$. From the list $L_{z_{fault}}$, **R** will come to know the identity of all incorrect $Q(x,i)$'s that **R** had received during **Phase I** (see Theorem 3), neglects them, interpolates $Q(x,y)$ using the remaining $Q(x,i)$'s and recovers $m = Q(0,0)$.

• If the list X is not present in the received pairs $(L_k, L_{k_{fault}})$, then **R** concludes that entire *bottom band* is corrupted and hence at most $t - u$ Byzantine errors occurred during **Phase I**. **R** then applies the Reed-Solomon decoding algorithm to each of the n tuples $[v'_{i1} v'_{i2} \ldots v'_{in}]$, $1 \leq i \leq n$ which **R** had received during **Phase I** to recover all $Q(x,i)'s$, $1 \leq i \leq n$ (see Theorem 4). Finally, he interpolates $Q(x,y)$ using $t + 1$ $Q(x,i)$ and recovers $m = Q(0,0)$.

had sent to **S** during **Phase II**. **R** will thus conclude that **S** had not received the actual *conflict graph* correctly because the entire *bottom band* is under the control of the adversary. Hence **R** also concludes that at most $t - u$ Byzantine errors had occurred during **Phase I**. Now as explained earlier, **R** can correct $t - u$ Byzantine errors by applying Reed-Solomon decoding algorithm to each of the codewords $[v'_{i1}v'_{i2} \ldots v'_{in}], 1 \leq i \leq n$, assuming the number of errors to be $t - u$ and recovers each of the polynomial $Q(x, i), 1 \leq i \leq n$ correctly. Finally, by taking any $t + 1$ $Q(x, i)'s$, **R** interpolates $Q(x, y)$ and recovers m. □

Theorem 5. *The communication complexity of* **Protocol I** *is* $O(n^3 u)$.

Proof: During **Phase I**, **S** sends over wire $f_i, 1 \leq i \leq n$ the polynomial $Q(x, i)$ which is of degree t and the value of the polynomials $Q(x, j), 1 \leq j \leq n$ at $x = i$. So the total number of field elements send during **Phase I** is $n(t + 1) + n^2$ which is $O(n^2)$ (for $n \geq 2t + 1, t = O(n)$). In **Phase II**, **R** sends the list of four tuples corresponding to the *conflict graph* to **S** through all the u wires. Since *conflict graph* in the worst case contains $O(n^2)$ edges, the total communication complexity of **Phase II** is $O(n^2 u)$. However, as explained in Theorem 4, **S** may receive u different *conflict graphs* during **Phase III**. In **Phase III**, corresponding to each received *conflict graph*, **S** broadcasts a conflict graph - fault list pair. Since there can be at most t faulty wires, each fault list will contain $O(t)$ field elements. Hence in the worst case, **S** needs to broadcast u *conflict graph - fault list* pairs which involves communicating $O(n * u * (n^2 + t))$ field elements which is $O(n^3 u)$. Hence total communication complexity of the protocol is $O(n^3 u)$. □

Note 1. In **Protocol I**, we have assumed that $0 < u < \lceil \frac{t}{2} \rceil$. If $\lceil \frac{t}{2} \rceil < u < t + 1$ then $3t - 2u + 1 < 2t + 1$ and hence $n = 2t + 1$. Even then **Protocol I** will work correctly because for $n = 2t + 1$, the error correcting capability of **R** using Reed-Solomon decoding will be $\frac{t}{2}$. So if during **Phase II**, **S** receives incorrect *conflict graph* through the *bottom band*, then **R** will conclude after **Phase III** that at most $t - u$ (which is at most $\frac{t}{2}$) errors had occurred during **Phase I**, which it can correct by applying Reed-Solomon decoding algorithm. If $u > t + 1$, then in **Protocol I**, **S** will always receive the actual *conflict graph* from **R** through at least one wire and hence from Theorem 3, after **Phase III**, **R** will be able to identify the faulty $Q(x, i)$ received during **Phase I**. **R** can now recover m by neglecting such faulty polynomials.

4 Three Phase Protocol with Reduced Message Complexity

In [1], the authors have shown that if there exists $n' = \max\{3t - u + 1, 2t + 1\}$ wires in the *top band*, then there exists a PSMT protocol which terminates in polynomial number of phases and hence has polynomial communication complexity. However, their communication complexity is much more than $O(n'^3)$. Here we show that if there are $n' = max\{3t - u + 1, 2t + 1\}$ wires from **S** to **R**, then the communication complexity of **Protocol I** can be reduced to $O(n'^3)$.

Protocol II - 3 Phase Protocol with reduced communication complexity

- **Phase I** and **Phase II** is same as in **Protocol I** except that here $n' = \max\{3t - u + 1, 2t + 1\}$.

Phase III: S to R

In **Protocol I**, **S** could receive u different list of four tuples corresponding to u different *conflict graphs* from **R** during **Phase II**. However, here **S** will only consider the list of four tuples that it receives from **R** over more than $\frac{u}{2}$ wires.

- If **S** does not receives a unique list of four tuples corresponding to a unique *conflict graph* over more than $\frac{u}{2}$ wires, then **S** broadcasts "ERROR" signal to **R** through all the wires $f_i, 1 \leq i \leq n'$ and terminates the protocol. On the other hand, if **S** receives some list L_k of four tuples corresponding to some *conflict graph* over more than $\frac{u}{2}$ wires, then similar to the previous protocol, **S** constructs the fault list $L_{k_{fault}}$ corresponding to the list L_k and broadcasts the pair $(L_k, L_{k_{fault}})$ to **R** over all the n' wires.

Message Recovery by R

- If **R** receives "ERROR" signal from **S** then **R** concludes that the original list of four tuples X has not reached correctly to **S** through more than $\frac{u}{2}$ wires because at least $\frac{u}{2} + 1$ Byzantine errors had taken place during **Phase II** in the *bottom band* implying that at most $t - \frac{u}{2} - 1$ Byzantine errors had occurred during **Phase I** in the *top band*. **R** then does the following: **R** concatenates each of the received codewords $[v'_{i1}v'_{i2} \ldots v'_{in'}], 1 \leq i \leq n'$ and applies Reed-Solomon decoding to each of these codewords assuming the number of errors in each of the codeword to be $t - \frac{u}{2}$ and correctly recovers each of the polynomials $Q(x, i), 1 \leq i \leq n'$ correctly (see Theorem 6). **R** then considers any $t + 1$ recovered $Q(x, i)$'s, interpolates the polynomial $Q(x, y)$ and recovers m from $Q(0, 0)$.

- If **R** receives a pair $(L_k, L_{k_{fault}})$ from **S**, then **R** checks whether L_k is same as X which is the original list corresponding to the *conflict graph* sent by **R** during **Phase II**. If $L_k = X$, then **R** concludes that **S** had received the actual *conflict graph* correctly. Then similar to the previous protocol, **R** will be able to interpolate $Q(x, y)$ correctly and hence recover m.
On the other hand, if $L_k \neq X$, then **R** concludes that **S** had not received the original list X through more than $\frac{u}{2}$ wires because at least $\frac{u}{2} + 1$ Byzantine errors had occurred during **Phase II**. **R** also concludes that at most $t - \frac{u}{2} - 1$ Byzantine errors had occurred during **Phase I**. **R** then do the same steps which it does if it receives "ERROR" signal from **S** as explained above and recovers m correctly.

We call the new protocol as **Protocol II**. Without loss of generality we assume that $0 < u \leq t$, hence $n' = 3t - u + 1$. **Phase I** and **Phase II** is same as in **Protocol I**. Also during **Phase III**, only a single *conflict graph* - fault list pair is broadcast which does not give any extra information about the message to the adversary. Hence security of **Protocol II** follows from Theorem 2. We now argue for the correctness of the new protocol.

Theorem 6. *In* **Protocol II,** **R** *will always be able to recover the message correctly in three phases.*

Proof. From Theorem 1, by putting $d = 0$, the error correcting capability by **R** in received codewords is now bounded by $(3t - u + 1) - (t) - 1 \geq 2c$ which gives $c \leq (t - \frac{u}{2})$ which is more than in **Protocol I**. In **Protocol II**, if **R** receives "ERROR" signal from **S** during **Phase III**, then **R** concludes that **S** has not received the original *conflict graph* over more than $\frac{u}{2}$ wires during **Phase II** because at least $\frac{u}{2} + 1$ Byzantine errors occurred in the *bottom band*. This implies that at most $t - \frac{u}{2}$ Byzantine errors occurred during **Phase I**. So **R** applies Reed-Solomon decoding algorithm to each of the received codeword assuming the number of errors to be at most $t - \frac{u}{2}$ and correctly recovers all the polynomials $Q(x, i), 1 \leq i \leq n'$. **R** then considers any $t + 1$ $Q(x, i)'s$, interpolate the polynomial $Q(x, y)$ and recovers the message m.

If **R** receives the pair $(L_k, L_{k_{fault}})$ from **S** during **Phase III**, then **R** checks whether $L_k = X$, where X is the original list corresponding to the original *conflict graph* sent by **R** during **Phase II**. If $L_k = X$, then it implies that **S** had received the original *conflict graph* correctly over more than $\frac{u}{2}$ wires. Now from Theorem 3, **R** will identify all the corrupted $Q(x, i)$'s wires received during **Phase I**. Neglecting them, **R** interpolates $Q(x, y)$ and recovers m.

On the other hand, if $L_k \neq X$, then again **R** concludes that **S** had not received the original *conflict graph* correctly because at least $\frac{u}{2} + 1$ Byzantine errors occurred in the *bottom band* during **Phase II**. **R** also concludes that at most $t - \frac{u}{2}$ Byzantine errors occurred during **Phase I**. Now **R** can apply the Reed-Solomon decoding algorithm to each codeword received during **Phase I** assuming the number of errors to be at most $t - \frac{u}{2}$, recovers all the polynomials $Q(x, i)$ correctly, interpolates $Q(x, y)$ and finally recovers m.   □

Theorem 7. *The communication complexity of* **Protocol II** *is* $O(n'^3)$.

Proof. The communication complexity of **Phase I** and **Phase II** is same as in **Protocol I**. During **Phase III**, **S** broadcasts only a single *conflict graph* - fault list pair through n' wires which involves a communication complexity of $O(n' * (n'^2 + t))$ which is $O(n'^3)$. Thus the total communication complexity of the protocol is $O(n'^2) + O(n'^2 u) + O(n'^3)$ which is $O(n'^3)$ because $0 < u \leq t$ and hence $u = O(t) = O(n')$ because $n' \geq 2t + 1$. Thus the total communication complexity of the protocol is $O(n'^3)$.   □

Note 2. In **Protocol II**, we have assumed that $0 < u \leq t$. If $t + 1 \leq u \leq 2t$, then also the protocol will work. If $u \geq 2t + 1$, then the protocol will work by slightly modifying it. In this case $n = 2t + 1$ and $u \geq 2t + 1$. So **R** will always be able to send the *conflict graph* reliably to **S** because the *conflict graph* will be now sent over at least $2t + 1$ wires, out of which at most t can be corrupted. Once, **S** receives the *conflict graph* correctly, it will identify all the wires over which the polynomial $Q(x, i)$ is changed during **Phase I**, sends this information to **R**, using which **R** will recover the message correctly. It can be seen easily that the communication complexity of the protocol in this case will be $O(n'^3)$.

5   Two Phase PSMT Tolerating Threshold Adversary

One of the significant attribute contributing to the quality of a PSMT protocol is the number of phases taken by the protocol. For PSMT in undirected graphs, $2t + 1$ wires (bi-directional) between **S** and **R** is necessary and sufficient for the existence of any r-phase ($r \geq 2$) PSMT protocol [4]. Thus, the connectivity requirement is same for any r-phase ($r \geq 2$) PSMT protocol in undirected graph. However, this is not true in the case of directed networks. The characterization for two phase PSMT in directed networks is given by the following theorem.

Theorem 8. *Let $G = (V, E)$ be a directed graph and* **S**, **R** $\in V$. *Then there exists a two phase PSMT protocol against a t-active Byzantine adversary between* **S** *and* **R** *iff there exist $n \geq 2t+1$ vertex disjoint paths from* **S** *to* **R** *and $u \geq 2t+1$ vertex disjoint paths from* **R** *to* **S**.

Proof: Necessity: In any two phase PSMT protocol, the first phase is from **R** to **S** and the second phase is from **S** to **R**. Moreover, the actual message is sent by **S** to **R** only in the second phase. Also, to send the message, **S** will always make use of the information that **R** had sent it during **Phase I** because if **S** does not make use of this information, then the two phase PSMT protocol reduces to a single phase PSMT protocol between **S** and **R** against a t-active adversary for which there should exist at least $3t + 1$ wires from **S** and **R** [4]. Thus in any two phase PSMT protocol, **S** always makes use of the information sent to it by **R** during **Phase I**. Since the information send by **R** during **Phase I** is used by **S** to send the message, this information should reach reliably to **S**. Otherwise **S** will make use of incorrect information to send the message and hence **R** will not be able to receive the message reliably. However, from [4], for the existence of any PRMT (perfectly Reliable Message Transmission) protocol between **S** and **R** or **R** and **S** against a t-active adversary, there should exist at least $2t + 1$ wires between them. So in order that the information send by **R** reaches reliably to **S**, there should exist $2t + 1$ wires in the *bottom band*. As mentioned above, the secret message is send during **Phase II** by **S**. So the message should reach reliably to **R**. Again from [4], the necessary condition for this is that there should exist $n \geq 2t+1$ wires in the *top band*. This proves the necessity condition.

Sufficiency: Suppose there exists $2t + 1$ wires $f_1, f_2, \ldots, f_{2t+1}$ from **S** to **R** and $2t + 1$ wires $b_1, b_2, \ldots, b_{2t+1}$ from **R** to **S**. From [8], it is well known that there exists a two phase PSMT protocol between **S** and **R**, in an undirected graph, when both of them are connected by $2t + 1$ vertex disjoint paths facilitating bi-directional communication. Let the protocol be denoted by $\mathcal{P}_{undirected}$. Here we have $2t + 1$ vertex disjoint paths facilitating communication from **S** to **R** and $2t + 1$ vertex disjoint paths facilitating communication from **R** to **S** which may or may not be vertex disjoint. However, irrespective of whether they are vertex disjoint or not, we can design a two phase PSMT protocol $\mathcal{P}_{directed}$ between **S** and **R** from $\mathcal{P}_{undirected}$. The protocol is as follows: In the first phase, **R** sends to **S** through the wires $b_1, b_2, \ldots, b_{2t+1}$, what ever **R** would had sent if it had executed the protocol $\mathcal{P}_{undirected}$ in an undirected graph to send the message m. In the second phase, **S** will send to **R** through the wires $f_1, f_2, \ldots, f_{2t+1}$, what ever it would had sent to **R**, if it had executed the protocol $\mathcal{P}_{undirected}$ to send m after receiving what ever it had received from **R** during the first phase of $\mathcal{P}_{directed}$. The reliability and security of the protocol $\mathcal{P}_{directed}$ follows from the reliability and security of the protocol $\mathcal{P}_{undirected}$ [8].   □

Significance of Theorem 8: Consider a network having five wires in the *top band* and two wires in the *bottom band*, which are disjoint from the *top band*. If we set $t = 2$, then there exists a three phase PSMT protocol between **S** and **R** (**Protocol I**) tolerating two adversaries. However, from Theorem 8, there does not exist any two phase PSMT protocol tolerating two adversaries. In fact, in this case, there does not exist any two phase PSMT protocol tolerating even a single adversary. Thus unlike undirected graphs, the connectivity requirement for two phase and three phase PSMT protocol in directed networks varies.

6   PSMT Tolerating Non-threshold Adversary

Non-Threshold adversary in the context of PSMT was first studied in [5]. Modeling the adversary by a threshold helps in easy characterization of PSMT. It also helps in analyzing protocols and proving lower bound on the communication complexity [10]. However, as mentioned in [5], modeling the (dis)trust in the network as a threshold adversary is not always appropriate since:

1. In the case of secure communication, not all scenarios of mutual (dis)trust can be captured by a threshold adversary.
2. The threshold model may lead to a gross overestimation of the connectivity requirement of the underlying network.

For instance, consider the network $\mathcal{N}$ and the Byzantine adversary $\mathcal{A}$ as given in Figure 1. As evident from Figure 1, there are *five* wires in the *top band* and *two* wires in the *bottom band*. Hence from [1], any protocol that tolerates a threshold adversary can tolerate only upto any *two* node failures. Therefore, there does *not* exist *any* threshold scheme for secure message transmission tolerating three node failures because to do so, we require six wires in the *top band* (by taking $u = 2, t = 3$ and $n = \max\{3t - 2u + 1, 2t + 1\}$) [1]. Thus the specified adversary is not tolerable. However, from our characterization for non-threshold adversary given in Theorem 10, the given adversary is indeed tolerable. Thus we see that the threshold protocol requires more stringent connectivity requirements. Therefore, we need a general way to characterize an adversary rather than just allow the adversary to corrupt some t players. Fortunately, such a characterization has been done in [5] using the notion of an *adversary structure*. We now briefly recall few definitions from [5] to deal with non-threshold adversary.

92   A. Patra et al.

In a non-threshold model, adversary is defined by an adversary structure where an adversary structure represents the collection of all possible subsets of nodes (excluding **S** and **R**) that are potentially corruptible. During the execution of the protocol the adversary can choose any set from this collection to corrupt through the execution of the protocol. More precisely, if $\mathcal{P}$ is the set of nodes then we define the adversary structure by $\mathcal{A}$, where $\mathcal{A} \subseteq 2^{\mathcal{P}}$. The adversary structure is *monotone* in the sense that if $\mathcal{B}_1 \in \mathcal{A}$, then $\forall \mathcal{B}_2$ such that $\mathcal{B}_2 \subseteq \mathcal{B}_1$, $\mathcal{B}_2 \in \mathcal{A}$. We note that $\mathcal{A}$ can be uniquely represented by listing the elements in its *maximal basis*. For any monotone adversary structure $\mathcal{A}$, its maximal basis $\overline{\mathcal{A}}$ is defined as $\overline{\mathcal{A}} = \{B | B \in \mathcal{A}, \nexists X \in \mathcal{A}, X \neq B, X \supseteq B\}$. Note that a threshold adversary is an adversary structure such that the size of each set in the maximal basis is bounded by a threshold value t.

The Byzantine adversary $\mathcal{A}$ corrupts any *one* of the subsets $\{1,2,3\}$ or $\{3,4,7\}$ or $\{2,5,6\}$

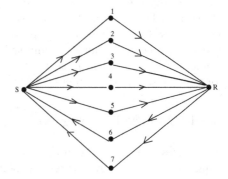

Fig. 1. Network $\mathcal{N}$ and the Adversary $\mathcal{A}$

Definition 2. *Given the adversary structure $\mathcal{A}$, the network is said to be $\mathcal{A}^{(k)}$-**connected** if for any k sets $X_{i_1}, X_{i_2}, \ldots, X_{i_{k-1}}$ and X_{i_k} from $\mathcal{A}$, the deletion of the nodes in $\bigcup_{\ell=1}^{k} X_{i_\ell}$ from the network does not disconnect the network. With respect to two nodes P_i and P_j, the network is said to be $\mathcal{A}^{(k)}(P_i, P_j)$-**subconnected** if for any k sets $X_{i_1}, X_{i_2}, \ldots, X_{i_{k-1}}$ and X_{i_k} from $\mathcal{A}$, the deletion of the nodes in $\bigcup_{\ell=1}^{k} X_{i_\ell}$ from the network does not render P_j unreachable from P_i; i.e., even after deleting the nodes from the k sets, there exists at least one directed path from P_i to P_j.*

6.1   Existing Results for Non-threshold Adversary

Non-threshold adversary in the context of *directed* graphs was first introduced in [3] where the authors have given the following characterization:

Theorem 9 ([3]). *Let $G = (V, E)$ be a directed graph. Let $\mathbf{S}, \mathbf{R} \in V$ and $\mathcal{A}$ be an adversary structure on $V - \{\mathbf{S}, \mathbf{R}\}$. If there are no directed paths from $\mathbf{R}$ to $\mathbf{S}$, then PSMT is possible between $\mathbf{S}$ and $\mathbf{R}$ iff G is $\mathcal{A}^{(3)}(\mathbf{S}, \mathbf{R})$-**subconnected**.*

It is easy to see that the above theorem is true only when there are no wires in the *bottom band*. Thus the above theorem characterize *only* single phase PSMT in directed networks. However, in many practical scenarios, there may exist wires in the *bottom band* and at the same time, the network may not satisfy the condition given in Theorem 9. Hence no single phase PSMT would be possible, but multiphase PSMT could be possible. For example the network in Figure 1 is not $\mathcal{A}^{(3)}(\mathbf{S}, \mathbf{R})$-**subconnected** and hence from Theorem 9, no single phase PSMT is possible. However, from our characterization of non-threshold adversary, given in Theorem 10, there exists a three phase PSMT in the network of Figure 1. Thus while our characterization shows the existence of protocol, the existing characterization [3] offers no such insight.

6.2   Characterization of PSMT Considering Feedback Paths

We now give the necessary and sufficiency conditions for PSMT in directed networks (considering feed-back paths) tolerating a non-threshold adversary. We first give the necessary lemma's before giving the characterization.

Lemma 1 ([5,3]). *Perfect Reliable Message Transmission (PRMT) from* **S** *to* **R** *in a network (directed or undirected) tolerating an adversary structure* $\mathcal{A}$ *is possible iff the network is* $\mathcal{A}^{(2)}(\mathbf{S}, \mathbf{R})$-**subconnected**.

Lemma 2. *Let* $G = (V, E)$ *be a directed graph. Let* **S**, **R** $\in V$ *and* $\mathcal{A}$ *be an adversary structure on* $V - \{\mathbf{S}, \mathbf{R}\}$. *Then PSMT between* **S** *and* **R** *is possible if and only if every monotone subset* $\mathcal{B} \subseteq \mathcal{A}$, *such that maximal basis of* $\mathcal{B}$ *is of size* **three**, *is tolerable.*

Proof: The only if condition is obvious because if the entire adversary structure $\mathcal{A}$ is tolerable, then every subset $\mathcal{B}$ of $\mathcal{A}$ with a maximal basis of size three is tolerable. We now prove the if condition. The proof is by induction. Suppose every monotone subset $\mathcal{B}$ of $\mathcal{A}$, such that $|\overline{\mathcal{B}}| = 3$ is tolerable where $\overline{\mathcal{B}}$ denotes the maximal basis of $\mathcal{B}$. Then, to show that every monotone subset $|\overline{\mathcal{B}}| = 4$ is also tolerable, we argue as follows: for any subset $\mathcal{B} \subseteq \mathcal{A}$ with $|\overline{\mathcal{B}}| = 4$, there exist four subsets each of size three such that any element in $\overline{\mathcal{B}}$ belongs to exactly three of them. Specifically, we may choose to divide $\overline{\mathcal{B}} = \{\mathcal{B}_1, \mathcal{B}_2, \mathcal{B}_3, \mathcal{B}_4\}$ into $\mathcal{A}_1 = \{\mathcal{B}_1, \mathcal{B}_2, \mathcal{B}_3\}$, $\mathcal{A}_2 = \{\mathcal{B}_1, \mathcal{B}_2, \mathcal{B}_4\}$, $\mathcal{A}_3 = \{\mathcal{B}_1, \mathcal{B}_3, \mathcal{B}_4\}$, $\mathcal{A}_4 = \{\mathcal{B}_2, \mathcal{B}_3, \mathcal{B}_4\}$. Now each of the set $\mathcal{A}_i, 1 \leq i \leq 4$ is of size three and hence from induction hypothesis there exists four PSMT protocols tolerating each of the $\mathcal{A}_i$'s individually. Therefore, if we run these four PSMT protocols in parallel then at most one of them will fail. Thus, if the shares of a 1-out-of-4 Shamir secret sharing scheme (which is nothing but four points on a straight line) are transmitted using these four sub-protocols, at least three points will be received correctly by **R** and hence **R** may recover the straight line and the secret (the y-axis intercept) easily [9]. The adversary will have the knowledge of only one point and the perfect secrecy follows from the correctness of Shamir's secret sharing scheme [9].

Applying the above procedure again, we find that any subset $\mathcal{B}$ of $\mathcal{A}$, such that $|\overline{\mathcal{B}}| = 5$, is tolerable — because any set of size five can be divided into four subsets of size four each such that every element occurs in at least three of the subsets. In general, any $\mu > 4$ sized set can be divided into four subsets, each of size $\lceil \frac{3\mu}{4} \rceil$, such that every element occurs in at least three of them. The proof now follows from induction.   □

Thus, the problem of characterizing the (im)possibility of PSMT tolerating non-threshold adversary $\mathcal{A}$ has been reduced to characterizing the (im)possibility of PSMT tolerating non-threshold adversary $\mathcal{B} \subset \mathcal{A}$, such that maximal basis of $\mathcal{B}$ is of size **three**[3]. We make further inroads with our next theorem.

Theorem 10. *Given a network consisting of several vertex disjoint directed paths between* **S** *and* **R**, *which is influenced by an adversary characterized by a Byzantine adversary structure* $\mathcal{A}$, *perfectly secure message transmission from* **S** *to* **R** *is possible if and only if PRMT (perfectly reliable message transmission) from* **S** *to* **R** *is possible and for every subset* $\mathcal{B} \subseteq \mathcal{A}$ *where* $\bar{\mathcal{B}} = \{\mathcal{B}_1, \mathcal{B}_2, \mathcal{B}_3\}$, *either of the following conditions holds:*

1. *There exists a directed path from* **S** *to* **R** *that does not involve nodes from* $(\mathcal{B}_1 \cup \mathcal{B}_2 \cup \mathcal{B}_3)$.
2. *There exists* $\alpha, \beta \in \{1, 2, 3\}$, $\alpha \neq \beta$ *such that two (not necessarily distinct) directed paths* q_α *and* q_β *exist from* **R** *to* **S** *such that* q_α *avoid nodes from* $\mathcal{B}_\alpha$ *and* q_β *avoid nodes from* $\mathcal{B}_\beta$.

Proof: We first give the sufficiency proof and later the necessity proofs.

Sufficiency: Suppose that PRMT is possible between **S** and **R**. Now there are two possible cases. The case where a honest path free from $\mathcal{B}_1, \mathcal{B}_2$ and $\mathcal{B}_3$ exists is easy to prove. The honest path can be used to generate and share a common secret between **S** and **R** and then one only needs to PRMT the blinded message to achieve PSMT. Suppose that second case is true, that is, there exist strong paths, say q_α and q_β, from **R** to **S** such that they do not contain nodes from $\mathcal{B}_\alpha$ and $\mathcal{B}_\beta$ respectively. Note that the existence of PRMT implies that corresponding to any two sets $\mathcal{B}_i$ and $\mathcal{B}_j$ in the adversary structure $\mathcal{A}$, there exists a path p that does not contain nodes from $\mathcal{B}_i \cup \mathcal{B}_j$ (see Lemma 1). However, p can contain nodes from some other set $\mathcal{B}_k \in \mathcal{A}$. Thus, there for each $i \in \{1, 2, 3\}$ there exists paths p_i from **S** to **R** such that p_i avoid nodes from $\mathcal{B}_k \cup \mathcal{B}_j$ where $\{k, j\} = \{1, 2, 3\} - \{i\}$. However, p_i can involve nodes from $\mathcal{B}_i$. We now design a three phase PSMT protocol called **Secure Protocol**, which securely sends a single field element m against $\bar{\mathcal{B}} = \{\mathcal{B}_1, \mathcal{B}_2, \mathcal{B}_3\}$. **Secure Protocol** is similar in spirit to the three phase PSMT protocol **Protocol I** designed for tolerating threshold adversary. The proof of correctness and security is given after proving the the necessity condition.

Necessity: We consider the following three cases:

1. If there does not exist any path from **R** to **S**, then the existence of a directed path from **S** to **R** free from $\mathcal{B}_1 \cup \mathcal{B}_2 \cup \mathcal{B}_3$ is necessary from Theorem 9.

---

[3] Note that the proof only shows the necessity and sufficiency of the condition. It does not explicitly shows a concrete protocol. The protocol is inductive and is inefficient. However, our goal is to just show the sufficiency of the condition.

Secure Protocol - A Three phase PSMT Protocol Tolerating $\bar{\mathcal{B}} = \{\mathcal{B}_1, \mathcal{B}_2, \mathcal{B}_3\}$

Phase I: S to R:

• **S** chooses uniformly at random a bivariate polynomial $Q(x,y) = \sum_{i=0}^{1} \sum_{j=0}^{1} r_{ij} x^i y^j$ such that $Q(0,0) = m$. The polynomial $Q(x,y)$ is symmetric; i.e, $Q(i,j) = Q(j,i)$. Next, along path $p_i, 1 \leq i \leq 3$, **S** sends the polynomial $Q(x,i)$.

Phase II: R to S:

R receives the polynomial $Q'_i(x) = Q'(x,i)$ along path $p_i, 1 \leq i \leq 3$. Out of the three $Q'_i(x)$'s, at most one can be corrupted. **R** then tries to reconstruct $Q(x,y)$. Since $Q(x,y)$ is symmetric, using $Q'_i(x)$'s, **R** checks $Q'_i(j) \overset{?}{=} Q'_j(i), 1 \leq i, j \leq 3$; i.e., $Q'(j,i) \overset{?}{=} Q'(i,j)$.

• If the above test is successful for each $1 \leq i, j \leq 3$, then **R** concludes that each $Q'_i(x), 1 \leq i \leq 3$ lie on $Q(x,y)$. **R** then reconstructs $Q(x,y)$, recovers m (see Lemma 3) and terminates the protocol.

• If the test fails for two pairs say (i,j) and (i,k) then **R** concludes that p_i is corrupted. Thus if **R** finds that $Q'(i,j) \neq Q'(j,i)$ and $Q'(i,k) \neq Q'(k,i)$, then **R** concludes that p_i and hence $Q'_i(x)$ is corrupted (see Lemma 4). Thus the remaining two $Q'_j(x)$'s lie on $Q(x,y)$, using which **R** reconstructs $Q(x,y)$, recovers m and terminates the protocol.

• If the test fails for only one pair say (i,j) such that $Q'_i(j) \neq Q'_j(i)$, then **R** concludes that either p_i or p_j is corrupted and the third path $\{1,2,3\} \backslash \{i,j\}$ is honest. Next along both the paths q_α and q_β, **R** sends the four tuple $\{i, j, Q'_i(j), Q'_j(i)\}$.

Phase III: S to R:

If **S** does not receives anything along q_α and q_β, then **S** does nothing and terminates the protocol. Otherwise let S receives the four tuples $(i'', j'', Q''_{i''}(j''), Q''_{j''}(i''))$ along q_α and $(i''', j''', Q'''_{i'''}(j'''), Q'''_{j'''}(i'''))$ along q_β. The two four tuples may or may not be same. Also both the four tuples can be different from the original four tuple sent by **R**.

• Corresponding to the four tuple $(i'', j'', Q''_{i''}(j''), Q''_{j''}(i''))$, **S** checks $Q''_{i''}(j'') \overset{?}{=} Q_{i''}(j'')$ and $Q''_{j''}(i'') \overset{?}{=} Q_{j''}(i'')$. Depending upon the outcome of the test, **S** concludes that either **R** has received faulty $Q''_{i''}(x)$ through $p_{i''}$ or faulty $Q''_{j''}(x)$ through $p_{j''}$ during **Phase I**. Accordingly, **S** appends an error message "Path γ is faulty" to the four tuple $(i'', j'', Q''_{i''}(j''), Q''_{j''}(i''))$ where γ is either $p_{i''}$ or $p_{j''}$.

• **S** performs similar test for the other four tuple $(i''', j''', Q'''_{i'''}(j'''), Q'''_{j'''}(i'''))$ and appends an error message to the four tuple.

• **S** finally reliably sends the two four tuples, along with the appended error messages to **R** by executing a PRMT protocol (PRMT is possible from **S** to **R**). While sending the two tuples, **S** also mentions which tuple is received along q_α and q_β respectively.

Message Recovery by R:

If during **Phase II**, **R** has already recovered the message, then **R** does nothing. Otherwise **R** recovers m as follows. **R** reliably receives two four tuples along with the appended error messages. **R** also identifies which tuple is received by **S** along q_α and q_β respectively. **R** then checks whether the original four tuple $\{i, j, Q'_i(j), Q'_j(i)\}$ sent by himself during **Phase II** is same as any of the two received tuples.

• If the four tuple $\{i, j, Q'_i(j), Q'_j(i)\}$ is same as $(i'', j'', Q''_{i''}(j''), Q''_{j''}(i''))$, then **R** concludes that **S** has correctly received the four tuple through q_α. **R** will also receive a message of the form "path γ is faulty" appended with this four tuple where γ is either $p_{i''}$ or $p_{j''}$. Hence **R** concludes that he has received faulty polynomial through path γ during **Phase I**. Let $\{a, b\} = \{1, 2, 3\} \backslash \{\gamma\}$. Now **R** recovers the polynomial $Q(x,y)$ using the polynomials $Q_a(x)$ and $Q_b(x)$ which are guaranteed to be correct. Finally, **R** outputs $m = Q(0,0)$ and halts (see Lemma 5). Similarly, if $\{i, j, Q'_i(j), Q'_j(i)\}$ is same as $(i''', j''', Q'''_{i'''}(j'''), Q'''_{j'''}(i'''))$, then **R** concludes that **S** has correctly received the four tuple through q_β recover m in the same way.

• If the four tuple $\{i, j, Q'_i(j), Q'_j(i)\}$ does not matches with any of the two received tuples, then **R** concludes that both q_α as well as q_β delivered wrong messages to **S** during **Phase II**. **R** then concludes that the path p_γ where $\gamma = (\{1,2,3\} \backslash \{\alpha\}) \cap (\{1,2,3\} \backslash \{\beta\})$ is corrupt in the *top band*. Let $\{a, b\} = \{1, 2, 3\} \backslash \{\gamma\}$. Now, **R** recovers the polynomial $Q(x,y)$ using the polynomials $Q_\alpha(x)$ and $Q_\beta(x)$ which are guaranteed to be correct. Finally, **R** outputs $m = Q(0,0)$ and halts (see Lemma 5).

2. Suppose that there does not exist any directed path from **S** to **R** free from $\mathcal{B}_1 \cup \mathcal{B}_2 \cup \mathcal{B}_3$ and each feed back path from **R** to **S** passes through nodes from all the sets $\mathcal{B}_1, \mathcal{B}_2$ and $\mathcal{B}_3$. It is easy to see that in this case, the entire *bottom band* is useless because it can be completely corrupted by any of the $\mathcal{B}_i$'s and neither **S** nor **R** will know the identity of the set due to which the *bottom band* is corrupted. So effectively, this case reduces to a single phase PSMT where there does not exist any directed path from **S** to **R** free from $\mathcal{B}_1 \cup \mathcal{B}_2 \cup \mathcal{B}_3$, which from Theorem 9 is not possible.

3. Suppose that there does not exist any directed path from **S** to **R** free from $\mathcal{B}_1 \cup \mathcal{B}_2 \cup \mathcal{B}_3$ and each feed back path from **R** to **S** passes through two of the Byzantine sets, say $\mathcal{B}_2$ and $\mathcal{B}_3$ (without loss of generality). In this case, we show that there exists an adversary strategy such that the views of **R** are identical for two different messages. We assume a stronger case where **R** knows that $\mathcal{B}_1$ is corrupted or not and still maintain the impossibility of PSMT. The proof is by contradiction. Suppose there exists a PSMT protocol Π not withstanding the fact that there does not exist a path from **S** to **R** free from $\mathcal{B}_1 \cup \mathcal{B}_2 \cup \mathcal{B}_3$ and each feed back path from **R** to **S** passes through $\mathcal{B}_2$ and $\mathcal{B}_3$. Hence the paths from **S** to **R** can be divided into three sets Λ_1, Λ_2 and Λ_3, such that $\Lambda_i, 1 \le i \le 3$ contains nodes from the set $\mathcal{B}_i$. Let $m_1 \ne m_2 \in \mathbb{F}$ be two different messages. Now consider four different executions $\mathbf{E}_1, \mathbf{E}_2, \mathbf{E}_3$ and $\mathbf{E}_4$ of protocol Π, where in $\mathbf{E}_1$, m_1 is transmitted and $\mathcal{B}_1$ is corrupt, in $\mathbf{E}_2$, m_1 is transmitted and $\mathcal{B}_2$ is corrupt, in $\mathbf{E}_3$, m_1 is transmitted and $\mathcal{B}_3$ is corrupt and in $\mathbf{E}_4$, m_2 is transmitted and $\mathcal{B}_3$ is corrupt. Note that in any of these four executions, the information sent over the paths Λ_1 is independent of the secret message. Thus, irrespective of whether Π transmits m_1 or m_2, the distribution of the messages sent along Λ_1 will be same. If not, then it implies that information sent over the paths in Λ_1 depends upon m_1 or m_2 and so the adversary may get some information regarding the message by passively controlling the paths in Λ_1, which violates the PSMT property (adversary does not get any information about the secret message). We now devise an adversary strategy such that **R** cannot distinguish between $\mathbf{E}_2$ and $\mathbf{E}_4$ while **S** cannot distinguish between $\mathbf{E}_1, \mathbf{E}_2$ and $\mathbf{E}_3$, there by maintaining the impossibility of PSMT. Suppose **S** while transmitting m_1, **S** sends α_1, β_1 and γ_1 through the paths Λ_1, Λ_2 and Λ_3 respectively. Similarly, suppose while transmitting m_2, **S** sends α_2, β_2 and γ_2 through the paths Λ_1, Λ_2 and Λ_3 respectively. The behavior of the adversary during the four executions is defined as follows:

   (a) The behavior of set $\mathcal{B}_1$ in the execution $\mathbf{E}_1$ is to remain passive.

   (b) In $\mathbf{E}_2$, the Byzantine set $\mathcal{B}_2$ sends to **R** β_2 instead of β_1 along the paths in the set Λ_2 and sends **S** exactly the same messages that are sent to **S** by the honest $\mathcal{B}_2$ in the execution $\mathbf{E}_1$.

   (c) In $\mathbf{E}_4$, the Byzantine set $\mathcal{B}_3$ sends to **R** γ_1 instead of γ_2 along the paths in the set Λ_3 and sends **S** exactly the same messages that are sent to **S** by the honest $\mathcal{B}_3$ in the execution $\mathbf{E}_1$.

Thus irrespective of the number of phases of Π, in $\mathbf{E}_2$ and $\mathbf{E}_4$, the view of **R** will be $\alpha_1\ \beta_2\ \gamma_1$ and $\alpha_2\ \beta_2\ \gamma_1$ respectively, while the view of **S** will be same as in $\mathbf{E}_1$. Since, the distribution of messages in α_1 and α_2 is same (the messages received along the paths in Λ_1 does not contain any information about the secret message, otherwise adversary can passively listen these paths and will get the secret message), the distribution of messages in $\alpha_1 \ \beta_2 \ \gamma_1$ and $\alpha_2 \ \beta_2 \ \gamma_1$ will be identical. Hence $\mathbf{R}$ cannot distinguish whether the set $\mathcal{B}_2$ is corrupt and the message transmitted by $\mathbf{S}$ is m_1 or the set $\mathcal{B}_3$ is corrupt and the message transmitted by $\mathbf{S}$ is m_2. The state of $\mathbf{S}$ is invariant at indistinguishably among $\mathbf{E}_1, \mathbf{E}_2$ and $\mathbf{E}_3$. This is a contradiction because Π is assumed to be a PSMT protocol. $\square$

Significance of Theorem 10: Consider the network and the adversary structure shown in Figure 1. From Theorem 9, there does not exist any PSMT protocol (single phase) in the network tolerating the given adversary structure. However, according to Theorem 10, there exists a three phase PSMT protocol (**Secure Protocol**) tolerating the given adversary structure. Thus there exists several practical scenarios where Theorem 10 shows the existence of PSMT protocol while the existing results offer no such insight. We now prove the correctness and security of **Secure Protocol**.

Lemma 3. *In* **Secure Protocol**, *if during* **Phase II**, $\mathbf{R}$ *does not find any pair* $(i, j), 1 \leq i, j \leq 3, i \neq j$, *such that* $Q_i'(j) \neq Q_j'(i)$, *then* $\mathbf{R}$ *will be able to correctly interpolate* $Q(x, y)$ *and recover* m *during* **Phase II**.

Proof: If during **Phase II**, $\mathbf{R}$ does not find any pair $(i, j), 1 \leq i, j \leq 3, i \neq j$, such that $Q_i'(j) \neq Q_j'(i)$ then it implies that no corruption occurred during **Phase I**. Hence each $Q_i'(x), 1 \leq i \leq 3$ received during **Phase II** is same as corresponding $Q_i(x), 1 \leq i \leq 3$. Since $Q(x, y)$ is a bivariate polynomial of degree one in both x and y, any two correct $Q_i(x) = Q(x, i)$'s suffice to interpolate $Q(x, y)$. Hence $\mathbf{R}$ can easily reconstruct $Q(x, y)$ using any two $Q_i(x)$'s and recovers m. $\square$

Lemma 4. *In* **Secure Protocol**, *if during* **Phase II**, $\mathbf{R}$ *finds two distinct pairs* (i, j) *and* (i, k) *such that* $Q_i'(j) \neq Q_j'(i)$ *and* $Q_i'(k) \neq Q_k'(i)$, *then path* p_i *is corrupted. Moreover,* $\mathbf{R}$ *will be able to recover* m *during* **Phase II** *itself.*

Proof: The proof follows from few important facts. Out of the three polynomials $Q_1'(x), Q_2'(x)$ and $Q_3'(x)$ received along paths p_1, p_2 and p_3 respectively, at most one can be corrupted because each path p_i contains nodes only from $\mathcal{B}_i$. Since $Q(x, y)$ is bivariate, $Q_a'(x)$'s which are received correctly will agree with each other. Thus if paths p_a and p_b are honest, then $Q_a'(x) = Q_a(x)$ and $Q_b'(x) = Q_b(x)$ and $Q_a'(b) = Q_b'(a)$. Thus two correctly received polynomials will never contradict each other. So if $\mathbf{R}$ finds a pair (i, j) such that $Q_i'(j) \neq Q_j'(i)$, then $\mathbf{R}$ is sure that either p_i or p_j is faulty. Now $Q_1'(x), Q_2'(x)$ and $Q_3'(x)$ are polynomials in x of degree one. So if $\mathbf{R}$ finds two distinct pairs (i, j) and (i, k) such that $Q_i'(j) \neq Q_j'(i)$ and $Q_i'(k) \neq Q_k'(i)$, then it definitely implies that path p_i is faulty because out of the three paths exactly one can be corrupted. Once $\mathbf{R}$ knows that p_i is corrupted, $\mathbf{R}$ can neglect $Q_i'(x)$ received over p_i and interpolate $Q(x, y)$ using the remaining two $Q_a'(x)$'s which are correct and recover m. $\square$

Lemma 5. *In* **Secure Protocol**, *if during* **Phase II**, $\mathbf{R}$ *finds only pair* (i, j) *such that* $Q_i'(j) \neq Q_j'(i)$ *then* $\mathbf{R}$ *will be able to recover* m *after* **Phase III**.

Proof: From previous lemma, if **R** finds a pair (i, j) such that $Q_i'(j) \neq Q_j'(i)$, then either path p_i or p_j is corrupted. If **R** finds only one such conflicting pair then it implies that the remaining path p_c where $c = \{1, 2, 3\} \backslash \{i, j\}$ is correct and hence the corresponding $Q_c'(x)$ is received correctly. **R** will now try to find whether p_i or p_j is corrupted. Towards this, **R** sends the four tuple $(i, j, Q_i'(j), Q_j'(i))$ to **S** along path q_α and q_β. Now there are two possible cases:

1. **At least one of the paths q_α or q_β correctly delivers the four tuple** $(i, j, Q_i'(j), Q_j'(i))$ **to S:** Without loss of generality, suppose the path q_α correctly delivers $(i, j, Q_i'(j), Q_j'(i))$ to **S**. Thus, the four tuple $(i'', j'', Q_{i''}'(j''), Q_{j''}'(i''))$ received by **S** during **Phase III** along q_α is same as the original four tuple $(i, j, Q_i'(j), Q_j'(i))$. During **Phase III**, **S** will locally verify $Q_{i''}''(j'') \stackrel{?}{=} Q_{i''}(j'')$ and $Q_{j''}''(i'') \stackrel{?}{=} Q_{j''}(i'')$. If the first test fails then **S** concludes that **R** has received incorrect $Q_{i''}(x)$ through path $p_{i''}$ during **Phase I**. On the other hand if second test fails then **S** concludes that **R** has received incorrect $Q_{j''}(x)$ through path $p_{j''}$ during **Phase I**. Accordingly, **S** appends an error message "path γ is faulty" to the four tuple $(i'', j'', Q_{i''}'(j''), Q_{j''}'(i''))$ and reliably sends the four tuple along with the appended error message to **R** by executing a PRMT protocol. **S** also indicates that the four tuple along with the appended error message is sent in response to the four tuple received along q_α. **R** will correctly receive this response and will find that the original four tuple $(i, j, Q_i'(j), Q_j'(i))$ sent during **Phase II** matches the four tuple in the response sent by **S**. **R** thus conclude that **S** correctly received the original four tuple along q_α. **R** will also receive an error message "path γ is faulty" along with the response and hence conclude that the polynomial received along path γ during **Phase I** is corrupted. Thus the remaining two polynomials received along paths p_a and p_b where $\{a, b\} = \{1, 2, 3\} \backslash \{\gamma\}$ during **Phase I** are correct. Thus the polynomials $Q_a'(x)$ and $Q_b'(x)$ will lie on $Q(x, y)$. So using them **R** interpolates $Q(x, y)$ and recovers m correctly.

2. **None of the paths q_α or q_β correctly delivers the four tuple** $(i, j, Q_i'(j),$ $Q_j'(i))$ **to S:** In this case, neither of the four tuples $(i'', j'', Q_{i''}'(j''), Q_{j''}'(i''))$ and $(i''', j''', Q_{i'''}'(j'''), Q_{j'''}'(i'''))$ received along q_α and q_β respectively matches the original four tuple $(i, j, Q_i'(j), Q_j'(i))$. So after receiving the response sent by **S** during **Phase III**, **R** will find that the original four tuple $(i, j, Q_i'(j), Q_j'(i))$ is not present in any of the two responses. **R** thus conclude that **S** has not received the original four tuple during **Phase II** because both q_α and q_β are corrupted by the adversary. Now q_α does not contain nodes from $\mathcal{B}_\alpha$ while q_β is free from the nodes in $\mathcal{B}_\beta$. Thus the only way that both these paths get corrupted is that the adversary $\mathcal{B}_\gamma$ is activated during the protocol where $\gamma = (\{1, 2, 3\} \backslash \{\alpha\}) \cap (\{1, 2, 3\} \backslash \{\beta\})$. This implies that during **Phase I**, p_γ is corrupted and hence $Q_\gamma'(x)$ received along this path is corrupted. Thus the remaining two polynomials received along p_a and p_b where $\{a, b\} = \{1, 2, 3\} \backslash \{\gamma\}$ during **Phase I** are correct. Thus the polynomials $Q_a'(x)$ and $Q_b'(x)$ will lie on $Q(x, y)$. So using them **R** interpolates $Q(x, y)$ and recovers m correctly.

Thus **R** will recover m correctly at the end of **Phase III**. $\square$

Theorem 11. *In* **Secure Protocol, R** *will always recover m correctly.*

Proof: The proof follows from Lemma 3, Lemma 4 and Lemma 5.   □

Theorem 12. *In* **Secure Protocol,** *any adversary corrupting nodes from one of the sets* $\mathcal{B}_1, \mathcal{B}_2$ *or* $\mathcal{B}_3$ *does not get any information about m.*

Proof: Without loss of generality suppose adversary corrupts nodes from the set $\mathcal{B}_1$. Since path p_1 contains nodes from the set $\mathcal{B}_1$, the adversary will know $Q_1(x)$. However, to interpolate $Q(x,y)$, the adversary requires two $Q_i(x)$'s. Hence adversary will fall short of one $Q_i(x)$ to interpolate $Q(x,y)$. The adversary can himself evaluate $Q_1(1) = Q(1,1)$ and $Q_1(2) = Q(2,1)$, using which the adversary can form two independent equations in the coefficients of $Q(x,y)$. However, the number of coefficients in $Q(x,y)$ is three because $Q(x,y)$ is a symmetric bivariate polynomial. Thus the message m which is the constant term of $Q(x,y)$ is information theoretically secure. Note that it may be possible that the paths q_α and q_β from **R** to **S** contains nodes from $\mathcal{B}_1$. So if during **Phase II**, **R** sends a four tuple $(i, j, Q_i'(j), Q_j'(i))$ to **S** through q_α and q_β, the adversary will know this information. However, it is easy to see that this does not give any extra information to the adversary to interpolate $Q(x,y)$ and recover m.   □

Relation between Non-Threshold and Threshold Adversary: As mentioned earlier, a threshold adversary with threshold t is a special kind of non-threshold adversary structure where the size of each adversary set in the maximal basis is t. In [1], it is shown that PSMT tolerating a t-active Byzantine adversary is possible iff there exists $n = max\{3t - 2u + 1, 2t + 1\}$ vertex disjoint paths (wires) in the *top band*, where u is the number of wires in the *bottom band*. We now briefly explain how we get this bound Theorem 10 by substituting the size of each adversary set as t. The first obvious condition in Theorem 10 is that PRMT should be possible from **S** to **R**, for which the network should be $\mathcal{A}^{(2)}$-(**S**, **R**)-connected (see Lemma 1). By substituting the size of each adversary set as t, this condition implies that the network should be at least $2t + 1$-(**S**, **R**)-connected. We now claim that if there exists u paths in the *bottom band* and if the size of each $\mathcal{B}_i, 1 \le i \le 3$ is t, then in order that conditions of Theorem 10 are satisfied, there should exist at least $3t - 2u + 1$ wires in the *top band*. Suppose on the contrary that even with $3t - 2u$ wires in the *top band*, the conditions of Theorem 10 are satisfied. We then define a distribution of nodes for each $\mathcal{B}_i, 1 \le i \le 3$ which leads to a contradiction. The distribution is as follows:

1. $\mathcal{B}_1$ contains t nodes, where $t - u$ nodes lie on $t - u$ vertex disjoint paths in *top band* and u nodes lie on u vertex disjoint paths in the *bottom band*. Thus each path in *bottom band* contains nodes from $\mathcal{B}_1$.

2. $\mathcal{B}_2$ contains t nodes, where $t - u$ nodes lie on $t - u$ vertex disjoint paths in *top band* (which are also disjoint from the $t - u$ paths containing nodes from $\mathcal{B}_1$) and u nodes lie on u vertex disjoint paths in the *bottom band*. Thus each path in *bottom band* contains nodes from $\mathcal{B}_2$.

3. $\mathcal{B}_3$ contains t nodes, all of which lie on t vertex disjoint paths in the *top band* (which are disjoint from the paths containing nodes from $\mathcal{B}_1$ and $\mathcal{B}_2$).

It is clear from the distribution of nodes that each of the $3t - 2u$ vertex disjoint paths in the *top band* contains nodes from $\mathcal{B}_1, \mathcal{B}_2$ or $\mathcal{B}_3$ and each of the u vertex disjoint paths in the *bottom band* contains nodes from $\mathcal{B}_1$ as well as $\mathcal{B}_2$. Now it is easy to verify that none of the two conditions mentioned in Theorem 10 is satisfied, contradicting the assumption that with $3t - 2u$ vertex disjoint paths in the *top band*, the conditions in Theorem 10 are satisfied. It is easy to verify that if there are $3t - 2u + 1$ vertex disjoint paths in the *top band*, then irrespective of the distribution of nodes in $\mathcal{B}_1, \mathcal{B}_2$ and $\mathcal{B}_3$, the conditions in Theorem 10 will be satisfied. Thus Theorem 10 strictly generalizes threshold adversary.

7   Conclusion and Open Problems

In this paper we have proposed a three phase polynomial time PSMT protocol in directed network whose total communication complexity is also polynomial. This is a significant improvement over the exponential phase PSMT protocol proposed in [1]. We further show how the communication complexity of our three phase PSMT protocol is significantly reduced under the same network settings in which a polynomial phase PSMT protocol is proposed in [1]. We characterize two phase PSMT protocols in the directed graphs, which bridges the gap between single phase and three phase PSMT protocols in directed graphs. We have also characterized PSMT in directed networks tolerating non-threshold adversary. Our characterization is a true characterization in the sense that it considers all possible paths from **S** to **R** and vice-versa. Our characterization shows that in many practical scenarios protocols exist while the existing characterization offers no such insight. It is an open problem to give an efficient protocol tolerating a non-threshold adversary given that the protocol exists. It should be noted that abstracting the network as a directed graph where **S** and **R** are assumed be to be connected by directed chains, directed either from **S** to **R** or vice-versa, has been proved as a weak network model in [11]. However, the wired abstraction in directed graphs will work when the underlying network is densely connected. Hence the protocols proposed in [1] as well in this paper can be applied to such networks. It is an interesting problem, to completely characterize PRMT and PSMT protocols in arbitrary directed graphs.

References

1. Desmedt, Y., Wang, Y.: Perfectly secure message transmission revisited. Cryptology ePrint Archive, Report 2002/128 (2002), http://eprint.iacr.org
2. Desmedt, Y., Wang, Y.: Perfectly secure message transmission revisited. In: Knudsen, L.R. (ed.) EUROCRYPT 2002. LNCS, vol. 2332, pp. 502–517. Springer, Heidelberg (2002)
3. Desmedt, Y., Wang, Y., Burmester, M.: A complete characterization of tolerable adversary structures for secure point-to-point transmissions without feedback. In: Deng, X., Du, D.-Z. (eds.) ISAAC 2005. LNCS, vol. 3827, pp. 277–287. Springer, Heidelberg (2005)

4. Dolev, D., Dwork, C., Waarts, O., Yung, M.: Perfectly secure message transmission. JACM 40(1), 17–47 (1993)
5. Kumar, M.V.N.A., Goundan, P.R., Srinathan, K., Pandu Rangan, C.: On perfectly secure communication over arbitrary networks. In: Proc. of 21st PODC, pp. 193–202. ACM Press, New York (2002)
6. MacWilliams, F.J., Sloane, N.J.A.: The Theory of Error Correcting Codes. North-Holland Publishing Company (1978)
7. Patra, A., Choudhary, A., Pandu Rangan, C.: Brief announcement: Constant phase efficient protocols for secure message transmission in directed networks. In: Proc of ACM PODC, pp. 322–323 (2007)
8. Sayeed, H., Abu-Amara, H.: Efficient perfectly secure message transmission in synchronous networks. Information and Computation 126(1), 53–61 (1996)
9. Shamir, A.: How to share a secret. Communications of the ACM 22(11), 612–613 (1979)
10. Srinathan, K., Narayanan, A., Pandu Rangan, C.: Optimal perfectly secure message transmission. In: Franklin, M. (ed.) CRYPTO 2004. LNCS, vol. 3152, pp. 545–561. Springer, Heidelberg (2004)
11. Srinathan, K., Pandu Rangan, C.: Possibility and complexity of probabilistic reliable communication in directed networks. In: Proc. of 25th PODC, pp. 265–274. ACM Press, New York (2006)

Forward-Secure Key Evolution in Wireless Sensor Networks

Marek Klonowski[1], Mirosław Kutyłowski[1], Michał Ren[2], and Katarzyna Rybarczyk[2]

[1] Wrocław University of Technology*
[2] Adam Mickiewicz University, Poznań, Poland**

Abstract. We consider a key distribution scheme for securing node-to-node communication in sensor networks. While most schemes in use are based on random predistribution, we consider a system of dynamic pairwise keys based on design due to Ren, Tanmoy and Zhou. We design and analyze a variation of this scheme, in which capturing a node does not lead to security threats for the past communication.

Instead of bit-flipping, we use a cryptographic one-way function. While this immediately guarantees forward-security, it is not clear whether the pseudorandom transformation of the keys does not lead to subtle security risks due to a specific distribution of reachable keys, such as existence of small attractor subspaces. (This problem does not occur for the design of Ren, Tanmoy and Zhou.) We show, in a rigorous, mathematical way, that this is not the case: after a small number of steps probability distribution of keys leaves no room for potential attacks.

Keywords: communication in sensor networks, key management, key distribution, forward security, directed random graphs.

1 Introduction

Applications of sensor networks are sometimes constrained by security requirements. In order to be attractive from economic point of view, nodes of a sensor network need to be very cheap. This results in lack of tamperproofness (and tamper-resistance), limited computing power and memory space, inability to perform public-key cryptography efficiently, and limited communication bandwidth (due to battery capacity). This creates challenges for communication security: no public-key cryptography can be used, only symmetric algorithms are admissible, communication volume of the security protocols should be kept as small as possible. However, one of the crucial security threats in sensor networks is that communication can be recorded and the secret keys can be retrieved from a captured device. This may lead to disclosure of all data sent so far with the keys contained in this device. On the other hand, lack of connection to the device captured is nothing uncommon – it can be due to battery exhaustion or any physical failure. Also,

* Partially supported by the EU within the 6th Framework Programme under contract 001907 (DELIS).
** Partially supported by Ministry of Science and Higher Education, grant N N206 2701 33, 2007–2010.

F. Bao et al. (Eds.): CANS 2007, LNCS 4856, pp. 102–120, 2007.

it might be hard to find a device that is not responding to radio signals, so it is difficult to check if a device has been captured.

Recently, a simple scheme of dynamically evolving keys [1] has been proposed. It supports pairwise symmetric keys for each pair of communicating nodes, which change the key at every transmission. Namely, the sender chooses a key bit at random, flips it, and encodes current data transmission with the obtained key. The receiver makes trial decryptions and, based on the results, recovers which bit has been changed.

The idea of this solution is remarkably simple; it is both efficient and easy to implement. Obviously, in this way it only takes a small number of steps to change a key into any other key. This solves a lot of problems – for instance if some encrypted transmission has been recorded and cryptanalysis reveals the key used for encryption, it cannot be used to eavesdrop later transmissions. Simply, in the meantime the sensors transformed their keys completely. An attack in this case requires uninterrupted monitoring communication activities of a sensor. Replay and replication attacks become very limited. A nice feature especially for the sensor networks is that there is no communication overhead due to evolution of keys – this is important, since energy consumption for communication is of order of magnitudes higher than for any internal computations by the processor. For further discussion see the original proposal [1].

Problem Description. The major weakness of the scheme [1] is that if the current key is compromised, and the adversary has recorded the traffic beforehand, it is possible to reverse key transitions step by step. Our goal is to design an efficient framework that shares all advantages of the scheme from [1], but is resistant to the mentioned security threat.

Previous work. Since the most energy-intensive operation for a sensor node is wireless communication, protocols dedicated to the sensor networks should be optimized with respect to communication volume. Sending a bit is a typically orders of magnitude more expensive than encryption or decryption. On specialized hardware, energy cost of $9nJ$ per bit is achievable for AES encryption [2], but sending a bit requires around 21 μJ, which is a difference of three orders of magnitude. It is to be expected that the relative difference will increase as processor technology matures; in fact, modern optimized hardware achieves energy costs of AES encryption on order of $60pJ$ per bit [3]. For these reasons any key management protocol should avoid large communication overhead, and most solutions designed for wired networks (such as the SSL protocol) are useless in the context of sensor networks. The second limitation of this type is memory size and communication speed. A typical sensor network node has no more than 4KB of memory, and is capable of communicating at speeds of about 38.4 Kbps to a distance of around 30m. The nodes are also usually equipped with coprocessors to handle AES encryption and decryption efficiently. Asymmetric methods, on the other hand, require millions of multiplications per asymmetric operation, as well as large amounts of memory and currently are not considered suitable for sensor networks.

Most of the recent work on the problem of key distribution and management in sensor networks has been focused on random predistribution schemes (see e.g. [4,5,6]). Let us recall their general framework:

1. *Key predistribution phase* is conducted offline. It consists of generating a large pool of keys and loading a small number of different randomly-drawn keys into each sensor device. An identifier should be assigned to each key.

2. *Shared key discovery phase* takes place in the target environment, after the sensor nodes are deployed. Every node discovers its neighbors, and tries to establish a common key with each neighbor. The simplest method of achieving this goal is that each node broadcasts in plaintext the list of identifiers of all keys it possesses. This phase establishes network topology, as two nodes are "linked" only if they share at least one pre-installed key.
3. *Path-key establishment phase* allows pairs of nodes that are in communication range to establish a common key, even if they did not share any after the previous phase.

Adversary model for sensor networks has some peculiarities. Due to reliance on radio communication it is quite easy to record the traffic, or at least a part of it. The second point is that it is hardly possible to prevent an adversary from compromising some of the sensor nodes and extracting their keys. Moreover, due to failures occurring in usual field conditions, lack of response from a node might be regarded as a normal failure. Checking a node on-site is seldom possible. This is a serious problem for predistribution schemes. In case of compromising a node all its keys should not be used anymore. However, in practice, is it hard to distinguish between node compromise and battery exhaustion or any other failure. Large pools of keys help a little: only a fraction of traffic becomes insecure in this way.

On the other hand, some assumptions about the capabilities of the adversary can be relaxed in the context of sensor nodes. For example, it can be assumed that an adversary is not omnipresent and can not eavesdrop on all communication links all the time. This allows for construction of counterintuitively secure protocols, such as the key infection protocol, which is based on broadcasting the keys in the clear [7]. We can assume that in real-world scenarios within a few seconds immediately after deployment of the network, the adversary is unable to eavesdrop on all communications, but only a certain fraction of them.

The solution presented in [1] works with keys that are derived dynamically from the initial pairwise keys (which might be established in the clear or be derived from predistributed keys). The principal advantage is that evolution of the pairwise keys does not require any communication overhead. It is performed at a very modest energy cost, provided that encryption and decryption could be done efficiently. It also forces the adversary to keep monitoring communication all the time after compromising a key; otherwise the adversary loses control of the key as it diverges.

2   KEP – Key Evolution Protocol

Initialization. As in [1], the system initializes the nodes so that each pair of neighbor nodes establishes a key for this pair. Any method can be used: preloading with a common key, key infection, or a random predistribution scheme. At the end of this phase, every node knows its neighbors and shares a separate pairwise key with each neighbor.

Communication with Key Divergence. Consider nodes A and B sharing a pairwise key, say k_{AB}. We describe the steps executed by A. It waits until either it sends a message to B, or it receives one addressed to itself from B.

Case 1: A initializes key transition while sending a message to B

The following steps are executed:

1. A encrypts the message to be sent with a key k', called *proposed key*, that is derived from k_{AB} as follows:

$$k' := F(k_{AB}, i) \tag{1}$$

where F is a cryptographic one-way function and $i \leq l$ is chosen uniformly at random. The parameter l is a small constant, $l \geq 2$, controlling convergence rate. In the second version of the protocol

$$k' := F(k_{AB}, i, t) \tag{2}$$

for t denoting the so called *current index of* k_{AB}. Initially, this index is set to 1, and then increased after each transformation of k_{AB}.

2. If A has to send more messages, but has not yet received a message from B (neither valid nor invalid), it sends every next message encrypted to proposed key k'.
3. Finally, A receives a message from B. If it is encrypted to proposed key k' and the message counter indicates the message is fresh, the message is accepted, A substitutes

$$k_{AB} := k' \, ,$$

and increments the current index of k_{AB} by one. If the message was encrypted to a different key than k', the message is rejected, node A abandons proposed key k' remembering that it tried to change k_{AB} to k' but failed. This situation occurs if B has not received any message with the proposed key k' and has proposed a key itself.
4. If the counter in the received message is older than the one stored by A, this indicates a replay attack — the adversary is trying to make A change the key using an old message (for instance a message sent by A itself). As before, A should reject the message and abandon proposed key k' remembering that it tried to change the key to k' but failed. Note that in this situation it might be the case that B has accepted k', but A is unaware of it. Recording k' will enable to accept k' in this case (see the procedure below).

Case 2: A receives a message from B while not waiting for a reply as in Case 1

1. If A receives a message from B encrypted with a certain key k'', then it tries to decrypt it by brute force. Namely,
   - A checks if $k'' = k_{AB}$,
   - if not, A tries keys of the form $F(k_{AB}, i)$ for all $i \leq l$ (or $F(k_{AB}, i, t)$ in the variant of the protocol, where t is the current index of k_{AB}),
   - if none of those keys work, and if A has previously tried to change the key to k' but failed, A tries keys of the form $F(k', i)$ (or $F(k', i, t)$ in the variant of the protocol). This option is necessary for the case in which B has accepted a new key k' proposed by A, while A received some invalid message and, according to the protocol, reverted to k_{AB}.

If a valid decryption key is found and the message is fresh, then A waits until an opportune time to send its reply encrypted to k''. If $k'' \neq k_{AB}$, then the current index is incremented by one and k_{AB} is set to k''. If the message can not be decrypted or is not fresh, it is discarded.
2. If A receives further messages encrypted to k'', it processes them normally.
3. When A wants to send a message to B, it encrypts it with key k''.

Protocol Properties. For space limitations we skip here the analysis of protocol correctness (which is essentially the same as for [1]). As in case of the scheme from [1], our protocol has several advantages: there is no communication overhead due to evolution of keys, rate of key evolution is automatically controlled by traffic volume, capturing a node does not compromise other nodes' keys, the scheme scales to any number of nodes, it can be used with any predistribution scheme. Extra energy consumption also remains negligible as in [1], as the only substantial difference is the addition of the one-way function, which can be based on AES [8], and performed using the same co-processor that handles AES encryption/decryption. Another important point is that if the adversary somehow breaks a pairwise key from some moment, but transmissions between these nodes are not constantly monitored, then after a while the broken key becomes worthless.

The most important point is that KEP offers an important advantage over the one described in [1] in the event of node compromise. Even if an adversary has been eavesdropping on communications of the node, and recording them, the key extracted after compromising the node cannot be used to decrypt any of the recorded messages, as it is impossible to reverse the function F.

Main Problem. In case of the protocol from [1] it is obvious that starting from an arbitrary key one can reach any key in the keyspace in a quite short time. Moreover, probability distribution describing the chances to reach each key converges quickly to the uniform distribution over the keyspace.

It is unclear whether these uniformity and reachability properties hold for our KEP protocol: function F is pseudorandom but fixed. For this reason, key divergence process can have certain peculiarities. Consider a directed graph $G = (K, E)$, where the set of vertices K is the keyspace, and an arc kk' is in E if it is possible to make transition from key k to k' using rule (1). Even if F is pseudorandom it is not clear whether G is strongly connected (due to some reasons analogous to the birthday paradox). If digraph G is not strongly connected, then it may happen that there is a small subgraph G' of G such that after entering G' it it is impossible to leave G' (so G' would be like a black hole). For such subgraphs G' time-memory tradeoff attack [9] becomes very effective and endangers all keys contained in G'. In particular, in this case it would be possible to reverse key evolution without reversing F. Similarly, it would be easier to find the current pairwise key after breaking an old key even if the intermediate transmissions have not been recorded. We show in a rigorous, mathematical way that this is not the case – under certain assumptions G is strongly connected and has a small diameter with high probability (depending on the choice of F). This result would be much easier to obtain for rule (2). However, we concentrate on a mathematically hard case of rule (1) which is more elegant and easier to implement. For undirected random graphs connectivity and the diameter length were already widely studied, see for example B. Bollobás [10,11] F. Chung and L. Lu [12]. Unfortunately those results can not be translated directly to the case of the directed graph model. Let us also remark that from combinatorial point of view connectivity for directed and undirected graphs are quite different issues.

Due to attacks like exhaustive search another property of key evolution is necessary. Namely, we have to show that there no "attractors", that is, the keys that are relatively often "visited" during key divergence process. If probability of visiting certain attractors is sufficiently large, an adversary can perform exhaustive search confined to the set of attractors. In such a way time complexity can be reduced considerably, while success probability might be still acceptable. We show that for rule (2) there are no attractors. Moreover, we show that probability distribution of a pairwise key is very close to uniform distribution after a small number of steps. By "similarity" we mean here a very strong measure of distance between probability distributions (much stronger than usually considered in papers on anonymous communication). Such a result for rule (1) is related to mixing time for directed graphs. However, known results concern undirected expander graphs [13]. Recent results were achieved for random graphs as well, but only undirected ones, or special forms of directed deterministic graphs [14,15,16]. These results are not applicable to our case. Moreover, our results are not asymptotic and apply in the case of relatively small graphs (on order of 2^{32}–2^{64} nodes).

Due to size limitation, we had to skip some details in the proof that we think can be reconstructed by a reader.

3   Key Reachability – Random Digraph Model

Preliminaries. In this section we consider directed graph $G = (K, E)$, where the set of vertices K is the keyspace, and an arc kk' is in E if it is possible to make transition from key k to k' in one step of KEP according to rule (1). Let $K = \{0, 1\}^n$ and $N = 2^n$ denote the size of K.

We assume that the one-way function F changes a key into one of l keys, picked independently, uniformly at random. As there is a possibility of a collision, the actual number of possible keys in every step and for any initial key is a random variable X strongly concentrated around l. So, more generally, we consider the model of the random digraph $G(X) = (K, E)$ introduced in [17] (see also [18]) which is constructed in the following way:

- each vertex v chooses its out-degree l_v according to the distribution of $X_v = X$ independently of all other vertices,
- then, also independently of all other vertices, it chooses the set of l_v out–neighbors uniformly from all l_v-element subsets of K.

In this section, for a graph $G(X)$ defined by X such that $E(X) \geq \ln N$ and X is concentrated around the expected value we shall formalize and find the lower bound on the probability that:

- $G(X)$ is strongly connected. This means, in the context of KEP protocol, that every key can eventually be transformed into every other key and there are no isolated groups of keys.

– The diameter of $G(X)$ is concentrated around $\frac{\ln N}{\ln l}$. So, any two keys can be transformed quickly into one another.

Let $d(u, v) = k$ mean that the shortest directed path from u to v has length k. Let us denote:

$$\Gamma_k^+(v) := \{w \in K : d(v, w) = k\}, \quad \Gamma_k^-(v) := \{w \in K : d(w, v) = k\},$$

$$N_k^+(v) := \bigcup_{i=0}^{k} \Gamma_i^+(v), \quad N_k^-(v) := \bigcup_{i=0}^{k} \Gamma_i^-(v),$$

$$\text{diam}G := \max\{d(u, v) : u, v \text{ are connected by a path}\}.$$

Since the the proofs include many estimations, and are rather technical, we will present sketches saving the exact calculations for the appendix. For clarity of calculations, we also make an assumption that $\frac{l}{2} \le X \le 2l$, which need not always be true in KEP. See Corollary 1 for remarks on a more general model.

Lemma 1. *Let X be a random variable such that $E(X) = l$ and $\Pr(\frac{l}{2} \le X \le 2l) = 1$. In a graph $G(X)$ let A and B be disjoint subsets of K. If P_{AB} is the probability that v has an out–neighbor in A conditioned by the event that v has no out–neighbor in B, then for $N - |A| - |B| \ge \frac{l}{2}$*

$$\frac{l|A|}{N-|B|} - \frac{l^2|A|^2}{(N-|B|)^2} \le P_{AB} \le \frac{l|A|}{N-|B|} + \frac{l^2|A|}{(N-|B|)(N-|B|-2l)}. \quad (3)$$

Furthermore, if Y is a random variable counting those vertices in $K \setminus (A \cup B)$, which have out-neighbors in A, under the assumption that they do not have out–neighbors in B, then Y is binomially distributed with parameters $N - |A| - |B|$ and P_{AB}.

Proof. See appendix.

Theorem 1. *Let X be a random variable such that $E(X) = l$. If $\Pr(\lceil \frac{l}{2} \rceil \le X \le 2l) = 1$, $N \ge 2^{32}$ and $\ln N \le l \le \sqrt{N}/90 - 1$, then with probability at least $1 - p(N)$*

$$\lfloor \ln N/\ln 2l \rfloor \le \text{diam } G(X) \le \lceil \ln N/(2\ln\lfloor l/2\rfloor)\rceil + \lceil \ln N/(2\ln\lceil l/4\rceil)\rceil + 4,$$

where: $p(N) = \frac{1.6(\ln N)^7}{N^{1.5}} + \frac{1+0.0016(\ln N)^{15}}{N^{1.99}} + \frac{1}{N^{0.59}} + \frac{1}{N^{0.16l}-1} + \frac{1}{N^{0.5}}$

In the proof we will frequently use simple probabilistic fact that if events H_1 and H_2 occur with probability at least $1 - r_1$ and $1 - r_2$ respectively and event H_3 conditioned on H_1 occurs with probability at least $1 - r_3$, then

$$\Pr(H_1 \cap H_2) = \Pr(H_1) + \Pr(H_2) - \Pr(H_1 \cup H_2) \ge 1 - r_1 - r_2 \text{ and}$$
$$\Pr(H_1 \cap H_3) = \Pr(H_3|H_1)\Pr(H_1) \ge (1 - r_1)(1 - r_3) \ge 1 - r_1 - r_3.$$

Proof (Sketch). To indicate the upper bound we will prove that with probability at least $1 - p(N)$ if there exists a path between two vertices, then the shortest one has length at most $\left\lceil \frac{\ln N}{2\ln\lfloor\frac{l}{2}\rfloor} \right\rceil + \left\lceil \frac{\ln N}{2\ln\lceil\frac{l}{4}\rceil} \right\rceil + 4$. Namely, for vertices v_1 and v_2 we will estimate the number of vertices in $\Gamma_{k_1}^+(v_1)$ and in $\Gamma_{k_2}^-(v_2)$. Then we will prove that with probability close to one either these sets intersect, or there is an edge pointing from $\Gamma^+_{k_1}(v)$ to $\Gamma^-_{k_2}(w)$ for $k_1 + k_2 + 1$ at most $\left\lceil \frac{\ln N}{2\ln\lfloor\frac{l}{2}\rfloor} \right\rceil + \left\lceil \frac{\ln N}{2\ln\lceil\frac{l}{4}\rceil} \right\rceil + 4$. To prove the lower bound on $\mathrm{diam}G(X)$ we will estimate the size of $N^+_k(v)$. In fact we will show that for any vertex v there are some vertices at distance larger than $\lfloor \frac{\ln N}{\ln 2l} \rfloor$ from v.

First, for a given vertex $v \in K$, we will be considering sets of out–neighbors. Let us consider the process of labeling vertices, starting in vertex v. After this process, the set of vertices with label i will be the set $\Gamma^+_i(v)$. First, we will label vertex v with label 0. Then we will proceed one by one from $i = 0$. For given i if $\{w_1, w_2, \ldots, w_t\}$ are vertices with label i, then w_1 first labels all its out-neighbors, which were not labeled before, with label $i + 1$. Then w_2 labels its out-neighbors in the same way, and so on. We will keep going as long as the set of vertices with label $i + 1$ is smaller than $\sqrt{N}$.

Let $W = W(v)$ be a set of vertices labeled during the process and $A^v(w)$ be the event that during the process vertex $w \in W$ labels at least $\lceil\frac{l}{4}\rceil$ vertices. If event $A^v = \bigcap_{w\in W} A^v(w)$ occurs, then each vertex with label i labels at least $\lceil\frac{l}{4}\rceil$ vertices. Thus, $|\Gamma^+_{i+1}(v)| \geq \lceil\frac{l}{4}\rceil|\Gamma^+_i(v)|$ and $|\Gamma^+_i(v)| \geq \lceil\frac{l}{4}\rceil^i$ for all i. Therefore, if A^v occurs, then the process will stop in at most $k' = \frac{1}{2}\frac{\ln N}{\ln\lceil\frac{l}{4}\rceil}$ steps (since $\lceil\frac{l}{4}\rceil^{k'} \geq \sqrt{N}$) thus there exists an index $k_1(v) = k_1 \leq k'$ such that $|\Gamma^+_{k_1}(v)| \geq \sqrt{N}$.

Then, using estimations on $\Pr(\overline{A^v(w)})$ (where $\overline{A^v(w)}$ is the complement of event $A^v(w)$), we can prove (see Appendix) that for $N \geq 2^{32}$

$$\Pr\left(\forall_{v\in K}\exists_{0\leq k_1(v)\leq k'}|\Gamma^+_{k_1(v)}(v)| \geq \sqrt{N}\right) \geq \Pr\left(\bigcap_{v\in K} A^v\right) \geq$$
$$\geq 1 - \Pr\left(\bigcup_{v\in K}\bigcup_{w\in W(v)} \overline{A^v(w)}\right) \geq \qquad (4)$$
$$\geq 1 - \sum_{v\in K}\sum_{w\in W(v)} \Pr\left(\overline{A^v(w)}\right) \geq 1 - p_1(N),$$

where $p_1(N) = 1.6 \cdot (\ln N)^7/N^{1.5}$.

Now we will estimate the sizes of sets of in–neighbors. Consider a vertex $v \in V$ such that v has at least two in–neighbors $u_1 \neq v$ and $u_2 \neq v$ or v has in–neighbor $u_1 \neq v$ which has in–neighbor $u_2 \neq v, u_1$. We will call such vertex v a "good" vertex. For a "good" vertex v, using Lemma 1 and the pigeonhole principle, we can prove (see Appendix) that with probability at least $1 - q_1(N)$ (where $q_1(N) = \frac{1+0.0016(\ln N)^{15}}{N^{2.99}}$) there exists i_0, $1 \leq i_0 \leq 3$, such that

$$|\Gamma^-_{i_0}(v)| \geq 6. \qquad (5)$$

From now on, we assume that v is "good". Let $k'' = \left\lceil \frac{1}{2}\frac{\ln N}{\ln\lfloor l/2\rfloor} \right\rceil + 3$.

For all $0 < j \leq k''$ let:
- $B_j(v) = B_j$ be the event that $|\Gamma^-_j(v)| \geq 3\sqrt{N}$.

For all $i_0 < j \leq k''$ let:
- $C_j(v) = C_j$ be the event that $3\lfloor\frac{l}{2}\rfloor^{j-i_0} \leq |\Gamma^-_j(v)| < 3\sqrt{N}$,
- $D_j(v) = D_j$ be the event that $|\Gamma^-_j(v)| \leq 3\lfloor\frac{l}{2}\rfloor^{j-i_0}$.

Also denote by:

- $C_{i_0}(v)$ the event that $6 \leq |\Gamma_j^-(v)| < 3\sqrt{N}$,
- $D_{i_0}(v)$ the event that $|\Gamma_j^-(v)| < 6$.

Notice that by (5) we get:

$$\Pr(D_{i_0}) \leq q_1(N). \tag{6}$$

We will find a lower bound on the probability of the event $\bigcup_{i=0}^{k''} B_i$. Notice that if Ω is the whole probability space, than for all $i_0 \leq i \leq k''$, we have $B_i \cup C_i \cup D_i = \Omega$. Thus

$$
\begin{aligned}
\Omega &= B_{i_0} \cup (C_{i_0} \cap \Omega) \cup D_{i_0} = \\
&= B_{i_0} \cup (C_{i_0} \cap B_{i_0+1}) \cup D_{i_0} \cup (C_{i_0} \cap D_{i_0+1}) \cup (C_{i_0} \cap C_{i_0+1}) = \ldots = \\
&= B_{i_0} \cup \bigcup_{i=i_0}^{k''-1} \left(B_{i+1} \cap \left(\bigcap_{j=i_0}^{i} C_j \right) \right) \cup D_{i_0} \cup \\
&\quad \cup \bigcup_{i=i_0}^{k''-1} \left(D_{i+1} \cap \left(\bigcap_{j=i_0}^{i} C_j \right) \right) \cup \left(\bigcap_{j=i_0}^{k''} C_j \right).
\end{aligned}
$$

Also, by definition, $\bigcap_{j=i_0}^{k''} C_j = \emptyset$ since $3\sqrt{N} \leq 3 \lfloor \frac{l}{2} \rfloor^{k''-i_0}$. Thus

$$\bigcup_{i=i_0}^{k''} B_i \supseteq B_{i_0} \cup \bigcup_{i=i_0}^{k''-1} \left(B_{i+1} \cap \left(\bigcap_{j=i_0}^{k''} C_j \right) \right) \cup \left(\bigcap_{j=i_0}^{k''} C_j \right).$$

Using Lemma 1 and Chernoff inequality we can prove that

$$\Pr(D_{i_0+1} \cap C_{i_0}) \leq \left(\frac{1}{N} \right)^{1.59} \quad \text{and} \quad \Pr\left(D_{i+1} \cap \bigcap_{j=i_0}^{i} C_j \right) \leq \left(\frac{1}{N} \right)^{0.33 \cdot (\frac{1}{2})^{i-i_0}} \tag{7}$$

for $i_0 + 1 \leq i \leq k'' - 1$. Thus from (6) and (7)

$$
\begin{aligned}
\Pr\left(\bigcup_{i=0}^{k''} B_i(v) \right) &\geq 1 - \Pr(D_{i_0}) - \sum_{i=i_0}^{k''-1} \Pr\left(D_{i+1} \cap \bigcap_{j=i_0}^{i} C_j \right) \geq \\
&\geq 1 - q_1(N) - \left(\frac{1}{N} \right)^{1.59} - \sum_{i=i_0+1}^{k''-2} \left(\frac{1}{N} \right)^{0.33(\frac{1}{2})^{i-i_0}} \geq 1 - q_2(N),
\end{aligned} \tag{8}
$$

where $q_2(N) = (1 + 0.0016(\ln N)^{15})/N^{2.99} + 1/N^{1.59} + 1/(N^{0.16l} - 1)$.

Assume that $\bigcup_{i=i_0}^{k''} B_i$ holds. Then there exists such $k \leq k''$ that $|\Gamma_k^-(v)| \geq 3\sqrt{N}$. Let $k_2 = k_2(v)$ be the smallest such index k. Using Lemma 1 and Chernoff inequality we can prove that

$$\Pr(|\Gamma_{k_2(v)}^-(v)| \geq 10\sqrt{N}) \leq 1/N^{1.5}. \tag{9}$$

Thus from (8) and (9)

$$
\begin{aligned}
&\Pr\left(\forall_{v \in K, v \text{ is "good"}} \exists_{1 \leq k_2 \leq k''} 3\sqrt{N} \leq |\Gamma_{k_2(v)}^-(v)| \leq 10\sqrt{N} \right) \geq \\
&\geq 1 - \sum_{v \in K} \left(1 - \Pr\left(\exists_{1 \leq k_2 \leq k''} 3\sqrt{N} \leq |\Gamma_{k_2(v)}^-(v)| \leq 10\sqrt{N} \right) \right) \geq 1 - p_2(N),
\end{aligned} \tag{10}
$$

where $p_2 = N \left(q_2 + 1/N^{1.5} \right)$.

From now on we will assume that v_1 and v_2 are the vertices such that

$$\exists_{1 \leq k_1 \leq k', 1 \leq k_2 \leq k''} |\Gamma_{k_1(v)}^+(v)| \geq \sqrt{N} \text{ and } 3\sqrt{N} \leq |\Gamma_{k_1(v)}^+(v)| \leq 10\sqrt{N} \tag{11}$$

holds. We will find a lower bound on the probability that these vertices are connected by a directed path of length at most $k_1 + k_2 + 1$. If $\Gamma_{k_1}^+(v_1) \cap \Gamma_{k_2}^-(v_2) \neq \emptyset$, then there exists such a path. Otherwise, using Lemma 1, we may prove that the probability that there is an edge pointing from $\Gamma_{k_1}^+(v_1)$ to $\Gamma_{k_2}^-(v_2)$ is at least $1 - 1/N^{\frac{8}{3}}$. Since there are at most N^2 pairs of vertices, thus with probability at least $1 - p_3(N)$ (where $p_3(N) = 1/N^{\frac{2}{3}}$) all pairs, for which (11) is fulfilled, are connected by a path of length at most $k' + k'' + 1$.

Concluding, since for any two vertices v_1 and v_2, such that v_2 is "good", (11) is fulfilled with probability at least $1 - p_1(N) - p_2(N)$, and so any pair of such vertices is connected by a directed path of length at most $k' + k'' + 1$ with probability at least $1 - p_1(N) - p_2(N) - p_3(N)$. Therefore, with probability at least $1 - p_1(N) - p_2(N) - p_3(N)$

$$\text{diam } G(X) \leq \lceil \ln N/(2 \ln \lfloor l/2 \rfloor) \rceil + \lceil \ln N/(2 \ln \lceil l/4 \rceil) \rceil + 4 .$$

Furthermore, if $k''' = \left\lfloor \frac{\ln N}{\ln(2l)} \right\rfloor - 1$, then $|N_{k'''}^+(v)| \leq \sum_{i=0}^{k'''} (2l)^i = \frac{(2l)^{k'''+1}-1}{2l-1} \leq \frac{N-1}{2l-1} < N$. Thus, there exists a vertex $w \in K \setminus N_k^+(v)$. So diam $G(X) \geq k+1 = \left\lfloor \frac{\ln N}{\ln(2l)} \right\rfloor$. Substituting $p(N) = p_1(N) + p_2(N) + p_3(N)$ finishes the proof. □

Theorem 2. *Let X be a random variable such that $E(X) = l \geq \ln N$ and $\Pr(\frac{l}{2} \leq X \leq 2l) = 1$. If $N \geq 2^{32}$ and $\ln N \leq l \leq \sqrt{N}/90 - 1$ then the graph $G(X)$ is strongly connected with probability at least $1 - p'(N, l)$, where $p'(N, l) = \frac{l}{N}$.*

$$\frac{N-l}{(N-2l)} \exp\left(\frac{2l(2l+1)}{N}\right) + N \exp\left(-l \cdot \frac{N-l-1}{N}\right) + \frac{1.6(\ln N)^7}{N^{1.5}} + \frac{1+0.0016(\ln N)^{15}}{N^{1.99}} + \frac{1}{N^{0.59}} + \frac{1}{N^{0.16l}-1} + \frac{1}{N^{0.5}}$$

Proof (Sketch). Now, we shall estimate the probability that for any two vertices $v, w \in K$, there exists a directed (w, v)-path. We will find the lower bound on probability that any vertex in K is "good". Let $v \in K$. Substitute in Lemma 1 for $A = \{v\}$ and $B = \emptyset$, then v does not have any in–neighbor in $K \setminus \{v\}$ with probability:

$$(1 - P_{AB})^{N-1} \leq \exp(-P_{AB}(N-1)) \leq p_1'(N, l), \tag{12}$$

where $p_1'(N, l) = \exp\left(-l \cdot \frac{N-l-1}{N}\right)$. Moreover, using Lemma 1, we can estimate the probability that v has in–neighbor u but there is no vertex which would be in–neighbor of v or u by

$$\sum_{u \in K \setminus \{v\}} (1 - P_{\{v,u\},\emptyset})^{N-2} \cdot P_{\{v\},\emptyset} \leq p_2'(N, l), \tag{13}$$

where $p_2'(N, l) = \frac{l}{N^2} \cdot \frac{N-l}{(N-2l)} \exp\left(\frac{2l(2l+1)}{N}\right)$. Thus

$$\Pr(\exists_{v \in K} v \text{ is not "good"}) \leq \sum_{v \in K} \Pr(v \text{ is not "good"}) \leq N(p_1'(l, N) + p_2'(l, N)).$$

From the proof of Theorem 1, we know that in the graph $G(X)$ any two vertices $v_1, v_2 \in K$, such that v_2 is "good", are connected by a directed path from v_1 to v_2 with probability at least $1 - p(N)$. Moreover, with probability at least $1 - N(p_1'(l, N) + p_2'(l, N))$ each vertex in $G(X)$ is "good". Thus with probability at least $1 - p(N) - N(p_1'(l, N) - p_2'(l, N))$ graph $G(X)$ is connected.

Corollary 1

(a) For $N = 2^{32}$ and $l = 32 \geq \ln N$ with probability larger than 0.98, graph $G(X)$ is connected and $5 \leq diam(G(X)) \leq 14$.

(b) For $N = 2^{64}$ and $l = 64 \geq \ln N$ with probability larger than $1 - \frac{3}{10^5}$, graph $G(X)$ is connected and $9 \leq diam(G(X)) \leq 19$.

(c) If $\Pr(\frac{l}{2} \leq X \leq 2l) = 1 - p$, then in graph $G(X)$ with probability at least $1 - Np$ for all vertices $v \in K$ we have $\frac{l}{2} \leq X_v \leq 2l$. Thus with probability at least $1 - p'(l, N) - Np$ graph $G(X)$ is connected and has diameter as stated in Theorem 1.

4   Equalizing Probability Distribution

Now we consider KEP with rule (2). We are interested in the state of a key for a pair of nodes after t random transitions executed for a given initial state. Here, we model one-way function $F(-, -, \tau)$ as random functions chosen independently for each τ. The state of the key is a random variable with values that are keys reachable from the initial key in t steps. The corresponding probability distribution can be described as a vector $P^t = (P_1^t, P_2^t \ldots P_N^t)$, assuming that for all non-reachable keys we have 0 in this vector. Clearly, this vector depends on function F. The main issue is that certain keys can be reached in multiple ways and, consequently, the corresponding coordinates P_i^t might be significantly higher.

While in the previous section we have been interested in how many steps are necessary so that we can potentially reach every key, now our goal is to put an upper bound for deviation of the coordinate P_i^t from $1/N$ (corresponding to the uniform distribution on the keyspace) that holds for almost all transition functions.

In order to model the behavior of the key transition mechanism we analyze a stochastic process $\mathcal{B}$ expressed in terms of balls and bins. Let us consider N distinct bins and a single ball put in the first bin at the beginning of the process, i.e. for $t = 0$. At each step of the protocol each bin is linked to exactly $l \geq 2$ distinct bins chosen uniformly at random out of the set of all N bins. We demand that the connections chosen for bin i at round t are stochastically independent of the connections chosen for bin j at round t, for $i \neq j$, and that the connections in round t are independent of the connections in the previous rounds.

N bins correspond to all possible keys. The location of a ball indicates the current state of the considered key, l connections from the current bin to other bins correspond to possible key transitions. In order to simplify the considerations we assume that the number of keys that can be reached in one transition is exactly l, despite a small collision probability of a one-way function.

If the ball is in a particular bin at step t, it can be moved with equal probability to each of l bins at step $t + 1$ linked to the bin holding the ball. Assume that for a given number of rounds, we fix the transitions. At time $t = 0$, we place the ball in the first bin. Then, for $t = 1$, it can be placed in each of l bins connected to the first bin with probability $1/l$. For $t = 2$, the potential number of reachable bins is within the interval $[l, l^2]$. Note that if a bin can be reached in multiple ways, then generally probability of placing the ball in it is higher. After a number of steps the situation becomes highly complex; the probabilities depend very much on the connections.

The Result. Assuming the randomness of the transitions, P_i^t becomes a random variable. (Recall that for a given realization of connections P_i^t is simply the probability that in step t of process $\mathcal{B}$ the ball is in bin i.)

Theorem 3. *For step t of process $\mathcal{B}$ described above, with parameters $N > l \geq 2$, for $\varepsilon > 0$, and $\delta = \frac{1}{l} - \frac{1}{N}$ we have:*

$$\Pr\left(\max_i \left|P_i^t - \tfrac{1}{N}\right| \geq \varepsilon\right) \leq \left(\delta^t + \tfrac{\delta(1-\delta^{t-1})}{N(1-\delta)}\right)\varepsilon^{-2}.$$

Proof of Theorem 3. In the proof we consider the deviation of random vector P^t from the uniform distribution in terms of the random variable $\mathcal{D}_N(P^t)$:

$$\mathcal{D}_N(P^t) = \sum_{i=1}^{N} \left(P_i^t - \tfrac{1}{N}\right)^2.$$

The proof is based on observations regarding the rate of decrease of the expectation of $\mathcal{D}_N(P^t)$ and finding a t such that this distance is close to zero. Since random variables P_i^{t+1} have the same distribution for each i, we get:

$$\mathrm{E}\left(\mathcal{D}_N(P^{t+1})|P^t\right) = \mathrm{E}\left(\left(P_1^{t+1} - \tfrac{1}{N}\right)^2 + \ldots + \left(P_N^{t+1} - \tfrac{1}{N}\right)^2 |P^t\right) =$$
$$= N \cdot \mathrm{E}\left(\left(P_1^{t+1} - \tfrac{1}{N}\right)^2 |P^t\right).$$

Let $\phi(i, j, t)$ be a random variable describing the connection in round t, defined as follows: $\phi(i, j, t) = 1$ if bin i is linked to bin j at step t. Otherwise $\phi(i, j, t) = 0$.

Obviously, $\mathrm{E}\left(\phi(i, j, t)\right) = \frac{l}{N}$. Moreover, according to our assumptions the random variables $\phi(i_0, j_0, t_0)$ and $\phi(i_1, j_1, t_1)$ are independent if $i_0 \neq i_1$ or $t_0 \neq t_1$. By the above definition,

$$\mathrm{E}\left(\left(P_1^{t+1} - \tfrac{1}{N}\right)^2 |P^t\right) = \mathrm{E}\left(\left(\sum_i \tfrac{1}{l} \cdot P_i^t \cdot \phi(i, 1, t) - \tfrac{1}{N}\right)^2 |P^t\right).$$

Since $\phi(i, 1, t)$ and $\phi(j, 1, t)$ are independent of P^t, we get

$$\mathrm{E}\left(\mathcal{D}_N(P^{t+1})|P^t\right) = N \cdot \mathrm{E}\left(\left(\sum_i \tfrac{1}{l}P_i^t \cdot \phi(i, 1, t) - \tfrac{1}{N}\right)^2 |P^t\right) =$$
$$= N \cdot \mathrm{E}\left(\left(\sum_i \tfrac{1}{l} \cdot P_i^t \cdot \phi(i, 1, t) - \sum_i \tfrac{1}{l} \cdot P_i^t \cdot \tfrac{l}{N}\right)^2 |P^t\right) =$$
$$= N \cdot \mathrm{E}\left(\left(\sum_i \tfrac{1}{l} \cdot P_i^t \cdot \left(\phi(i, 1, t) - \tfrac{l}{N}\right)\right)^2 |P^t\right) =$$
$$= N \sum_i \tfrac{1}{l^2} \cdot (P_i^t)^2 \cdot \mathrm{E}\left(\left(\phi(i, 1, t) - \tfrac{l}{N}\right)^2\right) +$$
$$+ N \sum_{i \neq j} \tfrac{1}{l^2} \cdot P_i^t \cdot P_j^t \cdot \mathrm{E}\left(\left(\phi(i, 1, t) - \tfrac{l}{N}\right) \cdot \left(\phi(j, 1, t) - \tfrac{l}{N}\right)\right).$$

Let us note that $\phi(i, 1, t)$ and $\phi(j, 1, t)$ are independent for $i \neq j$.

Since $\mathrm{E}(\phi(j, 1, t)) = l/N$, the second sum is equal to 0. Moreover, $\mathrm{Var}(\phi(i, 1, t)) = l/N \cdot (1 - l/N)$, so

$$\mathrm{E}\left(\mathcal{D}_N(P^{t+1})|P^t\right) = N \sum_i \tfrac{1}{l^2} \cdot (P_i^t)^2 \tfrac{l}{N} \cdot \left(1 - \tfrac{l}{N}\right) = \left(\tfrac{1}{l} - \tfrac{1}{N}\right) \sum_i (P_i^t)^2$$
$$= \left(\tfrac{1}{l} - \tfrac{1}{N}\right) \cdot \left(\sum_i \left((P_i^t)^2 - \tfrac{2 \cdot P_i^t}{N} + \tfrac{1}{N^2}\right) + 2 \cdot \sum_i \tfrac{P_i^t}{N} - \sum_i \tfrac{1}{N^2}\right) =$$
$$= \left(\tfrac{1}{l} - \tfrac{1}{N}\right)\left(\sum_i \left(P_i^t - \tfrac{1}{N}\right)^2 + \tfrac{1}{N}\right) = \left(\tfrac{1}{l} - \tfrac{1}{N}\right) \cdot \left(\mathcal{D}_N(P^t) + \tfrac{1}{N}\right).$$

Hence, we have shown

$$\mathrm{E}\left(\mathcal{D}_N(P^{t+1})|P^t\right) = \left(\tfrac{1}{l} - \tfrac{1}{N}\right) \cdot \left(\mathcal{D}_N(P^t) + \tfrac{1}{N}\right) .$$

Taking expectation of both sides of the above equality gives us:

$$\mathrm{E}\left(\mathcal{D}_N(P^{t+1})\right) = \left(\tfrac{1}{l} - \tfrac{1}{N}\right) \cdot \mathrm{E}\left(\mathcal{D}_N(P^t)\right) + \left(\tfrac{1}{l} - \tfrac{1}{N}\right) \cdot \tfrac{1}{N} .$$

Let $\delta = \tfrac{1}{l} - \tfrac{1}{N}$. It is easy to check that $\mathrm{E}\left(\mathcal{D}_N(P^1)\right) = \delta$. Therefore, solving the recursive relation we get:

$$\mathrm{E}\left(\mathcal{D}_N(P^t)\right) = \mathrm{E}(\mathcal{D}_N(P^1)) \cdot \delta^{t-1} + \frac{\delta}{N} \cdot \left(1 + \delta + \ldots + \delta^{t-2}\right) = \delta^t + \frac{\delta(1 - \delta^{t-1})}{N(1 - \delta)} .$$

Since $\mathcal{D}_N(P^t)$ is nonnegative, we can apply Markov inequality:

$$\mathrm{Pr}\left(\mathcal{D}_N(P^t) \geq \varepsilon^2\right) \leq \mathrm{E}(\mathcal{D}_N(P^t))/\varepsilon^2$$

and get:

$$\mathrm{Pr}\left(\mathcal{D}_N(P^t) \geq \varepsilon^2\right) \leq \left(\delta^t + \frac{\delta(1 - \delta^{t-1})}{N(1-\delta)}\right) \varepsilon^{-2} .$$

Therefore,

$$\mathrm{Pr}\left(\max_i |P_i^t - \tfrac{1}{N}| \geq \varepsilon\right) \leq \mathrm{Pr}\left(\sum_i \left(P_i^t - \tfrac{1}{N}\right)^2 \geq \varepsilon^2\right)$$
$$= \mathrm{Pr}\left(\mathcal{D}_N(P^t) \geq \varepsilon^2\right) \leq \left(\delta^t + \frac{\delta(1 - \delta^{t-1})}{N(1-\delta)}\right) \varepsilon^{-2} .$$

This concludes the proof of Theorem 3. ☐

From previous considerations we immediately obtain the following corollaries:

Corollary 2. *For $l = 2^{m_1}$ and $N = 2^{m_2}$*

$$\mathrm{Pr}\left(\max_i |P_i^t - \tfrac{1}{N}| \geq \varepsilon\right) < \left(\left(\frac{2^{m_2-m_1}-1}{2^{m_2}}\right)^t + \frac{2^{m_2-m_1}-1}{2^{2m_2}-2^{2m_2-m_1}+2^{m_2}}\right) \cdot \varepsilon^{-2} .$$

Corollary 3

$$\mathrm{Pr}\left(\max_i |P_i^t - \tfrac{1}{N}| \geq \varepsilon\right) < \left(\left(\frac{N-2}{2N}\right)^t + \frac{N-2}{N(N+2)}\right) \varepsilon^{-2} .$$

for $l = 2$. In particular, for $l = 2$ and $t = \log N$

$$\mathrm{Pr}\left(\max_i |P_i^t - \tfrac{1}{N}| \geq \varepsilon\right) < \left(\tfrac{2}{N}\right) \varepsilon^{-2} .$$

Acknowledgements. Katarzyna Rybarczyk and Michał Ren would like to thank their advisor – professor Jerzy Jaworski – for fruitful discussions, his invaluable advice and support.

References

1. Ren, M., Tanmoy, K.D., Zhou, J.: Diverging keys in wireless sensor networks. In: Katsikas, S.K., Lopez, J., Backes, M., Gritzalis, S., Preneel, B. (eds.) ISC 2006. LNCS, vol. 4176, pp. 3–540. Springer, Heidelberg (2006)
2. Carman, D.W., Kruus, P.S., Matt, B.J.: Constraints and approaches for distributed sensor network security. Technical Report 00-010, NAI Labs, Cryptographic Technologies Group Trusted Information Systems, NAI Labs, The Security Research Division Network Associates, Inc. 3060 Washington Road (Rt. 97) Glenwood, MD 21738-9745 (2000)
3. Tiri, K., Hwang, D., Hodjat, A., Lai, B., Yang, S., Schaumont, P., Verbauwhede, I.: Aes-based cryptographic and biometric security coprocessor ic in 0.18-um cmos resistant to side-channel power analysis attacks. In: 2005 Symposia on VLSI Technology and Circuits, pp. 216–219 (2005)
4. Eschenauer, L., Gligor, V.D.: A key-management scheme for distributed sensor networks. In: CCS 2002: Proceedings of the 9th ACM conference on Computer and communications security, pp. 41–47. ACM Press, New York (2002)
5. Chan, H., Perrig, A., Song, D.: Random key predistribution schemes for sensor networks. In: SP 2003: Proceedings of the 2003 IEEE Symposium on Security and Privacy, Washington, DC, USA, pp. 197–213. IEEE Computer Society, Los Alamitos (2003)
6. Chan, H., Perrig, A.: Pike: Peer intermediaries for key establishment in sensor networks. In: Infocom 2005. The 24th Conference of the IEEE Communications Society (2005)
7. Anderson, R., Chan, H., Perrig, A.: Key infection: Smart trust for smart dust. In: ICNP 2004. Proceedings of IEEE International Conference on Network Protocols (2004)
8. Daemen, J., Rijmen, V.: Rijndael specification. NIST AES Algorithm (Rijndael) Information webpage (2001)
9. Hellman, M.E.: A cryptanalytic time-memory tradeoff. IEEE Trans. Inform. Theory 26, 401–406 (1980)
10. Bollobás, B.: The diameter of random graphs. IEEE Trans. Inform. Theory 36, 285–288 (1990)
11. Bollobás, B.: Random Graphs. Academic Press, London (1985)
12. Chung, F., Lu, L.: The diameter of sparse random graphs. Adv. in Appl. Math. 26(4), 257–279 (2001)
13. Aldous, D., Fill, J.A.: Reversible markov chains and random walks on graphs-chapter 9: A second look at general markov chains
14. Nachmias, A., Peres, Y.: Critical random graphs: diameter and mixing time (2007)
15. Benjamini, I., Kozma, G., Wormald, N.: The mixing time of the giant component of a random graph (2006)
16. Montenegro, R., Tetali, P.: Mathematical aspects of mixing times in markov chains. Found. Trends Theor. Comput. Sci. 1(3), 237–354 (2006)
17. Jaworski, J., Smit, I.: On a random digraph. Annals of Discrete Mathathematics 33, 111–127 (1987)
18. Jaworski, J., Palka, Z.: Remarks on a general model of a random digraph. Ars Combinatoria 65, 135–144 (2002)
19. Janson, S., Łuczak, T., Ruciński, A.: Random Graphs. Wiley, Chichester (2001)

Appendix

Proof of Lemma 1

Lemma 2. *Let A and B be disjoint subsets of K, and let P^s_{AB} be the probability that in a graph $G(X)$ a given vertex v with degree s has an out-neighbor in A,* *conditioned by the event that it does not have any out-neighbor in B. Then for $N - |A| - |B| \geq s$:*

$$\frac{s|A|}{N-|B|} - \frac{s^2|A|^2}{2(N-|B|)^2} \leq P_{AB}^s \leq \frac{s|A|}{N-|B|} + \frac{s^2|A|}{2(N-|B|)(N-|B|-s)}. \tag{14}$$

Proof. Assume that vertex v with degree s does not have any out-neighbor in B. Then the probability that it does not have any out-neighbor in A is equal to $\frac{\binom{N-|A|-|B|}{s}}{\binom{N-|B|}{s}}$.

Substituting $k = N - |B|$ and $|A| = d$ we have:

$$\frac{\binom{N-|A|-|B|}{s}}{\binom{N-|B|}{s}} = \frac{\binom{k-d}{s}}{\binom{k}{s}} = \prod_{i=0}^{s-1}\left(1 - \frac{d}{k-i}\right).$$

Furthermore,

$$\prod_{i=0}^{s-1}\left(1 - \frac{d}{k-i}\right) \leq \left(1 - \frac{d}{k}\right)^s \leq 1 - \frac{sd}{k} + \binom{s}{2}\frac{d^2}{k^2} \leq 1 - \frac{sd}{k} + \frac{s^2d^2}{2k^2} =$$

$$= 1 - \frac{s|A|}{N-|B|} + \frac{s^2|A|^2}{2(N-|B|)^2}$$

and

$$\prod_{i=0}^{s-1}\left(1 - \frac{d}{k-i}\right) \geq 1 - \sum_{i=0}^{s-1}\frac{d}{k-i} = 1 - \sum_{i=0}^{s-1}\left(\frac{d}{k-i} - \frac{d}{k}\right) - \frac{sd}{k} =$$

$$= 1 - \frac{sd}{k} - \sum_{i=0}^{s-1}\frac{di}{k(k-i)} \geq 1 - \frac{sd}{k} - \frac{d}{k(k-s)}\binom{s}{2} \geq 1 - \frac{sd}{k} - \frac{s^2d}{2k(k-s)} =$$

$$= 1 - \frac{s|A|}{N-|B|} - \frac{s^2|A|}{2(N-|B|)(N-|B|-s)}$$

which implies (14).

Proof (of Lemma 1). Using Lemma 2, since $X < 2l$ with probability 1,

$$P_{AB} = \sum_{s=0}^{2l} P_{AB}^s \cdot \Pr(X = s) \leq$$

$$\leq \sum_{s=0}^{2l}\frac{|A|s}{N-|B|}\Pr(X=s) + \sum_{s=0}^{2l}\frac{|A|}{2(N-|B|)}\cdot\frac{s^2}{(N-|B|-s)}\cdot\Pr(X=s) \leq$$

$$\leq \frac{l|A|}{N-|B|} + 2l\cdot\frac{|A|}{2(N-|B|)\cdot(N-|B|-2l)}\sum s\Pr(X=s) =$$

$$\leq \frac{l|A|}{N-|B|} + \frac{l^2|A|}{(N-|B|)(N-|B|-2l)}$$

$$P_{AB} = \sum_{s=0}^{2l}P_{AB}^s \cdot \Pr(X=s) \geq$$

$$\geq \sum_{s=0}^{2l}\frac{|A|s}{N-|B|}\Pr(X=s) - \sum_{s=0}^{2l}\frac{|A|s^2}{2(N-|B|)^2}\cdot\Pr(X=s) \geq$$

$$\geq \frac{l|A|}{N-|B|} - 2l\cdot\frac{|A|}{2(N-|B|)^2}\sum_{s=0}^{2l}s\Pr(X=s) \geq \frac{l|A|}{N-|B|} - \frac{l^2|A|}{(N-|B|)^2}$$

Moreover each vertex in $K \setminus (A \cup B)$ chooses its out–neighbors independently, therefore Y has a binomial distribution with parameters $N - |A| - |B|$ and P_{AB}.

Upper Bound on $\Pr\left(\overline{\overline{A^v(w)}}\right)$

Assume that w has degree $s \geq \left\lceil \frac{l}{2} \right\rceil$ in $G(X)$. Notice that for $N \geq 2^{32}$ the procedure mentioned in the proof will not label more than $N^+ = k'\sqrt{N} \leq \frac{\ln N\sqrt{N}}{2\ln\lceil\frac{l}{4}\rceil} \leq \frac{\ln N\sqrt{N}}{4}$ vertices. Moreover, probability that w during procedure labels less than $\left\lceil \frac{l}{4} \right\rceil$ vertices is smaller than probability that w has at most $\left\lceil \frac{l}{4} \right\rceil - 1$ out–neighbors in the set of unlabeled vertices.

$$\Pr\left(\overline{\overline{A^v(w)}}\right) = \sum_{j=0}^{\lceil\frac{l}{4}\rceil-1} \frac{\binom{N-N^+}{j}\binom{N^+}{s-j}}{\binom{N}{s}} \leq \sum_{j=0}^{\lceil\frac{l}{4}\rceil-1} \binom{s}{s-j}\left(\frac{N^+}{N}\right)^{s-j} \leq$$

$$\leq \sum_{j=0}^{\lceil\frac{l}{4}\rceil-1} \left(\frac{se}{s-j}\right)^{s-j}\left(\frac{N^+}{N}\right)^{s-j} \leq \sum_{j=0}^{\lceil\frac{l}{4}\rceil-1} \left(\frac{\frac{l}{2}}{\frac{l}{2}-j}\right)^{s-j}\left(\frac{e\cdot N^+}{N}\right)^{s-j} \leq$$

$$\leq \sum_{j=0}^{\lceil\frac{l}{4}\rceil-1} \left(\frac{\frac{l}{2}}{\frac{l}{2}-\frac{l}{4}}\right)^{s-j}\left(\frac{e\cdot\ln N}{4\sqrt{N}}\right)^{s-j} \leq \sum_{j=0}^{\lceil\frac{l}{4}\rceil-1} \left(\frac{2e\cdot\ln N}{4\sqrt{N}}\right)^{s-j} \leq$$

$$\leq \left(\frac{e\cdot\ln N}{2\sqrt{N}}\right)^{s-\lceil\frac{l}{4}\rceil+1} \sum_{j=0}^{\lceil\frac{l}{4}\rceil-1} \left(\frac{e\cdot\ln N}{2\sqrt{N}}\right)^{\lceil\frac{l}{4}\rceil-1-j} \leq q_3(N),$$

where $g_3(N) = \left(\frac{e\cdot\ln N}{2\sqrt{N}}\right)^6 \frac{2\sqrt{N}}{2\sqrt{N}-e\ln N}$.
Thus for $N \geq 2^{32}$

$$\sum_{v\in K}\sum_{w\in W(v)} \Pr\left(\overline{\overline{A^v(w)}}\right) \leq N\frac{\ln N\sqrt{N}}{4}q_3(N) \leq \frac{1.6\cdot(\ln N)^7}{N^{1.5}}.$$

Proof of (5)

Let v be a good vertex. Let Z be a random variable counting number of vertices in $K \setminus \{v, u_1, u_2\}$ having an out–neighbor in $\{v, u_1, u_2\}$. Thus $\sum_{i=1}^{3}|\Gamma_i^-(v)| - 2 \geq |Z|$. According to Lemma 1, for $A := \{v, u_1, u_2\}$ and $B = \emptyset$, Z has binomial distribution $\mathrm{Bin}\,(N-3, P_{AB})$. For those A,B since $\frac{l+1}{N} \leq \frac{\sqrt{N}}{90N} + \frac{1}{N} < \frac{1}{3\cdot2^{20}}$ we have $P_{AB} \leq \frac{3l}{N}\left(1 + \frac{l}{N-2l}\right) < \frac{3l}{N}\left(1 + \frac{3l}{N}\right) < \frac{3(2^{20}+1)}{2^{40}}$ and $(N-3)P_{AB} \geq (N-3)\left(\frac{3l}{N} - \frac{9l^2}{N}\right) \geq 3l\left(1 - \frac{3(l+1)}{N}\right) > 3\ln N\frac{2^{20}-1}{2^{20}}$.
Furthermore

$$\Pr(Z \leq 15) = \sum_{i=0}^{15}\binom{N-3}{i}(P_{AB})^i(1-P_{AB})^{N-3-i} \leq$$

$$\leq (1-P_{AB})^{N-3} + \sum_{i=1}^{15}\left(\frac{(N-3)P_{AB}e}{i}\right)^i \exp\left(-(N-3-i)P_{AB}\right) \leq$$

$$\leq \left(1 + \exp(15\cdot P_{AB})\sum_{i=1}^{15}\left(\frac{(N-3)P_{AB}}{\frac{i}{e}}\right)^i\right)\exp(-(N-3)P_{AB}) <$$

$$< \left(1 + 15\cdot\exp\left(15\cdot\frac{3(2^{20}+1)}{2^{40}}\right)\left(\frac{3\ln N\frac{2^{20}-1}{2^{20}}e}{15}\right)^{15}\right)\exp\left(-3\ln N\frac{2^{20}-1}{2^{20}}\right) <$$

$$< \left(1 + 15\cdot\exp\left(15\cdot\frac{3(2^{20}+1)}{2^{40}}\right)\cdot(0.54\cdot\ln N)^{15}\right)\left(\frac{1}{N}\right)^{2.99} <$$

$$< \frac{1+0.0016(\ln N)^{15}}{N^{2.99}} = q_1(N),$$

since the function $f(x) = x^i \exp(-x)$ is decreasing for $x > i$ and the function $f(x) = \frac{a^x}{x^x}$ is increasing for $x < \frac{a}{e}$.

Therefore, for a "good" vertex v, $\sum_{i=1}^{3} |\Gamma_i^-(v)| - 2 \geq |Z| \geq 16$ with probability at least $1 - q_1(N)$, and thus by pigeonhole principle with probability at least $1 - q_1(N)$ there exists i_0, $1 \leq i_0 \leq 3$, such that

$$|\Gamma_{i_0}^-(v)| \geq 6, \tag{15}$$

which proves (5).

Proof of (7)

For any $i_0 < i \leq k'' = \left\lceil \frac{\ln N}{2 \ln \lfloor \frac{l}{2} \rfloor} \right\rceil + 3$ and v – a "good" vertex we will find a lower bound on the size of $\Gamma_i^-(v)$. Notice that a set $\Gamma_{i+1}^-(v)$ consists of all vertices from $K \setminus (\Gamma_i^-(v) \cup N_{i-1}^-(v))$ having an out–neighbor in $\Gamma_i^-(v)$, thus by Lemma 1, if we assume that $|\Gamma_i^-(v)| = \Gamma$ and $|N_{i-1}^-(v)| = N_i$ we have:

$$|\Gamma_{i+1}^-(v)| \sim \text{Bin}\left(N - N_i - \Gamma, P_{\Gamma N_i}\right), \tag{16}$$

and

$$\frac{\Gamma l}{N - N_i} - \frac{\Gamma^2 l^2}{(N - N_i)^2} \leq P_{\Gamma N_i}.$$

Furthermore if we condition that event $\bigcap_{j=i_0}^{i} C_j$ occurs, then: $3 \left(\frac{l}{2}\right)^{i-i_0} \leq |\Gamma_i^-(v)| < 3\sqrt{N}$ and $|N_{i-1}^-(v)| \leq 3k''\sqrt{N}$. Moreover since $l \leq \frac{\sqrt{N}}{90} - 1$ for $\Gamma \leq 3\sqrt{N}$ and $N_i \leq (\frac{1}{2} \ln N + 3)\sqrt{N}$

$$E\Gamma_{i+1}^- = (N - N_i - \Gamma)P_{\Gamma N_i} \geq$$
$$\geq \Gamma l - \frac{\Gamma^2 l^2}{(N-N_i)} - \frac{\Gamma^2 l}{(N-N_i)} + \frac{\Gamma^3 l^2}{(N-N_i)^2} \geq \Gamma l \left(1 - \frac{\Gamma(l+1)}{(N-N_i)}\right) \geq a\Gamma l$$

Where $a = \frac{28999}{30000}$.

By $F_i(\Gamma)$ we denote event that $\bigcap_{j=i_0}^{i} C_j$ and $\Gamma_i^-(v) = \Gamma$. Then by Chernoff inequality (see for example [19] theorem 2.1), for $i \geq i_0$

$$\Pr(|\Gamma_{i+1}^-| \leq b\Gamma_i^- l | F_i(\Gamma)) =$$
$$= \Pr\left(|\Gamma_{i+1}^-| \leq \frac{b}{a} E(|\Gamma_{i+1}^-||F_i(\Gamma))|F_i(\Gamma)\right) \leq$$
$$\leq \Pr\left(|\Gamma_{i+1}^-| \leq E(|\Gamma_{i+1}^-||F_i(\Gamma)) - \left(1 - \frac{b}{a}\right)E(|\Gamma_{i+1}^-||F_i(\Gamma))|F_i(\Gamma)\right) \leq \tag{17}$$
$$\leq \exp\left(-\frac{(1-\frac{b}{a})^2(E(|\Gamma_{i+1}^-||F_i(\Gamma)))^2}{2E(|\Gamma_{i+1}^-||F_i(\Gamma))}\right) \leq \exp\left(-\frac{(1-\frac{b}{a})^2}{2}a\Gamma l\right)$$

Thus substituting $i = i_0$, $a = \frac{28999}{30000}$ and $b = 0.25$ for $6 \leq \Gamma \leq 3\sqrt{N}$:

$$\Pr(|\Gamma_{i_0+1}^-| \leq 0.25|\Gamma_{i_0}^-|l||\Gamma_{i_0}^-| = \Gamma) \leq \exp\left(-\frac{(1-0.25\frac{30000}{28999})^2}{2}\frac{28999}{30000}\Gamma l\right) \leq \left(\frac{1}{N}\right)^{1.59}.$$

Therefore since $0.25 \cdot 6 \cdot l \geq 3 \lfloor \frac{l}{2} \rfloor$ thus:

$$\Pr(D_{i_0+1}|C_{i_0}) \leq \sum_{\Gamma=6}^{3\sqrt{N}} \Pr(\Gamma_{i+1}^- \leq 0.3\Gamma_{i_0}^- l | \Gamma_{i_0}^- = \Gamma) \leq \left(\tfrac{1}{N}\right)^{1.59}$$

and

$$\Pr(D_{i_0+1} \cap C_{i_0}) = \Pr(D_{i_0+1}|C_{i_0})\Pr(C_{i_0}) \leq \left(\tfrac{1}{N}\right)^{1.59},$$

which is the first part of (7).

Furthermore for $i > i_0$ substituting $a = \frac{28999}{30000}$ and $b = \frac{1}{2}$ for $3 \lfloor \frac{l}{2} \rfloor^{i-i_0} \leq \Gamma \leq 3\sqrt{N}$:

$$\Pr(|\Gamma_{i+1}^-| \leq \tfrac{1}{2}|\Gamma_i^-||l|F_i(\Gamma)) \leq \exp\left(-\frac{(1-\frac{1}{2}\frac{30000}{28999})^2}{2}\frac{28999}{30000}\Gamma l\right) \leq \left(\tfrac{1}{N}\right)^{0.33\left(\frac{1}{2}\right)^{i-i_0}}.$$

Therefore since $\frac{1}{2} \cdot 3 \lfloor \frac{l}{2} \rfloor^{i-i_0} \cdot l \geq 3 \lfloor \frac{l}{2} \rfloor^{i+1-i_0}$ and $\bigcap_{j=i_0}^i C_j = \bigcup_{\Gamma=3\left(\frac{1}{2}\right)^{i-i_0}}^{3\sqrt{N}} F_i(\Gamma)$ thus

$$\Pr\left(D_{i+1}\Big|\bigcap_{j=i_0}^i C_j\right) \leq \frac{\sum_{\Gamma=3\left(\frac{1}{2}\right)^{i-i_0}}^{3\sqrt{N}} \Pr(|\Gamma_{i+1}^-| \leq \frac{1}{2}|\Gamma_i^-||l|F_i(\Gamma))\Pr(F_i(\Gamma))}{\Pr(\bigcap_{j=i_0}^i C_j)} \leq \left(\tfrac{1}{N}\right)^{0.33\lfloor\frac{l}{2}\rfloor^{i-i_0}}$$

and

$$\Pr\left(D_{i+1} \cap \bigcap_{j=i_0}^i C_j\right) \leq \left(\tfrac{1}{N}\right)^{0.33\lfloor\frac{l}{2}\rfloor^{i-i_0}},$$

which is the second part of (7).

Proof of (9) – An Upper Bound on $\Gamma_{k_2}^-(v)$

Assume that there exists $k_2 \leq k''$ - the smallest index such that $\Gamma_{k_2}^-(v)$ is larger then $3\sqrt{N}$. Thus $1 \leq |\Gamma_{k_2-1}^-(v)| \leq 3\sqrt{N}$ and $|N_{k_2-1}| \leq 3k''\sqrt{N}$. Since (16) holds thus from Lemma 1 we have

$$P_{\Gamma N_i} \leq \frac{\Gamma l}{N-N_i} + \frac{\Gamma l^2}{(N-N_i)(N-N_i-2l)}$$

and

$$E|\Gamma_{i+1}^-| = (N-N_i-\Gamma)P_{\Gamma N_i} \leq (N-N_i)P_{\Gamma N_i} \leq$$
$$\leq \Gamma l\left(1 + \frac{l}{N-N_i-2l}\right) \leq \Gamma l\left(1 + \frac{3l}{N-N_i}\right).$$

Then by Chernoff bound for $1 \leq \Gamma \leq 3\sqrt{N}$ and $|N_{k_2-1}| \leq 3k''\sqrt{N}$:

$$\Pr(|\Gamma_{k_2}^-| \geq 10\sqrt{N}||\Gamma_{k_2-1}^-| = \Gamma) \leq$$
$$\leq \Pr\left(|\Gamma_{k_2}^-| \geq 3\Gamma l\left(1 + \frac{3l}{N-|N_{k_2-1}|}\right) ||\Gamma_{k_2-1}^-| = \Gamma\right) \leq$$
$$\leq \Pr\left(|\Gamma_{k_2}^-| \geq E(|\Gamma_{k_2}^-||\Gamma) + 2\Gamma l\left(1 + \frac{3l}{N-|N_{k_2-1}|}\right) ||\Gamma_{k_2-1}^-| = \Gamma\right) \leq$$
$$\leq \exp\left(-\frac{4\Gamma^2 l^2\left(1 + \frac{3l}{N-|N_{k_2-1}|}\right)^2}{2\left(E(|\Gamma_{k_2}^-||\Gamma) + \frac{1}{3}\Gamma l\left(1 + \frac{3l}{N-|N_{k_2-1}|}\right)\right)}\right) \leq$$
$$\leq \exp\left(-\tfrac{3}{2}\Gamma l\left(1 + \frac{3l}{N-|N_{k_2-1}|}\right)\right) \leq \frac{1}{N^{\frac{3}{2}}}$$

Thus conditioned on the fact that $1 \leq \Gamma \leq 3\sqrt{N}$ and $|N_{k_2-1}| \leq 3k''\sqrt{N}$ holds

$$\Pr(|\Gamma_{k_2}| \geq 10\sqrt{N}) \leq \sum_{\Gamma=1}^{3\sqrt{N}} \Pr(|\Gamma_{k_2}^-| \geq 10\sqrt{N} \mid |\Gamma_{k_2-1}^-| = \Gamma) \Pr(|\Gamma_{k_2-1}^-| = \Gamma) \leq N^{\frac{3}{2}},$$

which implies (9)

Existence of Paths

From Lemma 1 substituting $A = \Gamma_{k_2}^-(v_2)$, and $B = \emptyset$ we know that the probability that vertex $u \in \Gamma_{k_2}^-(v_2)$ does not have any out-neighbor in $\Gamma_{k_2}^-(v_2)$ is equal to $1 - P_{AB}$. Thus for $\Gamma_{k_1}^+(v_1)$ and $\Gamma_{k_2}^-(v_2)$ such that $|\Gamma_{k_1}^+(v_1)| \geq \sqrt{N}$ and $3\sqrt{N} \leq |\Gamma_{k_2}^-(v_2)| \leq 10\sqrt{N}$, since $l \leq \frac{\sqrt{N}}{90}$, the probability that there are no edges pointing from $\Gamma_{k_1}^+(v)$ to $\Gamma_{k_2}^-(w)$ is:

$$(1 - P_{AB})^{|\Gamma_{k_1}^+|} \leq \left(1 - \frac{|\Gamma_{k_2}^-|l}{N} + \frac{|\Gamma_{k_2}^-|^2 l^2}{N^2}\right)^{|\Gamma_{k_1}^+|} \leq$$

$$\leq \exp\left(\left(-\frac{|\Gamma_{k_2}^-|l}{N} + \frac{|\Gamma_{k_2}^-|^2 l^2}{N^2}\right)|\Gamma_{k_1}^+|\right) \leq$$

$$\leq \exp\left(-|\Gamma_{k_2}^-| \cdot |\Gamma_{k_1}^+|l\left(1 - \frac{|\Gamma_{k_2}^-|l}{N}\right)\right) \leq \left(\frac{1}{N}\right)^{3\left(1 - \frac{|\Gamma_{k_2}^-|l}{N}\right)} \leq \frac{1}{N^{\frac{8}{3}}}.$$

Proof of (12) and (13)

For $A = \{v\}$ and $B = \emptyset$ from Lemma 1

$$(1 - P_{AB})^{N-1} \leq \exp(-P_{AB}(N-1)) \leq$$
$$\leq \exp\left(-(N-1) \cdot \frac{l}{N}(1 - \frac{l}{N})\right) =$$
$$= \exp\left(-\left(l\left(1 - \frac{l}{N}\right) - \frac{l}{N}\left(1 - \frac{1}{N}\right)\right)\right) =$$
$$= \exp\left(-l\left(1 - \frac{l}{N} - \frac{1}{N} + \frac{l}{N^2}\right)\right) \leq \exp\left(-l\left(1 - \frac{l+1}{N}\right)\right).$$

Using Lemma 1 twice we have

$$\sum_{v_1 \in K \setminus \{v\}}(1 - P_{\{v,v_1\},\emptyset})^{N-2} \cdot P_{\{v\},\emptyset} \leq$$
$$\leq (N-1) \cdot \left(1 - \frac{2l}{N} + \frac{4l^2}{N^2}\right)^{N-2} \cdot \left(\frac{l}{N} + \frac{l^2}{N(N-2l)}\right) \leq$$
$$\leq (N-1) \cdot \exp\left(-2l + \frac{2l}{N} + \frac{4l^2}{N} - \frac{8l^2}{N^2}\right) \cdot \left(\frac{l}{N} + \frac{l^2}{N(N-2l)}\right) \leq$$
$$\leq (N-1) \cdot \frac{1}{N^2} \cdot \exp\left(\frac{2l}{N} + \frac{4l^2}{N}\right) \cdot \left(\frac{l}{N} + \frac{l^2}{N(N-2l)}\right) \leq$$
$$\leq \exp\left(\frac{2l}{N}(1 + 2l)\right) \cdot \frac{l}{N^2}\left(1 + \frac{l}{(N-2l)}\right).$$

A Secure Location Service for Ad Hoc Position-Based Routing Using Self-signed Locations*

Jihwan Lim[1], Sangjin Kim[2], and Heekuck Oh[1]

[1] Hanyang University, Department of Computer Science and Engineering,
Republic of Korea
jhlim@cse.hanyang.ac.kr, hkoh@hanyang.ac.kr
[2] Korea University of Technology and Education,
School of Information and Media Engineering, Republic of Korea
sangjin@kut.ac.kr

Abstract. Location service, which provides current geographic positions of nodes, is one of the key elements of position-based routing schemes for ad hoc networks. In this paper, we define security threats of location service and propose a new secure location service protocol that uses self-signed locations. In our proposed protocol, nodes register their public keys in other nodes during the initialization phase and these registered keys are used to verify the locations of other nodes and to generate their self-signed locations. In this paper, we show that our protocol is robust against traditional attacks and new attacks that may occur in position-based routings. We also analyze the efficiency of our protocol using various simulations.

Keywords: ad hoc network, position-based routing, secure location service.

1 Introduction

An ad hoc network is a network that does not use any existing infrastructure and is formed autonomously by mobile nodes. Participating nodes communicate with other nodes that are outside their transmission range by using multi-hop routing. In other words, a node plays the role of a router as well as a host. These nodes can also move freely causing the network topology to change dynamically. These characteristics make designing a scalable and robust routing protocols a real challenge.

Earlier researches on routing for ad hoc networks are based on table-driven or on-demand methods [1]. Recently, position-based routing methods are attracting many researches since these types of methods use geographical coordinates of nodes to effectively route messages [2,3]. In position-based routing, participating nodes can recognize their own geographic locations using equipments such as GPS (Global Positioning System). However, to route messages using the destination node's location, one must obtain

---

* This research was supported by the MIC (Ministry of Information and Communication), Korea, under the HNRC (Home Network Research Center) - ITRC (Information Technology Research Center) support program supervised by the IITA (Institute of Information Technology Assessment). This work was also supported by the Korea Science and Engineering Foundation(KOSEF) grant funded by the Korea government(MOST) (No. R01-2006-000-10957-0).

F. Bao et al. (Eds.): CANS 2007, LNCS 4856, pp. 121–132, 2007.

such information. Therefore, in position-based routings, there must be a way for nodes to obtain locations of other nodes.

Location service of position-based routing provides such mechanism. Location service may also refer to locating a data item, but in this paper, this service refers to locating the position of the destination node. Generally, a node queries another node to retrieve such information. A node who maintains locations of other nodes are referred to as a location server. We can use a single centralized server that maintains locations of all the participating nodes. However, since true ad hoc networks do not have any central administration, distributed approach is more suitable. In such approach, each participating nodes normally manage locations of some other nodes.

The location service is composed of three components: location update, location request, and location response. Location servers must maintain the latest location of nodes it manages. In other words, location service is sensitive to nodes' mobility. To accomplish this task, a node reports its new location to the server as it moves around the network. This process is referred to as a location update. This update can occur periodically or when a node moves a certain distance from the previous reported location. A node requests the location of the destination node if it does not have that information in its cache. The location server responds by sending the latest location information it maintains to the requesting node.

Most of the current researches on position-based routings for ad hoc network do not deal with new security threats caused by location service. For example, messages can be routed to wrong location if the location information obtained from a server is false. In this paper, we propose a new secure location service for position-based routing that uses self-signed locations. However, we do not deal with location privacy of nodes. The reason is that making location information private conflicts with the inherent nature of position-based routing. In other words, the location servers must know the location information of other nodes and these servers cannot be regarded as trusted entities in ad hoc networks.

The remainder of this paper is organized as follows. In section 2, we briefly introduce related work. Our proposed scheme will be present in section 3. In section 4, we analyze the security and the efficiency of our scheme using various simulations. Finally, we conclude this paper in section 5.

2   Related Work

2.1   Location Services for Position-Based Routing

At one extreme, we can think of a scheme where each node maintains the locations of all the nodes in the system [4]. In such schemes, it is inevitable that a node must flood its location to other nodes periodically. Therefore, efficiency of a location update and storage burden on each node may be too heavy. To reduce the cost of a location update, most of the schemes send an update message to only a subset of nodes. At another extreme, a single location server can be assigned to each node [2]. These approaches, compared to flooding-based, are sometimes referred to as rendezvous-based protocol, since location servers serve as rendezvous point for updates and lookups. Rendezvous-based approach can be further divided into hash-based or quorum-based [2,3]. In this paper, we divide rendezvous-based approach into static-based and dynamic-based depending on whether the rendezvous point is fixed or not.

Location services that use a HR (Home Region) [5,6] are typical examples of static-based approach. In these approaches, a universal hash function maps each node's identifier to a HR and nodes residing in that region serve as location servers of that node. When a node in a region receives an update request, it shares this information with other nodes in the region through local flooding. A node that wants to acquire the location information of a node sends a query to the HR of that node.

XYLS (column-row quorum-based Location Service) protocol [7,8] is a typical example of dynamic-based approach. In this protocol, a node reports its position to the nodes currently residing in the north-south direction of its current position. A node requests other nodes' location by sending a request message in the east-west direction. Therefore, there is always an intersection between an update message and a request message which guarantees that lookups will always be satisfied by some node.

2.2 Security of Ad Hoc Routing

Since participating nodes act as routers in ad hoc network, there are many security threats such as black hole, replay, worm hole, blackmail, and routing table poisoning [9]. However, current proposals to defend these attacks use unrealistic assumptions. For example, some assume that each pair of nodes shares a common secret with each other when nodes can freely join and leave the network [10,11]. Others assume that all nodes have a certificate issued by a common CA (Certification Authority) when it is difficult to predetermine which kind of nodes will participate in the network [12,13]. Therefore, we suggest a protocol that uses only self-signed certificates. In our scheme, nodes pre-register their public keys in other nodes and use an assumption that vast majority of nodes are honest.

2.3 Security of the Location Service

Positioning-based routing brings about new threats that do not exist in ad hoc networks based on other routing methods. The most obvious attacks on location service are as follows.

- False location update attack: An attacker may try to update the location of another node causing the server to maintain false location.
- False location response attack: An attacker may try to alter the response from a server causing a node to receive wrong location of another node.

In order to defend against these attacks, authentication of the sender and authentication of update and response messages must be provided. However, since nodes in ad hoc network cannot be regarded as trusted entities, authenticating the sender of a message is not sufficient to provide a secure location service. To this end, we use self-signed locations. More precisely, nodes sign their current location using their own private key and these signatures are maintained in location servers. Location servers also use these signatures to respond to location requests. Therefore, nodes receiving a location response do not have to trust the location servers.

Our idea requires some sort of PKI (Public Key Infrastructure). However, as stated earlier, using existing PKI is not a feasible solution due to the fact that there is no prior knowledge of the participants involved. Furthermore, true ad hoc networks may not have any access points. In other words, participating nodes may not have any certificates or even if nodes possess certificates it may not be possible to verify other parties' certificates while participating in the ad hoc network.

3   Proposed Protocol

3.1   Overview

Our proposal is not affected by the location service mechanism used by the network. In other words, our scheme can also operate in ad hoc networks that use static-based location service. However, in this paper, we will explain our protocol using the XYLS scheme proposed by Stojmenovic and Pena [7]. This scheme is based on the fact that a vertical and a horizontal line in a square always intersect with each other. In this scheme, as shown in Fig 1, a node updates by broadcasting its new position to the north and south of the current location and requests locations of other nodes by broadcasting the message to the east and west. As a result, there is always an intersecting point between location update and request messages. This enables nodes to receive the latest location information of other nodes. As with most of position-based routing protocols, a node updates when it moves a certain distance from the previous position or periodically. However, in our scheme, a node must send an update message in both cases. This is required since location servers remove old information from its table as time elapses.

To provide a secure location service, a node generates a public key pair and registers its public key in other nodes when it joins the network. If the majority of the nodes are honest, then this process will be sufficient to provide a safe public key environment. A node updates its position by sending its location digitally signed and a node receives this digitally signed location when requesting other node's location. If a node cannot obtain other node's private key, it will be infeasible for nodes to alter or generate a valid update or response message. The security of this mechanism will be discussed in more detail in section 4.1.

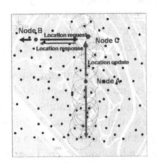

Fig. 1. Overview of Our Proposed Location Service

3.2 Assumption and Notation

We assume the followings about the ad hoc network environment and the nodes participating in our protocol.

– Nodes are assumed to be located uniformly in the given network. We also assume that they move at arbitrary speed and direction.
– All nodes are equipped with the same transmission radius and calculation capacity. That is, links between nodes are symmetric.
– Participating nodes can obtain their own geographical location through GPS and can accurately synchronize time through GPS.
– Participating nodes know in advance the protocols and algorithms used in the network to communicate with each other.
– Participating nodes know the unique ID of the respective node that they want to communicate with.
– Participating nodes can generate a public key pair by themselves and can generate and verify digital signatures.

Throughout this paper, we will use the notations given in Table 1.

Table 1. Notation

A	the identifier of node A.
A_{PK}, A_{PR}	the public and private key of node A.
$Sig_A(M)$	A's signature on message M using A_{PR}.
$Cert_A$	the self-signed certificate of A's public key.
T_{A_I}	the timestamp representing the time A_{PR} was first generated.
T_{A_C}	the timestamp representing the current time generated by A.
Pos_A	A's geographical location (coordinate) obtained from GPS.
Loc_A	the self-signed geographical location of node A.
	$Loc_A = Sig_A(A\|\|Pos_A\|\|T_{A_I}\|\|T_{A_C})$

3.3 Registration and Initialization

We use self-signed locations to provide a secure location service. To use our idea, we require a public key system that can be used in true ad hoc networks. As stated earlier, using an existing PKI in ad hoc network may not be plausible. Therefore, we propose the following public announcement method instead of traditional PKI. However, if there is a more suitable way to provide a PKI for ad hoc network exists, such mechanism can be used instead.

A node who wants to join the network follows the following steps to announce and register its public key in other nodes.

– **Step 1.** A node A generates a public key pair (A_{PK}, A_{PR}). It then creates a simple self-signed certificate of A_{PK} as follows:

$$Cert_A = Sig_A(A\|\|A_{PK}\|\|T_{A_I}).$$

- **Step 2.** The node A creates and vertically broadcast the following public key registration message (PK_init):

$$PK\_init = [Type, Seq, witdth, Cert_A, Loc_A],$$

where $Type$ refers to the type of the message such as such as 'public key registration', 'location update', and 'location request', Seq indicates a sequence number used to prevent loops and duplicate messages, and $width$ is a system parameter denoting the transmission width in hop distances. As one can see, this message also includes the initial location update.

In ad hoc network, a broadcasted message is received by all the nodes within one hop distance of the sender and one of the receiver will forward the message to the next hop. The width of a message is sometimes referred to as the thickness of reporting. For example, if the width is 1, a node located one hop east and a node located one hop west also forward the message vertically.

We do not flood the PK_init message to reduce the cost of registration and storage requirement. Instead, a node broadcasts its PK_init message vertically. When a message is broadcasted vertically, there are several ways to process the message. We use the following method 1 for normal location updates and method 2 for PK_init messages.

- Method 1. A node receiving the message unconditionally stores the certificate. If there are total n nodes and they are uniformly distributed, about $2r/l \times n$ nodes will store the certificate, where r is the transmission range of a node and l is the width of the terrain of the network assuming that the terrain is a square.
- Method 2. A node receiving the message determines the geographic location of the original source of the message and stores the certificate if the location is within certain boundary. If the boundary is divided into s disjoint columns, then n/s nodes will store the certificate.

When a node receives a message, depending on the policy used, the node may be responsible for determining the validity of the message. Obviously, due to the efficiency consideration, all nodes receiving a message do not have to verify it. Most of the messages in our protocol include a digital signature such as self-signed locations. To verify these signatures, nodes use self-signed certificates maintained in their storages. If a message is invalid, the node broadcasts an error alarm message in the reverse direction. However, nodes may not be able to verify a message because it does not have the required certificate. Since nodes moves around the network, the large number of nodes that receives this message will have the required certificate. However, when a node receives an error alarm message or when it is the target node it must always verify the received message. In this case, if a node does not have the necessary certificate, it requests the certificate from other nodes. If node B needs node A's certificate, the node B broadcasts the the following message horizontally:

$$PK\_request = [Type, Seq, A, Loc_B].$$

If a node has the requested certificate, it sends the following message to B:

$$PK\_response = [Type, Seq, Cert_A].$$

3.4 Location Update

When a node moves a certain distance from the previous location or if a certain time has elapsed from the last update, the node broadcasts the following message vertically:

$$Loc\_update = [Type, Seq, width, Loc_A].$$

Unlike PK_init messages, method 2 is always used. In other words, all nodes receiving this message will update the given location. If the width value is large, more nodes will preserve the location information which results in more nodes that can respond to location request messages. On the other hand, the cost of location update increases as the width value increases.

A node receiving an update message stores the message in its location table. An entry in a location table is maintained as follows:

$$[A, Cert_A, Loc_A, \Gamma_A],$$

where Γ_A denotes reliability of node A. When a node's reliability level falls below a certain level, the node is excluded from the network. The reliability threshold and adjustment of a node's reliability will be determined by the policy established prior to network deployment. All nodes receiving the location update message do not have to verify the validity of the message. We can use policies such as the followings.

– Policy 1. A message is verified every h hops.
– Policy 2. Every node randomly determines by itself whether it will verify the message or not.
– Policy 3. A node verifies a message only if it has the required certificate.

3.5 Location Request and Response

A node B broadcasts the following message horizontally to request the location of node A:

$$Loc\_request = [Type, Seq, A, Loc_B].$$

When a node receives this message, it first looks for node A's location information in its table. If the node has the requested information, it unicasts a location response message. A location response message from C in response to node B's query about node A's location is formed as follows:

$$Loc\_response = [Type, Seq, Loc_B, Loc_A, Loc_C].$$

3.6 Error Alarm

When a node A receives a message, depending on the policy, it verifies the signature included in the message. If the message is invalid, it broadcasts the following message in the reverse direction:

$$Err\_alarm = [msg, Sig_A(msg)],$$

where $msg = (Type, Seq, err\_type)$. Nodes receiving this message must verify the validness of this message and perform necessary actions such as removing the previous location update and changing the reliability of a node.

4   Analysis

4.1   Security Analysis

Analysis of Public Key Registration. Our scheme uses a public key system that uses only self-signed certificates to provide secure location service. Obviously, in a normal environment, this kind of public key system cannot provide a safe environment, since it is difficult to prevent false registrations. However, as stated earlier, using an existing PKI in an ad hoc environment may not be a plausible solution. Therefore, it is inevitable that systems such as ours must be used in such environment. In our scheme, nodes register their self-signed certificates when they join the network. Since nodes cannot determine whether the received certificate is valid or not, they accept the registration unconditionally. In this case, we have to consider the outcome of the following attacks. In this discussion, we assume that the current request is a legitimate one.

- Attack 1. Someone else has already register a public key using the same ID as the current one.
- Attack 2. Someone else may later try to register a public key using the same ID as the current one.
- Attack 3. Someone may simultaneously send a registration message using the same ID as the current one in a different location.
- Attack 4. Someone swaps the public key in the current message with another one and forwards the altered message.

We assume that it is difficult for nodes to know in advance the IDs of participants that will join the network. If this assumption holds, then attack of type 1 and type 3 cannot occur. In our scheme, nodes reject duplicate registrations using the timestamp included in the certificate. As a result, nodes that have already accepted a registration for that ID in the past will reject this attack. However, there may be nodes that are receiving such registration for the first time. In this case, these nodes will accept this fraud registration. However, due to our grouping policy, there will be nodes in the current column who have accepted the legitimate registration in the past. These nodes will send an error alarm message which will cause nodes to reject the fraud registration. Our scheme also assume that each node monitors neighboring nodes' behavior by using techniques suggest in [14]. Therefore, attack of type 4 can also be detected with high probability.

Security against Attack Threat. If the PKI used in our protocol is secure, our new location service is robust against various attacks.

- False location update attack/False response attack: In our protocol, we use self-signed locations. Therefore, without acquiring the private key of a certain node, one cannot generate a false but valid self-signed location. As a result, these kinds of attacks cannot succeed.
- Replay: In our protocol, old replayed messages will be discarded using the timestamp included in that message.

- Blackmail attack: This kind of attack is related to false error alarm messages. In our protocol, nodes receiving an error alarm message will verify both the current message and the previous message that is reported to be invalid. Therefore, assuming that the PKI used in our protocol is secure, nodes can detect a false error alarm message.
- Blackhole/Wormhole attack: These kinds of attacks are not applicable to position-based routing protocols.

4.2 Efficiency Analysis

In our scheme, additional measures are used to provide a secure location service. Compared to the basic XYLS scheme, our scheme requires the following additional costs:

- public key registration cost,
- signature generation cost needed when constructing a self-signed location,
- signature verification cost, and
- public key query costs for signature verification.

The costs for signature creation and verification can be regarded as basic costs for secure communication when using a public key system. In other words, these costs are inevitable. Therefore, in this paper, we analyze the number of additional messages exchanged instead of analyzing the number of public key operations performed by a node. Compared to the basic XYLS scheme, additional messages used in our scheme are related to public key queries and error alarm messages. However, public key registration messages should not be regarded as additional messages. This is because nodes also report their locations during this registration. That is, public key registration is a special case of location update message. However, there is an obvious increase in the size of messages we use. If we assume majority of nodes are honest, the frequency of error alarm messages will be low. Therefore, in this analysis, we will focus on public key queries only.

In our scheme, a node maintains only a subset of self-signed certificates of other nodes. Therefore, when a message arrives, nodes may not be able to verify the validity of the received message. A node can always use a public key query to obtain the required certificate to verify the message. If a node maintains $x\%$ of entire nodes' certificate, then this node will request on the average $(1 - x)\%$ of messages it must verify. However, if nodes cache previous obtain certificates and they tend to only communicate with a subset of nodes, then this percentage will be lower than $(1 - x)\%$. Moreover, even if a public key query is required, this query will only require a single hop once the nodes are uniformly distributed from their initial locations. Therefore, the cost of public key queries will not effect the network performance.

We will show that this argument holds using a hypothetical ad hoc network of 200 nodes. The terrain of this network is assumed to be a square of 1km^2 and the communication radius of a node is assumed to be 200m. If a PK_init message is sent vertically using the $width = 0$ and method 1 is used, about $80 (= 200\text{nodes} \times 400\text{m}/1\text{km})$ nodes will store the certificate. This is because approximately nodes residing in a column of 400m will receive this message. Let's assume the policy 3 given in section 3.4 is used and a certain amount of time has elapsed since the network was initially formed. This means that nodes that maintain the same certificate are uniformly distributed throughout the network. In this case, the number of neighbors of a node is as follows:

$$\text{The number of neighbor nodes} = d \times r^2 \times \pi = (200/km^2) \times (0.2km)^2 \times \pi \approx 25,$$

where d is the node density of the network. Since 40% of nodes maintains the same certificate, the same percentage of neighbors, which is about $10(25 \times 0.4)$, will have the required certificate. Even if a node started at the edge of the terrain, about 40 nodes will have that node's certificate. In this case, 20% of the neighbors, which is about 5, will have the required certificate. If we assume that 50% of the nodes are honest, some node will always detect and report invalid messages. If method 2 is used and 6 segments are used, about $33(= 200/6)$ nodes will store the certificate. In this case, 17% of the neighbors, which is about 4, will have the required certificate.

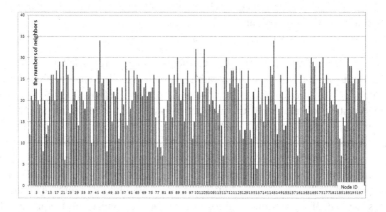

Fig. 2. The Number of Neighbor Nodes of Participating Nodes at Time $t = 100$

We ran a simulation to verify our above analysis. In this simulation, we assumed the same environment as used in above analysis. Moreover, we assumed that all 200 nodes participate from the start and we set the average movement speed of each node at 2.5m/sec and the maximum movement speed at 5m/sec. We ran the simulation for 180 seconds. We used method 2 with 6 segments which resulted in six distinct group and the size of each group was $A = 35$, $B = 30$, $C = 45$, $D = 29$, $E = 30$, and $F = 31$. Fig 2, shows the number of neighbor nodes of each nodes at time $t = 100$sec. The number of neighbors of a node ranged from 4 to 34 and the average was 22. We also observed the number of neighbors of a certain node numbered 0 which is given in Fig 3. We also observed the changes in neighbors of that node. This is also illustrated in Fig 3. As can be seen in the figure, during the simulation, except for group C at time 100sec to 120sec, there always exists a member from each group as the neighbor of node 0. If we think of the hops a message travels, it is reasonable to argue that there will always be an honest node that receives the message who has the required certificate.

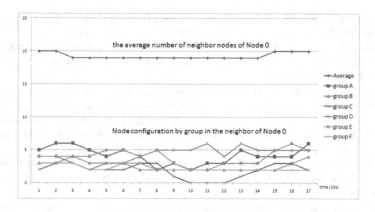

Fig. 3. Change of the Average Number of Neighbor Nodes and Change of Their Composition

5   Conclusion

In this paper, we proposed a new secure location service for ad hoc position-based routing. In our scheme, a node updates its location by sending its location digitally signed which we call a self-signed location. The use of this mechanism allows nodes to authenticate locations of others without relying on any trust on location servers. Our mechanism can be used in any position-based routing. However, the security of our mechanism depends on the PKI used in ad hoc network. Although, we have introduce an idea of using a public key announcement method, the security of our protocol can be enhanced further if a more efficient and secure way of deploying a PKI in ad hoc network can be devised.

References

1. Royer, E.M., Toh, C.: A Review of Current Routing Protocols for Ad hoc Mobile Wireless Networks. IEEE Personal Communications 2(6), 46–55 (1999)
2. Das, S.M., Pucha, H., Hu, Y.C.: Performance Comparison of Scalable Location Services for Geographic Ad hoc Routing. In: Proc. of the IEEE INFOCOM 2005, vol. 2, pp. 1228–1239. IEEE, Los Alamitos (2005)
3. Friedman, R., Kliot, G.: Location Services in Wireless Ad hoc and Hybrid Networks: A Survey. Tech. Rep. CS-2006-10. Haifa Univ. (2006)
4. Camp, T., Boleng, J., Wilcox, L.: Location Information Services in Mobile Ad hoc Networks. In: Proc. of the IEEE Int. Conf. on Communications, vol. 5, pp. 3318–3324. IEEE, Los Alamitos (2005)
5. Woo, S.C., Singh, S.: Scalable Routing in Ad hoc Networks. Wireless Networks 7(5), 513–529 (2001)
6. Cheng, C.T., Lemberg, H.L., Philip, S.J., van den Berg, E., Zhang, T.: SLALoM: A Scalable Location Management Scheme for Large Mobile Ad-hoc Networks. In: Proc. of the IEEE Wireless Communications and Networking Conf., vol. 2, pp. 574–578. IEEE, Los Alamitos (2002)

7. Stojmenović, I., Peña, P.: A Scalable Quorum based Location Update Scheme for Routing in Ad hoc Wireless Networks. Tech. Rep. TR-99-09. Ottawa Univ. (1999)
8. Melamed, R., Keidar, I., Barel, Y.: Octopus: A Fault-Tolerant and Efficient Ad-hoc Routing Protocol. In: Proc. of the 24th IEEE Symp. on Reliable Distributed Systems, pp. 39–49. IEEE, Los Alamitos (2005)
9. Argyroudis, P.G., Mahony, D.O.: Secure Routing for Mobile Ad hoc Networks. In: IEEE Communications Surveys & Tutorials, vol. 73, pp. 2–27. IEEE, Los Alamitos (2005)
10. Hu, Y.C., Johnson, D.B., Perrig, A.: SEAD: Secure Efficient Distance Vector Routing for Mobile Wireless Ad hoc Networks. In: Proc. of the IEEE Workshop on Mobile Computing Systems and Applications, pp. 3–13. IEEE, Los Alamitos (2002)
11. Hu, Y.C., Perrig, A., Johnson, D.B.: Ariadne: A Secure On-Demand Routing Protocol for Ad hoc Networks. In: Proc. of the 8th ACM Int. Conf. on MobiCom, pp. 12–23. ACM, New York (2002)
12. Zapata, M.G.: Secure Ad hoc On-demand Distance Vector routing. In: ACM Mobile Computing and Communications Review, vol. 6(3), pp. 106–107. ACM, New York (2002)
13. Sanzgiri, K., Dahill, B., Levine, B.N., Shields, C., Belding-Royer, E.M.: A Secure Routing Protocol for Ad hoc Networks. In: Proc. of the 10th IEEE Int. Conf. on Network Protocols, pp. 78–87. IEEE, Los Alamitos (2002)
14. Marti, S., Giuli, T.J., Lai, K., Baker, M.: Mitigating Routing Misbehavior in Mobile Ad Hoc Networks. In: Proc. of the 6th ACM Int. Conf. on Mobile Computing and Networking, pp. 255–265. ACM, New York (2000)

An Intelligent Network-Warning Model with Strong Survivability

Bing Yang, Huaping Hu, Xiangwen Duan, and Shiyao Jin

School of Computer Science, National University of Defense Technology,
Changsha Hunan, 410073, P.R. China
ybnudt@gmail.com

Abstract. Over the past decades more and more network security devices, such as IDS, Firewall and scanner, are distributed in the network. So superfluous alerts are generated, and do not have unified format. How to organize and utilize those alerts to enhance network security becomes a hot topic of research. Network-warning system, which can correlate alerts and predict future attacks, appears as one promising solution for the problem. In this paper, an intelligent strong-survivability network-warning model is introduced, which consists of a lot of intelligent agents. And a prototype is implemented based on the model. We propose a self-adaptive data-processing algorithm for classifying and reducing alerts automatically, and design a strong-survivability structure. The intelligence of self-adaptive algorithm depends on machine learning. In the prototype we adopt three methods (C5.0, Neural Net and CART) to construct the self-adaptive algorithm, and choose the best method fitting the algorithm, which is CART. The prototype can not only reduce and classify the original alert data from different network security devices, but also correlate alerts and generate intrusion scenario graphs. The equality of all agents makes the model strong-survivable. Furthermore, the model can predict potential attacks based on scenario graphs and track the attack sources[1].

Keywords: Strong Survivability, Intelligence, Network-Warning, Equality.

1 Introduction

Over the past decades more and more network security devices, such as IDS, Firewall and scanner, are distributed in the network. So superfluous alerts are generated, and do not have unified format. How to organize and utilize those alerts to enhance network security becomes a hot topic of research. Network-warning system, which can correlate alerts and predict future attacks, appears as one promising solution for the problem. It can not only deal with superfluous alerts, but also can derive alert information missed and predict potential attacks. With the network-warning system, network security managers may prevent attacks as soon as possible.

---

[1] This work was Supported by the National Natural Science Foundation of China under Grant No. 60573136.

F. Bao et al. (Eds.): CANS 2007, LNCS 4856, pp. 133–145, 2007.

Recently, some network-warning models [1, 2, 3, 4] have been presented, but the structure of these models is relatively simple. These models' shortages are:

1. Weak anti-destroy capability (weak survivability). The hierarchical structure of most traditional models has a control center in each level. Once the center is destroyed, the domain which is controlled by the center will be uncontrollable, so the alert data and attack can not be collected any more, the most important is that the performance of the model will fall off greatly.
2. Little intelligence. The bottom components of traditional models are not intelligent. They can only do some simple things, like unifying alerts format, uploading alerts and receiving commands from top components. They can not reduce or fuse superfluous alerts, so the burdens of the top components will be increased and a great deal network bandwidth is occupied. If the network scale becomes large or the network traffic becomes huge, the performance of the traditional models will fall off greatly.

With above mentioned in mind, we propose a new network-warning model, which named an Intelligent Network-Warning Model with Strong-Survivability, namely INWMSS. The model can process alerts and predict potential attacks. The characteristics of the INWMSS include intelligence and strong survivability (which means that the system based on INWMSS is highly survivable when environment changes or some parts of the system go wrong).

This paper is organized as following. The second section describes the architecture of INWMSS and the procedure of data-processing. The third section discusses how to implement the main functions and algorithms in the model. In the fourth section, we test the prototype base on INWMSS, and discuss the test result. Finally, we conclude the paper with the future work.

2   The Architecture and Data-Processing Procedure of INWMSS

2.1   The Architecture of INWMSS

The total functions of INWMSS include:

1. To predict potential attacks based on scenario graphs and alert data.
2. To generate attack Scenario graphs and track attack sources.

Figure 1 presents the architecture of INWMSS. The INWMSS includes several domains, and it is composed of three layers, such as detecting layer, agent layer and domain agent layer. The detecting layer, which is showed in domain 1 in figure 1, is responsible for alert data collection and provides alert data to other layers to process. For the case of space, we only focus on the processing of alert data, so we mainly focus on the agent layer and the domain agent layer and just give a brief introduction to detecting layer.

The detecting layer is composed of various security devices, like IDS, Firewall, scanner, and so on. They acquire and provide alert data to the intelligent agents periodically. There are a lot of devices in each domain. These devices communicate with at least one agent in the same domain.

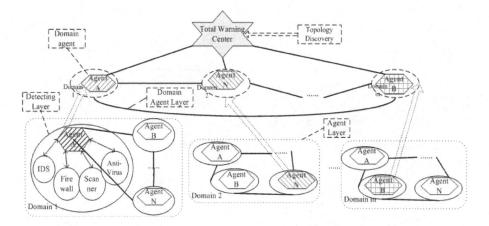

Fig. 1. Architecture of INWMSS

The agent layer includes several intelligent agents, which are distributed into several domains. All agents in the same domain can communicate with each other in the same domain and monitor each other, so as to know other agents' status, like whether an agent is alive or dead. All agents in the same domain are equal, which make the model more survivable. Once an agent is wrong, all other agents can substitute its work. Especially when the domain agent is wrong, a new domain agent will be chosen from other normal agents automatically. So the domain still can communicate with other domain smoothly.

The domain agent layer includes the agents picked up from all domains, one agent for each domain. Those agents picked up are the domain agent. The domain agents communicate with each other, and can exchange scenario graphs between each other. Thus, all domain agents can share alert data, so as to derive alerts missed and increase the accuracy of predicting.

The model has a total warning center which is the top layer of the hierarchy. The warning center is only an interface between security managers and the model, its task includes three aspects. First, it synthesizes scenario graphs provided by domain agents and network topology, and provides it to network security managers to help them make decision as quickly as they could; second, the center can receive predicting information from domain agents to help managers to take measures to prevent possible attacks; third, an important task of the center is to track attack sources, so as to cut off attacks as soon as possible. It can distribute some orders to the domain agents to track or prevent the attack sources based on the synthesized scenario graphs.

"Topology Discovery" can operate with INWMSS and provide network topology to INWMSS, so the network managers can get a clear view of the network state.

Figure 2 illustrates the structure of an intelligent agent. An intelligent agent mainly includes three modules, namely inside-domain communication module, outside-domain communication module and alert data processing module. The inside-domain module is responsible for communicating with other agents in the same domain. The outside-domain module is used to communicate with other agents in different domains, but only when the agent becomes a domain agent, the outside-domain module

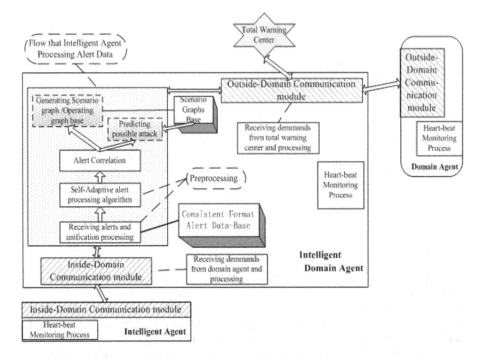

Fig. 2. Structure of an Intelligent Agent

will be triggered. The data processing module is the core of an agent, which can intelligently reduce and correlate the alert data, generate attack scenario graphs, or predict possible attacks. Heart-beat monitoring Process can monitor the health of the domain agent. If the domain agent is wrong, the process will trigger the choice about a new domain agent. This can make INWMSS strongly survivable.

A normal agent can only generate attack scenarios and save them, but when a normal agent in a domain becomes a domain agent, it can not only generate attack scenarios and save scenarios into scenario base, but also predict potential attacks. In the following section we will illustrate the implementation of each module in a intelligent agent.

2.2 The Data-Processing Procedure of INWMSS

Because of the comparability of data-processing procedure in each domain, we only illustrate the procedure in a domain. Detailed procedure is:

1) Security devices monitor the network and the hosts. as soon as discovering Intrusion action, they will provide alerts to intelligent agents.
2) After intelligent agents receive alerts from security devices, they first transform alerts into unified format, and save them into memory cache for alert dada.
3) Agent may utilize self-adaptive data-processing algorithm to reduce and delete false alerts, repeated alerts and unrelated information which are hold in memory

cache. The aim is to make a single attack corresponding to a real alert. Next alert correlation module deals with unified-format alerts.

4) Non domain agents (normal agents) send the results of correlation to a domain agent, the domain agent synthesizes all results from the agents in the same domain and generates intrusion scenario graphs. Finally, the domain agent returns scenario graphs to each normal agent in the same domain and save them to scenario base.

5) There are several concurrent processes in this step. First, a domain agent contrasts correlation results synthesized with scenario graphs in scenario base to estimate whether attacks are occurring or not. If attacks occurring, the domain agent may predict the next action of the attacker and uploads the results to the total warning center; second, the domain agent receives commands and data from the total warning center, include intrusion scenario graphs and information about confirmation of attack source, then executes corresponding operations which is to distribute messages to other agents in the same domain to prevent attacks and distribute scenario graphs to other agents. If the total warning center is wrong, the domain agent exchanges intrusion scenario graphs with other domain agents in the same layer and save them.

6) Once the total warning center receives the predicting results and intrusion scenario graphs from domain agents, by analyzing and estimating, it makes final warning reports. At the same time, it tracks attack sources and sends the result to lower-layer domain agents.

3   The Analysis and Implementation of Main Functions and Algorithms

Based on INWMSS, we implement a prototype. This section analyzes and implements the main functions and algorithms in the prototype.

3.1   Implementation of Strong Survivability for Prototype

Because of the equality among all agents in the same domain, the structure of INWNSS becomes reliable and highly survivable.

In the prototype, each agent in the same domain has the same functions and states. The domain agent is picked up by random from all agents in the same domain. The domain agent is denoted as symbol "D", other normal agents are all denoted as symbol "N". Each agent runs a heart-beat monitoring program, which can monitor the domain agent in the same domain. If the domain agent goes wrong, the normal agents in the same domain immediately pick up another agent as the new domain agent by random. The new domain agent will substitute the wrong domain agent to execute corresponding operation.

Figure 3 describes the mechanism of the heart-beat monitoring program. By receiving and sending UDP messages between the domain agent and other normal agents, we can monitor whether the domain agent is good or not. If the normal agents can not receive messages from the domain agent within deadtime, the domain agent is considered dead, and the action of picking up a new domain agent will be triggered.

Fig. 3. Heart-beat Monitoring Program

3.2 Implementation of Intelligent Data-Processing Function

The key component of network-warning model is the intelligent agent. And the key of the intelligent agent is the two modules on processing alert data, which are alert pre-processing module and alert correlation module. It is said that a quality input data should in theory help in producing good results [5]. Thus, data preprocessing is an important aspect for the practicability of the model. Therefore, we first consider how to adequately get alert data and preprocess data from network security devices. The data preprocessed are input of alert correlation module.

1. Alert preprocessing (self-adaptive data-processing algorithm)

Alert preprocessing consists of two steps. The first step is to unify the format of alert data. We use IDMEF XML [6] which is fit for IDS (Intrusion Detection System) as a unified format of output data, because most of alert data come from IDS, and some are from Firewalls or scanners in the experiment. The emphasis of alert preprocessing lies in the second step. It is to reduce and classify false alerts, repeated alerts and some unrelated information [7, 8, 9, 10, 11], so as to provide the alert correlation module with clear and high-quality alert data. We propose a self-adaptive data-processing algorithm on data processing which is fit for INWMSS. The alert data with IDMEF XML format are input of the algorithm.

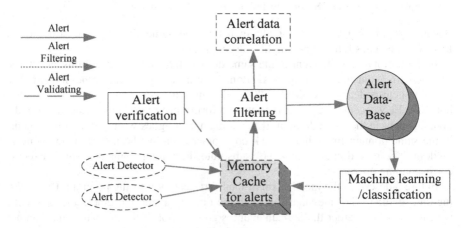

Fig. 4. Structure of the Self-adaptive Data-preprocessing Algorithm

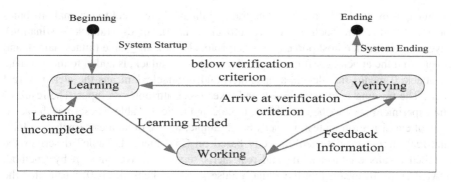

Fig. 5. The transition of three different states of self-adaptive algorithm

The structure of the self-adaptive algorithm is described in figure 4. It consists of five parts, including alert-filtering module, alert-verification module, machine-learning module (or classifier) and alert data-base. Alert-filtering module filters those alerts which are denoted as false alerts and uploads suspicious alerts; alert-verification module verifies the authenticity of input alerts and marks those alerts in memory cache; machine-learning module learns from denoted alerts in alert data-base and constructs a classification model. The classification model automatically distinguishes all alerts in memory cache and denoting them as suspicious alerts or false alerts; alert data-base saves those denoted alerts.

Figure 5 describes three different states of the algorithm, including learning state, validating state and working state. In learning state, classification model is being built, alert-verification module and machine-learning module start up; in working state, classification model begins to work, but alert-verification module and machine-learning module stop working; in verifying state, classification model is working, and alert-verification module starts up. Next we illustrate the implementation of the ma-chine-learning module of the self-adaptive algorithm.

We adopt three methods to implement the machine-learning module. One is a su-pervised-Learning multi-layer perceptron model which belongs to Neural Network [12], the other is a learning method based on rule induction which is called C5.0 [13, 14], and the last one is Classification and Regression Tree (namely CART) [15]. The CART classification does not require expert knowledge, automatically selects useful spectral and ancillary data from data supplied by the analyst, and can be used with continuous and categorical ancillary data.

We use two training data to test above-mentioned two methods. The training data are DARPA1999 Datasets [16] and DARPA2000 DataSets [17]. The 1, 2 week data of DARPA1999 Datasets are used to training, and the 4, 5 week data are used to testing. And DARPA2000 DataSets are used to test the performance of the two methods when environment is changed appreciably. All test datasets are entered into the database management system by Snort. Snort is one of the most famous network intrusion detection programs.

In experiment, the attributes of the training datasets are equal to original attributes of the Snort alert, such as ip_src (attack source), ip_dst (attack destination), layer4_sport (source host port), ip_proto (protocol type), sig_name (attack name), and so on. And the attack classification symbol, such as is_attack, is added to the test data, is_attack=0 means the alert is a false alert and is_attack=1 means the alert is a real alert. The training outputs is_attack and takes other attributes as input. The result of the experiment is described in table 1, table 2 and table 3. Table 1 describes the accuracy of classification on test datasets. For example, 87.9% of all alerts (including false and real alerts) are detected correctly based on C5.0 method. Table2 describes the detailed results on false alerts and real alerts separately. We show it by (method, DARPA). (0, 0) means that the actually false alerts is checked; (1, 0) means that the

Table 1. Accuracy of Classification on test datasets

	DARPA1999 Week4,5(%)	DARPA2000(%)
C5.0	87.9	52.3
Neural Net	98.35	56.06
CART	96.23	54.65

Table 2. Classification on test datasets

		DARPA1999 Week4,5		DARPA2000	
		0	1	0	1
C5.0	0	20042	2748	1066	124
	1	15	29	900	56
Neural Net	0	22460	330	1188	2
	1	29	15	941	15
CART	0	21926	864	1136	54
	1	38	6	920	36

Table 3. Average Training Time and Detection Time

	TrainingTime (hh:mm:ss)	DARPA1999 Week4,5(cpu Time)	DARPA2000 (cpu Time)
C5.0	0:00:40	1.56	0.17
Neural Net	1:06:46	1.40	0.15
CART	0:00:24	0.76	0.11

actually real alerts are regarded as false alerts; (0, 1)means that the actually false alerts are regarded as suspicious alerts; (1, 1) means that the actually real alerts is checked. Table3 describes training time and detection time based on three methods, and detection time is shown by cpu time.

According to the experiment result, we can draw some conclusions.

1) The accuracy of classification of the two methods is high, but Neural Net is a little better than CART, and C5.0 is third.
2) The time of model construction is different. Neural Net takes more time than C5.0 and CART, but the latter two is almost equal.
3) The time spent on verification is both in sec. level. But CART takes shortest than the other two. So we think that CART is more real-time than C5.0.

In short, because we think that the real-timeness is the most important for a practicable system, we mainly concern the real-timeness of a method besides accuracy. Although Neural net seems to perform a little better in both hit and miss rate than CART, CART can provides better support for the real-time requirement of INWMSS than other two methods and CART and C5.0 both can generate more readable and comprehensible rules. So we think that CART is more adaptive to INWMSS and we choose CART to construct the classification model.

2. Alert data correlation and attack prediction

Based on the output of self-adaptive data-processing algorithm, we refer to the traditional alert correlation algorithm which is on the basis of prerequisites and consequences of attacks [18]. We make a little improvement on the traditional algorithm. We add probability matching method based on alert attributes to the tradional alert correlation algorithm, and make it more suitable for those attacks which have the same source/destination addresses and ports. In other words, the improved algorithm not only correlates alert data, but also gets matching index based on probability matching. Finally the algorithm can generate intrusion scenario graphs.

Based on intrusion scenario graphs, the INWMSS can predict and analyze the potential attacks, so as to do active defense. The function of prediction is one of the main functions of INWMSS. Figure 6 describes two examples of scenario graph, which is extracted from the experiment.

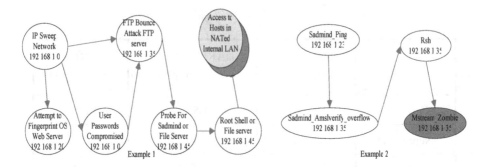

Fig. 6. Two Examples of Scenario Graph Extracted from the Experiment

4 Total Test Environment and Results for Prototype

Because of the limitation of conditions, total test of prototype and part of functions test only can be executed in a relatively simple network environment. The test network is described in figure 7. It consists of three routers, three Local Area Networks (include two Ethernets and one loop network), a lot of network security devices (such as IDS, Firewall, scanner) and several intelligent Agents. Three Local Area Networks respectively represent three domains, each domain has one domain agent and several normal agents.

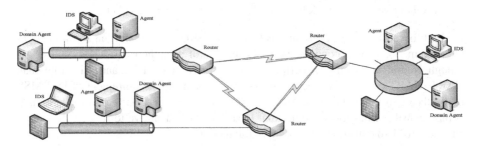

Fig. 7. Structure of Test Network

Figure 8 describes a relatively simple interface of the total warning center in the prototype. Now its function is simple and we will develop it further. The interface is designed for the network security managers to detect the situations of network protected, analyze the situations about Intrusion, and adjust the dangerous level about the network, so as managers can take actions to prevent attacks, predict attacks, and distribute commands to track attacks.

The emphasis of total test is the applicability of the prototype. We mainly test strong survivability of the prototype, alert data processing and generation of scenario graphs.

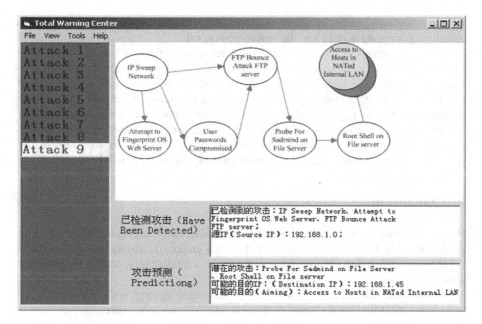

Fig. 8. The Interface of the Total Warning Center of the Pprototype

1. Test of strong survivability

Based on the result of previous experiment, we set the "deadtime" as 20s [19].Test of strong survivability consists of two steps.

● After a domain agent is destroyed artificially, we test whether the destroyed domain agent can be substituted successfully by a new normal agent in the same domain or not. This verifies whether the heart-beat monitoring program works or not. If the new picked-up domain agent's symbol becomes "D", the heart-beat program works. In addition, we test the communication between the new picked-up domain agent and other two domain agents. If the new domain agent updates its scenario graph base, we believe the new domain agent works.

● When we resume the destroyed domain agent, it becomes a normal agent. We test the resumed agent whether communicating with other agents in the same domain by detecting its symbol and its scenario graph base. If the symbol becomes "N" and its graph base is updated, the prototype is considered good.

2. Test of alert data processing and generation of scenario graphs

The test of data-processing and generation of scenario graphs is based on above-mentioned DARPA2000 datasets and real attack sequences similar to figure 6. We test whether intrusion scenario graphs can take on to the network security managers. If we can get scenario graphs like figure 6, the test is successful.

Through the tests, we can see that the Destroyed domain agent became a normal agent, its symbol is "N', and it can update its scenario graph base; the new picked-up domain agent change its symbol as "D", and it can communicate with other two domain agents and total warning center. The network security managers can get intrusion scenario graphs similar to figure 6. All situations show that the heart-beat monitoring program is right and the prototype is good.

Finally, the result of test shows that the intelligent Network-Warning Model with Strong-Survivability not only has a good theoretical basis, but also has good practicability. The model can reduce and fuse alerts, generate good intrusion scenarios, and has better warning capability based on intrusion scenario. The model can provide network security managers with simple and comprehensible scenario graphs, which can greatly decrease managers' burden. Of course, because of the relatively simple test environment, the prototype is not interfered greatly. So how to optimize the model and its algorithms to fit complicated network environment will be challenging.

5 Conclusion

We propose an intelligent network-warning model with strong-survivability. The model not only fits large-scale network, but also emphasize strong survivability and intelligence, which make the model to process alerts intelligently, predict the potential attack and increase the system survivability.

Although the model presented in this paper aimed at large-scale network, to be used in practical large-scale network, there is a lot of work to be done:

1) Because the alert correlation algorithm based on prerequisites and consequences of attacks depends on known attack types, and it can not discover the new unknown attack types, we need develop an intelligent algorithm, which can learn from the known attacks and scenario graphs to discover new attack types.
2) To develop an algorithm on tracking attack sources. The algorithm will make the model to actively track and prevent attacks.
3) In order to increase practicality, we need further improve the real-timeness for the model.
4) Because of the limitation of the heart-beat monitoring program in distance, we need enhance the strong-survivability mechanism for the practical large-scale networks.
5) To develop a multifunctional and more practicable interface of total warning center for managers.

References

1. Hu, H., Zhang, Y.: The Study of Large Scale Networks Intrusion Detection and Warning System. Journal of National University of Defence Technology 25(1), 21–25 (2003)
2. Sun, J., Zeng, H.: Network Security Testing and Alarming. Computer Engineering 27(7), 109–111 (2001)
3. Li, Z., Li, W.: Research on Early-warning and Quarantine System of Large-scale Network Intrusion. Application Research of computers 21(12), 100–104 (2004)
4. Zhang, X., Qin, Z., Liu, J.: Research on the Network Security Architecture for Distributed Early Warning. Computer Applications 24(5), 36–39 (2004)
5. Bakar, N.A., Belaton, B.: Towards Implementing Intrusion Alert Quality Framework. In: DFMA 2005, pp. 198–205 (2005)

6. Curry, D., Debar, H.: Intrusion Detection Message Exchange Format Data Model and Extensible Markup Language (XML) Document Type Definition. draft-itetf-idwg-idmef-xml-03.txt (February 2001)
7. Julisch, K.: Clustering Intrusion Detection Alarms to Support Root Cause Analysis. ACM Transactions on Information and System Security 6(4) (2003)
8. Wang, J., Lee, I.: Measuring False-Positive by Automated Real-Time correlated Hacking Behavior Analysis. In: Davida, G.I., Frankel, Y. (eds.) ISC 2001. LNCS, vol. 2200, pp. 512–535. Springer, Heidelberg (2001)
9. Law, K.H., Kwok, L.F.: IDS False Alarm Filtering Using KNN Classifier. In: Lim, C.H., Yung, M. (eds.) WISA 2004. LNCS, vol. 3325, pp. 114–121. Springer, Heidelberg (2005)
10. Tadeusz, P.: Using Adaptive Alert Classification to Reduce False Positives in Intrusion Detection. In: Jonsson, E., Valdes, A., Almgren, M. (eds.) RAID 2004. LNCS, vol. 3224, pp. 102–124. Springer, Heidelberg (2004)
11. Shin, M.S., Kim, E.H.: False Alarm Classification Model for Network-Based Intrusion Detection System. In: Yang, Z.R., Yin, H., Everson, R.M. (eds.) IDEAL 2004. LNCS, vol. 3177, pp. 259–265. Springer, Heidelberg (2004)
12. Su, L., Hou, C., Dai, Z.: Alarm Correlation based on Neural Net. Journal of Beijing Institute of Technology(Natural Science Edition) 22(3), 297–299 (2002)
13. Ji, W., Zhou, A., Zhang, L.: Application of C5.0 Algorithm in Passing Ball Training of RoboCup. Journal of Software 13(2), 245–249 (2002)
14. Zhang, J., Han, G., Zhang, W.: Application of C5.0 Algorithm in Passing Ball Training of RoboCup. Compuer Simulation 23(4), 131–134 (2006)
15. Lewis, R.J.: An Introduction to Classification and Regression Tree (CART) Analysis. The 2000 Annual Meeting of the Society for Academic Emergency Medicine in San Francisco, California (2000)
16. DARPA 2000 intrusion detection evaluation datasets. Lincoln Lab MIT (2000), http://www.ll.mit.edu/IST/ideval/data/2000/2000_data_index.html
17. DARPA Intrusion Detection Evaluation datasets, MIT Lincoln Laboratory, http://www.ll.mit.edu/IST/ideval/2000/1999_data_index.html
18. Ning, P., Cui, Y., Reeves, D.S., Xu, D.: Techniques and tools for analyzing intrusion alerts. ACM Trans. Inf. Syst. Secur 7(2), 274–318 (2004)
19. Yang, B., Hu, H.: Research on fine-Grained equal dynamic migration technique based WAN. Compuer Engineer and Science 26(2), 4–7 (2004)

Running on Karma –
P2P Reputation and Currency Systems

Sherman S.M. Chow

Department of Computer Science
Courant Institute of Mathematical Sciences
New York University, NY 10012, USA
schow@cs.nyu.edu

Abstract. Peer-to-peer (P2P) systems allow users to share resources with little centralized control. Malicious users can abuse the system by contributing polluted resources. Moreover, selfish users may just connect for their own benefits without donating any resources. The concepts of reputation and currency give possible approaches to address these problems. However, to implement these ideas is non-trivial, due to the non-existence of a single trusted party. Existing works circumvent this by placing trust assumption on certain nodes of an overlay network. This work presents a new reputation system and a new currency system. Our designs are simple thanks to the full use of the trust assumption.

Keywords: Decentralized systems, peer-to-peer, reputation, currency, micropayments, free riding, Byzantine agreement.

1 Introduction

In a peer-to-peer (P2P) network, every user is playing the roles of server and client simultaneously, i.e. there is a minimum central control. The last decade demonstrated many successful applications of the P2P computing model. The most popular one may be P2P file sharing, such as BitTorrent [5], Gnutella [12], etc. Thanks to the network's flat structure, P2P systems scale very well with the number of nodes. However, the lack of centralized control makes P2P systems suffer from many security problems.

Since every user can play the role of the "server" and share their resources (e.g. music files) to others, malicious users can abuse the system by contributing polluted resources. On the other hand, P2P systems suffer from the "free rider" problem, which means users only connect to the network for the resources they want, but not contribute any resources. A traffic study has shown that 70% of Gnutella network's users (at the time of the study) are not donating any file at all [1].

You will not ask for a file from someone who is notorious in polluting the network. This is where a reputation system comes to play. Generally speaking, a reputation system establishes trust among members of a community where each member does not have prior knowledge of each other, by integrating feedback from the peers to conjecture the trustworthiness of other peers.

F. Bao et al. (Eds.): CANS 2007, LNCS 4856, pp. 146–158, 2007.
© Springer-Verlag Berlin Heidelberg 2007

To fight against free riders, a natural solution is to offer users some "tokens" for their contributions, which enables them to retrieve their wanted resources at a later stage. Old approaches realize this concept in the software level. For example, KaZaA uses a measure of participation level [17], defined by upload/download ratio and the integrity rating, to prioritize among peers during periods of high demand. The participation level is stored locally. As one may expect, cracking tools are available. What we need is some kind of currency or barter that is transferable for exchanging resources, i.e. an electronic currency system over P2P networks.

1.1 Our Contribution

Putting a reputation system or an electronic currency system over P2P networks is non-trivial, due to the non-existence of a trusted party. Existing works circumvent this by placing a trust assumption on certain nodes of an overlay network. However, these solutions are rather inefficient, in terms of bandwidth or computational requirements.

Since we place trust on some nodes in the network anyway, why don't we fully utilize this trust assumption to avoid unnecessary operations? This work tries to make full use of these trusted nodes, to propose two simple and efficient systems.

1. Simple P2P Reputation System from Byzantine Agreement (SPRBA): Current approaches either require cryptographic schemes that cannot be realized in a P2P network (e.g. [9]), or require contacting with every online node to get responses about one's behavior history (e.g. [6]). The latter approach is expensive in terms of storage capacity and bandwidth. Moreover, it is difficult to enforce security in a large-scale dynamic system. In the face of a sybil attack that returns many negative comments, the security of the system depends on whether most of the responding nodes are trustworthy. On the other hand, SPRBA just places trust on a smaller set of nodes that are determined by a cryptographic hash function.
2. Simplified Karma (Karma$^+$): Off-line Karma [8] is a completely decentralized currency system for dynamic P2P networks. Extensive use of digital signatures is used to certify the transfer of electronic coins (e-coins), which means that the size of a e-coin will eventually get huge[1]. To resolve this issue, it is assumed that a set of nodes in the overlay network chosen by a cryptographic hash function will reduce the coin size by re-issuing signatures. Since the new signatures certify the current ownership of the coin, these re-issuing nodes are assumed trustworthy. If such an assumption is made, why don't we just assume these nodes to take the role of a "bank"? This gives the underlying idea of our proposed Karma$^+$.

---

[1] Even an aggregate signature scheme [3] is used; the messages being signed must be stored, which makes the coin bulky.

2   System Model

2.1   Reputation System

Our system only cares about the retrieval, casting and maintenance of the votes. Issues like how the reputation is modeled (e.g. [10]) and assessed (e.g. [11]), and whether a bad vote is cast even the resource is good, are beyond the scope of this work.

Our general mechanism is as follows. Before initiating the download, *requestors* can assess the reliability of the sources by polling peers (*vote maintainers*, or VM). After the transfer, the requestors now take the role of voters, returning their opinions to the peers for later retrieval by others. We also discuss how these votes are maintained in face of offline VMs.

Apart from the obvious constraint of no centralized control, our system should satisfy the following properties.

1. *Scalability.* Transaction cost should be independent of the size of the network. For example, our system would not flood the whole network.
2. *Load balance.* The overhead incurred by our system should be evenly distributed over the nodes, on average.
3. *Robustness.* Our system should be robust against denial-of-service attack. For example, the adversary cannot manipulate the protocol messages to turn the internal state distributively held by different nodes into an inconsistent state.

2.2   Currency System

There are only three components in our currency system: minting, spending and double-spending detection. Users first mint their own e-coins. In spending, the ownership of a coin is transferred. When a coin is spent, the receiver should check whether the coin has been double-spent. It is possible to come up with a proof when some user double-spends his coin. In additional to the above properties for a P2P reputation system, the objectives of our e-coin system are:

1. *Efficient verification.* It is efficient to verify the validity of the coin (e.g. whether it has been double-spent). This also implies the e-coin size should be small.
2. *Oblivious transaction history.* The transaction history related to the coin should not be included in the coin.

Other issues, like coin stripping and the fair exchange of coins and resources, are outside our scope. We note that double-spending *prevention* is generally not possible for an offline currency system, without tamper-proof hardware.

2.3   Overlay Network

This work assumes the existence of an underlying overlay network that provides primitives for both user look-up and message routing. In such a network, every node is assigned a uniform random identifier $u \in \mathcal{U}$ from an identifier space, and one can always efficiently and reliably compute the neighbor set $\aleph(u)$, which consists of all currently online nodes *close* to an identifier u. The exact definition of "close" depends on the actual overlay network one is using, but it is one of the essential and well-defined components of overlay network. Readers are suggested to refer routing overlays like CAN [13], Chord [15], Pastry [14] and Tapestry [16], as reviewed in [4].

We assume an ideal situation for the updating of routing information, where the overlay network instantaneously detects any change in the network topology. This depends on how well the underlying overlay network emulates this ideal functionality by a discrete approximation from constantly fingering to see whether a joined node has left. We also assume joining and leaving are atomic operations.

Finally, we assume that the overlay network has a blacklist mechanism. Whenever a fraud is detected, a user can somehow submit a proof of it to the overlay network and a blacklist will then be safely distributed.

In the rest of the paper, we use a cryptographic hash function $h : \{0,1\}^* \to \mathcal{U}$ to map an arbitrary bit-string to an element in the identifier space $\mathcal{U}$ of the overlay network. We use the notation of $\aleph^*(y) = \aleph(h(y))$ to denote the "neighbor set" corresponding to the bit-string y.

2.4 Certificate Authority

In Karma$^+$, we assume every user has his/her own public key and private key pair (PK, SK) along with a certificate certifying the binding between the public key and a node identifier. A certificate authority (CA) is only needed when a new user joins the system, and no other communication with the CA is needed. We require the CA to perform any task that substantiates the assumption required in the unforgeability of the underlying signature scheme, e.g. the knowledge of secret key assumption. No CA is required in SPRBA.

2.5 Threat Model

Our basic threat model assumes the network has a total of n users, and at most t of which are under the adversary's control.

For an overlay network, one can actually make a distinction between adding a user to the network and compromising an existing user. Let c $(0 \le c \le t)$ be an integer denoting the number of users corrupted by the adversary after they join the overlay network. An adversary who can compromise whoever he wishes means $c = t$, while $c = 0$ means all he can do is injecting random users. We also assume the adversary cannot make excessively many nodes to join the system. In practice, this can be done by requiring a node to compute a time-intensive operation (e.g. [7]) for each joining. Looking ahead, this is also the way an e-coin is minted in Karma$^+$.

3   Related Work

3.1   A Reputocracy System

A "reputocracy" system is presented in [9], which is a reputation system based on electronic voting from homomorphic encryption and storage enforcement protocols. The votes are for the resource requesters to make comments which affect the reputation of a resource contributor. The enforcement protocol is for showing a file of a certain complexity has been transmitted. We discuss this work to exemplify that some required cryptographic schemes cannot be easily deployed in a P2P setting.

Reputation is maintained by the votes that one receives. These votes are stored by the nodes responsible for tallying, which are called the tallying center. The tallying center of a node is determined by some globally-known hash function, i.e. different nodes will have different tallying centers, instead of a single global one. After a file transfer is done, the tallying center uses the storage enforcement protocol to get the cost of the communication $ > 0$. Then, the requester will cast an encrypted vote that is either +$ or −$, depending on whether he/she is satisfied with the file obtained. A zero-knowledge proof of the vote is either +$ or −$ is prepared. The tallying center has no idea whether a vote is good.

Problems: Note that only a single node is assigned as the vote maintainer, thus attack is relatively easy. Besides, it is not specified that who is responsible for the decryption of the tally. A natural choice is the tallying center, but it is meaningless to have the zero-knowledge proof in this case since he/she can decrypt anyway. Moreover, to the best of our knowledge, e-voting systems require the use of a bulletin board, even for those that are "self-tallying". Such a bulletin board is essentially a public-broadcast channel *with memory*, which is costly, if not unavailable, in a P2P network.

3.2   P2PRep

P2PRep [6] is a reputation system enabled by a peer review process. Each node keeps track of and shares with others the information about the reputation of their peers. Reputation sharing is based on a distributed polling protocol. After locating a list of servants who owns the wanted resources, the requester polls his/her peers about the reputation of servants in this list. Peers wishing to respond send back a reply, then the requestor selects a subset of them and contacts them directly. Their replies are integrated to make a decision. Additional mechanism can be added to poll for servant credibility, representing the trustworthiness of a servant in providing correct votes.

Problems: The requesters just ask around about one's reputation, and these broadcast messages occupy the network bandwidth significantly. Moreover, one's reputation depends on whether the peers in the previous transaction remain online. In the face of the free rider problem, this reliance is not desirable.

Regarding security, no mechanism is controlling who can respond. It is entirely possible that a whole bunch of malicious nodes respond with negative comments.

The suggested solution in [6] is to have "suspects identification", by computing cluster of voters whose characteristics suggest that they may have been created by a single malicious user. However, it depends on how good the clustering algorithm distinguishes between "consistent votes for bad behavior from many users" and "forged votes from a single malicious user". Even such an algorithm exists, it is implemented in the software level. Nothing prevents the adversary from re-engineering the algorithm and tailor-making bad votes accordingly.

3.3   Off-Line Karma

Off-line Karma [8] is a decentralized electronic currency system. A coin is minted by finding a collision of a hash function (of "small" output domain size) [2] with hash input including the owner of the coin, a serial number and the current time. At the very beginning, a user finds collisions and prepares a list of coins. Specifically, the user needs to find a y such that $H(U||sn||ts) = H'(y)$, where $H(\cdot)$ and $H'(\cdot)$ are two different hash functions, U is his node identifier, sn is a serial number and ts is a time stamp.

Transfer of a coin (i.e. spending) is done by a chain of signing. Suppose y is a coin corresponding to node A (i.e. $H'(y) = H(A||sn'||ts')$ for some serial number sn' and time stamp ts'), A gives it to another node B by signing on $(y, A \to B, z_A)$ where z_A is a random nonce. B spends this coin with U_C by signing on $(y, B \to C, z_B)$. Everyone can verify that C is the current owner of the coin since it is originally owned by A, A has certified the transfer $A \to B$ and B has certified $B \to C$.

As a result of a series of spending, the coin size will get huge eventually. To slim it, *re-minting* is done. Re-minting party is the neighbor set of the coin $\aleph(y)$ (i.e. treating the coin as a user) of the overlay network. *All* of them sign on y and the current time to certify the current ownership.

The timestamp associated with a coin also serves as an expiry time. Re-minting must be done before expiration. Double-spending is detected in re-minting. The nodes in the set $\aleph^*(y)$ will check whether there exists two different signatures signed by the same party. A random nonce is introduced to avoid the uncertainty about who is the traitor when a user spends the same coin twice with the same user.

Problems: Before re-minting, the coin size is large. One needs to do a series of signature verifications to verify the current ownership of a coin. Yet, these computations do not help double-spending detection at all. A shorter time frame can make the re-minting happen more often, but keep in mind that one needs to contact every node in $\aleph^*(y)$ for re-minting. On one hand, the coin may expire before every such node can be reached. On the other hand, it gives a higher computational burden (to verify all signatures associated with the coin and issue a new one) to these nodes.

Double-spending can only be detected at the stage of re-minting, but not when the coin is spent. To make the double-spending detection "happens earlier", the suggested solution in [8] is to ask each user to spend a coin that is the nearest (in the context of neighbor set) to the one whom he wants to initiate a transaction.

However, a malicious user who wants to double-spend a coin can do anything deviated from the protocol. Only having good users following such a suggestion is clearly not sufficient to make double-spending detection any earlier.

Finally, the transaction history is included in every coin, which violates the requirement of oblivious transaction history and is undesirable.

4 SPRBA – Simple P2P Reputation System from Byzantine Agreement

The main components of our proposed SPRBA are as follows.

4.1 Retrieval

Suppose A is the requestor and B is a candidate who owns some resources A wants. A performs the following:

1. A computes $\aleph^*(B)$ to get the VM groups maintaining B's reputation,
2. A sends an enquiry to each node in $\aleph^*(B)$ for B's reputation.
3. A makes a decision according to the information received (e.g. taking the majority).

Suppose a node C is being asked for B's reputation, C first performs a (one-time) verification to confirm his/her membership in the set $\aleph^*(B)$. If C has no record about B, he/she just returns so. From this point, C knows the list of VMs for B, which will be used in the maintenance phase.

4.2 Casting

After the file transfer, A now wants to cast a vote about B. The voting information will include his/her identity A, the current time ts and other auxiliary information (e.g. the name of the file being transferred). What A needs to do is just broadcasting his/her vote to $\aleph^*(B)$. The consistency functionality we want from the broadcast is ensured by a Byzantine agreement protocol among the nodes in $\aleph^*(B)$.

4.3 Maintenance

VMs may go offline. When they go online next time, they should catch up with other VMs. The first retrieval request gives the list of the "partners" in maintaining the reputation of someone. Synchronization is done by identifying which vote is missing in one's own record but exists in a threshold portion of the partners.

4.4 Analysis

Our system is scalable in the sense that no flooding of the whole network is needed to retrieve one's reputation. Due to the uniformity of the hash function's output, the incurred computational burden and the storage load are uniformly distributed across the network. Thus load balance is achieved.

There is a subtle difference between a resource requestor retrieving the reputation and VMs retrieving the reputation. For the former case, it just affects the one-time decision of whether a transaction should be carried. On the other hand, VMs do it for updating their own record to truly reflect the reputation of those nodes they are responsible for, which affects all the future reputation requests. Consider a malicious voter who sends different votes to different VMs, VMs who were offline before have no idea which vote is the "real" one during synchronization. Eventually, nothing useful can be inferred from the votes maintained distributively across the VMs. This is why Byzantine agreement is needed for each vote.

Byzantine agreement is a rather costly procedure, so we should keep the size of the VM group $\aleph^*(B)$ as small as possible. However, this parameter also governs the probability for the adversary to succeed in biasing the reputation.

Suppose r denotes the number of nodes output by $\aleph^*(B)$, f denotes the percentage of malicious nodes in this set of r nodes ($0 \leq f \leq 1$). Under the basic threat model that the adversary can only inject random nodes to the network; if 50% majority is the rule to make a decision, the probability for an adversary to succeed, i.e. having more than a half of nodes under his control, is given by $C_{r/2}^r(f(1-f))^{r/2}$. Depending on the actual scenario, says the security level we want, we should tune r accordingly.

5   Karma$^+$ – Simple Offline Electronic Currency System

Utilizing SPRBA, we can actually realize a simple electronic currency system. Instead of having the node-group chosen by the function $\aleph^*(\cdot)$ to manage the reputation of a node, we require the node-group to certify the current ownership of a coin. However, different from the reputation system that every node can cast a vote, there is only one node that can "change" the current ownership of a coin – the coin owner. We thus require cryptographic primitives providing authentication and non-repudiation to make it possible, i.e. digital signature schemes.

If signatures are used, Byzantine agreement is not necessary in our case since the recipient of the coin will actively check whether he/she is the new owner of the coin, and signatures signing on different messages can be used as a proof of misbehavior.

With these ideas in mind, our system turns out to be a simplified version of Off-line karma. We assume all nodes in the P2P network get the same set of system parameters, e.g. the maximum number of coins one can mint, the description of the hash function, and the signature scheme to be used, etc. The main components of our proposed SPRBA are as follows.

5.1   Minting

Minting of a coin involves finding a hash function collision [2] similar as that in Off-line Karma [8].

The user needs to find a $p + q$-long bit-string $y \in \{0,1\}^{(p+q)}$ such that[2] $H(x) = H'(y)$, for $x = (U||sn)$, where U is his node identifier of length p, sn is a bit string denoting a coin's serial number of length $|sn| = q$. This length restriction, together with the logic governing how the nodes managing this coin is determined, limits every user to mint up to 2^q karma coins.

The node identifier and the serial number uniquely determine the coin. The coin is defined as $\langle x, y \rangle$. For brevity, we call it "coin y". In contrast to Off-line Karma, a coin does not include the timestamp denoting the minting time.

5.2 Spending

We start by the case that a newly-minted coin is spent, followed by the case that a coin is spent by the one who did not mint it.

Suppose node A is spending a coin $\langle x, y \rangle$ minted by him/her with another node B. A sends y to each node in $\aleph^*(y)$ and notifies them B is now the coin owner of y by signing y together with a current timestamp ts.

The current owner of coin y is determined by the record held by the node-group $\aleph^*(y)$. We can view the node-group $\aleph^*(y)$ is performing the bank function of the coin y. They will keep track of the current coin ownership. We call these nodes the "bank-nodes".

Even though a bank-node obtains the collision pair from someone else and is the authority to say who is the current owner of the coin. It is not true that a bank-node of a coin cannot be the initial owner of a coin, (when he/she is lucky enough to mint a coin y having the node-group $\aleph^*(y)$ including him/herself). The reason is that the minting node is specified in the x component of the coin. No other node would mint a coin on other's behalf. Even a malicious bank-node claims the ownership of a coin after obtained a collision pair $\langle x, y \rangle$ from some other node is not convincing since the node identifier in x does not match.

Each bank-node needs to check whether x is in the correct form (i.e. including A's identifier and a bit-string sn of length q), $\langle x, y \rangle$ really gives a collision, and A gives a signature that signs on the coin, the recipient's node identifier, and a recent enough timestamp, i.e. $(y||B||ts)$. If all the verifications go through, the coin $\langle x, y \rangle$ is then sent to B. B is convinced he/she is the new owner if responses from a threshold number of bank-nodes are obtained.

In the second case, the spender is not the original owner. Suppose B is the spender and C is the "merchant" that B is dealing with. B signs on the coin with the recipient C's identifier and a new timestamp, and gives the coin to C. C contacts each bank-node in $\aleph^*(y)$ to see whether B is the current owner of the coin. Specifically, this is done by taking the latest ownership status purported by $\aleph^*(y)$ as the current ownership status of the coin.

---

[2] Instead of using two different hash functions, one can actually use a single hash function by appending x with a bit 0 and y with a bit 1. Otherwise, an attack exploiting the symmetry is possible so that a single coin can be interpreted in two ways corresponding to different minting-node.

5.3   Maintaining the Current Ownership

In a dynamic P2P network, the bank-nodes of a coin may not be online at the same time. Each of them should keep the signatures certifying the transfer of ownership, until a threshold number of the bank-nodes got the same set of signatures and update their own records. In this way, the storage requirement on the bank-node is minimized. The latest ownership can be easily identified since the signature is binding with a timestamp. It can be considered as a hybrid approach that combines a pure-updating of the coin ownership and the signature chain approach used in Off-line Karma.

5.4   Double-Spending Detection

Double spending means the current owner of a coin spends it at two different users. To do so, the double-spender must have signed on two different messages specifying different recipients, which give a cryptographic evidence of the misbehavior.

On the other hand, someone who wants to "spend" the coin once he/she owned will not be treated as a double-spending. It will be treated as just an invalid request instead since it is essentially the same thing as having a random node claiming for the ownership of someone else's coin. Depending on the level of service one desires, the signature can also be submitted to the blacklist mechanism of the network to impose a certain kind of penalty on the one making the invalid request.

On the other hand, a bank-node may be malicious in falsely-accusing someone has double-spent. An accusation thus requires a signature by a bank-node on a message stating the current owner as well. If any abnormality is observed, one can simply forward the signature to all other bank-nodes for further investigation of whether a bank-node is being malicious or just not-up-to-date.

5.5   Efficiency Analysis

Load balancing follows from the uniform distribution of the hash output. Scalability can be seen from the simple design of our system. We require no flooding of the network and no complex operations other than minting of the coin. The complexity involved in minting a coin is actually a good thing to hinder the extent of sybil attack.

No heavy cryptographic operations are involved other than signature generation and verification. The current state-of-art signatures offer a short signature size that makes the protocol bandwidth-efficient. In contrast with Off-line Karma [8], each node only needs to verify a single signature instead of a series of them.

The storage and complexity requirements of the bank-nodes are minimal. Each node needs to sign every time the current owner of the coin is about to change, but it can always be pre-computed. Besides, the message to be signed is short, in contrast with the signature on the huge coin in Off-line Karma. It is true that the bank-node needs to perform signature verification every time the coin ownership is changed. The total number of signature verification is the same as

that in the re-minting phase in Off-line Karma. However, the computational cost
is amortized in our case.

5.6   Security Analysis

It is easy to see that as long as there exists one honest node with up-to-date information among the bank-nodes, security is guaranteed. Here we assume the extended
threat model that t nodes are controlled by the adversary and c of them are corrupted after they joined the overlay network (i.e. after they became the bank-nodes
of a certain coin). Our analysis is similar to that of Off-line Karma [8].

Theorem 1. *Let r be the size of the bank-node set $\aleph^*(y)$ of a coin y. If $r > \gamma s + c$
for some constant γ, the probability that $\aleph^*(y)$ contains no honest nodes is less
than 2^{-s}.*

Proof. By assumption, the adversary can compromise c nodes in the set $\aleph^*(y)$.
All we need to show the probability that the remaining $r - c$ nodes happen to be
taken from the remaining $t - c$ corrupted nodes to be included in the set $\aleph^*(y)$.
Let X be the random variable of the number of honest nodes in the set $\aleph^*(y)$,
we have

$$
\begin{aligned}
\Pr[X = 0] &= \frac{C_{r-c}^{t-c}}{C_{r-c}^{n-c}} \\
&= \frac{(t-c)!/((r-c)!(t-r)!)}{(n-c)!/((r-c)!(n-r)!)} \\
&< \left(\frac{t-c}{n-c}\right)^{(r-c)}
\end{aligned}
$$

Since we want to upper-bound the success probability of the adversary by
2^{-s}, note that $\frac{t-c}{n-c} < 1$, we have

$$
\left(\frac{t-c}{n-c}\right)^{(r-c)} < 2^{-s}
$$
$$
r - c \geq \log_{(t-c)/(n-c)} 2^{-s}
$$
$$
r \geq -s(\log_{(t-c)/(n-c)} 2) + c
$$

Setting $\gamma = -(\log_{(t-c)/(n-c)} 2)$ completes the proof.

5.7   Improvements over Off-Line Karma

Apart from the efficiency gain like smaller coin size as revealed in the previous
analysis sections, Karma$^+$ enjoys the following features over Off-line Karma.

No Coin Expiration. Timestamp is used in Off-line Karma for expiring the
coin, and it forces the re-minting and let the re-minting party to have a chance
to do double-spending detection. In Karma$^+$, a coin would not expire so the
situation that a coin cannot be re-minted before its expiration is avoided. Besides,
Karma$^+$ detects double-spending in every transaction, but not well after the coin
is double-spent as in Off-line Karma.

Limit on the Maximum Number of Minting. Off-line Karma aims to limiting the number of coin one can mint by imposing a maximum length on the serial numbers. It is claimed that (U, sn) uniquely determines a coin. However, in addition to the owner identifier U and the serial number sn , time stamp ts is another varying factor. Note that the bank-node group $\aleph^*(U||sn||ts)$ is unlikely to contain a node that also appears in $\aleph^*(U||sn||ts')$ for a timestamp $ts' \neq ts$. It is difficult to discover two coins in the world are actually sharing the same U and sn. The number of coin one can mint is thus limited within a time period, and depends on the granularity of the time periods. However, the time-complexity of finding a collision already imposes an inherent limit on the number of coins one can mint at a given time.

Since the expiration mechanism is not necessary in our system, we can remove the inclusion of the timestamp in finding a collision pair, which means (U, sn) really serves as a unique identifier of a coin. In this way, we pose a limit on the maximum number of coins one can mint.

Higher Security in a Dynamic Network. Karma$^+$ works better in the case of dynamic network when compared with Off-line Karma [8]. The security of Off-line Karma depends on the nodes that are responsible for re-minting at the re-minting time, since the re-minting of the coin is done by asking all those nodes to give signatures to certify the new ownership of the coin. One has no information about the state of the network at that time, so an adversary may have unfairly constructed a re-mint set with only nodes that are under his control, giving signatures certifying himself, and claiming all other nodes were offline at that time. Karma$^+$ does not have this problem, since it is the verifier who computes this set and contacts the nodes according to the protocol for his own good.

6 Conclusion

We have presented two completely decentralized systems to address the pollution problem and the free-rider problem in peer-to-peer resources sharing applications. One is a reputation system and the other is an electronic currency system. Our systems outperform existing systems of similar functionalities under similar trust assumptions. Our simple design and efficiency gain are obtained from making full use of the trusted nodes.

Acknowledgements

Thanks to Lakshminarayanan Subramanian for his comments and support. Also thanks to Joël Alwen, Saurabh Kumar and Ning Ma for the discussions.

References

1. Adar, E., Huberman, B.A.: Free Riding on Gnutella. First Monday 5(10) (October 2000), http://firstmonday.org/issues/issue5_10/adar
2. Back, A.: Hashcash - a Denial of Service Counter Measure, http://www.hashcash.org/papers/hashcash.pdf

3. Boneh, D., Gentry, C., Lynn, B., Shacham, H.: Aggregate and Verifiably Encrypted Signatures from Bilinear Maps. In: Biham, E. (ed.) EUROCRPYT 2003. LNCS, vol. 2656, pp. 416–432. Springer, Heidelberg (2003)
4. Castro, M., Druschel, P., Ganesh, A., Rowstron, A., Wallach, D.S.: Secure Routing for Structured Peer-to-Peer Overlay Networks. SIGOPS Operating Systems Review 36/SI, 299–314 (2002)
5. Cohen, B.: Incentives Build Robustness in BitTorrent. In: Workshop on Economics of Peer-to-peer Systems (2003)
6. Damiani, E., De Capitani di Vimercati, S., Paraboschi, S., Samarati, P., Violante, F.: A Reputation-based Approach for Choosing Reliable Resources in Peer-to-Peer Networks. Computer and Communications Security 2002 , 207–216 (2002)
7. Dwork, C., Goldberg, A., Naor, M.: On Memory-Bound Functions for Fighting Spam. In: Boneh, D. (ed.) CRYPTO 2003. LNCS, vol. 2729, pp. 426–444. Springer, Heidelberg (2003)
8. Garcia, F.D., Hoepman, J.-H.: Off-line Karma: A Decentralized Currency for Peer-to-peer and Grid Applications. In: Ioannidis, J., Keromytis, A.D., Yung, M. (eds.) ACNS 2005. LNCS, vol. 3531, pp. 364–377. Springer, Heidelberg (2005)
9. Garcia-Martinez, A., Chuang, J.: A Cryptographic Reputation Scheme for Peer-to-peer Networks, http://citeseer.ist.psu.edu/550626.html
10. Gupta, M., Judge, P., Ammar, M.: A Reputation System for Peer-to-Peer Networks. In: NOSSDAV 2003. Network and Operating Systems Support for Digital Audio and Video, pp. 144–152 (2003)
11. Kamvar, S.D., Schlosser, M.T., Garcia-Molina, H.: The Eigentrust Algorithm for Reputation Management in P2P Networks. In: World Wide Web Conference 2003, pp. 640–651 (2003)
12. Kirk, P.: Gnutella, http://rfc-gnutella.sourceforge.net
13. Ratnasamy, S., Francis, P., Handley, M., Karp, R., Shenker, S.: A Scalable Content-Addressable Network. Computer Communication Review 31(4), 161–172
14. Rowstron, A., Druschel, P.: Pastry: Scalable, Distributed Object Location and Routing for Large-Scale Peer-to-peer Systems. In: Guerraoui, R. (ed.) Middleware 2001. LNCS, vol. 2218, pp. 329–350. Springer, Heidelberg (2001)
15. Stoica, I., Morris, R., Karger, D., Kaashoek, M.F., Balakrishnan, H.: Chord: A Scalable Peer-to-peer Lookup Service for Internet Applications. In: SIGCOMM 2001, pp. 149–160
16. Zhao, B.Y., Huang, L., Rhea, S.C., Stribling, J., Joseph, A.D., Kubiatowicz, J.D.: Tapestry: A Global-Scale Overlay for Rapid Service Deployment. IEEE J-SAC 22(1), 41–53 (2004)
17. KaZaA.com. The Guide - The Glossary: Participation Level, Available at http://www.kazaa.com/us/help/glossary/participation_ratio.htm

Generic Combination of Public Key Encryption with Keyword Search and Public Key Encryption

Rui Zhang and Hideki Imai

Research Center for Information Security (RCIS)
National Institute of Advanced Industrial Science and Technology, AIST
{r-zhang,h-imai}@aist.go.jp

Abstract. In this paper, we study the problem of secure integrating public key encryption with keyword search (PEKS) with public key data encryption (PKE). We argue the previous security model is not complete regarding keyword privacy and the previous constructions are secure only in the random oracle model. We solve these problems by first defining a new security model, then give a generic construction which is secure in the new security model without random oracles. Our construction is based on secure PEKS and tag-KEM/DEM schemes and achieves modular design. We also point some applications and extensions for our construction. For example, instantiate our construction with proper components, we have a concrete scheme without random oracles, whose performance is even competitive to the previous schemes with random oracles.

1 Introduction

Public key encryption with keyword search (PEKS) [7] is very useful to provide the functionality of "searching on encrypted data" for public key cryptosystems. For instance, it can be used to build a gateway to route an encrypted email without knowing the content. We briefly review this mechanism here. Let (pk, sk) be Alice's public/secret key pair. Bob encrypts his message (email body) m with a public key encryption (PKE) scheme under Alice's public key pk and let's call the encrypted email σ. Bob also encrypts a keyword w using PEKS, under Alice's public key pk and let's call the encrypted keyword τ. The resulting ciphertext $c = \tau||\sigma$ will be sent to Alice's email server. Alice is able to specify a few keywords, and upon receiving a trapdoor t_w associated with a keyword w from Alice, the server can check whether τ encrypts w. Then if the keyword is "urgent", the server sends c to Alice's mobile phone, and if the keyword is "lunch", the server sends c to Alice's desktop to be read later. The security of PEKS is that the server should not know anything beyond the keyword. Readers are recommended to refer [7] and the references thereafter for details.

The security requirements discussed in [7,1] have considered semantic security of encryption of keywords against a powerful adversary that adaptively corrupts

F. Bao et al. (Eds.): CANS 2007, LNCS 4856, pp. 159–174, 2007.

gateways. Since a PEKS scheme cannot be used alone but have to be paired with a public key encryption (PKE) scheme, we have to consider the security of the whole system rather than separate components. Hereafter we refer the integrated scheme as PEKS/PKE. Unfortunately, secure PEKS and secure PKE schemes may not remain secure when they are composed together, which was pointed out by Baek, Safavi-Naini and Susilo [3]. Basically, they gave a counterexample as follows: When an adversary observes a PEKS/PKE ciphertext $\tau \| \sigma$, it can produce another valid ciphertext $\tau' \| \sigma$, where τ' is a valid tag under different keyword. Querying $\tau' \| \sigma$ to a decryption oracle, the adversary obtains the plaintext m.

We remark that the above attack is realistic in practice, since for most encrypted email systems, headers of an email remain even after routing, and the decryption is done without integrity check on the header. On the other hand, for keyword privacy, nothing was considered against chosen keyword/ciphertext attack before this work.

Known Solutions and Their Limitations. As mentioned in [3], a trivial solution may be simply appending an authentication tag generated from a message authentication code (MAC), with a shared key between the sender and receiver. While it works, the solution destroys the asymmetric nature of public key encryption. Another possible solution is to attach a signature on the ciphertext. However, this requires the sender has a pair of verification/signing keys, which is not applicable for many practical scenarios.

Additionally, two solutions were given in [3], assuming that a MAC is provided by the PKE component. One is based on the Boneh-Franklin identity based encryption (IBE) [8] as a PEKS [7] with ElGamal [16] as a PKE. The other is a generic construction based on a PEKS and a PKE with a MAC. The intuition behind both constructions is borrowed from REACT [22], where a MAC is used to protect the integrity of both parts of the ciphertext. However, to prove their security, the authors of [3] have to assume the hash functions are random oracles [6] and the underlying PKE is secure against plaintext checking attack (PCA), which is inherent in all variants of REACT. These requirements may be too stringent, and it is desirable to have other solutions, better without random oracles.

1.1   Our Contributions

Formal Security Model of PEKS/PKE. Authors of [3] have given a security model on data privacy of PEKS/PKE against adaptive chosen keyword attack and chosen ciphertext attack, however, it is not clear which attack model is posed on keyword privacy. Actually, no concrete discussions were given regarding this point in [3].

Here we show an example with no keyword privacy at all when the attack model of [3] is considered. To see this, one just appends the keyword as a part of the ciphertext of data encryption scheme. It is easily verified that this doesn't violate the data privacy of the PEKS/PKE scheme, as long as the keyword is chosen independent from the encrypted message, but the scheme is not a secure PEKS/PKE scheme since it leaks the information of the keyword. It seems that keyword privacy has been assumed to remain even after compositions by [3].

We thus conclude the previous security model of PEKS/PKE is not complete regarding keyword privacy, however, we emphasize that the two concrete constructions proposed in [3] are secure. In this paper, we formalize the requirement of keyword privacy for secure PEKS/PKE schemes.

Generic Construction of PEKS/PKE. Principally, the design of PEKS/PKE schemes without assuming random oracles is not new, e.g., one first put together PEKS and PKE components (each without random oracles), then applies non-interactive zero-knowledge proof of "well-formness" for this integration, but this is only theoretical and very inefficient. When speaking of practical schemes, all known constructions have to assume random oracles. It is well-known that a scheme with a security proof in the random oracle model implies no security in the real world [11], therefore, it is desirable to build proofs without random oracles. In this paper, we present such a generic construction.

Interesting Extensions. We also give some applications and extensions of the generic construction. For example, instantiating the above construction with concrete components, one obtains various PEKS/PKE schemes with many good properties. For instance, combining a PEKS scheme from the Gentry IBE [18], and the Kurosawa-Desmedt tag-KEM/DEM [20], we have a PEKS/PKE scheme secure without random oracles. The scheme is quite efficient, which is even comparable to previous constructions with random oracles. In fact, a secure PEKS/PKE is achievable from a variety of assumptions, e.g., from the Waters IBE [28] using asymmetric pairing [10], however, our scheme from the Gentry IBE provides better efficiency.

1.2   Related Work

Public key encryption (PKE) is an important primitive in modern cryptography which guarantees privacy of communications. The standard security notion for PKE is indistinguishability against adaptively chosen ciphertext attack (IND-CCA) [19,21,23,15,5]. While it is comparatively easy to build CCA-secure schemes assuming random oracles [6], to have CCA-secure schemes such that security reduction without random oracles is not easy. Only theoretical constructions of CCA-secure PKE schemes [21,15,24] were known before Cramer and Shoup gave the first practical solution [14]. Another recent approach was proposed by Boneh, Canetti, Halevi and Katz [12,9] based on identity based encryption (IBE).

An IBE scheme is a public key encryption scheme where any string can be the public key of a user, say, the identity of a user. It was advocated by Shamir [25], whose original intuition was to simplify the management of public key certificates. It has been an open problem to construct full-fledged IBE schemes for many years until [8], when Boneh and Franklin proposed the first IBE scheme based on pairings. Cocks [13] independently proposed another IBE scheme based on decisional quadratic residue problem. Public key encryption with keyword search (PEKS) was proposed in [7]. It was shown that to build a PEKS with exponential keyword space is at least as hard as build an identity based encryption (IBE) [7].

Another security notion for public key encryption is key privacy [4], which captures an adversary's inability to know a receiver's identity from a given ciphertext. For identity based encryption, this was studied under the name "anonymity" [1] (the precise definition postponed to Appendix A). Basically, public key encryption schemes with key privacy provides the functionality of PEKS, however, currently anonymous PKE schemes only provide polynomially bounded keyword space [7,1], and one may need anonymous IBE schemes for a keyword space of exponential size.

2   Preliminary

In this section, we give some notations and definitions.

Notations. If x is a string, let $|x|$ denotes its length, while if S is a set then $|S|$ denotes its size. If S is a set then $s \leftarrow S$ denotes the operation of picking an element s of S uniformly at random. We write $z \leftarrow \mathcal{A}(x, y, \ldots)$ to indicate that $\mathcal{A}$ is an algorithm with inputs $(x, y, \ldots)$ and an output z. Denote $x\|y$ as the string concatenation of x and y. If $k \in \mathbb{N}$, a function $f(k)$ is negligible if $\exists\, k_0 \in \mathbb{N}, \forall\, k > k_0,\ f(k) < 1/k^c$, where $c > 0$ is a constant.

2.1   Public Key Encryption

A public key encryption scheme consists of three algorithms $\mathcal{PKE} = ($PKEkg, PKEenc, PKEdec$)$.

PKEkg: a randomized algorithm, taking a security parameter k as input, generates a public key pk and a corresponding secret key sk, denoted as $(pk, sk) \leftarrow$ PKEkg(1^k).

PKEenc: a possibly randomized algorithm, taking a public key pk, and a plaintext m taken from the message space as input, with internal coin flipping, outputs a ciphertext c, denoted as $c \leftarrow$ PKEenc(pk, m).

PKEdec: a deterministic algorithm, taking a secret key sk and a ciphertext c as input, outputs the corresponding m, or "$\perp$" (indicating invalid ciphertext), denoted as $m \leftarrow$ PKEdec(sk, c).

We require a PKE scheme should satisfy the standard correctness requirement, namely for all $(pk, sk) \leftarrow$ PKEkg(1^k) and all m, PKEdec(sk, PKEenc(pk, m)) $= m$.

Data Privacy. We say a public key encryption scheme is (ϵ, q, T)-IND-CCA secure, if the advantage of any adversary $\mathcal{A}$ with at most q queries to a decryption oracle $\mathcal{DO}$, is at most ϵ within time T in the following experiment.

$$\mathrm{Adv}^{\mathsf{ind\text{-}cca}}_{\mathcal{PKE}, \mathcal{A}}(k) = |\Pr[(pk, sk) \leftarrow \mathsf{PKEkg}(1^k); (m_0, m_1, s) \leftarrow \mathcal{A}^{\mathcal{DO}}(pk);$$
$$b \leftarrow \{0, 1\}; c^* \leftarrow \mathsf{PKEenc}(pk, m_b); b' \leftarrow \mathcal{A}^{\mathcal{DO}}(c^*, s) : b' = b] - 1/2|$$

where $\mathcal{DO}$ returns the corresponding decryption result on a query on ciphertext c, whereas $\mathcal{A}$ is forbidden to query c^* to $\mathcal{DO}$. We say a PKE scheme is IND-CCA-secure, if for polynomially bounded q and T, ϵ is negligible.

2.2 Tag-KEM/DEM

Shoup introduced key encapsulation mechanism (KEM) and data encapsulation mechanism (DEM) [27], to deal with efficient hybrid encryption. Tag-KEM/DEM is a form of KEM which also takes as input a tag, which was introduced in [2]. A tag-KEM is a generalization of KEM/DEM, and together with a passively secure DEM, it can be easily be extended to threshold settings.

Tag-KEM. Our definition of tag-KEM runs parallel with [2]. A tag-KEM consists of four algorithms $\mathcal{TK} = (\mathsf{TKkg}, \mathsf{TKkey}, \mathsf{TKenc}, \mathsf{TKdec})$.

TKkg: a randomized algorithm, taking a security parameter k as input, generates a public key pk and a secret key sk, denoted as $(pk, sk) \leftarrow \mathsf{TKEMgen}(1^k)$.

TKkey: a randomized algorithm, taking a public key pk as input, outputs a random session key $dk \in \mathcal{K}_D$, where $\mathcal{K}_D$ is a key space, and internal state information η, denoted as $(dk, \eta) \leftarrow \mathsf{TKEMkey}(pk)$.

TKenc: a possible randomized algorithm, taking the internal state η and a tag λ as input, encrypts dk (embedded in η) into ψ, denoted as $\psi \leftarrow \mathsf{TKenc}(\eta, \lambda)$.

TKdec: a deterministic algorithm, taking a secret key sk, a ciphertext ψ and a tag λ as input, recovers dk from ψ and λ, denoted as $dk \leftarrow \mathsf{TKdec}(sk, \psi, \lambda)$. We require $\mathsf{TKdec}(\psi, \lambda) = dk$ must hold for any sk, dk, ψ and λ, associated by the above three algorithms. The algorithm outputs "$\perp$" when encountering an error.

Additionally, we require that given a public key pk, a tag λ, and an internal state η for the encryption algorithm TKenc, the session key dk of a tag-KEM should be uniquely decided. We call this property uniqueness of tag-KEM/DEM.

Security Notion. We define the security of tag-KEM as indistinguishability against adaptive chosen ciphertext attack (IND-TK-CCA). We say a tag-KEM scheme is (ϵ, q, T)-IND-TK-CCA secure, if the advantage of any adversary $\mathcal{A}$ with at most q queries to a decryption oracle $\mathcal{DO}$, is at most ϵ within time T in the following experiment.

$$\mathrm{Adv}_{\mathcal{TK}, \mathcal{A}}^{\mathsf{ind\text{-}tk\text{-}cca}}(k) = |\mathrm{Pr}[(pk, sk) \leftarrow \mathsf{TKkg}(1^k); b \leftarrow \{0,1\};$$
$$dk_0 \leftarrow \mathcal{K}_D; (\eta, dk_1) \leftarrow \mathsf{TKkey}(pk); (\lambda^*, s) \leftarrow \mathcal{A}^{\mathcal{DO}}(pk, dk_b);$$
$$\psi^* \leftarrow \mathsf{TKenc}(\eta, \lambda^*); b' \leftarrow \mathcal{A}^{\mathcal{DO}}(\psi^*, s) : b' = b] - 1/2|$$

where $\mathcal{DO}$ returns corresponding dk on input (ψ, λ), and $\mathcal{A}$ cannot query (ψ^*, λ^*) to $\mathcal{DO}$. We say a tag-KEM is IND-TK-CCA-secure, if for polynomially bounded q and T, ϵ is negligible.

DEM. A DEM consists of two deterministic algorithms, $\mathcal{DEM} = $ (DEMenc, DEMdec), which is associated with a key space and a plaintext space defined by a security parameter k.

DEMenc: taking a symmetric key $dk \in \mathcal{K}_D$, where $\mathcal{K}_D$ is defined by k and a plaintext $m \in \{0,1\}^*$ as input, outputs a ciphertext χ, denoted as $\chi \leftarrow$ DEMenc(dk, m).

DEMdec: taking a symmetric key $dk \in \mathcal{K}_D$ and a ciphertext χ as input, outputs a plaintext m, denoted as $m \leftarrow$ DEMdec(dk, χ).

We require that for all m and all dk, DEMdec$(dk, $DEMenc$(dk, m)) = m$.

Semantic Security. We only require passive security for DEM. We say a DEM scheme is (ϵ, T)-semantically secure, if the advantage of any adversary $\mathcal{A}$, is at most ϵ within time T in the following experiment.

$$\mathrm{Adv}^{ss}_{\mathcal{DEM},\mathcal{A}}(k) = |\Pr[b \leftarrow \{0,1\}; dk \leftarrow \mathcal{K}_D; (m_0, m_1, s) \leftarrow \mathcal{A}(1^k);$$
$$\chi \leftarrow \mathsf{DEMenc}(m_b); b' \leftarrow \mathcal{A}(\chi, s) : b' = b] - 1/2|$$

We say a DEM scheme is (ϵ, T)-semantically secure, if for polynomially bounded T, ϵ is negligible.

2.3 PEKS

A public key encryption with keyword search (PEKS) scheme [7,1] consists of four algorithms $\mathcal{PEKS} = $ (PEKSkg, PEKSenc, PEKStd, PEKStest).

PEKSkg: a randomized algorithm, taking a security parameter k as input, the probabilistic key generation algorithm generates a public key pk and a secret key sk, denoted as $(pk, sk) \leftarrow$ PEKSkg(1^k).

PEKSenc: a possibly randomized algorithm, taking a public key pk and a keyword w as input, computes a ciphertext τ, denoted as $\tau \leftarrow$ PEKSenc(pk, w).

PEKStd: a possibly randomized algorithm, taking a secret key sk and a keyword w as input, computes a trapdoor t_w, denoted as $t_w \leftarrow$ PEKStd(sk, t_w).

PEKStest: a deterministic algorithm, taking a trapdoor t_w and a ciphertext τ as input, tests whether c encrypts w and outputs a bit b, with 1 meaning "**yes**" and 0 meaning "**no**", denoted as $b \leftarrow$ PEKStest(t_w, τ).

Here we assume there is only one receiver (one public key) in the system, and it is straightforward to extend the above definitions to multi-user settings.

Consistency. Several flavors of consistency were discussed in [1], and we only define computational consistency here, since this notion suffices for most practical applications. A PEKS scheme is said to be computationally consistent, if the advantage is negligible for all computationally bounded adversary $\mathcal{A}$ in the following experiment.

$$\mathrm{Adv}^{peks\text{-}consist}_{\mathcal{PEKS},\mathcal{A}}(k) = \Pr[(pk, sk) \leftarrow \mathsf{PEKSkg}(1^k); (w, w') \leftarrow \mathcal{A}(pk);$$
$$t_{w'} \leftarrow \mathsf{PEKStd}(sk, w'); \tau^* \leftarrow \mathsf{PEKSenc}(pk, w) : \mathsf{PEKStest}(t_{w'}, c^*) = 1]$$

Keyword Privacy. We define indistinguishability of keywords against adaptive chosen keywords attack (IK-CKA), as considered in [7,1]. We say a PEKS scheme is (ϵ, q, T)-IK-CKA secure, if the advantage of any adversary $\mathcal{A}$ with at most q queries to a trapdoor generation oracle $\mathcal{TO}$, is at most ϵ within time T in the following experiment.

$$\mathrm{Adv}_{\mathcal{PEKS},\mathcal{A}}^{\mathrm{ik\text{-}cka/cca}}(k) = |\Pr[(pk, sk) \leftarrow \mathsf{PEKSkg}(1^k); (w_0, w_1, s) \leftarrow \mathcal{A}^{\mathcal{TO}}(pk);$$

$$b \leftarrow \{0, 1\}; \tau^* \leftarrow \mathsf{PEKSenc}(pk, w_b); b' \leftarrow \mathcal{A}^{\mathcal{TO}}(\tau^*, s) : b' = b] - 1/2|$$

where $\mathcal{TO}$ is a trapdoor oracle, returns the corresponding trapdoor t_w upon a query on keyword w, whereas $\mathcal{A}$ cannot query w_0 or w_1 to $\mathcal{TO}$. A PEKS scheme is said to be IK-CKA-secure, if for polynomially bounded q and T, ϵ is negligible.

2.4   Bilinear Groups

We review some facts about bilinear groups for future use. Let $\mathbb{G}_1$ and $\mathbb{G}_T$ be two multiplicative cyclic groups of prime order p and g be a generator of $\mathbb{G}_1$. A bilinear map $e : \mathbb{G}_1 \times \mathbb{G}_1 \to \mathbb{G}_T$ satisfies the following properties: (i) *Bilinearity:* For all $x, y \in \mathbb{G}_1$ and $a, b \in \mathbb{Z}$, $e(x^a, y^b) = e(x, y)^{ab}$. (ii) *Non-degeneracy:* $e(g, g) \neq 1$. (iii) *Computability:* There is an efficient algorithm to compute $e(x, y)$ for any $x, y \in \mathbb{G}_1$.

3   Our Model of PEKS/PKE

In this section, we give the syntax and security definitions for PEKS/PKE schemes. The advantage of our model is that we have notational convenience to define keyword privacy and data privacy.

3.1   PEKS/PKE

We focus on the integration of PEKS/PKE. A PEKS/PKE scheme consists of five algorithms $\mathcal{PEKS}/\mathcal{PKE} = (\mathsf{Kg}, \mathsf{Enc}, \mathsf{Dec}, \mathsf{Td}, \mathsf{Test})$.

Kg: a randomized algorithm, taking a security parameter k as input, generates a public key pk and a secret key sk, denoted as $(pk, sk) \leftarrow \mathsf{Kg}(1^k)$.

Enc: a possibly randomized algorithm, taking a public key pk, a keyword w and a plaintext m as input, outputs a PEKS/PKE ciphertext c, denoted as $c \leftarrow \mathsf{Enc}(pk, w, m)$.

Dec: a deterministic algorithm, taking a secret key sk and a PEKS/PKE ciphertext c, outputs the decryption result m (or "$\perp$" if c is invalid). We denote this as $m \leftarrow \mathsf{Dec}(sk, c)$.

Td: a possibly randomized algorithm, taking a secret key sk and a keyword w as input, computes a trapdoor t_w for keyword w, denoted as $t_w \leftarrow \mathsf{Td}(sk, w)$.

Test: a deterministic algorithm, tests whether a given PEKS/PKE ciphertext c encrypts keyword w, and outputs a bit b, with 1 meaning "**yes**" and 0 meaning "**no**", denoted as $b \leftarrow \mathsf{Test}(t_w, c)$.

Our model simplifies the one in [3]. In the encryption algorithm Enc, we don't explicitly require a tag in the ciphertext, since otherwise the security definition should additionally consider the tag. We remark the model is general enough because the tag can be regarded as a part of the ciphertext.

Consistency. A PEKS/PKE scheme is said to be computationally consistent, if the advantage is negligible for all computationally bounded adversary $\mathcal{A}$ in the following experiment.

$$\mathrm{Adv}_{\mathcal{PEKS}/\mathcal{PKE},\mathcal{A}}^{\mathsf{peks/pke\text{-}consist}}(k) = \Pr[(pk, sk) \leftarrow \mathsf{Kg}(1^k); (w, w', m) \leftarrow \mathcal{A}(pk);$$
$$t_{w'} \leftarrow \mathsf{Td}(sk, w'); c^* \leftarrow \mathsf{Enc}(pk, m, w) : \mathsf{Test}(t_{w'}, c^*) = 1]$$

3.2 Security Notions

We consider two security requirements, keyword privacy, namely, indistinguishability of keywords against adaptive chosen keyword attack and chosen ciphertext attack (IK-CKA/CCA), and data privacy, namely, indistinguishability of ciphertexts against adaptive chosen keyword attack and chosen ciphertext attack (IND-CKA/CCA). Note that in a PEKS/PKE scheme, PEKS and PKE are both regarded as components of the whole system.

Principally, the adversary is given two oracles, a trapdoor generation oracle $\mathcal{TO}$, that on a keyword w, generates the corresponding trapdoor t_w and a decryption oracle that on a ciphertext c, returns the corresponding plaintext m.

Keyword Privacy. We say a PEKS/PKE scheme is (ϵ, q_t, q_d, T)-IK-CKA/CCA secure, if the advantage of any adversary $\mathcal{A}$ with at most q_t queries to a trapdoor generation oracle $\mathcal{TO}$, at most q_d queries to a decryption oracle $\mathcal{DO}$, is at most ϵ within time T in the following experiment.

$$\mathrm{Adv}_{\mathcal{PEKS}/\mathcal{PKE},\mathcal{A}}^{\mathsf{ik\text{-}cka/cca}}(k) = |\Pr[(pk, sk) \leftarrow \mathsf{Kg}(1^k); (w_0, w_1, m, s) \leftarrow \mathcal{A}^{\mathcal{TO},\mathcal{DO}}(pk);$$
$$b \leftarrow \{0, 1\}; c^* \leftarrow \mathsf{Enc}(pk, m, w_b); b' \leftarrow \mathcal{A}^{\mathcal{TO},\mathcal{DO}}(c^*, s) : b' = b] - 1/2|$$

where $\mathcal{TO}$ is a trapdoor oracle, upon a query on keyword w returns the corresponding trapdoor t_w, and $\mathcal{DO}$ is a decryption oracle, upon a query on ciphertext c returns the corresponding plaintext, whereas $\mathcal{A}$ cannot query w_0 or w_1 to $\mathcal{TO}$. We say a PEKS/PKE is IK-CKA/CCA-secure, if for polynomially bounded q_t, q_d and T, ϵ is negligible.

Data Privacy. We say a PEKS/PKE scheme is (ϵ, q_t, q_d, T)-IK-CKA/CCA secure, if the advantage of any adversary $\mathcal{A}$ with at most q_t queries to a trapdoor generation oracle $\mathcal{TO}$, at most q_d queries to a decryption oracle $\mathcal{DO}$, is at most ϵ within time T in the following experiment.

$$\mathrm{Adv}_{\mathcal{PEKS}/\mathcal{PKE},\mathcal{A}}^{\mathsf{ind\text{-}cka/cca}}(k) = |\Pr[(pk, sk) \leftarrow \mathsf{Kg}(1^k); (w, m_0, m_1, s) \leftarrow \mathcal{A}^{\mathcal{TO},\mathcal{DO}}(pk);$$
$$b \leftarrow \{0, 1\}; c^* \leftarrow \mathsf{Enc}(pk, w, m_b); b' \leftarrow \mathcal{A}^{\mathcal{TO},\mathcal{DO}}(c^*, s) : b' = b] - 1/2|$$

where $\mathcal{TO}$ is a trapdoor oracle, upon a query on keyword w returns the corresponding trapdoor t_w, and $\mathcal{DO}$ is a decryption oracle, upon a query on ciphertext c returns the corresponding plaintext, whereas $\mathcal{A}$ cannot query c^* to $\mathcal{DO}$. We say a PEKS/PKE is IK-CKA/CCA-secure, if for polynomially bounded q_t, q_d and T, ϵ is negligible.

4   A Generic Construction of Secure PEKS/PKE

We need two ingredients for our generic construction, one is an IK-CKA secure PEKS scheme, and the other is an IND-TK-CCA secure tag-KEM/DEM. The main idea is to regard the ciphertext of PEKS as a proportion of the tag for tag-KEM/DEM. The tag-KEM/DEM framework covers almost all the known PEK schemes (see [2] for details), and can be built flexibly from a variety of assumptions. Since a tag is a natural component for a tag-KEM/DEM scheme, the structures of both parts persist. Another advantage of our methodology is that a tag-KEM/DEM can be easily extended to threshold settings, since the DEM only require passive security. We give our construction in Figure 1.

$\mathsf{Kg}(1^k)$	$\mathsf{Dec}(sk, c)$
$\quad (pk_1, sk_1) \leftarrow \mathsf{PEKSkg}(1^k);$	$\quad sk = (sk_1, sk_2);$
$\quad (pk_2, sk_2) \leftarrow \mathsf{TKkg}(1^k);$	$\quad c = (\tau, \psi, \chi);$
$\quad pk = (pk_1, pk_2);$	$\quad dk \leftarrow \mathsf{TKdec}(sk_2, \psi, \tau\|\chi);$
$\quad sk = (sk_1, sk_2);$	$\quad m \leftarrow \mathsf{DEMdec}(dk, \chi);$
$\quad \text{return } (pk, sk);$	$\quad \text{return } m;$
$\mathsf{Enc}(pk, w, m)$	$\mathsf{Td}(sk, w)$
$\quad pk = (pk_1, pk_2);$	$\quad sk = (sk_1, sk_2);$
$\quad \tau \leftarrow \mathsf{PEKSenc}(pk_1, w);$	$\quad t_w \leftarrow \mathsf{PEKStd}(sk_1, w);$
$\quad (dk, \eta) \leftarrow \mathsf{TKkey}(pk_2);$	$\quad \text{return } t_w;$
$\quad \chi \leftarrow \mathsf{DEMenc}(dk, m);$	
$\quad \lambda \leftarrow (\tau\|\chi);$	$\mathsf{Test}(t_w, c)$
$\quad \psi \leftarrow \mathsf{TKenc}(\eta, \lambda);$	$\quad c = (\tau, \psi, \chi);$
$\quad c \leftarrow (\tau, \psi, \chi);$	$\quad b \leftarrow \mathsf{PEKStest}(t_w, \tau);$
$\quad \text{return } c;$	$\quad \text{return } b;$

For each algorithm of PEKS/PKE, we require it should terminate and return "$\perp$" (denoting "abnormal termination"), if any of its sub-algorithms terminates abnormally.

Fig. 1. Generic Construction of PEKS/PKE

It is easily verified that if both the PEKS and PKE used in the construction are consistent, the resulting PEKS/PKE is consistent. We focus on the keyword privacy and data privacy of the construction.

Theorem 1. *The construction of PEKS/PKS shown in Figure 1 is* IK-CKA/ CCA-*secure and* IND-CKA/CCA *secure, provided that the underlying PEKS* *scheme is* IK-CKA-*secure, the tag-KEM scheme is* IK-TK-CCA-*secure and the DEM scheme is semantically secure.*

Intuitions. First, notice that a PEKS scheme aims at providing keywords privacy, while "naturally", ciphertext χ of the tag-KEM/DEM will not leak information of the keywords. By uniqueness property of tag-KEM, ψ is determined once the public key pk_2, the tag $\lambda = (\psi||\chi)$ and internal state η of the tag-KEM are determined, and will be independent from a keyword w if τ doesn't leak information on w. Moreover, because dk only depends on pk_2 and internal random coin-flipping of TKkey, and the algorithm DEMenc is deterministic, we have χ is also independent from w. Finally, we conclude, if τ doesn't leak information on w, neither will ψ and χ. On the other hand, from our construction, τ does not depend on m, thus leaks no information on m. Additionally, taking τ as a part of the tag provides integrity guarantee also for τ, i.e., any adversary cannot gain advantage in obtaining knowledge on a plaintext m by modifying this part. Otherwise, the adversary breaks indistinguishability of session key for the tag-KEM. We elaborate the above discussions in two lemmas.

Lemma 1. *The construction shown in Figure 1 is* $(\epsilon_K + \epsilon_D, q_t, q_d, T_K + T_D)$-IND-CKA/CCA *secure, provided that the tag-KEM scheme is* (ϵ_K, q_d, T_K)-IK-TK-CCA-*secure and the DEM scheme is* (ϵ_D, T_D)-*semantically secure.*

Proof. First, notice that τ is independent from m_b from the encryption algorithm. Assume there is an IND-CKA/CCA adversary $\mathcal{A}$, we can build an adversary $\mathcal{B}$ against IND-TK-CKA/CCA of tag-KEM or semantic security of DEM. $\mathcal{A}$ flips a fair coin, and runs in either of the following modes.

Mode 0 (Adversary against tag-KEM/DEM): $\mathcal{A}$ generates a pair of public/secret keys for PEKS. Since $\mathcal{A}$ has the secret key, trapdoor queries are handled perfectly. Decryption queries are forwarded to $\mathcal{A}$'s own decryption oracle and are also handled perfectly. For challenge, after receiving a pair of plaintext (m_0, m_1) and a keyword w from $\mathcal{B}$ and dk_b from its own challenger, $\mathcal{A}$ chooses uniformly $\beta \leftarrow \{0, 1\}$ and computes $\tau = \mathsf{PEKSenc}(pk_1, w)$, and computes $\chi \leftarrow \mathsf{DEMenc}(dk_b, m_\beta)$, where $b \leftarrow \{0, 1\}$. $\mathcal{A}$ then sets $\lambda = (\tau, \chi)$ as the tag to its challenger. After receiving its challenge ψ, $\mathcal{A}$ gives $\mathcal{B}$ the challenge $c = (\tau, \psi, \chi)$. When $\mathcal{B}$ outputs a guess on β, $\mathcal{A}$ checks whether this equals to β. $\mathcal{A}$ outputs 1 if yes and otherwise, 0. It is easily verified when dk_b is the real session key, then the challenge for $\mathcal{B}$ is valid and $\mathcal{A}$ will succeed at least the probability as $\mathcal{B}$. If dk_b is a random session key, β is perfectly hiding from $\mathcal{B}$, and $\mathcal{B}$'s probability in guessing b is exactly $1/2$. Summarize above discussions, we have the success probability of $\mathcal{A}$ is at least that of $\mathcal{B}$.

Mode 1 (Adversary against DEM): For setup, $\mathcal{A}$ generates a pair of public/secret keys for PEKS and tag-KEM. Trapdoor oracle queries and decryption oracle queries can perfectly simulated, since $\mathcal{A}$ has the secret keys. After receiving a pair of plaintext (m_0, m_1) and a keyword w from $\mathcal{B}$, $\mathcal{A}$ outputs (m_0, m_1) to its challenger. After obtains a challenge χ^* from its challenger, $\mathcal{A}$ computes a ciphertext τ of PEKS and a ciphertext ψ with some random

$dk \in \mathcal{K}_D$ from a tag $\lambda = (\tau || \psi)$. After $\mathcal{B}$ stops and outputs a guess, $\mathcal{A}$ also outputs the same bit. Since neither τ or ψ contains information on b, $\mathcal{B}$ can only gain advantage by inferring b from χ. One case to mention is that if $\mathcal{B}$ is able to distinguish ψ is not a valid ciphertext, then the result of $\mathcal{B}$ cannot be utilized and $\mathcal{A}$ should abort. However, in this case, we can construct an attack against the tag-KEM. However, according to our assumption, this happens at most ϵ_K. We then have in this case $\mathcal{A}$'s success probability breaking the DEM is at least that of $\mathcal{B}$ plus ϵ_K.

Summarizing the above two cases, we see the advantage of $\mathcal{A}$ is upper-bounded by $\epsilon_K + \epsilon_D$ and the queries and the running time of $\mathcal{A}$ are exactly the same as the claim.   □

Lemma 2. *The construction shown in Figure 1 is* $(\epsilon_P, q_t, q_d, T_P)$-IK-CKA/CCA-*secure, provided that the PEKS scheme is* (ϵ_P, q_t, T_P)-IK-CKA-*secure.*

Proof Sketch. The proof for the lemma is quite simple and we only give the sketch. From the algorithms shown in Figure 1, only τ depends on a keyword w, since the tag-KEM/DEM does not even take w as an input. a PEKS adversary $\mathcal{A}$ generates the public/secret keys (pk_2, pk_2) for the tag-KEM/DEM scheme and sets the public key as $pk = (pk_1, pk_2)$, where pk_1 is the public key of its target PEKS scheme. Since $\mathcal{A}$ knows the the secret key of the tag-KEM scheme, all decryption queries from a PEKS/PKE adversary $\mathcal{B}$ can be answered perfectly. For $\mathcal{B}$'s challenge query, $\mathcal{A}$ forwards (w_0, w_1) to its own trapdoor oracle and extracts τ^* from its challenge as the challenge for $\mathcal{B}$, it is easy to verify that τ^* is a valid challenge for $\mathcal{B}$. Then $\mathcal{A}$'s success probability is exactly the same as $\mathcal{B}$. This proves our claim.   □

Theorem 1 follows Lemma 1 and Lemma 2 naturally.

5   Applications and Extensions

In this section, we give some possible extensions of our generic construction. In particular, we show a concrete PEKS/PKE scheme, whose security can be proven without random oracles.

5.1   A Concrete Instantiation Without Random Oracles

We instantiate our generic construction with an anonymous IBE by Gentry [18], and the Kurosawa-Desmedt tag-KEM/DEM [20]. The resulting PEKS/PKE is secure without random oracles. The scheme is given in Figure 2.

The notion of anonymous IBE is reviewed in Appendix A. The consistency condition is easy verified to be met since it is a straightforward instantiation of BDOP construction of PEKS (based Gentry IBE) and a secure tag-KEM/DEM scheme.

$\mathsf{Kg}(1^k)$	$\mathsf{Enc}(pk, w, m)$
$\quad g, h \leftarrow \mathbb{G}_1;$	$\quad s_1, s_2 \leftarrow \mathbb{Z}_p;$
$\quad z \leftarrow e(g_1, g_2);$	$\quad u_1 \leftarrow g_1^{s_1} g^{-s_1 w};$
$\quad \alpha \leftarrow \mathbb{Z}_p;$	$\quad u_2 \leftarrow e(g, g)^{s_1};$
$\quad g_1 \leftarrow g^\alpha;$	$\quad u_3 \leftarrow H(e(g, h)^{-s_1});$
$\quad pk_1 \leftarrow (g, g_1, h);$	$\quad c_1 \leftarrow (u_1, u_2, u_3);$
$\quad sk_1 \leftarrow \alpha;$	$\quad v_1 \leftarrow z_1^{s_2};$
$\quad z_1, z_2 \leftarrow \mathbb{G}_2;$	$\quad v_2 \leftarrow z_2^{s_2};$
$\quad x_1, x_2, y_1, y_2 \leftarrow \mathbb{Z}_p;$	$\quad K \leftarrow c^{s_2} d^{s_2 H(u_1, u_2)};$
$\quad c \leftarrow z_1^{x_1} z_2^{x_2};$	$\quad (K_1, K_2) \leftarrow F(K);$
$\quad d \leftarrow z_1^{y_1} z_2^{y_2};$	$\quad v_3 \leftarrow G(K_2) \oplus m;$
$\quad pk_2 \leftarrow (c, d, G, F, H);$	$\quad v_4 \leftarrow \mathsf{Mac}(K_2, v_3 \| c_1);$
$\quad sk_2 \leftarrow (x_1, x_2, y_1, y_2);$	$\quad c \leftarrow (c_1, c_2);$
$\quad pk \leftarrow (pk_1, pk_2);$	$\quad$ return $c;$
$\quad sk \leftarrow (sk_1, sk_2);$	
$\quad$ return $(pk, sk);$	$\mathsf{Td}(sk, w)$
	$\quad r_w \leftarrow \mathbb{Z}_p;$
	$\quad d_w \leftarrow hg^{r_w};$
	$\quad t_w \leftarrow (r_w, d_w);$
$\mathsf{Dec}(sk, c)$	$\quad$ return $t_w;$
$\quad c = (c_1, c_2),$ where $c_1 = (u_1, u_2, u_3)$	
$\quad\quad$ and $c_2 = (v_1, v_2, v_3);$	$\mathsf{Test}(t_w, c)$
$\quad f \leftarrow v_1^{x_1 + y_1 H(v_1, v_2)} v_2^{x_1 + y_1 H(v_1, v_2)};$	$\quad c = (c_1, c_2),$ where $c_1 = (u_1, u_2, u_3)$
$\quad (K_1, K_2) \leftarrow F(K);$	$\quad\quad$ and $c_2 = (v_1, v_2, v_3);$
$\quad$ if $v_4 \neq \mathsf{Mac}(K_1, v_3 \| c_1);$	$\quad$ if $u_3 = H(e(u_1, d_w) u_2^{r_w});$
$\quad\quad$ return "$\perp$";	$\quad\quad$ return 1;
$\quad m \leftarrow v_3 \oplus G(K_2);$	$\quad$ otherwise
$\quad$ return $m;$	$\quad\quad$ return 0;

‡ Let $e : \mathbb{G}_1 \times \mathbb{G}_1 \rightarrow \mathbb{G}_2$ be a bilinear group pair with prime order p. $\mathcal{MAC} =$ (Mac, Vrfy) is a message authentication code. F is a key derivition function (KDF) [27], G is a pseudorandom generator and H is a collision resistant hash function. Without further descriptions, we simply assume the input domain and output domain match.

Fig. 2. A Concrete Instantiation without Random Oracles

Theorem 2. *The PEKS/PKE scheme shown in Figure 2 is* IND-IK-CKA/CCA-*secure, provided that the Kurosawa-Desmedt tag-KEM/DEM is secure and the Gentry IBE is anonymous.*

The above proof is easily derived from Theorem 1 and known results [2,18].

Performance. Though our scheme relies on the DADHE assumption that seems strong, however, the scheme is quite efficient in of key size and computation cost. Note that the previous schemes have to adopt a large key size to compensate security loss due to loose security reductions. Moreover, our scheme needs no Map-to-Point computations [8], and it can be further optimized with a trick mentioned in [17] and pre-computations. Consider all these and the fact that our scheme is without random oracles, we conclude our scheme is efficient.

PEKS/PKE without MACs. Our instantiation of tag-KEM/DEM is based on Kurosawa-Desmedt, where a MAC is inevitable. One can use other tag-KEM schemes, e.g., Cramer-Shoup tag-KEM [14,2], or OAEP+ [26,2], such that the MAC is not explicitly needed.

5.2 Other Extensions

PEKS/PKE from General Assumptions. Our generic construction has implicitly assumed an exponential keyword space, thus the constructions of PEKS is restricted to anonymous IBE schemes. In fact, it is possible to base the PEKS on general assumptions, e.g., existence of trapdoor one-way functions, with relaxation to a polynomial keywords space [7].

Randomness Reuse. We have required that the encryption algorithms of PEKS and PKE choose independent randomness in our generic construction, however, one can actually reuse the randomness without harming the security of the scheme. The technique is standard, and the details are omitted here due to space limitation.

PEKS/PKE with Threshold Decryption. Since a tag-KEM can be easily extended to the threshold setting, it is natural to follow the strategy of [2] to have non-interactive threshold decryption for PEKS/PKE.

Multi-Keyword and Multi-Receiver PEKS/PKE. PEKS/PKE with multi-keywords and multi-receivers have been considered in [3]. We remark the same problem of keyword privacy occurs when considering the ciphertext of PKE leaks information on keyword. It is not hard to generate all our above discussions to these settings. The techniques are quite standard, and again, we omit the details here.

Acknowledgement

We thank the anonymous referees of CANS'07 for many helpful comments.

References

1. Abdalla, M., Bellare, M., Catalano, D., Kiltz, E., Kohno, T., Lange, T., Malone-Lee, J., Neven, G., Pallier, P., Shi, H.: Searchable Encryptino Revisited: Consistnecy Properties, Relation to Anonymous IBE, and Extensions. In: Shoup, V. (ed.) CRYPTO 2005. LNCS, vol. 3621, pp. 205–222. Springer, Heidelberg (2005)
2. Abe, M., Gennaro, R., Kurosawa, K.: Tag-KEM/DEM: A New Framework for Hybrid Encryption. Cryptology ePrint Archive (2005), http://eprint.iacr.org/2005/027/
3. Baek, J., Safavi-Naini, R., Susilo, W.: On the Integration of Public Key Data Encryption and Public Key Encryption with Keyword Search. In: Katsikas, S.K., Lopez, J., Backes, M., Gritzalis, S., Preneel, B. (eds.) ISC 2006. LNCS, vol. 4176, pp. 217–232. Springer, Heidelberg (2006)

4. Bellare, M., Boldyreva, A., Desai, A., Pointcheval, D.: Key-Privacy in Public-Key Encryption. In: Boyd, C. (ed.) ASIACRYPT 2001. LNCS, vol. 2248, pp. 566–582. Springer, Heidelberg (2001)

5. Bellare, M., Desai, A., Pointcheval, D., Rogaway, P.: Relations among notions of security for public key encryption schemes. In: Krawczyk, H. (ed.) CRYPTO 1998. LNCS, vol. 1462, pp. 26–45. Springer, Heidelberg (1998)

6. Bellare, M., Rogaway, P.: Random oracles are practical: A paradigm for designing efficient protocols. In: ACM CCS 1993, pp. 62–73. ACM Press, New York (1993)

7. Boneh, D., Di Crescenzo, G., Ostrovsky, R., Persiano, G.: Public Key Encryption with Keyword Search. In: Cachin, C., Camenisch, J.L. (eds.) EUROCRYPT 2004. LNCS, vol. 3027, pp. 506–522. Springer, Heidelberg (2004)

8. Boneh, D., Franklin, M.: Identity-Based Encryption from the Weil Pairing. In: Kilian, J. (ed.) CRYPTO 2001. LNCS, vol. 2139, pp. 213–229. Springer, Heidelberg (2001)

9. Boneh, D., Katz, J.: Improved Efficiency for CCA-Secure Cryptosystems Built Using Identity-Based Encryption. In: Menezes, A.J. (ed.) CT-RSA 2005. LNCS, vol. 3376, pp. 87–103. Springer, Heidelberg (2005)

10. Boyen, X., Waters, B.: Anonymous Hierarchical Identity Based Encryption (without Random Oracles). In: Dwork, C. (ed.) CRYPTO 2006. LNCS, vol. 4117, pp. 290–307. Springer, Heidelberg (2006)

11. Canetti, R., Goldreich, O., Halevi, S.: The Random Oracle Methodology, Revisited. In: STOC 1998, pp. 557–594. ACM, New York (1998), Full version available at http://eprint.iacr.org/1998/011.pdf

12. Canetti, R., Halevi, S., Katz, J.: Chosen-Ciphertext Security from Identity-Based Encryption. In: Cachin, C., Camenisch, J.L. (eds.) EUROCRYPT 2004. LNCS, vol. 3027, pp. 207–222. Springer, Heidelberg (2004)

13. Cocks, C.: An Identity Based Encryption Scheme Based on Quadratic Residues. In: Honary, B. (ed.) Cryptography and Coding. LNCS, vol. 2260, pp. 360–363. Springer, Heidelberg (2001)

14. Cramer, R., Shoup, V.: A Practical Public Key Cryptosystem Provably Secure against Adaptive Chosen Ciphertext Attack. In: Krawczyk, H. (ed.) CRYPTO 1998. LNCS, vol. 1462, pp. 13–25. Springer, Heidelberg (1998)

15. Dolev, D., Dwork, C., Naor, M.: Non-Malleable Cryptography. In: STOC 1991, pp. 542–552. ACM, New York (1991)

16. ElGamal, T.: A Public Key Cryptosystem and a Signature Scheme Based on Discrete Logarithms. IEE Transactions on Information Theory 31(4), 469–472 (1985)

17. Gennaro, R., Shoup, V.: A Note on An Encryption Scheme of Kurosawa and Desmedt. Eprint Report 2004/194 (2004), Available at http://eprint.iacr.org/2004/194

18. Gentry, C.: Practical Identity-Based Encryption Without Random Oracles. In: Vaudenay, S. (ed.) EUROCRYPT 2006. LNCS, vol. 4004, pp. 445–464. Springer, Heidelberg (2006)

19. Goldwasser, S., Micali, S.: Probabilistic Encryption. Journal of Computer and System Sciences 28(2), 270–299 (1984)

20. Kurosawa, K., Desmedt, Y.: A New Paradigm of Hybrid Encryption Scheme. In: Franklin, M. (ed.) CRYPTO 2004. LNCS, vol. 3152, pp. 426–442. Springer, Heidelberg (2004)

21. Naor, M., Yung, M.: Public-key Cryptosystems Provably Secure against Chosen Ciphertext Attacks. In: STOC 1990, pp. 427–437. ACM, New York (1990)

22. Okamoto, T., Pointcheval, D.: REACT: Rapid Enhanced-security Asymmetric Cryptosystem Transform. In: Naccache, D. (ed.) CT-RSA 2001. LNCS, vol. 2020, pp. 159–175. Springer, Heidelberg (2001)

23. Rackoff, C., Simon, D.R.: Non-Interactive Zero-Knowledge Proof of Knowledge and Chosen Ciphertext Attack. In: Feigenbaum, J. (ed.) CRYPTO 1991. LNCS, vol. 576, pp. 433–444. Springer, Heidelberg (1992)

24. Sahai, A.: Non-Malleable Non-Interactive Zero Knowledge and Adaptive Chosen-Ciphertext Security. In: FOCS 1999, pp. 543–553. IEEE Computer Society, Los Alamitos (1999)

25. Shamir, A.: Identity-Based Cryptosystems and Signature Schemes. In: Blakely, G.R., Chaum, D. (eds.) CRYPTO 1984. LNCS, vol. 196, pp. 47–53. Springer, Heidelberg (1985)

26. Shoup, V.: OAEP Reconsidered. In: Kilian, J. (ed.) CRYPTO 2001. LNCS, vol. 2139, pp. 239–259. Springer, Heidelberg (2001)

27. Shoup, V.: ISO 18033-2: An Emerging Standard for Public-Key Encryption (committee draft) (June 2004), Available at http://shoup.net/iso/

28. Waters, B.: Efficient Identity-Based Encryption Without Random Oracles. In: Cramer, R.J.F. (ed.) EUROCRYPT 2005. LNCS, vol. 3494, pp. 114–127. Springer, Heidelberg (2005)

A   Identity Based Encryption

An identity based encryption (IBE) can be regarded as a special public key encryption, where the receiver's public key can be any string. Compared with traditional public key encryption, an IBE scheme is equipped with an additional extraction algorithm, with a master secret key and an identity as input, outputs a secret key that is capable to decrypt ciphertext corresponding to this identity. An IBE scheme consists of four algorithms $\mathcal{IBE} = (\mathsf{IBEkg}, \mathsf{IBEext}, \mathsf{IBEenc}, \mathsf{IBEdec})$.

IBEkg: a randomized algorithm, taking a security parameter k as the input, outputs a public parameter $params$ and a master secret key msk, denoted as $(params, msk) \leftarrow \mathsf{TBEkg}(1^k)$.

IBEext: a possibly randomized algorithm, takes inputs of $params$, msk and an identity id, outputs a secret key sk_{id} for id, denoted as $sk_{id} \leftarrow \mathsf{IBEext}$ $(params, msk, id)$, in brief $sk_{id} \leftarrow \mathsf{IBEext}(msk, id)$.

IBEext: a possibly randomized algorithm, taking $params$, an identity id and a plaintext m taken from the message space as input, with internal coin flipping r, outputs a ciphertext c, which is denoted as $c \leftarrow \mathsf{IBEenc}(params, id, m, r)$, in brief $c \leftarrow \mathsf{IBEenc}(params, id, m)$.

IBEdec: a deterministic algorithm, taking a secret key sk_{id}, an identity id and a ciphertext c as input, outputs a plaintext m, or a special symbol "$\perp$", which is denoted $m \leftarrow \mathsf{IBEdec}(sk_{id}, id, c)$.

We require for all $(params, msk) \leftarrow \mathsf{IBEkg}(1^k)$, $sk_{id} \leftarrow \mathsf{IBEext}(msk, id)$ and all m, we have $\mathsf{IBEdec}(sk_{id}, id, \mathsf{IBEenc}(params, id, m)) = m$.

Anonymity. We consider anonymity of receiver against adaptively chosen-ID and chosen plaintext attack (AONT-ID-CPA) [1]. We say an identity based encryption is (ϵ, q, T)-IND-sID-CPA-secure if the advantage of any adversary $\mathcal{A}$ is at most ϵ, with access q times to an extraction oracle $\mathcal{EO}$ within time T in the following experiment.

$$\mathrm{Adv}_{\mathcal{JBE},\mathcal{A}}^{\mathrm{aont\text{-}id\text{-}cpa}}(k) = \Pr[(params, msk) \leftarrow \mathsf{IBEkg}(1^k);$$
$$(id_0, id_1, m, s) \leftarrow \mathcal{A}^{\mathcal{EO}}(params); b \leftarrow \{0,1\};$$
$$c^* \leftarrow \mathsf{IBEenc}(params, id_b, m); b' \leftarrow \mathcal{A}^{\mathcal{EO}}(c^*, s) : b' = b] - 1/2$$

where $\mathcal{EO}$ returns the corresponding secret key on a query on identity id, whereas $\mathcal{A}$ is forbidden to query (id_0, id_1) at $\mathcal{EO}$. We say an IBE is AONT-ID-CPA-Secure, if for polynomially bounded q and T, ϵ is negligible.

Extended Private Information Retrieval and Its Application in Biometrics Authentications*

Julien Bringer[1], Hervé Chabanne[1], David Pointcheval[2], and Qiang Tang[2]

[1] Sagem Sécurité
[2] Departement d'Informatique, École Normale Supérieure
45 Rue d'Ulm, 75230 Paris Cedex 05, France

Abstract. In this paper we generalize the concept of Private Information Retrieval (PIR) by formalizing a new cryptographic primitive, named Extended Private Information Retrieval (EPIR). Instead of enabling a user to retrieve a bit (or a block) from a database as in the case of PIR, an EPIR protocol enables a user to evaluate a function f which takes a string chosen by the user and a block from the database as input. Like PIR, EPIR can also be considered as a special case of the secure two-party computation problem (and more specifically the oblivious function evaluation problem). We propose two EPIR protocols, one for testing equality and the other for computing Hamming distance. As an important application, we show how to construct strong privacy-preserving biometric-based authentication schemes by employing these EPIR protocols.

1 Introduction

This paper describes a new primitive, Extended Private Information Retrieval (EPIR) which is a natural generalization of PIR, and two EPIR protocols, one for testing equality and the other for computing Hamming distance. This work is partially motivated by the growing privacy requirements in processing sensitive information such as biometrics.

1.1 Related Work

With respect to the functionality, an EPIR is indeed a combination of a PIR [10] and a general secure two-party computation protocol [26,49]. Next, we briefly review the literature in both areas.

The concept of PIR was proposed by Chor et al. [10]. A PIR protocol enables a user to retrieve a bit from a database which contains a bit string. Chor et al. defined user privacy for PIR in the information-theoretical setting, which captures the concept that the database (with unlimited resources) learns nothing about which bit the user has retrieved. They also proposed a number of multi-database protocols that are secure in the information-theoretical setting. Chor

---

* This work is partially supported by french ANR RNRT project BACH.

F. Bao et al. (Eds.): CANS 2007, LNCS 4856, pp. 175–193, 2007.

and Gilboa [9] proposed to construct multi-database PIR under computational assumptions. Kushilevitz and Ostrovsky [32] presented a definition of user privacy in computational setting, where a PIR protocol achieves user privacy if, for any query for i-th bit, the database learns nothing about the index i. They showed that one can achieve single-database PIR under the Quadratic Residuosity assumption with communication complexity $O(N^c)$ for any $c > 0$, where N is the database size throughout the paper. Cachin, Micali, and Stadler [7] proposed a single-database PIR scheme with poly-logarithmic communication complexity $O((\log N)^8)$ based on the Φ-hiding assumption.

Chor et al. [10] also proposed the notion of Private Block Retrieval (PBR), a natural extension to single-bit PIR, in which instead of retrieving only one bit, the user retrieves a d-bit block. They proposed an efficient method for the transformation from PIR to PBR. Lipmaa [34] proposed a PBR scheme with communication complexity $\Theta(\Omega((\log N)^{3-o(1)})(\log N)^2 + d\log N)$. Gentry and Ramzan [23] proposed a single-database PBR protocol based on the decision subgroup problem, with communication complexity $O(k + d)$ where $k \geq \log N$ is the security parameter.

Gertner et al. [24] introduced the notion of data privacy in the computational setting, where a PIR protocol achieves database privacy if, for any query, the user cannot tell whether it is an ideal-world execution or a real-world execution. In an ideal-world execution the user interacts with a simulator which takes only a single bit from the database as input, while in a real-world execution the user interacts with the database. If a PIR protocol achieves both user privacy and data privacy, then it is said to be SPIR (symmetrically-private information retrieval) which is also referred to as one-out-of-N oblivious transfer [13]. Mishra and Sarkar [35] proposed a single-server SPIR protocol which can have communication complexity $O(N^\epsilon)$ for any $\epsilon > 0$. Their protocol is proven secure under the XOR assumption defined by Mishra and Sarkar.

Gasarch [22] provides a very detailed summary of PIR/PBR protocols and lower/upper bounds on communication complexity, and Ostrovsky and Skeith III [37] also provides a summary. To facilitate our discussion, we use the notation PIR to denote both PIR and PBR, and generalise the setting of PIR to be: a database $\mathcal{DB}$ contains a list of N blocks $\mathbf{R} = (R_1, R_2, \cdots, R_N)$, and a user $\mathcal{U}$ can run a PIR protocol to retrieve R_i from $\mathcal{DB}$, for any $1 \leq i \leq N$.

As a special case of secure two-party computation problem, the concept of EPIR is relevant to the oblivious function evaluation [8,20,36]. Canetti et al. [8] study the problem that a client privately evaluate a public function which takes inputs from one or more servers. Note that the client does not have any private input to the function. Naor and Pinkas [36] study the problem that a receiver privately evaluates a function f(a) by interacting with a sender, where f is a secret polynomial of the sender and a is a secret input of the receiver. Freedman et al. [20] study the keyword search problem that a client privately evaluates whether a keyword is contained in a database. EPIR can be considered to be a generalization of the these problems (in the single database case). Next, we briefly review some works which are related to equality test and hamming distance computation. In [11,19], the authors studied how to compare two commonly shared strings and determine whether they are the same. Freedman, Nissim, and Pinkas [21] studied two-party set-interaction problems and proposed a number of protocols. Du and Atallah [48,17] considered the secure computation in an environment similar to that of EPIR, and proposed protocols based on solutions to Yao's millionaire problem. Goethals *et al.* [25] showed the weakness in the private scalar product protocols [16,46] and proposed a new protocol based on homomorphic encryption schemes. Kiltz, Leander, and Malone-Lee [31] proposed some methods for a user to compute the mean (and other statistics) over the data in a database. However, they did not propose any specific security model for this type of computation, and their protocols either require a semi-trusted third party or are very inefficient in round and communication complexity. Note that Kiltz, Leander, and Malone-Lee [31] showed that some approach in [17] leaks information in some applications. Boneh, Goh, and Nissim [3] proposed an encryption scheme (referred to as the BGN encryption scheme) and used it for evaluating 2-DNF formulas. As an application, they showed how to construct efficient PIR protocols based on their encryption scheme.

1.2   Practical Motivation

Biometrics, such as fingerprint and iris, have been used to a high level of security in order to cope with the increasing demand for reliable and highly-usable information security systems, because they have many advantages over cryptographic credentials. However, there are some obstacles for a wide adoption of biometrics in practice. Among them, one is that biometric features are volatile over the time so that it cannot be integrated into most of the legacy systems. This means that approximate matching might be necessary for an identification or authentication. The other is that biometrics are usually considered to be sensitive, so that there is big privacy concern in using them. To address the volatility of biometrics, error-correction concept is widely used in the literature (e.g. [4,5,12,15,14,29,30,40]). Employing this concept, some public information is firstly generated based on a reference biometric template, and later, a newly-captured template could help to recover the reference template if their distance (in a certain space) is not too large. In [33,42,43,44,47], the authors attempted to enhance privacy protection in biometric authentication schemes, where the privacy means that the compromise of the database will not enable the attacker to recover the biometric template. Ratha, Connell, and Bolle [2,39] introduced the concept of *cancelable biometrics* in an attempt to solve the revocation and privacy issues related to biometric information. More recently, Ratha *et al.* [38] intensively elaborated this concept in the case of fingerprint-based authentication systems. In addition, Atallah *et al.* [1] proposed a method, in which biometric templates are treated as bit strings and subsequently masked and permuted during the authentication process. Schoenmakers and Tuyls [41] proposed to use homomorphic encryption schemes for biometric authentication schemes by employing multi-party computation techniques. Practical concerns, security issues, and challenges about biometrics have been discussed in a number of papers (e.g. [2,39,45]).

Despite these efforts, there are still some concerns which require further investigation. The most important one is that privacy may mean much more than recovering the biometric template. For example, an application server may not be trusted to store biometric information, and, even if an independent database stores biometric information, the application server's access to the biometric information still needs to be restricted. In addition, it is desirable to simplify the storage requirements for the human users and the (communication) client. Bringer *et al.* [6] proposed a biometric-based authentication protocol which protects the sensitive relationship between a biometric feature and relevant pseudorandom identity. Their protocol makes use of the Goldwasser-Micali encryption scheme and is less efficient in communication than those described in Section 5.

1.3   Our Contributions

We generalize the concept of PIR by formalizing a new cryptographic primitive, named Extended Private Information Retrieval (EPIR). Instead of enabling a user to retrieve a block from a database as in the case of PIR, an EPIR protocol enables a user to evaluate a function f which takes a string chosen by the user and a block from the database as input[1]. If f is defined to be a function that simply returns the block from the database then the EPIR protocol is indeed a traditional PIR protocol. Analogous to the privacy properties of PIR, we define two privacy properties for EPIR, including (1) user privacy which captures the concept that, for any query, the database should know nothing about block index the user has queried and the user's input to f, (2) database privacy captures the concept that, from a single query, the user should obtain no more information than the output of function f. Note that we focus on the single-database computational setting in this paper.

We further propose two EPIR protocols: one for testing equality and the other for computing Hamming distance. The first protocol is based on a PIR protocol and the ElGamal encryption scheme (described in Appendix A)[18], and the second protocol is based on a PIR protocol and the BGN encryption scheme (described in Appendix B) [3]. In both EPIR protocols, in order to achieve database privacy, the PIR protocols employed do not need to achieve database privacy.

As an important application, we show a modular way to construct biometric-based authentication schemes by employing an EPIR protocol. Due to the privacy properties of EPIR, these schemes achieve strong privacy properties against a malicious server and a malicious database which will not collude. It is worth noting that our proposal is not focused on a specific biometric, but rather on a generalization of biometrics which can be represented as binary strings in the Hamming space. Iris is such a type of biometric that can be easily encoded into a binary string [28].

---

[1] We assume that the index of the block from the database is also chosen by the user.

1.4 Organization of the Paper

The remainder of the paper is organized as follows. In Section 2 we present the security definitions for EPIR. In Section 3 we describe an EPIR protocol for testing equality of two binary strings based on the ElGamal encryption scheme. In Section 4 we describe an EPIR protocol for computing Hamming distance of two binary strings based on the BGN encryption scheme. In Section 5 we propose two biometric-based authentication schemes by employing these two EPIR protocols. In Section 6 we conclude the paper.

2 Privacy Definitions for EPIR

Formally, a (single-database) EPIR protocol involves two principals: a database $\mathcal{DB}$ which holds a set of N blocks $\mathbf{R} = (R_1, R_2, \cdots, R_N)$ where $R_j \in \{0,1\}^{\ell_1}$ and ℓ_1 is an integer, a user $\mathcal{U}$ which retrieves the value of a function $\mathsf{f}(R_i, X)$ where $X \in \{0,1\}^{k_1}$ is chosen by the user, k_1 is an integer, and the index i is also chosen by the user. We assume that the description of f is public and N is a public constant integer. Without loss of generality, we further assume that the retrieval is through a $\mathsf{retrieve}(\mathsf{f}, i, X)$ query.

2.1 Notation

We first describe some conventions for writing probabilistic algorithms and experiments. The notation $x \xleftarrow{R} S$ means x is randomly chosen from the set S. If $\mathcal{A}$ is a probabilistic algorithm, then $\mathcal{A}(\mathsf{Alg}; \mathsf{Func})$ is the result of running $\mathcal{A}$, which can have any polynomial number of oracle queries to the functionality Func, interactively with Alg which answers the oracle query issued by $\mathcal{A}$. For clarity of description, if an algorithm $\mathcal{A}$ runs in a number of stages then we write $\mathcal{A} = (\mathcal{A}_1, \mathcal{A}_2, \cdots)$. As a standard practice, the security of a protocol is evaluated by an experiment between an attacker and a challenger, where the challenger simulates the protocol executions and answers the attacker's oracle queries. Without specification, algorithms are always assumed to be polynomial-time.

Specifically, in our case, there is only one functionality, namely $\mathsf{retrieve}$. If the attacker is a malicious $\mathcal{DB}$, the challenger samples the index i and X from the distribution specified in the protocol and issues $\mathsf{retrieve}$ queries to the attacker. If the attacker is a malicious $\mathcal{U}$ then it can freely chooses the index i and X (that may derivate from the distribution specified in the protocol) and issues $\mathsf{retrieve}$ queries to the challenger.

In addition, we have the following definitions for negligible and overwhelming probabilities.

Definition 1. *The function $P(\ell) : \mathbb{Z} \to \mathbb{R}$ is said to be negligible if, for every polynomial $f(\ell)$, there exists an integer N_f such that $P(\ell) \leq \frac{1}{f(\ell)}$ for all $\ell \geq N_f$. If $P(\ell)$ is negligible, then the probability $1 - P(\ell)$ is said to be overwhelming.*

2.2   User Privacy

This property is an analog to the user privacy property in the case of PIR where user privacy captures the concept that $\mathcal{DB}$ knows nothing about block index that $\mathcal{U}$ has queried. However, in the case of EPIR, we wish user privacy to imply more than that $\mathcal{DB}$ knows nothing about the block index $\mathcal{U}$ has queried. Consider a toy example, in which an EPIR protocol is constructed as follows: $\mathcal{U}$ simply sends X to the database which computes $\mathsf{f}(R_j, X)$ $(1 \leq j \leq N)$, and $\mathcal{U}$ then runs a PIR to retrieve $\mathsf{f}(R_i, X)$. It is clear that, if the PIR protocol achieves user privacy then $\mathcal{DB}$ learns nothing about the index in the toy protocol. However, if $\mathsf{f}(R_j, X)$ $(1 \leq j \leq N)$ are equal then $\mathcal{DB}$ knows the result obtained by $\mathcal{U}$.

Informally, the user privacy for EPIR captures the concept that, for any retrieve(f, i, X) query, $\mathcal{DB}$ knows nothing about the queried block index i and the user's string X. Formally, an EPIR protocol achieves user privacy if any attacker $\mathcal{A} = (\mathcal{A}_1, \mathcal{A}_2, \mathcal{A}_3, \mathcal{A}_4)$ has only a negligible advantage in the following game, where the attacker's advantage is $|\Pr[b' = b] - \frac{1}{2}|$.

$$
\begin{array}{ll}
\mathbf{Exp}_{\mathcal{A}}^{\text{user-privacy}} & \\
\mathbf{R} = (R_1, R_2, \cdots, R_N) & \leftarrow \mathcal{A}_1(1^\ell) \\
1 \leq i_0, i_1 \leq N; X_0, X_1 \in \{0,1\}^{k_1} & \leftarrow \mathcal{A}_2(Challenger; \mathsf{retrieve}) \\
b & \xleftarrow{R} \{0,1\} \\
\emptyset & \leftarrow \mathcal{A}_3(Challenger; \mathsf{retrieve}(\mathsf{f}, i_b, X_b)) \\
b' & \leftarrow \mathcal{A}_4(Challenger; \mathsf{retrieve})
\end{array}
$$

In this game, the attacker $\mathcal{A}$ is a malicious $\mathcal{DB}$. For the clarity, we rephrase the game as follows.

1. The attacker $\mathcal{A}_1$ generates N blocks $\mathbf{R} = (R_1, R_2, \cdots, R_N)$.
2. The attacker $\mathcal{A}_2$ can request the challenger to start any (polynomial) number of retrieve queries. At some point, $\mathcal{A}_2$ outputs (i_0, i_1, X_0, X_1) for a challenge.
3. The challenger randomly chooses $b \in \{0,1\}$ and issues a retrieve(f, i_b, X_b) query to the attacker $\mathcal{A}_3$.
4. The attacker $\mathcal{A}_4$ can continue requesting the challenger to start any (polynomial) number of retrieve queries. At some point, $\mathcal{A}_4$ outputs a guess b'.

Note that the symbol $\emptyset$ means that the attacker $\mathcal{A}_3$ has no explicit output (besides the state information).

2.3   Database Privacy

This property is an analog to the database privacy property in the case of SPIR [24] and the formalization follows that for secure two-party computation [49,26]. Informally, database privacy captures the concept that, from a retrieve(f, i, X) query, $\mathcal{U}$ obtains no more information than $\mathsf{f}(R_{i'}, X')$ for some $1 \leq i' \leq N$ and $X' \in \{0,1\}^{k_1}$. As in [24], we do not require that $i' = i$ and $X' = X$ because a malicious $\mathcal{U}$ may construct the query without following the specification. The concept can also be rephrased as follows: $\mathcal{U}$ cannot tell whether it is an ideal-world execution and a real-world execution. In an ideal-world execution $\mathcal{U}$ interacts with a simulator which takes $(i', f(R_{i'}, X'))$ as input, while in a real-world execution $\mathcal{U}$ interacts with $\mathcal{DB}$.

For the clarity of formalization, let $\mathsf{simulator}_0$ denote $\mathcal{DB}$. Formally, an EPIR protocol achieves database privacy, if there exists a simulator $\mathsf{simulator}_1$ such that any attacker $\mathcal{A} = (\mathcal{A}_1, \mathcal{A}_2)$ has only a negligible advantage in the following game, where the attacker's advantage is $|\Pr[b' = b] - \frac{1}{2}|$. For every retrieve query, $\mathsf{simulator}_1$ has an auxiliary input from a hypothetical oracle $\mathcal{O}$, where the input is $(i', f(R_{i'}, X'))$ for some $1 \le i' \le N$ and $X' \in \{0, 1\}^{k_1}$.

$$\mathbf{Exp}_{\mathcal{A}}^{\text{database-privacy}}$$

$$\left|
\begin{array}{ll}
b & \xleftarrow{R} \{0, 1\} \\
\mathbf{R} = (R_1, R_2, \cdots, R_N) & \leftarrow \mathcal{A}_1(1^{\ell}) \\
b' & \leftarrow \mathcal{A}_2(\mathsf{simulator}_b; \text{retrieve})
\end{array}
\right.$$

In this game, the attacker $\mathcal{A}$ is a malicious $\mathcal{U}$. For the clarity, we rephrase the game as follows.

1. The challenger randomly chooses $b \in \{0, 1\}$. If $b = 0$ then $\mathsf{simulator}_0$ answers the retrieve queries from the attacker; otherwise $\mathsf{simulator}_1$ answers such queries.
2. The attacker $\mathcal{A}_1$ generates N blocks $\mathbf{R} = (R_1, R_2, \cdots, R_N)$.
3. The attacker $\mathcal{A}_2$ can start any (polynomial) number of retrieve queries. At some point, $\mathcal{A}_2$ outputs a guess b'.

We emphasize that the hypothetical oracle $\mathcal{O}$ may have unlimited computing resources. In an attack game, a malicious $\mathcal{U}$ may or may not generate a query by following the protocol specification, nonetheless, in order to answer the attacker's query, $\mathsf{simulator}_1$ only needs to obtain $f(R_{i'}, X')$ for some $1 \le i' \le N$ and $X' \in \{0, 1\}^{k_1}$. As a result, if the attacker cannot distinguish the interactions with $\mathsf{simulator}_0$ and $\mathsf{simulator}_1$, then, for each query, it obtains no more information about $\mathbf{R}$ than i' and $f(R_{i'}, X')$, which is what $\mathsf{simulator}_1$ needs to answer the query.

2.4   Security of EPIR

Analogous to the case of other primitives, a (useful) EPIR protocol should be sound, which means that if both $\mathcal{U}$ and $\mathcal{DB}$ follow the protocol specification then $\text{retrieve}(f, i, X)$ always returns the correct value of $f(R_i, X)$ with an overwhelming probability.

Definition 2. *An EPIR protocol is said to be secure if any attacker has only negligible advantage in the attack games for user privacy and database privacy.*

3   EPIR Protocol for Testing Equality

In this section we present an EPIR protocol which enables $\mathcal{U}$ to compare a string with a block from $\mathcal{DB}$. The function $f(R_i, X)$ is defined to be 1 if $R_i = X$ and to be 0 otherwise. Suppose every block in $\mathcal{DB}$ has bit-length ℓ_1, X also has bit-length ℓ_1, and N has bit-length ℓ_2.

The construction is based on the ElGamal scheme and a PIR protocol. It is worth noting that, due to the randomization in step 3, the employed PIR protocol does not need to be SPIR (achieving database privacy) in order to guarantee the database privacy for the EPIR.

3.1   Description of the Protocol

The EPIR protocol is as follows.

1. $\mathcal{U}$ generates an ElGamal key pair (pk, sk), where $pk = (p, q, g, y)$, $y = g^x$, and $sk = x$ is randomly chosen from $\mathbb{Z}_q$. It is required that the bit-length of q is at least $\ell_1 + \ell_2 + 1$. Let "$||$" be the string concatenation operator.
2. To retrieve the value $f(R_i, X)$, for any $1 \le i \le N$ and $X \in \{0,1\}^{\ell_1}$, $\mathcal{U}$ first sends pk and an ElGamal ciphertext $(g^r, y^r g^{i||X})$ to $\mathcal{DB}$, where r is randomly chosen from $\mathbb{Z}_q$.
3. After receiving pk and $(g^r, y^r g^{i||X})$ from $\mathcal{U}$, $\mathcal{DB}$ first checks that pk is a valid ElGamal public key[2] and $(g^r, y^r g^{i||X})$ is a valid ElGamal ciphertext. If the check succeeds, $\mathcal{DB}$ computes C_j for every $1 \le j \le N$, where r_j, r'_j are randomly chosen from $\mathbb{Z}_q$ and

$$C_j = (g^{r'_j}(g^r)^{r_j}, y^{r'_j}(y^r g^{i||X}(g^{j||R_j})^{-1})^{r_j}).$$

4. $\mathcal{U}$ runs a PIR protocol to retrieve C_i from $\mathcal{DB}$. $\mathcal{U}$ then sets $f(i, X) = 1$ if $\text{Dec}(C_i, sk) = 1$ and sets $f(i, X) = 0$ otherwise.

It is clear that, in our case, no encoding algorithm Ω is required to guarantee the semantic security of the ElGamal scheme. As to the performance, the communication complexity is dominated by that of the PIR protocol. The computational complexity is dominated by the computation of C_j $(1 \le j \le N)$, say $O(N)$ exponentiations for $\mathcal{DB}$. Moreover, it is straightforward to verify the following observation.

Observation 1. *For every $1 \le j \le N$, if $g^{i||X}(g^{j||R_j})^{-1} \ne 1$, the components of $C_j = (C_{j1}, C_{j2})$ are uniformly and independently distributed over $\mathbb{G}$; otherwise C_{j1} is uniformly distributed over $\mathbb{G}$ and $C_{j2} = (C_{j1})^x$.*

Due to the bit-length requirement on q, if $\ell_1 + \ell_2 + 1$ is very large then the protocol may become impractical. Note that ℓ_2 will be bounded by a reasonably small integer (say 50), because it is hard to imagine that we have a database

---

[2] In practice, the validity of pk can be certified by a TTP, and the same pk can be used by the user for all his queries.

with 2^{50} records. As a result, in this situation, a simple solution is to work on the records $\mathbf{R}' = (R'_1, R'_2, \cdots, R'_N)$ instead of $\mathbf{R}$, where $R'_j = \mathsf{H}(R_j)$ $(1 \leq j \leq N)$ and H is a collision-resistant hash function with a reasonable output bit-length. Inherently, $\mathcal{U}$ issues a $\mathsf{retrieve}(\mathsf{f}, i, \mathsf{H}(X))$ query to retrieve the value of $\mathsf{f}(R_i, X)$. It is clear that $\mathcal{U}$ gets the correct answer with an overwhelming probability.

Instead of employing the ElGamal encryption scheme, other homomorphic encryption schemes may also be used here though we will need a different randomization method in step 3.

3.2 Security Analysis

It is straightforward to verify that if the PIR protocol is sound then the EPIR protocol for equality is also sound. The following lemmas show that the EPIR protocol achieves user privacy and database privacy but their proofs will appear in the full version of this paper.

Lemma 1 (user privacy). *If the PIR protocol achieves user privacy, then the EPIR protocol for testing equality achieves user privacy based on the DDH assumption.*

Lemma 2 (database privacy). *The EPIR protocol for testing equality achieves database privacy (unconditionally).*

4 EPIR Protocol for Computing Hamming Distance

In this section we present an EPIR protocol which enables $\mathcal{U}$ to compute Hamming distance between a string chosen by itself and a block from $\mathcal{DB}$. Especially, the protocol allows the user to assign a weight for every bit. For an ℓ_1-bit string S, let $S^{(k)}$ denote the k-th bit of S. Let the weight vector be $(w_1, w_2, \cdots, w_{\ell_1})$ where w_k $(1 \leq k \leq \ell_1)$ are integers. The function f is defined as follows.

$$\mathsf{f}(R_i, X) = \sum_{k=1}^{\ell_1} w_k (R_i^{(k)} \oplus X^{(k)})$$

The construction is based on the BGN encryption scheme [3], the GOS NIZK protocol [27], and a PIR protocol. It is worth noting that, due to the randomization in step 3, the employed PIR protocol does not need to be SPIR (achieving database privacy) in order to guarantee the database privacy for the EPIR.

4.1 Description of the Protocol

Suppose every block in $\mathcal{DB}$ has bit-length ℓ_1. The EPIR protocol is as follows.

1. $\mathcal{U}$ generates a key pair (pk, sk) for the BGN encryption scheme, where $pk = (n, \mathbb{G}, \mathbb{G}_1, \hat{e}, g, h)$, and $sk = q_1$.

2. To retrieve the value of $f(R_i, X)$, for any $1 \leq i \leq N$ and $X \in \{0,1\}^{\ell_1}$, $\mathcal{U}$ first sends BGN ciphertexts c and c_k $(1 \leq k \leq \ell_1)$ to $\mathcal{DB}$, where $c = g^i h^r$, $c_k = g^{X^{(k)}} h^{s_k}$ $(1 \leq k \leq \ell_1)$, r and s_k $(1 \leq k \leq \ell_1)$ are randomly chosen from $\mathbb{Z}_n$. In addition, $\mathcal{U}$ also sends $proof_k$ $(1 \leq k \leq \ell_1)$ to $\mathcal{DB}$, where, for every $1 \leq k \leq \ell_1$, $proof_k$ is the GOS NIZK parameter for proving $X^{(k)} \in \{0,1\}$.

3. After receiving c, c_k $(1 \leq k \leq \ell_1)$, and $proof_k$ $(1 \leq k \leq \ell_1)$ from $\mathcal{U}$, $\mathcal{DB}$ first checks that pk is a valid BGN public key[3] and c, c_k $(1 \leq k \leq \ell_1)$ are valid BGN ciphertexts. If the check succeeds, $\mathcal{DB}$ verifies $proof_k$ $(1 \leq k \leq \ell_1)$. If the verification succeeds, $\mathcal{DB}$ computes C_j for every $1 \leq j \leq N$ as follows.

   (a) For every $1 \leq k \leq \ell_1$, compute $m_{j,k}$ where

$$
\begin{aligned}
m_{j,k} &= \frac{\hat{e}(c_k g^{R_j^{(k)}}, g)}{\hat{e}(c_k, g^{R_j^{(k)}})^2} \\
&= \frac{\hat{e}(g^{X^{(k)}} h^{s_k} g^{R_j^{(k)}}, g)}{\hat{e}(g^{X^{(k)}} h^{s_k}, g^{R_j^{(k)}})^2} \\
&= \frac{\hat{e}(g^{X^{(k)}} g^{R_j^{(k)}}, g)\hat{e}(h^{s_k}, g)}{\hat{e}(g^{X^{(k)}}, g^{R_j^{(k)}})^2 \hat{e}(h^{s_k}, g^{R_j^{(k)}})^2} \\
&= \hat{e}(g, g)^{X^{(k)} + R_j^{(k)} - 2X^{(k)} R_j^{(k)}} \hat{e}(h, g)^{s_k(1 - 2R_j^{(k)})} \\
&= \hat{e}(g, g)^{X^{(k)} \oplus R_j^{(k)}} \hat{e}(h, g)^{s_k(1 - 2R_j^{(k)})}
\end{aligned}
$$

   (b) Compute C_j, where r_j, r_j' are randomly chosen from $\mathbb{Z}_n$ and

$$
\begin{aligned}
C_j &= \hat{e}(cg^{-j} h^{r_j'}, g)^{r_j} \prod_{k=1}^{\ell_1} (m_{j,k})^{w_k} \\
&= \hat{e}(g^{i-j} h^{r+r_j'}, g)^{r_j} \prod_{k=1}^{\ell_1} \hat{e}(g, g)^{w_k(X^{(k)} \oplus R_j^{(k)})} \hat{e}(h, g)^{w_k s_k(1 - 2R_j^{(k)})} \\
&= \hat{e}(g, g)^{r_j(i-j) + \sum_{k=1}^{\ell_1} w_k(X^{(k)} \oplus R_j^{(k)})} \hat{e}(h, g)^{r_j(r+r_j') + \sum_{k=1}^{\ell_1} w_k s_k(1 - 2R_j^{(k)})}
\end{aligned}
$$

   Otherwise, $\mathcal{DB}$ aborts the protocol execution.

4. $\mathcal{U}$ runs a PIR protocol to retrieve C_i from $\mathcal{DB}$, and sets $f(i, X) = d$ if $C_i^{q_1} = \hat{e}(g^{q_1}, g)^d$.

As to the performance, the communication complexity is dominated by that of the PIR protocol and the transmission of $c_k, proof_k$ $(1 \leq k \leq \ell_1)$. For $\mathcal{U}$, the computational complexity is dominated by generating $c_k, proof_k$ $(1 \leq k \leq \ell_1)$: $O(\ell_1)$ exponentiations. For $\mathcal{DB}$, the computational complexity is dominated by checking the GOS NIZK proofs and the computation of C_j $(1 \leq j \leq N)$: $O(N + \ell_1)$

---

[3] In practice, the validity of pk can be certified by a TTP, and the same pk can be used by the user for all his queries.

pairing computations and $O(N)$ exponentiations. Moreover, it is straightforward to verify the following observation.

Observation 2. *For every* $1 \leq j \leq N$, *given that* $i \neq j$, *the components of* $C_j = (C_{j1}, C_{j2})$, *where*

$$C_{j1} = \hat{e}(g,g)^{r_j(i-j)+\sum_{k=1}^{\ell_1} w_k(X^{(k)} \oplus R_j^{(k)})}, \; C_{j2} = \hat{e}(h,g)^{r_j(r+r_j')+\sum_{k=1}^{\ell_1} w_k s_k (1-2R_j^{(k)})},$$

are uniformly and independently distributed over $\mathbb{G}_1$ *and the subgroup of order* q_1 *of* $\mathbb{G}_1$, *respectively. If* $i = j$, *then* $C_{j1} = \hat{e}(g,g)^{\sum_{k=1}^{\ell_1} w_k(X^{(k)} \oplus R_j^{(k)})}$ *and* C_{j2} *is uniformly distributed over the subgroup of order* q_1 *of* $\mathbb{G}_1$.

4.2 Security Analysis

It is straightforward to verify that if the PIR protocol is sound then the EPIR protocol is also sound. First, we have the following lemma whose proof will appear in the full version of this paper.

Lemma 3. *Given any* $M \geq 1$, *the attacker's advantage in the following game is negligible for the BGN encryption scheme.*

$$\mathbf{Exp}_{\mathcal{A}}^{P\text{-}IND\text{-}CPA}$$

$$
\begin{aligned}
(pk, sk) &\leftarrow \mathsf{Gen}(1^{\ell}) \\
((m_{0,1}, \ldots, m_{0,M}), (m_{1,1}, \ldots, m_{1,M})) &\leftarrow \mathcal{A}_1(pk) \\
b &\leftarrow \{0, 1\} \\
\mathbf{c} &\leftarrow (\mathsf{Enc}(m_{b,1}, pk), \ldots, \mathsf{Enc}(m_{b,M}, pk)) \\
b' &\leftarrow \mathcal{A}_2(\mathbf{c})
\end{aligned}
$$

The following lemmas show that the EPIR protocol achieves user privacy and database privacy but their proofs will appear in the full version of this paper.

Lemma 4 (user privacy). *If the PIR protocol achieves user privacy, the EPIR protocol for computing Hamming distance achieves user privacy based on the subgroup decision assumption.*

Lemma 5 (database privacy). *The EPIR protocol for computing Hamming distance achieves database privacy (unconditionally).*

5 Authentication Schemes Using Biometrics

5.1 Preliminaries

In our security model, besides human users, we assume that a biometric-based (remote) authentication system consists of the following types of components:

- Authentication client $\mathcal{C}$, which is responsible for extracting human user's biometric template using some biometric sensor and communicating with authentication server.
- Authentication server $\mathcal{S}$, which is responsible for dealing with the human user's authentication requests by querying the database which stores user's biometric template.

- Centralized database $\mathcal{DB}$, which stores the relevant biometric information for authentication[4].

Like most existing biometric-based systems (and many traditional cryptosystems), a biometric-based authentication scheme consists of two phases: an enrollment phase and a verification phase.

1. In the enrollment phase, user U_i registers his biometric template b_i at the database $\mathcal{DB}$ and his identity information ID_i at the authentication server $\mathcal{S}$.
2. In the verification phase, user U_i issues an authentication request to the authentication server $\mathcal{S}$ through a client $\mathcal{C}$. The authentication server $\mathcal{S}$ retrieves U_i's biometric information from the database $\mathcal{DB}$ and makes a decision.

Human users and $\mathcal{S}$ trust $\mathcal{C}$ to be honest, and $\mathcal{S}$ trusts $\mathcal{DB}$ to provide the correct biometric information. We further make the following assumptions on the system components: The communication links between any two components are authenticated and encrypted. In practice, the security links can be implemented using a standard protocol such as SSL or TLS. In addition, the following assumptions are indispensable for all biometrics-based systems.

1. Biometric Distribution assumption: Let H be the distance function in the Hamming space. We assume that, there is a threshold value λ, the probability that $H(b_i, b_j) > \lambda$ is close to 1[5], where b_i is Alice's biometric template and b_j is Bob's biometric template, while the probability that $H(b_i, b_i') \leq \lambda$ is close to 1, where b_i and b_i' are Alice's biometric templates in two measurements.
2. Liveness assumption: We assume that, with a high probability, the biometric template captured by the sensor is from a live human user. In other words, it is difficult to produce a faked biometric template that can be accepted by the sensor.

For a biometric-based authentication scheme, two types of security properties are mainly concerned. One is the resistance to impersonation attacks, in which case we only consider outside adversaries by assuming that all the system components are honest. The other is preserving privacy properties, in which case we only consider malicious inside adversaries including a malicious $\mathcal{S}$ and a malicious $\mathcal{DB}$. But we assume that $\mathcal{S}$ and $\mathcal{DB}$ will not collude. In practice, many methods (for example, issuing a smart-card to every user) can be used to guarantee these properties against other kinds of adversaries, but we omit them in this paper since our main aim is to demonstrate the application of the EPIR protocols.

---

[4] It is worth emphasizing that $\mathcal{DB}$ and $\mathcal{S}$ are two different principles and $\mathcal{DB}$ may serve as a trusted storage for a number of authentication servers. This is different from the conventional environment where we say a server has its own database for storing the authentication secrets.

[5] Note that this probability is related to the false accept and false reject rates of biometrics, but we omit a detailed discussion in this paper.

5.2   The First Biometric-Based Authentication Scheme

This biometric-based authentication scheme is constructed based on the EPIR protocol for equality as described in Section 3.1. In this scheme, due to the secure sketch scheme, the user does not need to store any private information and the client C does not need to store any user specific information. The enrollment phase works as follows.

- C implements a (m, m', λ)-secure sketch $(\mathsf{SS}, \mathsf{Rec})$ (an example is described in Appendix C),where m' is the system security parameter.
- S generates an ElGamal key pair (pk, sk).
- U_i generates his unique pseudorandom identifier ID_i and registers it at the server S, and registers (ID_i, R_i) at the database $\mathcal{DB}$, where b_i is U_i's reference biometric template and

$$R_i = \mathsf{Enc}(g^{ID_i||b_i}, pk)$$
$$= (R_{i1}, R_{i2}).$$

In addition, U_i publicly stores a sketch $sketch_i = \mathsf{SS}(b_i)$.

If U_i wants to authenticate himself to the server S through the authentication client C, then the procedure is as follows.

1. C extracts U_i's biometric template b_i^* and computes the adjusted template $b_i' = \mathsf{Rec}(b_i^*, sketch_i)$. Then C sends ID_i to S and sends X to $\mathcal{DB}$, where $X = \mathsf{Enc}(g^{ID_i||b_i'}, pk)$. Otherwise, C aborts the operation.
2. After receiving X, $\mathcal{DB}$ performs as in the EPIR protocol for testing equality as described in Section 3.1, where $\mathcal{DB}$ computes C_j for every $1 \leq j \leq N$, where r_j, r_j' are randomly chosen from $\mathbb{Z}_q$ and

$$C_j = (g^{r_j'}(g^r(R_{i1})^{-1})^{r_j}, y^{r_j'}(y^r g^{ID_i||X}(R_{i2})^{-1})^{r_j})$$

3. The server runs a PIR to retrieve C_i. If $\mathsf{Dec}(C_i, sk) = 1$, S accepts the request; otherwise rejects it.

It is easy to verify that impersonation attacks are prevented based on the biometric distribution assumption, i.e. an adversary can not force C to output U_j's template by letting C measure $U_i's$ biometric if U_i and U_j are different human users.

Every authentication is indeed an execution of the EPIR protocol for testing equality between S and $\mathcal{DB}$, though X is sent to $\mathcal{DB}$ by a trusted C. From the user privacy property of the EPIR protocol, $\mathcal{DB}$ learns nothing about which user is authenticating himself and what is the authentication result. In addition, $\mathcal{DB}$ obtains nothing about the registered biometric templates because they are encrypted by S's public key. From the database privacy property of the EPIR protocol, S learns nothing about a user's biometric template. In fact, S only obtains the information whether the authentication request is made by the legitimate user or not.

5.3   The Second Biometric-Based Authentication Scheme

This biometric-based authentication scheme is constructed based on the EPIR protocol for computing Hamming distance as described in Section 4.1. In this scheme, the user does not need to store any private or public information and the client $\mathcal{C}$ does not need to store any user specific information. The server $\mathcal{S}$ is enabled to make its decision based on an exact matching between a user's biometric templates. The overall matching result can be more accurate by allocating a score (or a weight) for the matching result of every single bit. The enrollment phase works as follows.

- $\mathcal{S}$ generates a BGN encryption key pair (pk, sk).
- U_i generates his pseudorandom identifier ID_i and registers it at the server $\mathcal{S}$, and registers $(ID_i, \alpha_i^{(k)}\ (1 \leq k \leq \ell_1))$ at the database $\mathcal{DB}$, where b_i is U_i's reference biometric template with bit-length ℓ_1, $\alpha_i^{(k)} = g^{b_i^{(k)}} h^{\beta_{ik}}\ (1 \leq k \leq \ell_1)$, and $\beta_{ik}\ (1 \leq k \leq \ell_1)$ are randomly chosen from $\mathbb{Z}_n$.

If U_i wants to authenticate himself to the server $\mathcal{S}$ through the authentication client $\mathcal{C}$, then the procedure is as follows.

1. $\mathcal{C}$ extracts U_i's biometric template b_i', and sends c and $c_k\ (1 \leq k \leq \ell_1)$ to $\mathcal{DB}$, where $c = g^{ID_i} h^r$, $c_k = g^{b_i'^{(k)}} h^{s_k}\ (1 \leq k \leq \ell_1)$, r and $s_k\ (1 \leq k \leq \ell_1)$ are randomly chosen from $\mathbb{Z}_n$. Simultaneously, $\mathcal{C}$ sends ID_i to $\mathcal{S}$.
2. After receiving c and $c_k\ (1 \leq k \leq \ell_1)$, $\mathcal{DB}$ performs in a similar way as in the EPIR protocol for computing Hamming distance except that it computes C_j for every $1 \leq j \leq N$ as follows.
   (a) For every $1 \leq k \leq \ell_1$, compute $m_{j,k}$ where

$$
\begin{aligned}
m_{j,k} &= \frac{\hat{e}(c_k \alpha_j^{(k)}, g)}{\hat{e}(c_k, \alpha_j^{(k)})^2} \\
&= \frac{\hat{e}(c_k g^{b_j^{(k)}} h^{\beta_{jk}}, g)}{\hat{e}(c_k, g^{b_j^{(k)}} h^{\beta_{jk}})^2} \\
&= \frac{\hat{e}(g^{b_i'^{(k)}} h^{s_k + \beta_{jk}} g^{b_j^{(k)}}, g)}{\hat{e}(g^{b_i'^{(k)}} h^{s_k}, g^{b_j^{(k)}} h^{\beta_{jk}})^2} \\
&= \frac{\hat{e}(g^{b_i'^{(k)}} g^{b_j^{(k)}}, g) \hat{e}(h^{s_k + \beta_{jk}}, g)}{\hat{e}(g^{b_i'^{(k)}}, g^{b_j^{(k)}})^2 \hat{e}(h, g)^{2(s_k b_j^{(k)} + b_i'^{(k)} \beta_{jk} + s_k \beta_{jk} \log_g h)}} \\
&= \hat{e}(g, g)^{b_i'^{(k)} + b_j^{(k)} - 2 b_i'^{(k)} b_j^{(k)}} \hat{e}(h, g)^{s_k(1 - 2\beta_{jk} \log_g h - 2b_j^{(k)}) + \beta_{jk}(1 - 2b_i'^{(k)})} \\
&= \hat{e}(g, g)^{b_i'^{(k)} \oplus R_j^{(k)}} \hat{e}(h, g)^{s_k(1 - 2\beta_{jk} \log_g h - 2b_j^{(k)}) + \beta_{jk}(1 - 2b_i'^{(k)})}
\end{aligned}
$$

   (b) Let $x_{jk} = s_k(1 - 2\beta_{jk} \log_g h - 2b_j^{(k)}) + \beta_{jk}(1 - 2b_i'^{(k)})\ (1 \leq k \leq \ell_1)$, compute C_j, where r_j, r_j' are randomly chosen from $\mathbb{Z}_n$ and

$$C_j = \hat{e}(cg^{-ID_j}h^{r'_j}, g)^{r_j} \prod_{k=1}^{\ell_1} (m_{j,k})^{w_k}$$

$$= \hat{e}(g^{ID_i - ID_j}h^{r+r'_j}, g)^{r_j} \prod_{k=1}^{\ell_1} \hat{e}(g, g)^{w_k(b'^{(k)}_i \oplus b^{(k)}_j)} \hat{e}(h, g)^{w_k x_{jk}}$$

$$= \hat{e}(g, g)^{r_j(ID_i - ID_j) + \sum_{k=1}^{\ell_1} w_k(b'^{(k)}_i \oplus b^{(k)}_j)} \hat{e}(h, g)^{r_j(r+r'_j) + \sum_{k=1}^{\ell_1} w_k x_{jk}}$$

3. $\mathcal{S}$ runs a PIR to retrieve C_i, and computes d satisfying $C_i^{q_1} = \hat{e}(g^{q_1}, g)^d$. $\mathcal{S}$ accepts the request if d is smaller than a threshold value; otherwise rejects it.

We first emphasize that the GOS NIZK proofs are omitted in this authentication scheme because c and c_k ($1 \leq k \leq \ell_1$) are sent by $\mathcal{C}$ which is trusted by all parties.

It is easy to verify that impersonation attacks are prevented based on the biometric distribution assumption. Every authentication is indeed an execution of the EPIR protocol for computing Hamming distance between $\mathcal{S}$ and $\mathcal{DB}$, though we have made some small modifications. As a result, this scheme achieves the same security properties as those of the previous scheme.

Compared with the previous scheme, this scheme is more convenient for human users and the the client $\mathcal{C}$, where a human user does not need to store any information and secure sketch is not needed to be implemented in $\mathcal{C}$. Another advantage of this protocol is that it works even when secure sketches are not practical (i.e. when noise is high).

6   Conclusion

In this paper we formulated the concept of EPIR and proposed two protocols: one for testing equality and the other for computing Hamming distance. The randomizations in both protocols are performed to avoid using a SPIR protocol in order to achieve the privacy for the database. In addition, the randomizations also guarantee that the privacy for the database is unconditionally achieved (without any computational assumption). It is a challenging task to design more efficient EPIR protocols, especially to reduce the computational complexity. In this paper, we also showed how to construct strong privacy-preserving biometric-based authentication schemes by employing these EPIR protocols. Some further work is required to evaluate the performance of these schemes in practice.

References

1. Atallah, M.J., Frikken, K.B., Goodrich, M.T., Tamassia, R.: Secure biometric authentication for weak computational devices. Financial Cryptography, 357–371 (2005)
2. Bolle, R.M., Connell, J.H., Ratha, N.K.: Biometric perils and patches. Pattern Recognition 35(12), 2727–2738 (2002)

3. Boneh, D., Goh, E., Nissim, K.: Evaluating 2-DNF formulas on ciphertexts. In: Kilian, J. (ed.) TCC 2005. LNCS, vol. 3378, pp. 325–341. Springer, Heidelberg (2005)
4. Boyen, X.: Reusable cryptographic fuzzy extractors. In: Atluri, V., Pfitzmann, B., McDaniel, P.D. (eds.) CCS 2004: Proceedings of the 11th ACM conference on Computer and communications security, pp. 82–91. ACM Press, New York (2004)
5. Boyen, X., Dodis, Y., Katz, J., Ostrovsky, R., Smith, A.: Secure remote authentication using biometric data. In: Cramer, R.J.F. (ed.) EUROCRYPT 2005. LNCS, vol. 3494, pp. 147–163. Springer, Heidelberg (2005)
6. Bringer, J., Chabanne, H., Izabachène, M., Pointcheval, D., Tang, Q., Zimmer, S.: An application of the Goldwasser-Micali cryptosystem to biometric authentication. In: Pieprzyk, J., Ghodosi, H., Dawson, E. (eds.) Information Security and Privacy, 12th Australasian Conference, ACISP 2007 Proceedings. LNCS, vol. 4586, pp. 96–106. Springer, Heidelberg (2007)
7. Cachin, C., Micali, S., Stadler, M.: Computationally private information retrieval with polylogarithmic communication. In: Stern, J. (ed.) EUROCRYPT 1999. LNCS, vol. 1592, pp. 402–414. Springer, Heidelberg (1999)
8. Canetti, R., Ishai, Y., Kumar, R., Reiter, M.K., Rubinfeld, R., Wright, R.N.: Selective private function evaluation with applications to private statistics. In: PODC 2001: Proceedings of the twentieth annual ACM symposium on Principles of distributed computing, pp. 293–304. ACM Press, New York (2001)
9. Chor, B., Gilboa, N.: Computationally private information retrieval (extended abstract). In: Proceedings of the Twenty-Ninth Annual ACM Symposium on the Theory of Computing, pp. 304–313 (1997)
10. Chor, B., Kushilevitz, E., Goldreich, O., Sudan, M.: Private information retrieval. J. ACM 45(6), 965–981 (1998)
11. Crepeau, C., Salvail, L.: Oblivious verification of common string. CWI Quarterly, special issue for Crypto Course 10th Anniversary 8(2), 97–109 (1995)
12. Crescenzo, G.D., Graveman, R., Ge, R., Arce, G.: Approximate message authentication and biometric entity authentication. In: Patrick, A.S., Yung, M. (eds.) FC 2005. LNCS, vol. 3570, pp. 240–254. Springer, Heidelberg (2005)
13. Crescenzo, G.D., Malkin, T., Ostrovsky, R.: Single database private information retrieval implies oblivious transfer. In: Preneel, B. (ed.) EUROCRYPT 2000. LNCS, vol. 1807, pp. 122–138. Springer, Heidelberg (2000)
14. Dodis, Y., Katz, J., Reyzin, L., Smith, A.: Robust fuzzy extractors and authenticated key agreement from close secrets. In: Dwork, C. (ed.) CRYPTO 2006. LNCS, vol. 4117, pp. 232–250. Springer, Heidelberg (2006)
15. Dodis, Y., Reyzin, L., Smith, A.: Fuzzy extractors: How to generate strong keys from biometrics and other noisy data. In: Cachin, C., Camenisch, J.L. (eds.) EUROCRYPT 2004. LNCS, vol. 3027, pp. 523–540. Springer, Heidelberg (2004)
16. Du, W., Atallah, M.: Privacy-preserving cooperative statistical analysis. In: ACSAC 2001: Proceedings of the 17th Annual Computer Security Applications Conference, pp. 102–110. IEEE Computer Society, Los Alamitos (2001)
17. Du, W., Atallah, M.J.: Secure multi-party computation problems and their applications: a review and open problems. In: NSPW 2001: Proceedings of the 2001 workshop on New security paradigms, pp. 13–22. ACM Press, New York (2001)
18. ElGamal, T.: A public key cryptosystem and a signature scheme based on discrete logarithms. In: Blakely, G.R., Chaum, D. (eds.) CRYPTO 1984. LNCS, vol. 196, pp. 10–18. Springer, Heidelberg (1985)
19. Fagin, R., Naor, M., Winkler, P.: Comparing information without leaking it. Communications of the ACM 39(5), 77–85 (1996)

20. Freedman, M.J., Ishai, Y., Pinkas, B., Reingold, O.: Keyword search and oblivious pseudorandom functions. In: Kilian, J. (ed.) TCC 2005. LNCS, vol. 3378, pp. 303–324. Springer, Heidelberg (2005)

21. Freedman, M.J., Nissim, K., Pinkas, B.: Efficient private matching and set intersection. In: Cachin, C., Camenisch, J.L. (eds.) EUROCRYPT 2004. LNCS, vol. 3027, pp. 1–19. Springer, Heidelberg (2004)

22. Gasarch, W.: A survey on private information retrieval, http://www.cs.umd.edu/~gasarch/pir/pir.html

23. Gentry, C., Ramzan, Z.: Single-database private information retrieval with constant communication rate. In: Caires, L., Italiano, G.F., Monteiro, L., Palamidessi, C., Yung, M. (eds.) ICALP 2005. LNCS, vol. 3580, pp. 803–815. Springer, Heidelberg (2005)

24. Gertner, Y., Ishai, Y., Kushilevitz, E., Malkin, T.: Protecting data privacy in private information retrieval schemes. In: Proceedings of the Thirtieth Annual ACM Symposium on the Theory of Computing, pp. 151–160 (1998)

25. Goethals, B., Laur, S., Lipmaa, H., Mielikäinen, T.: On private scalar product computation for privacy-preserving data mining. In: Park, C.-s., Chee, S. (eds.) ICISC 2004. LNCS, vol. 3506, pp. 104–120. Springer, Heidelberg (2005)

26. Goldreich, O.: Foundations of Cryptography: Basic Applications, vol. 2. Cambridge University Press, Cambridge (2004)

27. Groth, J., Ostrovsky, R., Sahai, A.: Perfect non-interactive zero knowledge for NP. In: Vaudenay, S. (ed.) EUROCRYPT 2006. LNCS, vol. 4004, pp. 339–358. Springer, Heidelberg (2006)

28. Hao, F., Anderson, R., Daugman, J.: Combining crypto with biometrics effectively. IEEE Transactions on Computers 55(9), 1081–1088 (2006)

29. Juels, A., Sudan, M.: A fuzzy vault scheme. Des. Codes Cryptography 38(2), 237–257 (2006)

30. Juels, A., Wattenberg, M.: A fuzzy commitment scheme. In: ACM Conference on Computer and Communications Security, pp. 28–36 (1999)

31. Kiltz, E., Leander, G., Malone-Lee, J.: Secure computation of the mean and related statistics. In: Kilian, J. (ed.) TCC 2005. LNCS, vol. 3378, pp. 283–302. Springer, Heidelberg (2005)

32. Kushilevitz, E., Ostrovsky, R.: Replication is NOT needed: Single database, computationally-private information retrieval. In: FOCS 1997. 38th Annual Symposium on Foundations of Computer Science, pp. 364–373 (1997)

33. Linnartz, J.M.G., Tuyls, P.: New shielding functions to enhance privacy and prevent misuse of biometric templates. In: Kittler, J., Nixon, M.S. (eds.) AVBPA 2003. LNCS, vol. 2688, pp. 393–402. Springer, Heidelberg (2003)

34. Lipmaa, H.: An oblivious transfer protocol with log-squared communication. In: Zhou, J., Lopez, J., Deng, R.H., Bao, F. (eds.) ISC 2005. LNCS, vol. 3650, pp. 314–328. Springer, Heidelberg (2005)

35. Mishra, S.K., Sarkar, P.: Symmetrically private information retrieval. In: Roy, B., Okamoto, E. (eds.) INDOCRYPT 2000. LNCS, vol. 1977, pp. 225–236. Springer, Heidelberg (2000)

36. Naor, M., Pinkas, B.: Oblivious polynomial evaluation. SIAM J. Comput. 35(5), 1254–1281 (2006)

37. Ostrovsky, R., Skeith III, W.E.: A survey of single database PIR: Techniques and applications. Cryptology ePrint Archive: Report 2007/059 (2007)

38. Ratha, N., Connell, J., Bolle, R.M., Chikkerur, S.: Cancelable biometrics: A case study in fingerprints. In: ICPR 2006: Proceedings of the 18th International Conference on Pattern Recognition, pp. 370–373. IEEE Computer Society, Los Alamitos (2006)

39. Ratha, N.K., Connell, J.H., Bolle, R.M.: Enhancing security and privacy in biometrics-based authentication systems. IBM Systems Journal 40(3), 614–634 (2001)

40. Safavi-Naini, R., Tonien, D.: Fuzzy universal hashing and approximate authentication. Cryptology ePrint Archive: Report 2005/256 (2005)

41. Schoenmakers, B., Tuyls, P.: Efficient binary conversion for Paillier encrypted values. In: Vaudenay, S. (ed.) EUROCRYPT 2006. LNCS, vol. 4004, pp. 522–537. Springer, Heidelberg (2006)

42. Tuyls, P., Akkermans, A.H.M., Kevenaar, T.A.M., Jan Schrijen, G., Bazen, A.M., Veldhuis, R.N.J.: Practical biometric authentication with template protection. In: Kanade, T., Jain, A., Ratha, N.K. (eds.) AVBPA 2005. LNCS, vol. 3546, pp. 436–446. Springer, Heidelberg (2005)

43. Tuyls, P., Goseling, J.: Capacity and examples of template-protecting biometric authentication systems. In: Pajdla, T., Matas, J(G.) (eds.) ECCV 2004. LNCS, vol. 3021, pp. 158–170. Springer, Heidelberg (2004)

44. Tuyls, P., Verbitskiy, E., Goseling, J., Denteneer, D.: Privacy protecting biometric authentication systems: an overview. In: EUSIPCO 2004 (2004)

45. Uludag, U., Pankanti, S., Prabhakar, S., Jain, A.K.: Biometric cryptosystems: Issues and challenges. Proceedings of the IEEE 92(6), 948–960 (2004)

46. Vaidya, J., Clifton, C.: Privacy preserving association rule mining in vertically partitioned data. In: KDD 2002: Proceedings of the eighth ACM SIGKDD international conference on Knowledge discovery and data mining, pp. 639–644 (2002)

47. Verbitskiy, E., Tuyls, P., Denteneer, D., Linnartz, J.P.: Reliable biometric authentication with privacy protection. In: SPIE Biometric Technology for Human Identification Conf. (2004)

48. Atallah, M.J., Du, W.: Protocols for secure remote database access with approximate matching. Technical report, CERIAS, Purdue University. CERIAS TR (2000)-15 (2000)

49. Yao, A.: Protocols for secure computations. In: Proceedings of the twenty-third annual IEEE Symposium on Foundations of Computer Science, pp. 160–164 (1982)

Appendix A: Introduction to the ElGamal Encryption Scheme

The algorithms $(\mathsf{Gen}, \mathsf{Enc}, \mathsf{Dec})$ of the ElGamal public key encryption scheme [18] are defined as follows:

1. The key generation algorithm Gen takes a security parameter 1^k as input and generates two primes p, q satisfying $q | p - 1$. Let $\mathbb{G}$ be the subgroup of order q in $\mathbb{Z}_p^*$, g be a generator of $\mathbb{G}$. The private key x which is randomly chosen from $\mathbb{Z}_q$, and the public key is $y = g^x$. Let Ω be a bijective map from $\mathbb{Z}_q$ to $\mathbb{G}$.

2. The encryption algorithm Enc takes a message m and the public key y as input, and outputs the ciphertext $c = (c_1, c_2) = (g^r, y^r \Omega(m))$ where r is randomly chosen from $\mathbb{Z}_q^*$.

3. The decryption algorithm Dec takes a ciphertext $c = (c_1, c_2)$ and the private key x as input, and outputs the message $m = \Omega^{-1}((c_1^{-x}c_2)$.

It is well-known that the ElGamal scheme is semantically secure based on the DDH assumption.

Appendix B: Introduction to the BGN Scheme

The algorithms (Gen, Enc, Dec) of the BGN encryption scheme [3] are defined as follows:

1. The key generation algorithm Gen takes a security parameter 1^k as input and generates a tuple $(n, q_1, q_2, \mathbb{G}, \mathbb{G}_1, \hat{e}, g, u, h)$, where q_1 and q_2 are two primes, $n = q_1 q_2$, $\mathbb{G}$ and $\mathbb{G}_1$ are two cyclic groups of order n, g and u are generators of $\mathbb{G}$, and $h = u^{q_2}$. The private key $sk = q_1$, and the public key is $pk = (n, \mathbb{G}, \mathbb{G}_1, \hat{e}, g, h)$.
2. The encryption algorithm Enc takes a message $m \in \mathbb{Z}_{q_2}$ and the public key pk as input, and outputs the ciphertext $c = g^m h^r$ where r is randomly chosen from $\mathbb{Z}_n$.
3. The decryption algorithm Dec takes a ciphertext c and the private key sk as input, and outputs the message $c^{q_1} = (g^{q_1})^m$. Then compute the discrete log of c^{q_1} base g^{q_1}.

It is proved by Boneh, Goh, and Nissim that this scheme is semantically secure given the subgroup decision problem is hard for $(n, \mathbb{G}, \mathbb{G}_1, \hat{e})$.

Appendix C: Introduction to Secure Sketches

Roughly speaking, a secure sketch scheme (SS, Rec) allows recovery of a hidden value from any value close to this hidden value. Informally, the algorithm SS take a value x as input and outputs some public value y, and the algorithm Rec takes a value x' and y as input and outputs a value x''. If x' and x are close enough, then $x'' = x$.

We take the Code-Offset Construction given in [15] as an example. let C be a $[n, k, 2t + 1]$ error-correction code over a field $\mathbb{F}$. With input $x \in \mathbb{F}^n$, y is computed as $SS(x) = x - c$, where c is a random codeword. With input (x', y), Rec computes x'' in the following way: compute $c' = x' - y$, decode c' to obtain c'', and set $x'' = c'' + y$.

Strongly Secure Certificateless Public Key Encryption Without Pairing

Yinxia Sun[1], Futai Zhang[1], and Joonsang Baek[2]

[1] School of Mathematics and Computer Science,
Nanjing Normal University, Nanjing 210097, P.R. China
[2] Institute for Infocomm Research,
21 Heng Mui Keng Terrace, Singapore 119613, Singapore

Abstract. *Certificateless Public Key Cryptography* (CLPKC) enjoys the advantage of ID-based public key cryptography without suffering from the key escrow problem. In 2005, Baek et al. proposed the first certificateless encryption (CLPKE) scheme that does not depend on pairing. Although it provides high efficiency, one drawback of their scheme is that the security proof only holds for a weaker security model in which the Type I adversary is not allowed to replace the public key associated with the challenge identity. In this paper, we eliminate this limitation and construct a strongly secure CLPKE scheme without pairing. We prove that the proposed scheme is secure against adaptive chosen-ciphertext attack in the random oracle model, provided that the Computational Diffie-Hellman problem is intractable.

Keywords: public key encryption, certificateless public key encryption, Computational Diffie-Hellman problem.

1 Introduction

Motivation. In traditional public key cryptography, the authenticity of public keys is guaranteed in the form of certificate issued by a Certification Authority (CA). Anyone who wants to send a confidential message to someone else by using a public key encryption must first verify the corresponding certificate to check the validity of the public key. The problems of certificate-based cryptography have been well documented, especially the issues associated with the certificate management, including storage, distribution, and the computation cost of certificate verification.

In 1984, Shamir proposed the notion of *Identity-Based Cryptography* [15] in which an entity's public key is derived directly from its identity, such as IP address or an e-mail address, while the private key is generated by a trusted third party called a private key generator (PKG). The first fully-functional and secure identity-based public key encryption scheme was presented in [5]. The advantage of Identity-Based Cryptography is the elimination of the need for certificates. On the other hand, the full dependence on the Private Key Generator (PKG) to generate private keys for entities inevitably introduces key escrow problem.

F. Bao et al. (Eds.): CANS 2007, LNCS 4856, pp. 194–208, 2007.

In 2003, Al-Riyami and Paterson brought forth a new paradigm called *Certificateless Public Key Cryptography* [1] which enjoys the advantage of identity-based public key cryptography without suffering from the key escrow problem. Since then, a variety of certificateless public key encryption (CLPKE) schemes have been proposed [17,6,2,18,16,4,11,14,12]. In 2005, Baek et al. [3] proposed the first CLPKE scheme that does not depending on the pairings. Compared to the previous CLPKE schemes, an attractive feature of their scheme is the efficiency gained from removing computationally-heavy pairing operations. However, the security model for CLPKE, which Baek et al' uses in [3] to analyze their scheme is, as pointed out in [11], sightly weaker than Al-Riyami and Patersen's [1] original security model for CLPKE in a sense that the Type I adversary is not allowed to request a partial private key associated with the challenge (target) identity at any time during the attack. (In Al-Riyami and Patersen's security model for CLPKE, the Type I adversary *can* request a partial private key associated with the target identity if the public key associated with it has not been replaced.) In addition to this, we point out that Baek et al.'s security analysis for their scheme fails to consider the case when the Type I adversary replaces the public key associated with the challenge identity; and that when this public key replacement occurs, it is impossible to present a reduction from the Computational Diffie-Hellman (CDH) problem to the Type I security of Baek et al's CLPKE scheme as the CDH attack algorithm simulating the environment of the Type I adversary does not know the private corresponding to the public key that has been replaced, which is used to derive the Diffie-Hellman key at the end of the simulation.

Our Contributions. It seems to us that it is not easy to fix the above problem without modifying Baek et al's scheme nor introducing somewhat non-standard computational assumption related to the CDH assumption. In this paper we take the former approach. Namely, we modify Baek et al.'s CLPKE scheme to construct a new one, which is proven to be secure against the Type I and Type II adversaries in a strong sense that the Type I adversary *is able to* replace the public key associated with the challenge identity (before challenge phase) but is unable to extract partial private key associated with the challenge identity at any time during the attack, provided that the Computational Diffie-Hellman problem is intractable and the underlying hash functions are the random oracles.

The rest of our paper is organized as follows. Section 2 gives definitions of CLPKE and the security model. Our scheme is given in Section 3 followed by the security proof in Section 4. Section 5 concludes the paper.

2   Definitions

First we recall the definition of certificateless public key encryption, given by Baek et al. [3]. Note that their definition of CLPKE is slightly weaker than the one given by Al-Riyami and Patersen [1] in a sense that the user must authenticate himself/herself to the Key Generation Center (KGC) and obtain an appropriate partial public key to create a public key, while Al-Riyami and Patersen's original CLPKE does not require this. A formal definition follows.

Definition 1 (Certificateless Public Key Encryption Scheme). A certificateless public key encryption (CLPKE) scheme is defined by the following seven algorithms:

- Setup: Providing some security parameter k as input, the KGC runs this algorithm to create a master key mk and a list of public parameters params.
- PartialKeyExtract: Providing params, mk and a user's identifier ID as input, the KGC runs this algorithm to create a partial private key D_{ID} and a partial public key P_{ID}.
- SetSecretValue: Providing params and ID as input, the user (the owner of ID) runs this algorithm to create a secret value s_{ID}.
- SetPrivateKey: Providing params, D_{ID} and s_{ID} as input, the user runs this algorithm to set a private key SK_{ID}.
- SetPublicKey: Providing params, P_{ID} and s_{ID} as input, the user runs this algorithm to set a public key PK_{ID}.
- Encrypt: Providing params, PK_{ID}, ID and a message M as input, any entity runs this algorithm to create a ciphertext C. Note that C can be a special symbol $\perp$, meaning "Reject".
- Decrypt: Providing params, SK_{ID} and C, the user runs this algorithm to decrypt C into M. Note that M can be a special symbol $\perp$ ("Reject").

We now review Baek et al.'s definition of the security of the CLPKE scheme. As usual, their definition considers two types of adversaries, Type I and Type II. The difference between them is that a Type I adversary $\mathcal{A}_I$ does not have access to the master key but may replace public keys of arbitrary identities with values of its own choice, whereas a Type II adversary $\mathcal{A}_{II}$ does have access to the master key but may not replace public keys of entities. As pointed out in [11], Baek et al.'s security definition for a Type I adversary is weaker than Al-Riyami and Patersen's [1] in a sense that $\mathcal{A}_I$ does not extract partial private key for the target identity in any phase. That is, the security models we use here are the Strong Type I* and the Weak Type II models proposed by W.Dent [7].

Definition 2 (Security of CLPKE). Let $\mathcal{A}_I$ and $\mathcal{A}_{II}$ denote Type I and II adversaries for the CLPKE scheme respectively. We consider two games Game I and Game II where $\mathcal{A}_I$ and $\mathcal{A}_{II}$ interact with their Challenger. Note that the Challenger keeps a history of query-answer while interacting with the adversaries.

Game I (for a Type I adversary)

- **Setup:** The Challenger runs Setup by taking a security parameter k as input to generate a master key mk and a list of public parameters params. It gives params to the adversary $\mathcal{A}_I$ and keeps mk secret.
- **Phase 1:** Below, we describe $\mathcal{A}_I$'s various queries and the Challenger's responses to them:

- **Partial Key Extraction query** ID: The Challenger runs PartialKeyExtract to generate the partial private key D_{ID} and the partial public key P_{ID}, and returns them to $\mathcal{A}_I$.
- **Private Key Extraction** ID: The challenger runs PartialKeyExtract and SetSecretValue to generate (D_{ID}, P_{ID}) and s_{ID} respectively, and then runs SetPrivateKey to generate the private key SK_{ID}. It returns SK_{ID} to $\mathcal{A}_I$.
- **Public Key request** ID: The challenger runs PartialKeyExtract and SetSecretValue to generate (D_{ID}, P_{ID}) and s_{ID} respectively, and then runs SetPublicKey to generate the public key PK_{ID}. It returns PK_{ID} to $\mathcal{A}_I$.
- **Public Key Replacement:** The adversary $\mathcal{A}_I$ can repeatedly replace the public key for any identity with any value of its choice. The current value of an entity's public key is used by the challenger in any computation or response to the adversary's requests.
- **Decryption query:** The adversary supplies an identity ID and a ciphertext C. The challenger responds with the decryption of C under the private key that is associated with the current public key.

- **Challenge Phase:** Once $\mathcal{A}_I$ decides that Phase 1 is over, it outputs the challenge identity ID^* and two equal-length plaintext messages (M_0, M_1). Note that ID^* has not been queried to extract a partial private key nor a private key at any time. The Challenger picks $\beta \in_R \{0,1\}$ and creates a target ciphertext C^* which is the encryption of M_β under the current public key PK_{ID^*}. The Challenger returns C^* to $\mathcal{A}_I$.
- **Phase 2:** $\mathcal{A}_I$ makes more queries as in Phase 1. Note that ID^* should not be queried to extract a partial private key nor a private key at any time and no decryption query should be made on C^* for the combination of ID^* and PK_{ID^*} that was used to encrypt M_β.
- **Guess:** $\mathcal{A}_I$ outputs its guess $\beta' \in \{0,1\}$ for β.

Game II (for a Type II adversary)

- **Setup:** The Challenger runs Setup by taking a security parameter k as input to generate a master key mk and a list of public parameters params. It gives *both* mk and params to the adversary $\mathcal{A}_{II}$.
- **Phase 1:** As $\mathcal{A}_{II}$ knows mk, it can run PartialKeyExtract to generate the partial public/private key pair (D, P). Below, we describe $\mathcal{A}_{II}$'s various queries and the Challenger's responses to them:
  - **Private Key Extraction** ID: The challenger runs PartialKeyExtract and SetSecretValue to generate (D_{ID}, P_{ID}) and s_{ID} respectively, and then runs SetPrivateKey to generate the private key SK_{ID}. It returns SK_{ID} to $\mathcal{A}_{II}$.
  - **Public Key request** ID: The challenger runs PartialKeyExtract and SetSecretValue to generate (D_{ID}, P_{ID}) and s_{ID} respectively, and then runs SetPublicKey to generate the public key PK_{ID}. It returns PK_{ID} to $\mathcal{A}_{II}$.

- **Decryption query:** Adversaries can issue decryption queries for any identity and any ciphertext.
- **Challenge Phase:** Once $\mathcal{A}_{II}$ decides that Phase 1 is over, it outputs the challenge identity ID^* and two equal-length plaintext messages (M_0, M_1). Note that ID^* has not been queried to extract a private key at any time. The Challenger picks $\beta \in_R \{0, 1\}$ and creates a challenge ciphertext C^* which is the encryption of M_β under the public key for ID^*. The Challenger returns C^* to $\mathcal{A}_{II}$.
- **Phase 2:** $\mathcal{A}_{II}$ makes more queries as in Phase 1. Note that ID^* should not be queried to extract a private key and no decryption query should be made on C^* for ID^*.
- **Guess:** $\mathcal{A}_{II}$ outputs its guess $\beta' \in \{0, 1\}$ for β.

We define $\mathcal{A}_i$'s advantage in the above game i by $\mathsf{Adv}(\mathcal{A}_i) = 2(\Pr[\beta' = \beta] - \frac{1}{2}), i \in \{I, II\}$. A CLPKE scheme is said to be IND-CCA secure if no probabilistic polynomial-time adversary has non-negligible advantage in the above games.

A signature scheme consists of four algorithms: a parameter generation algorithm ParamGen, a key generation algorithm KeyGen, a signature generation algorithm Sign and a signature verification algorithm Ver.

Definition 3 (Security of Signature). A signature scheme $S = \langle$ParamGen, KeyGen, Sign, Ver$\rangle$ is existentially unforgeable under an adaptive chosen message attack (EUF-CMA secure) if it is infeasible for a forger $\mathcal{F}$ who only knows the public key to produce a valid message-signature pair with non-negligible advantage after obtaining polynomially many signatures on messages of its choice from the signer.

We define $\mathcal{F}$'s advantage to be

$$\mathsf{Adv}(\mathcal{F}) = \Pr \begin{bmatrix} \langle pk, sk \rangle \leftarrow \langle \mathsf{ParamGen}, \mathsf{KeyGen} \rangle; \\ for\ i = 1, 2, ..., k; \\ m_i \leftarrow \mathcal{F}(pk, m_1, \sigma_1, ..., m_{i-1}, \sigma_{i-1}), \sigma_i \leftarrow \mathsf{Sign}(sk, m_i); \\ \langle m, \sigma \rangle \leftarrow \mathcal{F}(pk, m_1, \sigma_1, ..., m_k, \sigma_k); \\ m \notin \{m_1, ..., m_k\}, \mathsf{Ver}(pk, m, \sigma) = accept. \end{bmatrix}$$

Finally we review the definition of the Computational Diffie-Hellman (CDH) problem as follows.

Definition 4 (Computational Diffie-Hellman (CDH)). Let p and q be primes such that $q|(p-1)$. Suppose g is an element selected from $\mathbb{Z}_p^*$ with order q. Let $\mathcal{B}$ be an attacker. $\mathcal{B}$ tries to solve the following problem: *Given* (g, g^a, g^b) *for uniformly chosen* $a, b \in \mathbb{Z}_q^*$ *at random, compute* g^{ab}. We define $\mathcal{B}$'s advantage in solving the CDH problem by $\mathsf{Adv}(\mathcal{B}) = \Pr[\mathcal{B}(g, g^a, g^b) = g^{ab}]$.

3   Our CLPKE Scheme

In this section, we describe our CLPKE scheme without pairing. The construction of our scheme is based on Baek et al's scheme but we make an important modification on the algorithm SetPublicKey to prevent some components of the public keys from being altered (by an attacker). Speaking informally, this is achieved by incorporating the signing algorithm of the Schnorr signature scheme into partial public key extraction and the verification algorithm to the CLPKE encryption algorithm. – By the unforgeability of the Schnorr signature, attackers are unable to replace the partial public key with the values of their choices.

A formal description of our CLPKE scheme is as follows.

- Setup: This algorithm takes as input a security parameter k to generate two primes p, q such that $q|(p-1)$. It then performs the following:
  1. Pick an element g from $\mathbb{Z}_p^*$ with order q.
  2. Select $x \in_R \mathbb{Z}_q^*$ and compute $y = g^x$.
  3. Choose cryptographic hash functions $H_1 : \{0,1\}^* \times \mathbb{Z}_p^* \to \mathbb{Z}_q^*, H_2 : \{0,1\}^* \times \mathbb{Z}_p^* \times \mathbb{Z}_p^* \to \mathbb{Z}_q^*, H_3 : \{0,1\}^* \to \mathbb{Z}_q^*, H_4 : \mathbb{Z}_p^* \times \mathbb{Z}_p^* \to \{0,1\}^{n+k_0}$. Here n, k_0 are the bit-length of a plaintext and a random bit string, respectively.

  The system parameters params are $\langle p, q, n, k_0, g, y, H_1, H_2, H_3, H_4 \rangle$. The master key mk is x. The plaintext space is $\mathcal{M} = \{0,1\}^n$ and the ciphertext space is $\mathcal{C} = \mathbb{Z}_p^* \times \{0,1\}^{n+k_0}$.
- PartialKeyExtract: Taking params, mk and an entity's identifier ID as input, this algorithm selects $s_0, s_1 \in_R \mathbb{Z}_q^*$, computes $w_0 = g^{s_0}, w_1 = g^{s_1}, d_0 = s_0 + xH_1(ID, w_0), d_1 = s_1 + xH_2(ID, w_0, w_1)$, and returns the partial private key $D_{ID} = d_0$ and the partial public key $P_{ID} = (w_0, w_1, d_1)$.
- SetSecretValue: Taking params and ID as input, this algorithm picks $z \in_R \mathbb{Z}_q^*$ and outputs the secret value $s_{ID} = z$.
- SetPrivateKey: Taking params, D_{ID} and s_{ID} as input, this algorithm returns the private key $SK_{ID} = (d_0, z)$.
- SetPublicKey: Taking params, P_{ID} and s_{ID} as input, this algorithm computes $u = g^z$ and returns the public key $PK_{ID} = (u, w_0, w_1, d_1)$.
- Encrypt: To encrypt a plaintext $M \in \{0,1\}^n$ for an entity with identifier ID and public key $PK_{ID} = (u, w_0, w_1, d_1)$, this algorithm performs the following steps:
  1. Check whether $g^{d_1} = w_1 y^{H_2(ID, w_0, w_1)}$. If not, output $\perp$ and abort encryption.
  2. Choose $\sigma \in_R \{0,1\}^{k_0}$ and compute $r = H_3(M, \sigma, ID, u)$.
  3. Compute and output the ciphertext $C = (U, V): U = g^r, V = (M\|\sigma) \oplus H_4(w_0^r y^{H_1(ID, w_0)r}, u^r)$.
- Decrypt: Suppose the ciphertext to be decrypted is $C = (U, V)$. To decrypt C using $SK_{ID} = (d_0, z)$, this algorithm conducts the following: Compute $M\|\sigma = V \oplus H_4(U^{d_0}, U^z), r = H_3(M, \sigma, ID, u)$. If $g^r = U$, return M. Otherwise, output $\perp$.

We remark that the reason why the intractability of the CDH problem could not be reduced to the security of Baek et al.'s [3] CLPKE scheme is that the s_0 value will be unknown to the CDH adversary when the public key is replaced. As mentioned earlier, our scheme avoids this problem by introducing another Schnorr signature to authenticate the $w_0(= g^{s_0})$ value.

4   Security Analysis

In this section, we analyze the security of our CLPKE scheme.

Theorem 1. *Our CLPKE scheme is IND-CCA secure in the random oracle model, assuming that the CDH problem is intractable.*

The above theorem is obtained by combining Lemma 1 and Lemma 2.

Lemma 1. *Suppose H_1, H_2, H_3, H_4 are random oracles and there exists a Type I IND-CCA adversary $\mathcal{A}_I$ against the CLPKE scheme with advantage ϵ when running in time t, making q_{pk} public key requests, q_{par} partial key queries, q_{pri} private key queries, q_{PR} public key replacement queries, q_D decryption queries and q_i random oracle queries to H_i $(1 \leqslant i \leqslant 4)$. Then, for any $0 \leqslant \nu \leqslant \epsilon$, there exists*

- *either an algorithm $\mathcal{B}$ to solve the CDH problem with advantage*

$$\epsilon' \geqslant \frac{1}{q_4}\left(\frac{\epsilon(1-\nu)^{q_{PR}}}{e(q_{par}+q_{pri}+1)} - \frac{q_3}{2^{k_0}} - \frac{q_D}{q} \right)$$

  and running in time $t' = \max\{t + (q_1 + q_2 + q_3 + q_4)O(1) + (q_{pk} + q_{PR} + q_D)(4T_{EX} + O(1)), cq_2 t/\epsilon\}$, where T_{EX} denotes the time for computing exponentiation in $\mathbb{Z}_p^*$, and c is some constant greater than 120686 assuming that $\epsilon \geq 10(q_{par}+1)(q_{par}+q_2)/q$.
- *or an attacker that breaks the EUF-CMA security of the Schnorr signature with advantage ν within time t'.*

Proof. To prove the lemma, we first assume that the Schnorr signature scheme is EUF-CMA secure with advantage ν $(0 \leqslant \nu \leqslant \epsilon)$ within time t'.

Let $\mathcal{A}_I$ be a Type I IND-CCA adversary against the CLPKE scheme. We show how to construct from A_I an algorithm $\mathcal{B}$ to solve the CDH problem.

$\mathcal{B}$ is given a random instance $\langle g, g^a, g^b \rangle$ of the CDH problem. $\mathcal{B}$ sets $y = g^a$ and simulates the Setup algorithm of the CLPKE scheme by supplying $\mathcal{A}_I$ with $\langle p, q, n, k_0, g, y, H_1, H_2, H_3, H_4 \rangle$ as public parameters, where H_1, H_2, H_3, H_4 are random oracles controlled by $\mathcal{B}$.

$\mathcal{A}_I$ may make queries to random oracles $H_i(1 \leqslant i \leqslant 4)$ at any time during its attack and $\mathcal{B}$ responds as follows:

H_1 **queries:** $\mathcal{B}$ maintains a H_1 list of tuples $\langle (ID_i, w_{0i}), e_{0i} \rangle$. On receiving such a query on (ID_i, w_{0i}), $\mathcal{B}$ does the following:

1. If there is a tuple $\langle (ID_i, w_{0i}), e_{0i} \rangle$ on the H_1 list, then $\mathcal{B}$ returns e_{0i} as answer.
2. Otherwise, $\mathcal{B}$ chooses $e_{0i} \in_R \mathbb{Z}_q^*$, adds $\langle (ID_i, w_{0i}), e_{0i} \rangle$ to the H_1 list and returns e_{0i} as answer.

H_2 **queries:** $\mathcal{B}$ maintains a H_2 list of tuples $\langle (ID_i, w_{0i}, w_{1i}), e_{1i} \rangle$. On receiving such a query on (ID_i, w_{0i}, w_{1i}), $\mathcal{B}$ first checks if there is a tuple $\langle (ID_i, w_{0i}, w_{1i}), e_{1i} \rangle$ on the H_2 list. If there is, return e_{1i} as answer. Otherwise, $\mathcal{B}$ picks $e_{1i} \in_R \mathbb{Z}_q^*$, adds $\langle (ID_i, w_{0i}, w_{1i}), e_{1i} \rangle$ to the H_2 list and returns e_{1i} as answer.

H_3 **queries:** $\mathcal{B}$ maintains a H_3 list of tuples $\langle(M_i, \sigma_i, ID_i, u_i), r_i\rangle$. On receiving such a query on $(M_i, \sigma_i, ID_i, u_i)$, $\mathcal{B}$ first checks if there is a tuple $\langle(M_i, \sigma_i, ID_i, u_i), r_i\rangle$ on the H_3 list. If there is, return r_i as answer. Otherwise, $\mathcal{B}$ picks $r_i \in_R \mathbb{Z}_q^*$ and returns r_i as answer.

H_4 **queries:** $\mathcal{B}$ maintains a H_4 list of tuples $\langle(A, B), h\rangle$. On receiving such a query on (A, B), if there is a tuple $\langle(A, B), h\rangle$ on the H_4 list, then $\mathcal{B}$ returns h as answer. Otherwise, $\mathcal{B}$ picks $h \in_R \{0,1\}^{n+k_0}$, adds $\langle(A, B), h\rangle$ to the H_4 list and returns h as answer.

Phase 1: $\mathcal{A}_I$ launches Phase 1 of its attack by making a series of requests, each of which is either a public key request, a partial key extraction, a private key extraction, a public key replacement or a decryption query.

Public Key request: $\mathcal{B}$ maintains a public key list of tuples $\langle ID_i, (u_i, w_{0i}, w_{1i}, d_{1i}), coin\rangle$. On receiving such a query on ID_i. $\mathcal{B}$ responds as follows:

1. If there is a tuple $\langle ID_i, (u_i, w_{0i}, w_{1i}, d_{1i}), coin\rangle$ on the list, return $(u_i, w_{0i}, w_{1i}, d_{1i})$ as answer.
2. Otherwise, pick $coin \in \{0,1\}$ with $\Pr[coin = 0] = \delta$ (δ will be determined later).

   (a) If $coin = 0$, choose $d_{0i}, d_{1i}, e_{0i}, e_{1i}, z_i \in_R \mathbb{Z}_q^*$, compute $w_{0i} = g^{d_{0i}}y^{-e_{0i}}$, $w_{1i} = g^{d_{1i}}y^{-e_{1i}}, u_i = g^{z_i}$. (Check the H_1 list and if there is a tuple of the form $\langle(ID_i, w_{0i}), e_0\rangle$, re-choose $d_{0i}, e_{0i} \in_R \mathbb{Z}_q^*$; Check the H_2 list and if there is a tuple of the form $\langle(ID_i, w_{0i}, w_{1i}), e_1\rangle$, re-choose $d_{1i}, e_{1i} \in_R \mathbb{Z}_q^*$.) Add $\langle(ID_i, w_{0i}), e_{0i}\rangle$ to the H_1 list, $\langle(ID_i, w_{0i}, w_{1i}), e_{1i}\rangle$ to the H_2 list, $\langle ID_i, d_{0i}, (w_{0i}, w_{1i}, d_{1i})\rangle$ to the partial key list, $\langle ID_i, (d_{0i}, z_i)\rangle$ to the private key list and $\langle ID_i, (u_i, w_{0i}, w_{1i}, d_{1i}), coin\rangle$ to the public key list. Return $(u_i, w_{0i}, w_{1i}, d_{1i})$ as answer.

   (b) Otherwise $(coin = 1)$, choose $s_{0i}, d_{1i}, e_{1i}, z_i \in_R \mathbb{Z}_q^*$, compute $w_{0i} = g^{s_{0i}}, w_{1i} = g^{d_{1i}}y^{-e_{1i}}, u_i = g^{z_i}$. (Check the H_2 list and if there is a tuple of the form $\langle(ID_i, w_{0i}, w_{1i}), e_1\rangle$, re-choose $d_{1i}, e_{1i} \in_R \mathbb{Z}_q^*$.) Add $\langle(ID_i, w_{0i}, w_{1i}), e_{1i}\rangle$ to the H_2 list and $\langle ID_i, (u_i, w_{0i}, w_{1i}, d_{1i}), s_{0i}, coin\rangle$ to the public key list. Return $(u_i, w_{0i}, w_{1i}, d_{1i})$ as answer.

Partial Key Extraction: $\mathcal{B}$ maintains a partial key list of tuples $\langle ID_i, d_{0i}, (w_{0i}, w_{1i}, d_{1i})\rangle$. On receiving such a query on ID_i, $\mathcal{B}$ responds as follows:

1. If there is a tuple $\langle ID_i, d_{0i}, (w_{0i}, w_{1i}, d_{1i})\rangle$ on the list, return d_{0i} as the partial private key and (w_{0i}, w_{1i}, d_{1i}) as the partial public key.
2. Otherwise, run the simulation algorithm for public key request taking ID_i as input to get a tuple $\langle ID_i, (u_i, w_{0i}, w_{1i}, d_{1i}), coin\rangle$. If $coin = 0$, search the partial key list for a tuple $\langle ID_i, d_{0i}, (w_{0i}, w_{1i}, d_{1i})\rangle$ and return d_{0i} as the partial private key and (w_{0i}, w_{1i}, d_{1i}) as the partial public key. Otherwise $(coin = 1)$, $\mathcal{B}$ aborts.

Private Key Extraction: $\mathcal{B}$ maintains a private key list of tuples $\langle ID_i, (d_{0i}, z_i)\rangle$. On receiving such a query on ID_i. $\mathcal{B}$ responds as follows:

1. If there is a tuple $\langle ID_i, (d_{0i}, z_i) \rangle$ on the list, return (d_{0i}, z_i) as answer.
2. Otherwise, run the simulation algorithm for public key request taking ID_i as input to get a tuple $\langle ID_i, (u_i, w_{0i}, w_{1i}, d_{1i}), coin \rangle$. If $coin = 0$, search the private key list for a tuple $\langle ID_i, (d_{0i}, z_i) \rangle$ and return (d_{0i}, z_i) as answer. Otherwise $(coin = 1)$, $\mathcal{B}$ aborts.

Public Key Replacement: $\mathcal{A}_I$ may replace the public key $(u_i, w_{0i}, w_{1i}, d_{1i})$ for any entity ID_i with any value $(u'_i, w'_{0i}, w'_{1i}, d'_{1i})$ of its choice. If $(w'_{0i}, w'_{1i}, d'_{1i}) \neq (w_{0i}, w_{1i}, d_{1i})$ satisfying $g^{d'_{1i}} = w'_{1i} y^{-H_2(ID_i, w'_{0i}, w'_{1i})}$, $\mathcal{B}$ aborts. Otherwise, $\mathcal{B}$ records the change.

Decryption queries: Suppose the request is to decrypt ciphertext $C = (U, V)$ for ID_i. $\mathcal{B}$ searches the public key list for a tuple $\langle ID_i, (u_i, w_{0i}, w_{1i}, d_{1i}), coin \rangle$. Then $\mathcal{B}$ does the following:

1. If the public key has not been replaced and $coin = 0$
   (a) Search the private key list for a tuple $\langle ID_i, (d_{0i}, z_i) \rangle$.
   (b) Compute $M \| \sigma = V \oplus H_4(U^{d_{0i}}, U^{z_i})$, $r = H_3(M, \sigma, ID_i, u_i)$. If $g^r = U$, return M. Otherwise, output $\perp$.
2. Otherwise, search the H_3 list for a tuple $\langle (M_i, \sigma_i, ID_i, u_i), r_i \rangle$ satisfying $U = g^{r_i}, V = (M_i \| \sigma_i) \oplus H_4(w_{0i}^{r_i} y^{H_1(ID_i, w_{0i}) r_i}, u_i^{r_i})$. Return the corresponding M_i if such a tuple exists. Otherwise, output $\perp$.

Challenge Phase: $\mathcal{A}_I$ outputs ID^* and two messages M_0, M_1 on which it wishes to be challenged. Upon receiving ID^*, $\mathcal{B}$ searches the public key list for the tuple $\langle ID^*, (u^*, w_0^*, w_1^*, d_1^*), coin \rangle$ and then conducts the following:

1. If $coin = 0$, abort the game.
2. Otherwise, do the following:
   (a) Pick $\sigma^* \in_R \{0,1\}^{k_0}, \beta \in_R \{0,1\}$ and $V^* \in_R \{0,1\}^{n+k_0}$.
   (b) Set $U^* = g^b$ and $e_0^* = H_1(ID^*, w_0^*)$.
   (c) Define $b = H_3(M_\beta, \sigma^*, ID^*, u^*)$ and $H_4(w_0^{*b} y^{e_0^* b}, u^{*b}) = V^* \oplus (M_\beta \| \sigma^*)$.
   (d) Output $C^* = \langle U^*, V^* \rangle$ as the challenge ciphertext. Note that from the construction above, $V^* = (M_\beta \| \sigma^*) \oplus H_4(w_0^{*b} y^{e_0^* b}, u^{*b}) = (M_\beta \| \sigma^*) \oplus H_4(g^{bs_0^*} g^{abe_0^*}, u^{*b})$.

Phase 2: $\mathcal{B}$ continues to respond to $\mathcal{A}_I$'s requests in the same way as it did in Phase 1. Note that $\mathcal{A}_I$ can not make a partial key extraction query or a private key extraction query on ID^*. No decryption query should be made on C^* for the combination of ID^* and $(u^*, w_0^*, w_1^*, d_1^*)$ that was used to encrypt M_β.

Guess: Eventually, $\mathcal{A}_I$ outputs its guess. $\mathcal{B}$ chooses a random pair $\langle (A, B), h \rangle$ from the H_4 list and outputs $\left(\frac{A}{g^{bs_0^*}} \right)^{\frac{1}{e_0^*}}$ as the solution to the CDH problem.

Analysis. We first evaluate the simulations of the random oracles. From the constructions of H_1 and H_2, it is clear that the simulations of H_1 and H_2 are perfect. And as long as $\mathcal{A}_I$ does not query $(M_\beta, \sigma^*, ID^*, u^*)$ to H_3 nor $(w_0^{*b} y^{e_0^* b}, u^{*b})$ to H_4, the simulations of H_3 and H_4 are perfect. Let AskH_3^* denote the event that $(M_\beta, \sigma^*, ID^*, u^*)$ has been queried to H_3 and AskH_4^* be the event that $(w_0^{*b} y_0^{e_0^* b}, u^{*b})$ has been queried to H_4.

Since we view H_3 and H_4 as random oracles, the simulated challenge ciphertext is identically distributed as the real one.

As to the simulation of decryption oracle, $\mathcal{B}$ will wrongly reject a valid ciphertext during the simulation with probability smaller than q_D/q. Namely, $\Pr[\mathsf{DecErr}] \leqslant q_D/q$, where DecErr denotes the event that $\mathcal{B}$ rejects a valid ciphertext during the simulation.

Let $\mathsf{E} = (\mathsf{AskH}_4^* \vee \mathsf{AskH}_3^* \vee \mathsf{DecErr}) | \neg \mathsf{Abort}$. It is clear that if E does not happen during the simulation, $\mathcal{B}$ will not gain any advantage greater than $1/2$ to guess β, due to the randomness of the output of H_4. Namely, $\Pr[\beta' = \beta | \neg \mathsf{E}] \leqslant 1/2$. We obtain

$$\Pr[\beta' = \beta] = \Pr[\beta' = \beta | \neg \mathsf{E}] \Pr[\neg \mathsf{E}] + \Pr[\beta' = \beta | \mathsf{E}] \Pr[\mathsf{E}]$$
$$\leqslant \frac{1}{2} \Pr[\neg \mathsf{E}] + \Pr[\mathsf{E}] = \frac{1}{2} + \frac{1}{2} \Pr[\mathsf{E}]$$

By definition of ϵ, we have

$$\epsilon \leqslant 2(\Pr[\beta' = \beta] - \frac{1}{2}) \leqslant \Pr[\mathsf{E}]$$
$$\leqslant \frac{\Pr[\mathsf{AskH}_4^*] + \Pr[\mathsf{AskH}_3^*] + \Pr[\mathsf{DecErr}]}{\Pr[\neg \mathsf{Abort}]}$$

The probability that $\mathcal{B}$ does not abort during the simulation is given by $\delta^{q_{par} + q_{pri}} (1 - \delta)(1 - \nu)^{q_{PR}}$ which is maximized at $\delta = 1 - \frac{1}{(q_{par} + q_{pri} + 1)}$. Hence $\Pr[\neg \mathsf{Abort}] \geqslant \frac{(1 - \nu)^{q_{PR}}}{e(q_{par} + q_{pri} + 1)}$, where e denotes the base of the natural logarithm.

Hence, It is not difficult for us to reach the following

$$\Pr[\mathsf{AskH}_4^*] \geqslant \epsilon \Pr[\neg \mathsf{Abort}] - \Pr[\mathsf{AskH}_3^*] - \Pr[\mathsf{DecErr}]$$
$$\geqslant \frac{\epsilon(1 - \nu)^{q_{PR}}}{e(q_{par} + q_{pri} + 1)} - \frac{q_3}{2^{k_0}} - \frac{q_D}{q}$$

If AskH_4^* happens, then $\mathcal{A}_I$ may be able to distinguish the simulation from the real life (it can tell that the challenge ciphertext C^* by the simulation is invalid), but $H_4(w_0^{*b} y_0^{e_0^* b}, u^{*b})$ has been recorded on the H_4 list. Then $\mathcal{B}$ wins if it chooses the correct element from the H_4 list. Hence we obtain the advantage for $\mathcal{B}$ to solve the CDH problem

$$\epsilon' \geqslant \frac{1}{q_4} \Pr[\mathsf{AskH}_4^*] \geqslant \frac{1}{q_4} \left(\frac{\epsilon(1 - \nu)^{q_{PR}}}{e(q_{par} + q_{pri} + 1)} - \frac{q_3}{2^{k_0}} - \frac{q_D}{q} \right)$$

The running time of the CDH attacker $\mathcal{B}$ is bounded by $t' = \max\{t + (q_1 + q_2 + q_3 + q_4)O(1) + (q_{pk} + q_{PR} + q_D)(4T_{EX} + O(1)), cq_2 t/\epsilon\}$, where T_{EX} denotes the time for computing exponentiation in $\mathbb{Z}_p^*$, and c is some constant greater than 120686 assuming that $\epsilon \geq 10(q_{par} + 1)(q_{par} + q_2)/q$. (This estimate in obtained from the result of [13].)

The following Lemma 2 shows that our CLPKE scheme is secure against the Type II adversary.

Lemma 2. *Suppose H_1, H_2, H_3, H_4 are random oracles and there exists a Type II IND-CCA adversary $\mathcal{A}_{II}$ against the CLPKE scheme with advantage ϵ when running in time t, making q_{pk} public key requests, q_{pri} private key extraction queries, q_D decryption queries and q_i random oracle queries to H_i ($1 \leqslant i \leqslant 4$). Then there exists an algorithm $\mathcal{B}$ to solve the CDH problem with advantage $\epsilon' \geqslant \frac{1}{q_4} \left(\frac{\epsilon}{q_{pri}+1} - \frac{q_3}{2^{k_0}} - \frac{q_D}{q} \right)$ running in time $t' < t + (q_1 + q_2 + q_3 + q_4)O(1) + (q_{pk} + q_D)(3T_{EX} + O(1))$, where T_{EX} denotes the time for computing exponentiation in $\mathbb{Z}_p^*$.*

The proof is presented in Appendix A.

5   Concluding Remarks

In this paper we have presented a CLPKE scheme that does not depend on the pairings but is provably secure in the security model where a Type I adversary is allowed to replace the public key associated with the challenge identity (before challenge phase). – Note that the security analysis of Baek et al's [3] CLPKE scheme without pairings does not consider this case. – The security of our CLPKE scheme is relative to the standard CDH problem.

We, however, could not prove whether the proposed scheme is still secure when the adversary extracts a partial private key associated with the challenge identity. Proving (or disproving) this is an interesting open problem.

References

1. Al-Riyami, S.S., Paterson, K.: Certificateless Public Key Cryptography. In: Laih, C.-S. (ed.) ASIACRYPT 2003. LNCS, vol. 2894, pp. 452–473. Springer, Heidelberg (2003)
2. Al-Riyami, S.S., Paterson, K.: CBE from CL-PKE: A generic construction and efficient schemes. In: Vaudenay, S. (ed.) PKC 2005. LNCS, vol. 3386, pp. 398–415. Springer, Heidelberg (2005)
3. Baek, J., Safavi-Naini, R., Susilo, W.: Certificateless public key encryption without pairing. In: Zhou, J., Lopez, J., Deng, R.H., Bao, F. (eds.) ISC 2005. LNCS, vol. 3650, pp. 134–148. Springer, Heidelberg (2005)
4. Bentahar, K., Farshim, P., Malone-Lee, J., Smart, N.P.: Generic Constructions of Identity-Based and Certificateless KEMs (2005), Available from http://eprint.iacr.org/2005/058
5. Boneh, D., Franklin, M.: Identity-based Encryption from the Weil Pairing. In: Kilian, J. (ed.) CRYPTO 2001. LNCS, vol. 2139, pp. 213–229. Springer, Heidelberg (2001)
6. Cheng, Z., Comley, R.: Efficient Certificateless Public Key Encryption. Cryptology ePrint Archive, Report 2005/012 (2005), http://eprint.iacr.org/2005/012
7. Dent, A.W.: A Survey of Certificateless Encryption Schemes and Security Models (2006), Available from http://eprint.iacr.org/2006/211

8. Fujisaki, E., Okamoto, T.: Secure Integration of Asymmetirc and Symmetric Encryption Schemes. In: Wiener, M.J. (ed.) CRYPTO 1999. LNCS, vol. 1666, pp. 537–554. Springer, Heidelberg (1999)

9. Fujisaki, E., Okamoto, T.: How to Enhance the Security of Public-key Encryption at Minimal Cost. In: Imai, H., Zheng, Y. (eds.) PKC 1999. LNCS, vol. 1560, pp. 53–68. Springer, Heidelberg (1999)

10. Galindo, D., Morillo, P., Rafols, C.: Breaking Yum and Lee Generic Constructions of Certificateless and Certificate-Based Encryption Schemes. In: Atzeni, A.S., Lioy, A. (eds.) EuroPKI 2006. LNCS, vol. 4043, pp. 81–91. Springer, Heidelberg (2006)

11. Libert, B., Quisquater, J.-J.: On Constructing Certificateless Cryptosystems from Identity based Encryption. In: Yung, M., Dodis, Y., Kiayias, A., Malkin, T.G. (eds.) PKC 2006. LNCS, vol. 3958, pp. 474–490. Springer, Heidelberg (2006)

12. Liu, J.K., Au, M.H., Susilo, W.: Self-Generated-Certificate Public Key Cryptography and Certificateless Signature/Encryption Scheme in the Standard Model. In: Proc. ACM Symposium on Information, Computer and Communications Security, ACM Press, New York (2007)

13. Pointcheval, D., Stern, J.: Security Arguments for Digital Signatures and Blind Signatures. J. Cryptology 13(3), 361–396 (2000)

14. Huang, Q., Wong, D.S.: Generic Certificateless Encryption in the Standard Model (2007), Available from http://eprint.iacr.org/2007/095

15. Shamir, A.: Identity-based Cryptosystems and Signature Schemes. In: Blakely, G.R., Chaum, D. (eds.) CRYPTO 1984. LNCS, vol. 196, pp. 47–53. Springer, Heidelberg (1985)

16. Shi, Y., Li, J.: Provable Efficient Certificateless Public Key Encryption (2005), Available from http://eprint.iacr.org/2005/287/

17. Yum, D., Lee, P.: Generic Construction of Certificateless Encryption. In: Laganà, A., Gavrilova, M., Kumar, V., Mun, Y., Tan, C.J.K., Gervasi, O. (eds.) ICCSA 2004. LNCS, vol. 3043, pp. 802–811. Springer, Heidelberg (2004)

18. Zhang, Z., Feng, D.: On the Security of a Certificateless Public-key Encryption (2005), Available from http://eprint.iacr.org/2005/426

A   Proof of Lemma 2

Proof. Let A_{II} be a Type II IND-CCA adversary against the CLPKE scheme. We show how to construct from A_{II} an algorithm B to solve the CDH problem.

B is given a random instance $\langle g, g^a, g^b \rangle$ of the CDH problem. B chooses $s \in_R \mathbb{Z}_q^*$, computes $y = g^s$ and simulates the Setup algorithm of the CLPKE scheme by supplying A_{II} with the public parameters $\langle p, q, n, k_0, g, y, H_1, H_2, H_3, H_4 \rangle$ and the master key s, where H_1, H_2, H_3, H_4 are random oracles controlled by B.

A_{II} may make queries to random oracles $H_i (1 \leqslant i \leqslant 4)$ at any time during its attack and B responds as follows:

H_1 **queries:** B maintains a H_1 list of tuples $\langle (ID_i, w_{0i}), e_{0i} \rangle$. On receiving such a query on (ID_i, w_{0i}), B does the following:

1. If there is a tuple $\langle (ID_i, w_{0i}), e_{0i} \rangle$ on the H_1 list , then B returns e_{0i} as answer.
2. Otherwise, B chooses $e_{0i} \in_R \mathbb{Z}_q^*$, adds $\langle (ID_i, w_{0i}), e_{0i} \rangle$ to the H_1 list and returns e_{0i} as answer.

H_2 **queries:** $\mathcal{B}$ maintains a H_2 list of tuples $\langle (ID_i, w_{0i}, w_{1i}), e_{1i} \rangle$. On receiving such a query on $\langle (ID_i, w_{0i}, w_{1i}), \mathcal{B}$ first checks if there is a tuple $\langle (ID_i, w_{0i}, w_{1i}), e_{1i} \rangle$ on the H_2 list. If there is, return e_{1i} as answer. Otherwise, $\mathcal{B}$ picks $e_{1i} \in_R \mathbb{Z}_q^*$, adds $\langle (ID_i, w_{0i}, w_{1i}), e_{1i} \rangle$ to the H_2 list and returns e_{1i} as answer.

H_3 **queries:** $\mathcal{B}$ maintains a H_3 list of tuples $\langle (M_i, \sigma_i, ID_i, u_i), r_i \rangle$. On receiving such a query on $(M_i, \sigma_i, ID_i, u_i)$, $\mathcal{B}$ first checks if there is a tuple $\langle (M_i, \sigma_i, ID_i, u_i), r_i \rangle$ on the H_3 list. If there is, return r_i as answer. Otherwise, $\mathcal{B}$ picks $r_i \in_R \mathbb{Z}_q^*$ and returns r_i as answer.

H_4 **queries:** $\mathcal{B}$ maintains a H_4 list of tuples $\langle (A, B), h \rangle$. On receiving such a query on (A, B), if there is a tuple $\langle (A, B), h \rangle$ on the H_4 list, then $\mathcal{B}$ returns h as answer. Otherwise, $\mathcal{B}$ picks $h \in_R \{0, 1\}^{n+k_0}$, adds $\langle (A, B), h \rangle$ to the H_4 list and returns h as answer.

Phase 1: $\mathcal{A}_{II}$ launches Phase 1 of its attack by making a series of requests, each of which is either a public key request, a private key extraction query or a decryption query.

Compute Partial Key: $\mathcal{A}_{II}$ computes the partial private key d_{0i} and the partial public key (w_{0i}, w_{1i}, d_{1i}) for ID_i. $\mathcal{B}$ keeps $\langle ID_i, d_{0i}, (w_{0i}, w_{1i}, d_{1i}) \rangle$ to the partial key list.

Public Key request: $\mathcal{B}$ maintains a public key list of tuples $\langle ID_i, (u_i, w_{0i}, w_{1i}, d_{1i}), z_i, coin \rangle$. On receiving such a query on ID_i. $\mathcal{B}$ responds as follows:

1. If there is a tuple $\langle ID_i, (u_i, w_{0i}, w_{1i}, d_{1i}), z_i, coin \rangle$ on the public key list, return $(u_i, w_{0i}, w_{1i}, d_{1i})$ as answer.
2. Otherwise, pick $coin \in \{0, 1\}$ with $Pr[coin = 0] = \delta$ (δ will be determined later).
   (a) If $coin = 0$, choose $z_i \in_R \mathbb{Z}_q^*$ and compute $u_i = g^{z_i}$. Search the partial key list to get the partial public key (w_{0i}, w_{1i}, d_{1i}), add $\langle ID_i, (u_i, w_{0i}, w_{1i}, d_{1i}), z_i, coin \rangle$ to the public key list and return $(u_i, w_{0i}, w_{1i}, d_{1i})$ as answer.
   (b) Otherwise $(coin = 1)$, $\mathcal{B}$ sets $u_i = g^a$, searches the partial key list to get the partial public key (w_{0i}, w_{1i}, d_{1i}), adds $\langle ID_i, (u_i, w_{0i}, w_{1i}, d_{1i}), ?, coin \rangle$ to the public key list and returns $(u_i, w_{0i}, w_{1i}, d_{1i})$ as answer.

Private Key Extraction: $\mathcal{B}$ maintains a private key list of tuples $\langle ID_i, (d_{0i}, z_i) \rangle$. On receiving such a query on ID_i. $\mathcal{B}$ responds as follows:

1. If there is a tuple $\langle ID_i, (d_{0i}, z_i) \rangle$ on the private key list, return (d_{0i}, z_i) as answer.
2. Otherwise, search the partial key list to get the partial private key d_{0i} and run the simulation algorithm for public key request taking ID_i as input to get a tuple $\langle ID_i, (u_i, w_{0i}, w_{1i}, d_{1i}), z_i, coin \rangle$. If $coin = 0$, return (d_{0i}, z_i) as answer. Otherwise $(coin = 1)$, $\mathcal{B}$ aborts.

Decryption queries: Suppose the request is to decrypt ciphertext $C = (U, V)$ for ID_i. $\mathcal{B}$ first runs the simulation algorithm for public key request taking ID_i as input to get a tuple $\langle ID_i, (u_i, w_{0i}, w_{1i}, d_{1i}), z_i, coin \rangle$. Then $\mathcal{B}$ does the following:

1. If $coin = 0$, search the private key list for a tuple $\langle ID_i, (d_{0i}, z_i) \rangle$. Compute $M \| \sigma = V \oplus H_4(U^{d_{0i}}, U^{z_i})$, $r = H_3(\sigma, M, ID_i, u_i)$. If $g^r = U$, return M. Otherwise, output $\bot$.
2. Otherwise, search the H_3 list for a tuple $\langle (M_i, \sigma_i, ID_i, u_i), r_i \rangle$ satisfying $U = g^{r_i}$, $V = (M_i \| \sigma_i) \oplus H_4(w_{0i}^{r_i} y^{H_1(ID_i, w_{0i})r_i}, u_i^{r_i})$. Return the corresponding M_i if such a tuple exists. Otherwise, output $\bot$.

Challenge Phase: $\mathcal{A}_{II}$ outputs ID^* and two messages M_0, M_1 on which it wishes to be challenged. Then $\mathcal{B}$ runs the simulation algorithm for public key request taking ID^* as input to get a tuple $\langle ID^*, (u^*, w_0^*, w_1^*, d_1^*), z_i, coin \rangle$ and then conducts the following:

1. If $coin = 0$, abort the game.
2. Otherwise, do the following:
   (a) Pick $\sigma^* \in_R \{0,1\}^{k_0}$, $\beta \in_R \{0,1\}$ and $V^* \in_R \{0,1\}^{n+k_0}$.
   (b) Set $U^* = g^b$ and $e_0^* = H_1(ID^*, w_0^*)$.
   (c) Define $b = H_3(M_\beta, \sigma^*, ID^*, u^*)$ and $H_4(w_0^{*b} y^{e_0^* b}, u^{*b}) = V^* \oplus (M_\beta \| \sigma^*)$.
   (d) Output $C^* = \langle U^*, V^* \rangle$ as the challenge ciphertext. Note that from the construction above, $V^* = (M_\beta \| \sigma^*) \oplus H_4(w_0^{*b} y^{e_0^* b}, u^{*b}) = (M_\beta \| \sigma^*) \oplus H_4(w_0^{*b} g^{be_0^*}, g^{ab})$.

Phase 2: $\mathcal{B}$ continues to respond to $\mathcal{A}_{II}$'s requests in the same way as it did in Phase 1. Note that $\mathcal{A}_{II}$ can not make private key extraction queries on ID^*. If any decryption query is equal to the challenge ciphertext C^* for ID^*, then $\mathcal{B}$ aborts.

Guess: Eventually, $\mathcal{A}_{II}$ outputs its guess. Then $\mathcal{B}$ chooses a random pair $\langle (A, B), h \rangle$ from the H_4 list and outputs B as the solution to the CDH problem.

Analysis. First we evaluate the simulations of the random oracles. From the constructions of H_1 and H_2, it is clear that the simulations of H_1 and H_2 are perfect. And as long as $\mathcal{A}_{II}$ does not query $(M_\beta, \sigma^*, ID^*, u^*)$ to H_3 nor $(w_0^{*b} y^{e_0^* b}, u^{*b})$ to H_4, the simulations of H_3 and H_4 are perfect. Let AskH_3^* denote the event that $(M_\beta, \sigma^*, ID^*, u^*)$ has been queried to H_3 and AskH_4^* be the event that $(w_0^{*b} y^{e_0^* b}, u^{*b})$ has been queried to H_4.

Since we view H_3 and H_4 as random oracles, the simulated challenge ciphertext is identically distributed as the real one.

As to the simulation of decryption oracle, $\mathcal{B}$ will wrongly reject a valid ciphertext during the simulation with probability smaller than q_D/q. Namely, $\Pr[\mathsf{DecErr}] \leqslant q_D/q$, where DecErr denotes the event that $\mathcal{B}$ rejects a valid ciphertext during the simulation.

Let $\mathsf{E} = (\mathsf{AskH}_4^* \vee \mathsf{AskH}_3^* \vee \mathsf{DecErr}) | \neg \mathsf{Abort}$. It is clear that if E does not happen during the simulation, $\mathcal{B}$ will not gain any advantage greater than $1/2$ to guess β, due to the randomness of the output of H_4. Namely, $\Pr[\beta' = \beta | \neg \mathsf{E}] \leqslant 1/2$. We obtain

$$\Pr[\beta' = \beta] = \Pr[\beta' = \beta | \neg \mathsf{E}] \Pr[\neg \mathsf{E}] + \Pr[\beta' = \beta | \mathsf{E}] \Pr[\mathsf{E}]$$
$$\leqslant \frac{1}{2} \Pr[\neg \mathsf{E}] + \Pr[\mathsf{E}] = \frac{1}{2} + \frac{1}{2} \Pr[\mathsf{E}]$$

By definition of ϵ, we have

$$\epsilon \leqslant 2(\Pr[\beta' = \beta] - \frac{1}{2}) \leqslant \Pr[E]$$

$$\leqslant \frac{\Pr[\mathsf{AskH}_4^*] + \Pr[\mathsf{AskH}_3^*] + \Pr[\mathsf{DecErr}]}{\Pr[\neg\mathsf{Abort}]}$$

The probability that $\mathcal{B}$ does not abort during the simulation is given by $\delta^{q_{pri}}(1 - \delta)$ which is maximized at $\delta = 1 - \frac{1}{q_{pri}+1}$. Hence $\Pr[\neg\mathsf{Abort}] \geqslant \frac{1}{e(q_{pri}+1)}$, where e denotes the base of the natural logarithm.

It is not difficult for us to reach the following

$$\Pr[\mathsf{AskH}_4^*] \geqslant \epsilon\Pr[\neg\mathsf{Abort}] - \Pr[\mathsf{AskH}_3^*] - \Pr[\mathsf{DecErr}]$$

$$\geqslant \frac{\epsilon}{e(q_{pri} + 1)} - \frac{q_3}{2^{k_0}} - \frac{q_D}{q}$$

If AskH_4^* happens, then $\mathcal{A}_{II}$ may be able to distinguish the simulation from the real life (it can tell that the challenge ciphertext C^* by the simulation is invalid), but $H_4(w_0^{*b}y^{e_0^*b}, u^{*b})$ has been recorded on the H_4 list. Then $\mathcal{B}$ wins if it chooses the correct element from the H_4 list. Hence we obtain the advantage for $\mathcal{B}$ to solve the CDH problem

$$\epsilon' \geqslant \frac{1}{q_4}\Pr[\mathsf{AskH}_4^*] \geqslant \frac{1}{q_4}\left(\frac{\epsilon}{e(q_{pri} + 1)} - \frac{q_3}{2^{k_0}} - \frac{q_D}{q}\right)$$

The running time of the CDH attacker is bounded by $t' < t + (q_1 + q_2 + q_3 + q_4)O(1) + (q_{pk} + q_D)(3T_{EX} + O(1))$, where T_{EX} denotes the time for computing exponentiation in $\mathbb{Z}_p^*$.

Modeling Protocol Based
Packet Header Anomaly Detector for
Network and Host Intrusion Detection Systems

Solahuddin B. Shamsuddin and Michael E. Woodward

Department of Computing, School of Informatics
University of Bradford, United Kingdom
{S.B.Shamsuddin,M.E.Woodward}@bradford.ac.uk

Abstract. This paper describes an experimental protocol based packet header anomaly detector for Network and Host Intrusion Detection System modelling which analyses the behaviour of packet header field values based on its layer 2, 3 and 4 protocol fields of the ISO OSI Seven Layer Model for Networking. Our model which we call as Protocol based Packet Header Anomaly Detector (PbPHAD) Intrusion Detection System is designed to detect the anomalous behaviour of network traffic packets based on three specific network and transport layer protocols namely UDP, TCP and ICMP to identify the degree of maliciousness from a set of detected anomalous packets identified from the sum of statistically modelled individually rated anomalous field values.

Keywords: Anomaly, Data base, Network Intrusion Detection System.

1 Introduction

The advent of Intrusion Detection System (IDS) technologies have contributed a lot to the Network Security domain which have been the much talked about issues after a wave of the infamous 'code red' worm and its like i.e. 'self propagating malicious code' flooding and choking the internet traffic which almost caused a nearly catastrophic effect to the internet connected network infrastructures during this early part of the decade. Two major technologies which are commonly used in the design and development of the IDS are the signature based and anomaly based IDSs. We are focusing our IDS model based on the anomalous behaviour of the packet headers which behaves differently depending on the protocol used in the transmisson of a particular packet at network and transport layers.

In this experiment, we used MIT Lincoln Lab 1999 off-line intrusion detection evaluation data set [1] as the training and testing data as this data set has become one of the *de facto* standards for test data set among the IDS researcher community. A lot of well documented experiments have been published using this data set i.e. [2], [3], [4], [5], [6], [7], [8] and [9]. By using a skilfully crafted publicly available data set with a large quantity of rich background traffic, we would foresee that the result of our experiment would be very appealing as it can be compared with the published results by a number of researchers from renowned research institutions.

F. Bao et al. (Eds.): CANS 2007, LNCS 4856, pp. 209–227, 2007.

The rest of the paper is organized as follows. In section 2, we discuss other related works in intrusion detection system. In section 3, we describe PbPHAD model which include its design concept, process flow and statistical modelling. In Section 4, we discuss PbPHAD experimental results on 1999 DARPA evaluation data set. In section 5, we compare PbPHAD experimental results with the 1999 DARPA IDS evaluation best system results on poorly detected attacks. In section 6, we discuss the conclusion of our experiment. We present our future work in section 7.

2   Related Work

The fundamental inspiration behind our experiment was drawn from a Technical Report written by M.V. Mahoney and P.K. Chan that learns the normal range of values for 33 fields of the Ethernet, IP, TCP, UDP and ICMP protocols using a generic statistical model for all values in the packet headers for all protocols [10]. Our experiment in essence is to expand this idea of using just the packet header field values to learn the anomalous behaviour of the packets during transmission in any TCP/IP network traffic. We extend the statistical analysis by modelling the detection algorithm based on three specific network and transport layer protocols namely UDP, TCP and ICMP. Future analysis will be done using the combination of knowledge engineering methodologies which would eventually determine to some extent the degree of maliciousness of the detected anomalous packets in a cluster which is suspected to be intrusive through their assigned anomaly scores.

3   Protocol Based Packet Header Anomaly Detection (PbPHAD) Model

Fig. 1. [11] shows of an isolated test bed network for the 1999 DARPA offline eva-luation. Scripting techniques were used to generate live background traffic which is similar to traffic that flows between the inside of one fictional Eyrie Air force base created for the evaluation to the outside internet. Rich background traffic was generated in the test bed which looks as if it were initiated by hundreds of users on

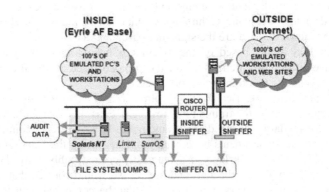

Fig. 1. Block Diagram of DARPA 1999 Test Bed

thousands of hosts. Automated attacks were launched against the UNIX victim machines and the router from outside hosts. Machines labelled 'sniffer' in Figure 1 run a program named *tcpdump* to capture all packets transmitted over the attached network segment. 5 weeks of data which comprise of 3 weeks of training data and 2 weeks of testing data are made available for evaluation in *tcpdump* format.

The packet header field values are taken from layer 2, 3 and 4 protocols which are the IP, Ethernet, TCP, UDP and ICMP which summed up to 33 fields as depicted in the Field Name column in Table 1. We designed our PbPHAD anomaly statistical model based on 3 specific protocols which are TCP, UDP and ICMP because of their unique behaviour when communicating among hosts, client and servers depending on the purpose and application used for a particular session. With this in mind, a more accurate statistical model with finer granularity which represents the 3 chosen protocols can be built for detecting the anomalous behaviour of the testing data.

For each protocol, if we index each field as i, $i=1,2,...,n$, the model is built based on the ratio of the normal number of distinct field values in the training data, R_i, against the total number of packets associated with each protocol, N_i. The ratio, $p_i = R_i/N_i$ represents the probability of the network seeing normal field values in a packet. Thus, the probability of anomalies will be $1- p_i$ for each corresponding field. Each packet header field containing values not found in the normal profile will be assigned a score of $1 - p_i$ and will be summed up to give the total value for that particular packet.

$$\text{Score}_{packet} = \sum_{i=1}^{n} (1 - p_i), \qquad i = 1,2,...n \qquad (1)$$

As the value of R_i varies greatly, we use log ratio in our model. The value of column TCP, UDP and ICMP in Table 1 is calculated based on:

Relative percentage ratio of $1-log(R_i/N_i)$

to give the total probability of 1 for each protocol.

Table 1 shows PbPHAD statistical model. It is obvious from the PbPHAD model that the bigger the number of anomalous fields (R), the smaller the anomaly score will be. The anomaly score of 0.000 shows that particular field is not related to that particular protocol. From table 1 we can see the distinct value of destination IP (ipdest=1934) and source IP (ipsrc=1918) fields which depict the number of hosts simulated in the DARPA 1999 Test Bed as shown in Fig. 1.

Fig. 2. shows the process flow of building the PbPHAD Network Intrusion Detection System model. The process flow can be divided into 3 stages as follows:

- **Stage I. Data Preparation.** In this stage, training and testing data are downloaded from MIT Lincoln Lab web site. The raw data are in the form of compressed *tcpdump* format. We wrote a C++ program to extract the data from the *tcpdump* files and write the output to comma separated values (.csv) files. We took this approach due to the volume of the raw data. By doing bulk copying into the Ingres database, the process will be a lot faster as the size of the raw data alone occupy almost 6GB of hard disk space. We used *ethereal* to read the data in *tcpdump* format in order to verify the converted data in the .csv file format.

Table 1. PbPHAD Statistical Model

i	Field Name	R	N	ANOMALY SCORE		
				TCP	UDP	ICMP
1	etherdesthi	9	12,814,738	0.045	0.057	0.060
2	etherdestlo	12	12,814,738	0.045	0.056	0.059
3	etherprotocol	4	12,814,738	0.048	0.060	0.063
4	ethersize	1456	12,814,738	0.031	0.040	0.041
5	ethersrchi	6	12,814,738	0.047	0.059	0.061
6	ethersrclo	9	12,814,738	0.045	0.057	0.060
7	icmpchecksum	2	7,169	0.000	0.000	0.038
8	icmpcode	3	7,169	0.000	0.000	0.037
9	icmptype	3	7,169	0.000	0.000	0.037
10	ipchecksum	1	12,715,589	0.052	0.065	0.068
11	ipdest	1934	12,715,589	0.031	0.039	0.040
12	ipfragid	12,489	12,715,589	0.025	0.032	0.034
13	ipfragptr	2	12,715,589	0.050	0.062	0.065
14	ipheaderlength	1	12,715,589	0.052	0.065	0.068
15	iplength	1463	12,715,589	0.031	0.040	0.041
16	ipprotocol	3	12,715,589	0.049	0.061	0.064
17	ipsrc	1918	12,715,589	0.031	0.039	0.040
18	iptos	4	12,715,589	0.048	0.060	0.063
19	ipttl	11	12,715,589	0.045	0.057	0.059
20	tcpack	6,015,527	10,617,293	0.008	0.000	0.000
21	tcpchecksum	2	10,617,293	0.049	0.000	0.000
22	tcpdestport	22,293	10,617,293	0.023	0.000	0.000
23	tcpflag	10	10,617,293	0.045	0.000	0.000
24	tcpheaderlength	3	10,617,293	0.048	0.000	0.000
25	tcpoption	3	10,617,293	0.048	0.000	0.000
26	tcpseq	7,357,319	10,617,293	0.007	0.000	0.000
27	tcpsrcport	22,293	10,617,293	0.023	0.000	0.000
28	tcpurgptr	2	10,617,293	0.049	0.000	0.000
29	tcpwindowsize	10,705	10,617,293	0.025	0.000	0.000
30	udpchecksum	2	2,091,127	0.000	0.056	0.000
31	udpdestport	8,050	2,091,127	0.000	0.027	0.000
32	udplength	129	2,091,127	0.000	0.042	0.000
33	udpsrcport	8,051	2,091,127	0.000	0.027	0.000
n	**TOTAL**	**13,463,719**		**1.000**	**1.000**	**1.000**

The attack identification file is available in the text format from the Lincoln Lab web site. We verified each attack in the testing table in the database using SQL query before converting it into .csv format file prior inserting it into the database. It is very interesting to note that the number of packets which constitute an attack instance differs greatly from only 1 packet for an attack (i.e. *land*, *syslogd*) to 179,983 packets for *udpstorm*. There are 201 attack instances embedded in the MIT Lincoln Lab evaluation data set for both inside and outside testing data. Out of 201 attack instances only 176 are found in the inside testing data used for this experiment. Our performance evaluation will be based on the 176 attack instances as we only use the inside testing data.

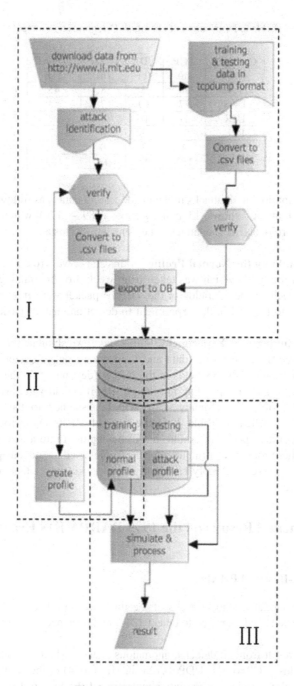

Fig. 2. PbPHAD Process Flow

Table 2. Distribution of all Attack Categories by Protocol

Category	TCP	UDP	ICMP	TOTAL
(a)	(b)	(c)	(d)	(e)
Probe	30	7	8	45
DOS	37	10	7	54
U2R	27	0	0	27
R2L	54	3	0	57
Data	4	2	0	6
Total	152	22	15	189

The distribution of all attacks in the inside testing data is as follows:

The total attacks shows 13 extra attacks (189 – 176) which is caused by duplicated protocols in the attacks. i.e. one attack instance uses more than 1 protocol.

- **Stage II. Building the Normal Profile.** In this stage, we wrote a program to build a normal profile table which was taken from week 3 of the training data. Distinct values for each of the 33 fields in the TCP/IP packet were inserted into normal profile table to be used in the experiment to detect anomalous packet header field values.

- **Stage III. Running the Experiment.** In this stage, we simulate the network traffic for the 2 weeks of the testing data and used our model to detect the anomalous packets. Each one of the 33 fields in the packet (depending on the protocol) was compared with its corresponding normal profile. If a field value was not found in the normal profile, an anomaly score will be assigned to the packet as was statistically modelled in Table 1. If the sum of all its anomalous field values surpassed a certain preset threshold, it will be captured into a detected anomalous table. Another program was run to compare the detected anomalous packets against the attack database to classify each and every packet into either true positive or false positive.

4   Experimental Results on the 1999 DARPA IDS Evaluation Data Set

4.1 Network-Based PbPHAD

We tested our model on the 2 weeks of the inside testing data which comprises of 22,095,072 packets and managed to detect 121 attack instances as depicted in Table 3 below:

This is the result from all detected anomalous packets which had surpassed certain preset thresholds (TCP=0.041, UDP=0.128, ICMP=0.034) of the anomaly score. The detected anomalous packets represents about 10% of the total test data including all false positives. It should be noted that no attack was detected on 30/03/1999 as the test data for this particular date was missing from the test data set.

Table 3. Detection Result

Date	ICMP	UDP	TCP	Sub-Total
29/03/1999	0	1	10	11
30/03/1999	0	0	0	0
31/03/1999	1	1	1	3
01/04/1999	2	0	9	11
02/04/1999	4	0	6	10
03/04/1999	1	0	1	2
04/04/1999	0	0	0	0
05/04/1999	6	0	9	15
06/04/1999	0	3	14	17
07/04/1999	0	1	14	15
08/04/1999	1	1	9	11
09/04/1999	0	4	17	21
10/04/1999	0	0	5	5
Total	15	11	95	121

The distribution of detected attack categories by protocol is tabulated in Table 4. Only one attack instance is counted even though it was detected through more than 1 protocol. The success rate percentage in column (f) is in relation to total attacks in the testing data as shown in column (e) of Table 2. Total success rate of 68.75% is calculated based on 176 total attack instances found in the experimented inside testing data.

Table 4. Distribution of Detected Attack Categories by Protocol

Category	TCP	UDP	ICMP	TOTAL	Success Rate
(a)	(b)	(c)	(d)	(e)	(f)
Probe	27	4	8	39	86.67%
DOS	23	7	7	37	68.52%
U2R	16	0	0	16	59.26%
R2L	28	0	0	28	49.12%
Data	1	0	0	1	16.67%
TOTAL	95	11	15	121	68.75%
Percentage	62.5%	50%	100%	68.75%	

18 packet header fields have been observed to have contributed to the anomaly score for the detected attacks. The distribution of the frequency of anomalous fields is tabulated in Table 5.

The rest of the 15 packet header fields have been noted as non-contributors to the anomaly scores of the detected anomalous packets. From Table 5, we can design our next model by just taking into account the contributing packet header fields only so that the processing time to detect anomalous packets can be reduced.

Table 5. Distribution of Contribution of Anomalous Packet Header Fields to Detected Attacks

Ser	Packet Header Field	Frequency
1	tcpseq	83
2	ipsrc	60
3	ipfragid	53
4	tcpack	50
5	ipdest	34
6	tcpsrcport	16
7	tcpdestport	11
8	tcpwindowsize	8
9	udpsrcport	8
10	ipfragptr	7
11	udpdestport	6
12	udplen	6
13	iplength	5
14	tcpflag	4
15	tcpurgptr	3
16	tcpchecksum	2
17	etherdesthi	1
18	etherdestlo	1

Table 6, 7 and 8 shows top 5 anomaly scores for ICMP, UDP and TCP protocols respectively. Anomalous field column shows fields that contributed to the score.

Duplicate attack names indicate the same attack on different destination hosts at different time of the day which are to be counted as separate attack instances.

Table 6. Top 5 Anomaly Scores for ICMP Packets

Ser	Attack Name	Score	Anomalous Field
1	ipsweep	0.132	ipfragid=20751; ipdest=204.233.047.021
2	pod	0.109	ipfragptr=x2000; ipsrc=202.077.162.213
3	pod	0.109	ipfragptr=x2000; ipsrc=202.077.162.213
4	smurf	0.109	ipfragptr=x2000; ipsrc=202.077.162.213
5	pod	0.109	ipfragptr=x2000; ipsrc=010.011.022.033

From table 6, for ICMP packets, it shows that ICMP protocol fields themselves are not exploited in the attack. For TCP and UDP packets, their corresponding protocol fields contributed significantly to the anomaly score for the detected anomalous packet.

Table 7. Top 5 Anomaly Scores for UDP Packets

Ser	Attack Name	Score	Anomalous Field

1	illegalsniffer	0.217	etherdesthi=x00104B;
			etherdestlo=xA26739;
			ipfragid=33248;
			ipdest=172.016.112.097;
			udpdestport=1024

2	portsweep	0.217	iplength=28;
			ipfragid=38809;
			ipsrc=153.010.008.174;
			udpsrcport=60716;
			udpdestport=513;
			udplen=8

3	teardrop	0.160	ipfragptr=x2000;
			ipsrc=207.230.054.203;
			udpsrcport=17631;
			udpdestport=23

4	teardrop	0.160	ipfragptr=x2000;
			ipsrc=199.227.099.125;
			udpsrcport=24891;
			udpdestport=23

5	syslogd	0.154	iplength=32;
			ipsrc=172.003.045.001;
			udpsrcport=514;
			udplen=12

Table 8. Top 5 Anomaly Scores for TCP Packets

Ser	Attack Name	Score	Anomalous Field

1	portsweep	0.236	iplength=28;
			ipfragid=58448;
			ipfragptr=x2000;
			ipsrc=206.048.044.050;
			tcpsrcport=50460;
			tcpseq=3192052884;
			tcpchecksum=x77F7

2	portsweep	0.175	ipsrc=192.168.001.001;
			ipdest=172.016.118.010;
			tcpdestport=63432;
			tcpseq=3269601754;
			tcpack=3303464411;
			tcpwindowsize=4128

3	phf	0.174	ipfragid=46639;
			ipsrc=206.048.044.050;
			tcpseq=242486627;
			tcpflag=x01;
			tcpchecksum=x9397

Table 8. (*continued*)

4	portsweep	0.173	ipfragid=47803;
			ipdest=153.010.008.174;
			tcpdestport=49998;
			tcpseq=1320219032;
			tcpack=36059013;
			tcpwindowsize=9112

5	dosnuke	0.165	ipfragid=59399;tcpseq=47711425;
			tcpack=47585391;
			tcpflag=x39;
			tcpurgptr=196

4.2 Host-Based PbPHAD

For Host-based PbPHAD, we built the normal profile for each host by taking the packet header field values from layer 3 and 4 protocols only which are the IP, TCP, UDP and ICMP without its layer 2 protocol, the ethernet. The total fields tested for anomaly in this model is 27 as depicted in the field name column in Table 1 minus the first 6 field names which belong to ethernet protocol. We built 2 different normal profiles, one for incoming packets and the other for outgoing packets for each inside host with the intention to acquire a more accurate statistical model with finer granularity for each of the 3 chosen protocols; TCP, UDP and ICMP.

We tested Host-based PbPHAD on the 2 weeks of the inside testing data which comprises of 22,095,072 packets. This is the same data set we used for testing the Network-based PbPHAD. Host-based PbPHAD managed to detect more attacks compared to its peer, the Network-based PbPHAD by 33 attacks (154 – 121) even though it only used layer 3 and 4 protocol fields for anomaly detection. See Table 9.

Table 9. Detection Result for Host-based PbPHAD

Date	ICMP	UDP	TCP	Sub-Total
29/03/1999	0	0	12	12
30/03/1999	0	0	0	0
31/03/1999	1	1	13	15
01/04/1999	2	0	11	13
02/04/1999	4	0	9	13
03/04/1999	3	0	0	3
04/04/1999	0	0	0	0
05/04/1999	4	0	10	14
06/04/1999	0	3	19	22
07/04/1999	0	1	17	18
08/04/1999	1	1	11	13
09/04/1999	0	4	22	26
10/04/1999	0	0	5	5
Total	**15**	**10**	**129**	**154**

This is quite a significant improvement as it shows an increment of 27.27%.

Table 10. Distribution of Detected Attack Categories by Protocol for Host-based PbPHAD

Category (a)	TCP (b)	UDP (c)	ICMP (d)	TOTAL (e)	Success Rate (f)
Probe	26	3	8	37	82.22%
DoS	28	7	7	42	77.78%
U2R	27	0	0	27	100.00%
R2L	45	0	0	45	78.95%
Data	3	0	0	3	50.00%
TOTAL	**129**	**10**	**15**	**154**	**81.48%**
Percentage	**84.87%**	**45.45%**	**100%**	**81.48%**	

Table 10 shows that Host-based PbPHAD managed to detect all attacks in U2R category as compared to its Network-based PbPHAD peer as depicted in Table 4. It decreases slightly by 4.45% on Probe category and increase by 9.26% on DoS category. For R2L category, it increases quite significantly by 29.83% and a bigger increment can be observed for attack category of Data which is 33.33%.

Host-based PbPHAD shows a significant improvement in terms of detecting number of anomalous fields as shown in Table 11. Host-based PbPHAD managed to detect 25 anomalous fields compared to only 18 by Network-based PbPHAD. Table 11 shows that the Host-based model could detect anomalous fields with a finer granularity. 9 packet header fields (Serial No. 17-25) are new anomalous fields detected by Host-based PbPHAD which are not detected by Network-based PbPHAD.

Table 11. Distribution of Contribution of Anomalous Packet Header Fields to Detected Attacks for Host-based PbPHAD

Ser	Packet Header Field	Frequency for Network-based PbPHAD	Frequency for Host-based PbPHAD
1	tcpseq	83	125
2	ipsrc	60	96
3	ipfragid	53	15
4	tcpack	50	55
5	ipdest	34	13
6	tcpsrcport	16	64
7	tcpdestport	11	49
8	tcpwindowsize	8	22
9	udpsrcport	8	6
10	ipfragptr	7	9
11	udpdestport	6	7
12	udplen	6	7

Table 11. (*continued*)

13	iplength	5	38
14	tcpflag	4	5
15	tcpurgptr	3	0
16	tcpchecksum	2	0
17	ipheaderlen	-	1
18	Iptos	-	1
19	Ipttl	-	1
20	ipprotocol	-	3
21	ipchecksum	-	1
22	tcpheaderlength	-	3
23	udpchecksum	-	2
24	icmptype	-	6
25	icmpcode	-	1

As described for the Network-based PbPHAD above, duplicate attack names indicate the same attack on different destination hosts at different time of the day which are to be counted as separate attack instances. Different anomalous field values for the same anomaly score shows each host has its own outgoing and incoming normal profile and the anomaly score for each host differs from other hosts as the normal profile for each host is unique to that particular host only as each host interact with different set of incoming and outgoing packets during training.

Table 12. Top 5 Anomaly Scores for ICMP Packets

Ser	Attack Name	Score	Anomalous Field
1	ipsweep	0.340	iplength=38; ipfragid=104; ipsrc=194.027.251.021; icmptype=8
2	ipsweep	0.340	iplength=38; ipfragid=2811; ipsrc=194.007.248.153; icmptype=8
3	ipsweep	0.339	iplength=38; ipfragid=15514; ipsrc=207.136.086.223; icmptype=8
4	ipsweep	0.339	ipsrc=204.233.047.021;
5	portsweep	0.318	ipdest=208.240.124.083; icmptype=3; icmpcode=3

From table 12, for ICMP packets, in contrary to network-based PbPHAD, Host-based PbPHAD managed to detect anomalous ICMP protocol fields. This shows that the ICMP fields are indeed being exploited in some of the attacks. This is a new interesting finding as the Network-based PbPHAD failed to detect any anomalous ICMP fields being exploited in any of the attacks. For UDP and TCP packets as shown in Table 13 and Table 14, their corresponding protocol fields contributed significantly to the anomaly score for the detected anomalous packets as similar as shown by the Network-based PbPHAD in Table 7 and Table 8 respectively.

Table 13. Top 5 Anomaly Scores for UDP Packets

Ser	Attack Name	Score	Anomalous Field

1	teardrop	0.312	ipfragptr=x2000;
			ipsrc=207.230.054.203;
			udpsrcport=17631;
			udpdestport=23;
			udplen=36

2	teardrop	0.312	ipfragptr=x2000;
			ipsrc=199.227.099.125;
			udpsrcport=24891;
			udpdestport=23;
			udplen=36

3	satan	0.277	ipsrc=209.030.070.014

4	syslogd	0.272	iplength=32;
			ipsrc=172.003.045.001;
			udpsrcport=514;
			udpdestport=514;
			udplen=12

5	portsweep	0.272	iplength=28;
			ipsrc=153.010.008.174;
			udpsrcport=60716;
			udpdestport=513;
			udplen=8

Table 14. Top 5 Anomaly Scores for TCP Packets

Ser	Attack Name	Score	Anomalous Field

1	portsweep	0.594	iplength=28;
			ipfragptr=x2000;
			ipsrc=206.048.044.050;
			tcpsrcport=49826;
			tcpdestport=514;
			tcpseq=2162256216;
			tcpack=1767401816;
			tcpheaderlen=x69

2	mscan	0.431	iplength=44;
			ipfragid=30133;
			ipdest=207.136.086.223;
			ipprotocol=6;
			tcpsrcport=25;
			tcpdestport=13074;
			tcpseq=1865002828;
			tcpack=3222202810;
			tcpheaderlen=x60

Table 14. (*continued*)

3	ipsweep	0.401	tcpsrcport=1885;
			tcpdestport=80;
			tcpseq=3295102387

4	dosnuke	0.356	ipfragid=46087;
			ipsrc=206.048.044.018;
			tcpsrcport=1734;
			tcpdestport=139;
			tcpseq=43860484;
			tcpflag=x02;
			tcpwindowsize=8192

5	tcpreset	0.319	ipfragid=35357;
			tcpdestport=26398;
			tcpseq=487325652;
			tcpack=3809752458

5   Comparison with the 1999 DARPA IDS Evaluation Best System Result

We made a comparison between PbPHAD with the combined 1999 DARPA evaluation best systems in each category of attack results on poorly detected attacks as documented by Lippman et al [11]. This analysis was performed to determine how well all 18 evaluated intrusion detection system models submitted by 8 research groups taken together detect attacks regardless of false alarm rates. The best system was first selected for each attack as the system which detects the most instances of that attack which will serve as a rough estimation for upper bound on composite system performance. Our results are in column (f) and (g) as shown in Table 15 below for Network-based PbPHAD and Host-based PbPHAD respectively.

5.1   Network-Based PbPHAD

Our initial analysis shows that Network-based PbPHAD managed to detect 48 attacks as compared to only 15 attacks detected by the composite best systems. This result shows an increment of 39.76% on detection rate for the poorly detected attacks. Our model managed to detect 9 out of 10 attacks which were not detected by all evaluated systems as compared to only 4 attacks we did not detect which were detected by the best systems.

Both Network-based PbPHAD and all DARPA evaluated systems failed to detect 1 attack which is *snmpget*. As for the type of attacks detected (58 total), Network-based PbPHAD managed to detect 53 attack types as compared to 48 attack types for composite systems. On this aspect, PbPHAD demonstrated an increment of 8.62% on the detection rate.

5.2   Host-Based PbPHAD

Column (g) in Table 15 shows attacks detected by Host-based PbPHAD for attacks which are classified as 'poorly detected' by the 1999 DARPA evaluation best

Table 15. Comparison between the 1999 DARPA Evaluation Best Systems and PbPHAD on Poorly Detected Attacks

Ser	Name	Cat.	Tot. Inst.	Instance Detected by Best System	Network-Based PbPHAD	Host-Based PbPHAD
(a)	(b)	(c)	(d)	(e)	(f)	(g)
1	ipsweep	Probe	7	0	7	7
2	lsdomain	Probe	2	1	2	2
3	portsweep	Probe	13	3	13	13
4	queso	Probe	4	0	2	3
5	resetscan	Probe	1	0	1	1
6	arppoison	DoS	5	1	0	0
7	dosnuke	DoS	4	2	4	4
8	selfping	DoS	3	0	1	1
9	tcpreset	DoS	3	1	2	2
10	warezclient	DoS	3	0	3	3
11	ncftp	R2L	5	0	4	5
12	netbus	R2L	3	1	2	2
13	netcat	R2L	4	2	0	4
14	snmpget *	R2L	4	0	0	0
15	sshtrojan	R2L	3	0	1	1
16	loadmodule	U2R	3	1	0	2
17	ntfsdos *	U2R	3	1	0	0
18	perl	U2R	4	0	3	3
19	sechole	U2R	3	1	1	2
20	sqlattack	U2R	3	0	1	2
21	xterm	U2R	3	1	1	3
Total			83	15	48	61
Percentage Detected				18.07%	57.83%	73.49%
Increment					39.76%	55.41%

systems. Host-based PbPHAD shows a significant improvement in terms of detection of number of attacks and new attacks. Host-based PbPHAD managed to detect 2 new attacks which were not detected by Network-based PbPHAD which are *netcat* and *loadmodule*. 2 attack instances which have been marked by an asterisk (* *snmpget* and *ntfsdos*) - are attacks which are only found in outside testing data, which PbPHAD did not attempt to detect as we only used inside testing data in our experiment.

For the 1999 DARPA category of 'poorly detected' attack, Host-based PbPHAD fails to detect only one attack which is *arppoison* and managed to detect 7 attacks which were totally missed by all systems participated in the second 1999 DARPA off-line intrusion detection evaluation. *Arppoison* operates at layer 2, which is the data link layer which Host-based PbPHAD excluded from its model.

6 Conclusions

Our PbPHAD model has been demonstrated as a very promising model to be used for an anomaly based IDS model by analyzing anomalous behaviour of the packet header fields on three prominent protocols.

To summarize, Network-based PbPHAD has shown the following results worthy of note:

- On the overall category of attack, Network-based PbPHAD has shown a good percentage of detection rate which is 68.75%. Network-based PbPHAD demonstrated a high percentage of detection rate for Probe and DOS which is 86.67% and 68.52% respectively.
- On the type of attacks by protocol, Network-based PbPHAD managed to detect 62.5% for TCP, a perfect 100% for ICMP and an average performance achievement for UDP at 50%. It can be seen from Table 2 and Table 4 that Network-based PbPHAD shows to be a perfect model to detect Probe and DOS attacks exploiting ICMP protocols.
- In comparison with the combined 1999 DARPA best systems for the best attack rate on poorly detected attacks, Network-based PbPHAD achieved 39.76% increment on the detection rate.
- On the number of attack types detected, Network-based PbPHAD demonstrated an increment of 8.62% on the detection rate as compared to all 1999 DARPA evaluated systems.
- On the number of 'poorly detected' attack instances which were not detected by all 1999 DARPA evaluated systems, Network-based PbPHAD is better by 60%. All DARPA evaluated combined systems failed to detect 10 attack instances as compared to only 4 attack instances not detected by Network-based PbPHAD. This clearly shows that Network-based PbPHAD could cover different attack space that could not be covered by all 1999 DARPA evaluated IDS models.

Host-based PbPHAD has demonstrated quite a significant improvement compared to its peer, the Network-based PbPHAD. Our Host-based PbPHAD anomaly based IDS model has shown that it has succeeded in complementing the existing techniques implemented by all 18 IDS models evaluated in the 1999 DARPA off-line intrusion detection evaluation exercise. This experiment has shown that it has paved a way for discovering new dimension of attack space. This shall bequeath a very promising optimism for IDS researcher community in designing new IDS model based on anomaly and host profiling.

By analyzing the detection results on both network and host based models, we can see that Network-based PbPHAD is better in terms of detecting number of attacks for Probe attack category compared to Host-based PbPHAD. This is not surprising as the Network-based PbPHAD is capable of seeing bigger attack horizon compared to the Host-based PbPHAD. Network-based PbPHAD model can see both horizontal and vertical scannings whereas Host-based PbPHAD is not capable to detect horizontal scanning as it only analyzes packets attacking its own IP only. These results show that deploying both Network-based and Host-based IDS models in a particular network installation could give a broader coverage of attack space in defending network infrastructure from malicious attacks.

7 Future Work

The percentage of false positive is still quite big for the detected anomalous packets based on the statistical model alone. Thus, we will be working on expert production rules to reduce the number of false positives. The format of the production rules is similar to other rules found in artificial intelligence techniques in the form of antecedent and consequent. Some example of the rules which will be inferred to the detected anomalous packets will be in the form as shown below:

Rule 1
Antecedent
IF   destination IP address is anomalous
AND   destination port number is the well known server port number which is in
         normal profile for that particular host
AND   session is initiated by the inside host
Consequent
THEN   Reduce the anomaly score by the destination IP anomaly value
i.e. normal internet connection for HTTP traffic using port 80.

Rule 2
Antecedent
IF   source IP address is anomalous
AND   destination port number is the well known server port number which is in
         normal profile for that particular host
AND   session is initiated by the outside host
Consequent
THEN   Reduce the anomaly score by the source IP anomaly value
i.e. normal FTP traffic for downloading file using port 21 as normal service offered by the inside host.

Fig. 3. shows a new detection process flow chart when expert production rules are included as part of the detection process. The process can be segregated into 3 stages as stage I, II & III as depicted in Fig. 3. In stage I, each packet will be examined for its anomaly using the statistical model and will be assigned an anomaly score accordingly. If the anomaly score is greater than the threshold for its protocol, it will go to stage II. Before entering stage II, the packet will be segregated based on its protocol. An ICMP packet will branch out to be inferred by an ICMP expert production rule whereas UDP and TCP packet will branch out to another production rule. In stage II, expert production rule will be inferred to the packet to examine its anomaly and a new anomaly score will be calculated. If the score is still greater than the threshold, the packet will have to go to stage III to be inferred with another layer of expert production rule. After completion of stage III, the packet anomaly score will be examined once again. If the score is still greater than the threshold it will be recorded as anomalous.

Our aim is to reduce the number of false positives to a maximum of only 10 FPs per day for our next performance evaluation benchmark.

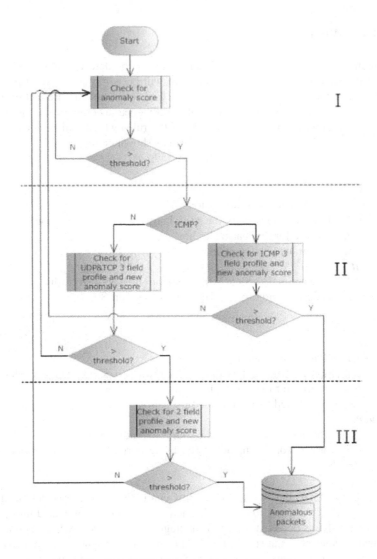

Fig. 3. PbPHAD Detection Process Flow Chart

References

1. MIT Lincoln Laboratory 1999 DARPA Intrusion Detection Data Sets (1999),
   http://www.ll.mit.edu/IST/ideval/data/1999/1999_data_index.html
2. Wang, K., Stolfo, S.J.: Anomalous Payload-based Network Intrusion Detection. In:
   Jonsson, E., Valdes, A., Almgren, M. (eds.) RAID 2004. LNCS, vol. 3224, pp. 201–222.
   Springer, Heidelberg (2004)
3. Mahoney, M.V., Chan, P.K.: Learning Rules for Anomaly Detection of Hostile Network
   Traffic. In: Proceeding of the 3rd IEEE International Conference on Data Mining (2003)

4. Luo, S., Marin, G.A.: Modeling Networking Protocols to Test Intrusion Detection Systems. In: LCN 2004. Proceedings of the 29th Annual IEEE International Conference on Local Computer Networks (2004)
5. Ertoz, L., Eilertson, E., Lazarevic, A., Tan, P.N., Dokas, P., Kumar, V., Srivastava, J.: Detection of Novel Network Attacks Using Data Mining. In: Proc. of SIAM Conf. Data Mining (2003)
6. Bolzoni, D., Etalle, S., Hartel, P., Zambon, E.: POSEIDON: A 2-Tier Anomaly Based Intrusion Detection System. In: IWIA 2006. Proceedings of the Fourth IEEE International Workshop on Information Assurance, pp. 144–156 (2006)
7. Vliet, F.V.: Turnover Poseidon: Incremental Learning in Clustering Methods for Anomaly based Intrusion Detection. In: Proceedings of Twente Student Conference on IT, University of Twente (2006)
8. Barbara, D., Couto, J., Jajodia, S., Popyack, L., Wu, N.: ADAM: Detecting intrusions by data mining. In: Proc. of the IEEE Workshop on Information Assurance and Security (June 2001)
9. Yin, C., Tian, S., Huang, H., He, J.: Applying Genetic Programming to Evolve Learned Rules for Network Anomaly Detection. In: Wang, L., Chen, K., Ong, Y.S. (eds.) ICNC 2005. LNCS, vol. 3612, pp. 323–331. Springer, Heidelberg (2005)
10. Mahoney, M.V., Chan, P.K.: PHAD: Packet Header Anomaly Detection for Identifying Hostile Network Traffic. Technical report, Florida Tech., technical report CS-2001-4 (April 2001)
11. Lippmann, R.P., Haines, J.W., Fried, D.J., Korba, J., Das, K.: The 1999 DARPA Off-Line Intrusion Detection Evaluation. MIT Lincoln Lab Technical Report (2000)

How to Secure Your Email Address Book and Beyond

Erhan J. Kartaltepe, T. Paul Parker, and Shouhuai Xu

Department of Computer Science, University of Texas at San Antonio
{ekartalt,tparker,shxu}@cs.utsa.edu

Abstract. Email viruses (or worms) have become a severe threat to the business utility of email systems. In spite of existing countermeasures such as email virus scanners, many people (including the authors) constantly receive suspicious emails. Most, if not all, email viruses proliferate by exploiting the email address books on the infected hosts, simply because the address books are not protected by any means whatsoever. In this paper we explore a novel method to protect email systems, based on appropriately encrypting the email addresses in the email address books and email boxes (or folders). To our knowledge, this work is the first to investigate robust methods for protecting email addresses. We have implemented two prototype systems based on our method, one for a cell phone platform and the other for a desktop platform. Simulation study shows that our method is effective, even if only some users deployed our mechanisms.

Keywords: self-spreading malicious emails, self-replicating malicious emails, email address book, encryption.

1 Introduction

Email has become an indispensable part of most people's daily routines. However, email was not originally designed as a utility in an adversarial environment, which may explain why there have been so many incidents related to its abuse. A severe threat imposed by email viruses (or worms) is that they can automatically replicate and spread themselves to users in the email address books of the infected hosts. Some concrete examples include the mass-mailing `W32.Klez.gen@mm`[15], `SirCam`[14], and `W32/Mydoom@MM` – one flavor of the latter even launched a *zero-day* attack targeting a Microsoft Internet Explorer IFRAME buffer overflow vulnerability [7]. These attacks are possible because the email address books – a special kind of data with important security and business utility – are not protected by any means whatsoever.

In this paper we explore a novel method to protect email systems, based on appropriately encrypting the email addresses in the email address books and email boxes (or folders). While instrumental, this turns out to be a non-trivial problem, as straightforward designs are either not secure at all or unlikely to be practically deployable. For example, the arguably most straightforward method, namely that an email address book is encrypted with a *single* key (whether that be a memorizable password or a non-memorizable cryptographically-strong key), is insufficient for preventing harvesting of email addresses from address books. This is because, even in the worst case scenario (where "worst" is from the perspective of the attacker), the attacker can simply reside

F. Bao et al. (Eds.): CANS 2007, LNCS 4856, pp. 228–246, 2007.

on the victim host and wait for the user to enter the key. This attack is certainly possible because the malicious email has already exploited some vulnerability in the victim host system anyway. As a consequence, the email virus can still spread itself soon after the victim user sends a *single* legitimate email, and the resulting delay in the spreading of email virus might not be significant enough to be of any practical impact. (As we will see in Section 6, the industrial attempts in encrypting email address books [11,18] suffer from this weakness.)

The above observation suggests that each record of an email address book should be encrypted with a different key. This can significantly slow down the proliferation of an email virus, because in order to spread to all email addresses in a victim's address book, the virus will have to wait until the user has sent at least one email to each of them. This waiting time varies, and mainly depends on the social behavior of the victim user; we suspect it would be at days or weeks at least. Such a delay would significantly increase the chance of the virus being removed because, for instance, the virus may be detected and countermeasures may become available. While theoretically possible, this approach might *not* be practically deployable due to the following reasons. First, the number of email address book entries is often quite large (as many as several hundred in the authors' experience), meaning that each user would need to keep a significant number of keys. Even if the keys are based on memorizable passwords, this is not practical because the resulting solution would eventually degenerate to the aforementioned case where a single password encrypts all entries (just as we often use the same password for multiple accounts). Of course, this problem can be alleviated if one only wants or needs to encrypt a small number of email addresses (rather than all of them); this flexibility actually will be offered by our solution. Second, special hardware devices do not necessarily help. On one hand, it is clear that devices such as cell phones and handheld computers are equally subject to virus attacks. On the other hand, even if one utilizes some trusted computing module [16], the virus can perfectly impersonate the user to the module (because the virus has already compromised the user's secrets for authenticating to the module), unless some form of human test [1,3] is imposed by the module. This extra assumption suggests that it would be ideal if we can achieve the same functionality without involving any special hardware devices.

1.1   Our Contributions

In this paper we present a scheme, called "encrypted address book," for facilitating the encryption of some or all — dependent upon users' needs — of the email addresses in the address books. The scheme offers the following desired properties: (1) each need-to-be-protected entry in an email address book is encrypted with a different key that is derived from a unique passphrase; (2) the users are relieved of memorizing any of the passphrases; (3) there is no need for any special purpose hardware. These are achieved via a novel use of some hard AI problems. Specifically, to relieve a user of memorizing any passphrase, we can embed one into an appropriate picture (e.g., a photo of the user corresponding to an address book entry), which will prompt the user to enter the embedded passphrase. Furthermore, this protection is extended to protect the corresponding appearances of the protected email addresses in the email boxes (or folders). We stress the design's flexibility in allowing one to *selectively* encrypt the email addresses in one's address book, which would ease the real-life deployment (because some users may have very large address books).

Another feature of our scheme is its immunity to offline dictionary attack. Since the cryptographic keys are based on low-entropy passphrases, it is crucial to be immune to this attack; otherwise, many, if not all, of the encrypted addresses could be recovered by an email virus. We achieve this desired feature via the following design. First, we encrypt only the non-structural information in the email addresses. In other words, we keep the structural information in email addresses such as the "@" and " . " in plaintext. Second, even if structural information is not encrypted, an email virus could still try to conduct a brute-force attack, because the decryption may not lead to legitimate email addresses. Fortunately, the virus is not necessarily able to tell whether the decryption is a true or "junk" email address, unless it tries to send email to that decrypted address. As a result, either the legitimate outgoing mail server (in the case the virus utilizes the victim user's SMTP engine) or the network firewall (in the case the virus utilizes its own SMTP engine) can detect such an explosion in outgoing email traffic or bounced undeliverable emails.

We have implemented two prototype systems based on our scheme: one is for a cell phone platform, and the other is for desktop platforms. Both prototype systems are based on the integration of our scheme into the open source email client software called Pooka [10]. The performance penalty incurred by our scheme is almost imperceptible to email users. Our prototype system has been tested by a small group of volunteers. We plan to conduct a wider and more thorough usability test, and will report the usability feedback in the full version of the present paper.

In order to show the effectiveness of our scheme, we conducted a simulation study. The result shows that the number of email addresses exposed to email viruses can be significantly reduced, even if only a portion (e.g., 60%) of the users deployed our mechanism. Our mechanism would be particularly useful in dealing with zero-day email attacks, whose cures are not available until after the attacks have been detected. Our scheme is orthogonal to other email virus protection mechanisms (e.g., scanners), and thus can be seamlessly integrated with them to provide more comprehensive protection.

Outline: The rest of the paper is organized as follows. In Section 2 we briefly review the functionalities of email systems. In Section 3 we explore our scheme for encrypting email addresses in the address books. In Section 4 we present the functionalities and the implementation of our prototype system, including the encryption of email addresses in the email boxes. In Section 5 we analyze the effectiveness of our mechanism. We discuss related works in Section 6. We conclude the paper in Section 7.

2   Functionalities of Current Email Systems – A Brief Review

We now briefly review the relevant functionalities of current email systems, since our system simply layers over an existing system. We denote by ces a current email system, and by ces.AB $= (A_0, A_1, A_2)$ the current email address book schema, where the A_i's are attributes. Without loss of generality, we assume that A_0 is the email address, A_1 is the username, and A_2 is the rest of the relevant attribute content. Note username denotes the "friendly name" or nickname used in the address book for the holder of the email address, not the portion of the email address preceding the @ sign. Let ces.ab be an instance of ces.AB, namely one's address book; an entry in ces.ab is denoted by (a_0, a_1, a_2). Let ces.folders be the folders of a current email system. We classify, in Table 1, the functionalities of ces into two categories: those of the address book services and those of the email services.

Table 1. Relevant functionalities of current email systems

Functionalities of address book services	Description
ces.addaddress(address, username)	Add a new entry into its email address book.
ces.deleteaddress(ces.ab, address)	Delete an entry of an email address book.
ces.modifyaddress(ces.ab, address)	Modify the email address in the entries of an email address book.
Functionalities of email services	Description
ces.compose()	Compose a message to be sent.
ces.insertaddress(address)	Insert an email address address (from its email address book) into an address bar when composing an email.
ces.attach(file)	Attach a file that is to be sent together with an email message.
ces.send(email)	Send an email to a recipient.
ces.receive()	Receive emails.
ces.reply(email)	Reply to the sender of an email.
ces.replyall(email)	Reply to all the email addresses in the email header.
ces.forward(email)	Forward an email to some users.
ces.search(parameter)	Search email address book entries based on some parameter.
ces.createfolder(ces.folders, folder)	Create an email folder.
ces.deletefolder(ces.folders, folder)	Delete an email folder.
ces.sort(parameter)	Sort the emails in an email folder based on some parameter.
ces.deliver(email)	Internal program function that delivers an email to some users.

3   Encrypted Address Book

In this section we present our mechanism for encrypting addresses in email address books. (The encryptions of addresses appearing in the emails of the email boxes are done at a higher layer; see Section 4.) We first discuss the needed building blocks, and then show how they are put together to implement encrypted address books.

3.1   Building Blocks

Building block I: embedding passphrases into pictures. As mentioned before, we require that each entry in an email address book is encrypted with a different key that is derived from a unique passphrase. This ensures that compromise of one email address (e.g., a user entering the passphrase for encrypting that specific email address on a compromised machine) does not entail the compromise of any other address in the email address book. The key challenge is to relieve the users from having to memorize any of the passphrases. For this purpose, we propose embedding a passphrase onto an appropriate picture (e.g., a photo of the user corresponding to an address book entry), which will prompt the user to enter the embedded passphrase. Fig. 1 shows an example

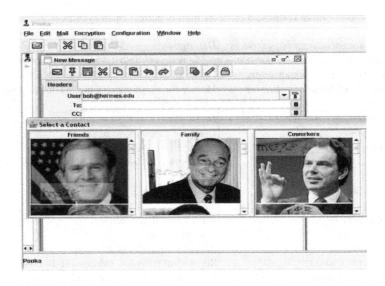

Fig. 1. Embedding passphrases onto pictures of the corresponding users

of encrypted email address book where, for instance, the passphrase used to encrypt the email address of G. W. Bush is "hpay." We abstract this building block as a function **embed**($passphrase$, image) that returns an icon that is obtained by embedding a string (e.g., a passphrase) onto a picture image. The concrete implementation of this function is orthogonal to the present work, as long as it ensures that there are no feasible ways for a computer program to extract the embedded passphrases. Our experiments are based on the output of CMU's CAPTCHA project [1,3], which is a special kind of Reverse Turing Test (RTT) for telling computer programs and human being users apart.

Note that since the decision of whether to encrypt an email address is left to the users, one may encrypt only the addresses of the peers whose pictures are easy to obtain or whose addresses are especially important to protect from address harvesting. When a user chooses to encrypt an email address of a peer whose picture is not available (e.g., an email list), a picture may be automatically generated with some appropriate software that takes as input a user-specified text (e.g., the name of the email list).

Building block II: needed encryption scheme and its security. In order to encrypt addresses, we need some cryptographic encryption scheme. It is interesting, however, that the needed security property of the encryption scheme is actually strictly weaker than the often required ones. Specifically, let us denote by κ the security parameter (in this paper, the length of the key in bits). A function negl is negligible in κ if $\mathsf{negl}(\kappa) < 1/poly(\kappa)$ for all polynomial $poly$ and all sufficiently large κ. Let h be an ideal hash function [2], which may be instantiated as SHA256 [13] in practice. Our mechanism utilizes a symmetric encryption scheme (keyGen, Enc, Dec), where keyGen is the key generation algorithm that takes as input a security parameter κ and returns a key $K \in_R \{0,1\}^\kappa$, Enc is the encryption algorithm that takes as input a key K and a plaintext message m and returns a ciphertext $c \leftarrow \mathsf{Enc}_K(m)$, and Dec is the decryption algorithm that takes as input a key K and a ciphertext c and returns a plaintext $m \leftarrow \mathsf{Dec}_K(c)$.

As in traditional symmetric key encryption schemes [6], we consider a probabilistic polynomial-time adversary $\mathcal{A}$. However, it is interesting to see that the well-known notions of indistinguishability under chosen-plaintext and chosen-ciphertext attacks become irrelevant in our application setting. This is because an adversary who can launch such an attack would have already been able to "steal" the keys (e.g., by residing on the victim host). Instead, the following security requirement, which we call *simple-security* as it reflects that the key and plaintext should not be recovered from the ciphertexts, would suffice for the purpose of our specific application. Formally, we say a symmetric key encryption scheme is of *simple-security* if

$$\Pr[K \leftarrow_R \mathsf{keyGen}(1^\kappa); c \leftarrow \mathsf{Enc}_K(m) : m \leftarrow \mathcal{A}(c)] = \mathsf{negl}(\kappa)$$

where the probability is taken over the coins of keyGen and the adversary algorithm $\mathcal{A}$. Note that the above requirement implies

$$\Pr[K \leftarrow_R \mathsf{keyGen}(1^\kappa); c \leftarrow \mathsf{Enc}_k(m) : K \leftarrow \mathcal{A}(c)] = \mathsf{negl}(\kappa).$$

In our experiments, we use the RC4 stream cipher (with appropriate truncation [8]) to encrypt email addresses. We assume that RC4 can be treated as a pseudorandom function [5]. This immediately means that the resulting encryption scheme has the desired simple-security property.

Building block III: how to encrypt email addresses while eliminating the offline dictionary attack. Having specified the encryption scheme, we now explore how the encryption scheme should be employed. This issue is important because the keys are derived from some low-entropy passphrases, meaning that special care must be taken to deal with the offline dictionary attack. Suppose the keys might be drawn from a relatively small passphrase dictionary D. Then, the above notion of simple-security needs to be amended to the following:

$$\left| \Pr[K \leftarrow_R \mathsf{keyGen}(1^\kappa); c \leftarrow \mathsf{Enc}_K(m) : m \leftarrow \mathcal{A}(c)] - \frac{n}{|D|} \right| = \mathsf{negl}(\kappa)$$

where n is the number of trials in sending emails to the (likely junk) addresses that are decrypted from guessed passphrases. This leads to the following instructions on how to encrypt email addresses.

First, we observe that a simple-minded encryption of email addresses is vulnerable to offline dictionary attack. This is because the keys are derived from low-entropy passphrases, and email addresses are well-structured (e.g., user@host.domain). For example, if the decryption obtained from a guessed passphrase does not have the email address structure or the (top) domain name is invalid (note that there are only a small number of domain names), then the attacker can conclude that guess is incorrect. Therefore, we do not encrypt those structured portions of the email addresses; they include the special symbols "@" and ".", and the top domain names. This also means that any "." in the username portion of an email address is not encrypted (note this username part is distinct from A_1, which we normally refer to as the username in this paper and is sometimes referred to as a nickname).

Second, we observe that if the decrypted address does not contain ASCII characters, or contains ASCII characters not suitable for email addresses and hostnames, then the attacker knows that its guess was wrong. Note also that the simple idea of encrypting only the 7 least significant bits of each character byte does not work because it still gives the attack enough information to launch the brute-force attack. To see this, notice that even though the IETF RFC 2821 and 2822 clearly state that only 7-bit ASCII characters are allowed in Internet email addresses, in practice only a subset of them are actually usable, either because they are disallowed (control characters fall into this category), or because of their confusing nature (the pipe and asterisk symbols fall into this category due to their use in UNIX shells). Indeed, it seems that the only legitimate characters (besides the reserved "@" and ".") that can appear in an email address include the following 64 characters: a-z, A-Z, 0-9, "_", and "-". If we simply encrypt the least significant 7 bits of each character, then the probability of the malicious program realizing its guess was incorrect is $1 - 1/(2^m)$, where m is the length of the email address (i.e., the number of characters other than "@" and "."). This is unacceptably high (e.g., when $m = 10$ the probability is very close to 1). We also observe that simply encrypting the least significant 6 bits of each character is also unacceptable. This is so because the allowed characters do not evenly correspond to $0000,0000$ and $0011,1111$. We overcome this problem by defining a table that maps the above 64 usable ASCII characters to the range between $0000,0000$ and $0011,1111$, and we only encrypt the least significant 6 bits of each byte. Of course, an inversion transformation is conducted when we execute the decryption algorithm.

Third, we observe that the first character in an email address is generally a letter, and many email services enforce this restriction. If the first decrypted character isn't a letter, the attacker virus or worm may assume, likely correctly, that its guess was incorrect. We can remove this liability by not encrypting the first character.

Now let us informally examine the security of the resulting scheme (a formal analysis is deferred to the full version of the present paper). We notice that all the above instructions are made public and thus known to the adversary; this means that security against offline dictionary attacks is merely based on standard cryptographic machinery. The objective of the attacker (i.e., the malicious email in this paper's context) is to recover the email addresses. There are two approaches for the attacker to obtain them. The first is to constantly monitor the client software until the victim user has sent emails to all (or most) of the users in the address book. This waiting time varies, and mainly depends on the social behavior of the victim user. Our solution has been successful if the attacker is forced to adopt this approach. The second is to conduct a dictionary attack against the passphrases. Fortunately, our careful design blocks any *offline* dictionary attack. This is because, without actually trying to send an email to an address decrypted with a guessed passphrase, the attacker cannot tell whether its guess is correct or not. As a result, the attacker's capability is essentially downgraded to an *online* dictionary attack, which can be easily detected and blocked either by a firewall or by a legitimate SMTP engine.

3.2 Encrypted Address Book – Putting Pieces Together

Let EAB be the schema of encrypted address books. The key difference between ces.AB (as reviewed in Section 2) and EAB is that attribute A_0 in the former is substituted by several attributes in the latter, whereas A_1 and A_2 are kept intact. An encrypted address book is an instance of EAB, called eab. Our mechanism consists of the functionalities that are formally specified in Figure 2 and intuitively presented below. The setup

```
eab.setup(ces.ab) {
    eab ← ∅
    For each (a₀, a₁, a₂) ∈ ces.ab {
        select a random r₀
        user picks a passphrase pa
        user picks a picture image for a₀
        icon ← embed(pa, image)
        c₀ ← Enc_{h(r₀,pa)}(a₀)
        c₁ ← a₁
        c₂ ← a₂
        eab ← eab ∪ {(icon, r₀, c₀, c₁, c₂)}
    }
}
```

```
eab.addaddress(eab, address, username) {
    select a random r₀
    user picks a passphrase pa
            that is embedded onto an icon
    user picks picture image for address
    user enters info for address
    icon ← embed(pa, image)
    c₀ ← Enc_{h(r₀,pa)}(address))
    c₁ ← username
    c₂ ← info
    eab ← eab ∪ {(icon, r₀, c₀, c₁, c₂)}
}
```

```
eab.modifyaddress(eab) {
    user browses eab
    users clicks icon such that
        (icon, r₀, c₀, c₁, c₂) ∈ eab
    user enters pa embedded onto an icon
    user types in new address newaddress
    c₀ ← Enc_{h(r₀,pa)}(address)
    update (icon, r₀, c₀, c₁, c₂) ∈ eab
}
```

```
eab.getaddress(eab, icon) {
    If ∃ r₀, c₀, c₁, c₂ such that
        (icon, r₀, c₀, c₁, c₂) ∈ eab {
        user enters pa
        address ← Dec_{h(r₀,pa)}(c₀))
        return address
    }
    Else return null
}
```

```
eab.deleteaddress(eab, icon) {
    If ∃ r₀, c₀, c₁, c₂ such that
        (icon, r₀, c₀, c₁, c₂) ∈ eab
    eab ← eab − {(icon, r₀, c₀, c₁, c₂)}
}
```

```
eab.geticon(eab, username) {
    If ∃ (icon, r₀, c₀, username, c₂) ∈ eab
        return icon
    Else return NULL
}
```

Fig. 2. Functionalities of encrypted address book subsystem

algorithm eab.setup(ces.ab) takes as input an existing email address book ces.ab $= \{(a_{i,0}, a_{i,1}, a_{i,2})\}_{1 \leq i \leq \ell}$, and transforms it into an encrypted email address book eab $= \{(\mathrm{icon}_i, r_{i,0}, c_{i,0}, c_{i,1}, c_{i,2})\}_{1 \leq i \leq \ell}$, where icon_i is the icon returned by embed($\cdot, \cdot$), $r_{i,0}$ is a random string of appropriate length (e.g., 160 bit), $c_{i,0} = \mathrm{Enc}_{h(r_{i,0}, pa_i)}(a_{i,0})$, $c_{i,1} = a_{i,1}$, and $c_{i,2} = a_{i,2}$. Notice that each record of eab is encrypted with a different key $h(r_{i,0}, pa_i)$; in other words, both $r_{i,0}$ and pa_i are unique to this record. Note further that only the email address itself ($a_{i,0}$) is encrypted.

The algorithm **eab.addaddress**(eab, *address*, *username*) takes as input the current encrypted address book eab, a new email address *address* and the corresponding username *username*, and updates eab by adding a new record for the new user.

The algorithm **eab.modifyaddress**(eab) allows the owner to browse the encrypted address book eab, and change the email address in an entry. Note that the browsing of eab can be indexed by the icon's or the $c_{i,1}$'s (i.e., the usernames). In order to accomplish this functionality, the owner needs to enter the passphrase pa corresponding to the record whose email address is to be changed. Note that pa need not be memorized by the owner, because it is embedded onto the icon that is presented to him.

The algorithm **eab.getaddress**(eab, icon) allows the owner to extract the email address of the record corresponding to icon in the encrypted address book eab. For this purpose, the owner also needs to enter the pa prompted by the icon.

The algorithm **eab.deleteaddress**(eab, icon) allows the owner to delete the record corresponding to icon from the encrypted address book eab. Note that the owner is not asked to enter the passphrase pa, because an attacker that already compromised the victim host can delete the records in eab anyway.

The algorithm **eab.geticon**(eab, *username*) returns the icon, if any, corresponding to the give username *username* in the encrypted address book eab. This algorithm does not ask the user to enter the passphrase pa.

4   Prototype System with Integrated Encrypted Address Books

In this section we describe our prototype system based on the above mechanism that encrypts the email addresses in the email address books. The email addresses appearing in the email boxes (or folders) are encrypted as well (see **initialize** below).

4.1   Functionalities of Our Prototype System

Our prototype system provides the same set of functionalities as a current email system does. Since our system is built upon the current email systems, it additionally provides an **initialize** functionality. As shown in Figure 3, most functionalities of the prototype system are provided by calling the counterpart functions that are offered by the current email system (ces) or the encrypted address book (eab) mechanism. Specifically, its **insertaddress, attach, send, search, createfolder, deletefolder, sort** and **deliver** functionalities are the same as **ces.insertaddress, ces.attach, ces.send, ces.search, ces.createfolder, ces.deletefolder, ces.sort** and **ces.deliver**, respectively. Its **addaddress** and **modifyaddress** functionalities are the same as the eab **addaddress** and **modifyaddress**, respectively. The other functionalities, namely **replyall** as well its special case **reply, receive, deleteaddress, compose**, and **forward**, are formally specified in Figure 4 and intuitively presented below.

Denote by eab an instance of EAB, and by **projection**(eab, $column_1$, $column_2$) the projection of eab on the two attributes $column_1$ and $column_2$. Each email system has a set of email folders folders, each of which consists of a set of emails. For each

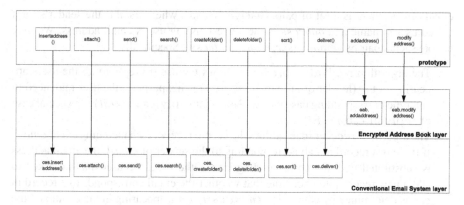

Fig. 3. Inheritance diagram for most prototype functions (others have pseudocode in Figure 4). The function at the base of the arrow essentially calls the function at the arrow's head.

initialize(ces.ab, ces.folders) {
  eab.setup(ces.ab)
  For each folder ∈ ces.folders {
    For each $email$ ∈ folder {
      For each $(email.address, email.user)$
        $email.address$ ← **eab.geticon**(eab,
          $email.user$)
    }
  }
  erase ces.ab
  new.folders ← ces.folders
}
	replyall(eab, $email$) {
	  // **reply** is a special case of **replyall**
	  t ← $email$
	  For each $(t.address, t.user)$ {
	    If $t.address$ is an icon
	      $t.address$ ← **eab.getaddress**(eab,
	        $t.address$)
	  }
	  ces.replyall(t)
	  erase t
	}

receive(eab) {
  EMAILS ← **ces.receive**()
  table ← **projection**(eab, icon, c_1)
  For each $email$ ∈ EMAILS {
    For each $(email.address, email.user)$ {
      If ∃ icon such that $(icon, email.user)$ ∈ table
        $email.address$ ← icon
      Else {
        user picks an icon for $email.user$
        eab.addaddress(eab, $email.address$,
          $email.user$)
        $email.address$ ← **eab.geticon**(eab,
          $email.user$)
    }
    ces.deliver($email$)
  }
}
	deleteaddress(eab, new.folders, icon) {
	  allowed ← TRUE
	  For each folder ∈ new.folders {
	    For each $email$ ∈ folder {
	      If icon $= email.address$ {
	        allowed ← FALSE
	        exit
	      }
	    }
	  }
	  If allowed
	    eab.deleteaddress(eab, icon)
	}

compose(eab) {
  ces.compose()
  If user clicks the "insert address" button {
    user browses eab and clicks on an icon
    $address$ ← **eab.getaddress**(eab, icon)
    ces.insertaddress($address$)
  }
  If user types in an email address $address$ {
    user types in $recipient$
    If **eab.geticon**(eab, $recipient$) = NULL
      eab.addaddress(eab, $address$, $recipient$)
  }
}
	forward(eab, $email$) {
	  If user clicks the "insert address" button {
	    user browses eab and clicks on an icon
	    $address$ ← **eab.getaddress**(eab, icon)
	    ces.insertaddress($address$)
	  }
	  If user types in an email address $address$ {
	    user types in $recipient$
	    If **eab.geticon**(eab, $recipient$) = NULL
	      eab.addaddress(eab, $address$,
	        $recipient$)
	  }
	}

Fig. 4. Functionalities of our prototype system

email *email*, there is a set of pairs (*user*, *address*), where *user* is the sender's (or a cc'ed user's) name and *address* is the corresponding user's email address. We may denote such a pair by (*email.user*, *email.address*). Specifically,

* The algorithm **replyall**(eab, *email*) allows the user to reply to all the users appearing in the (header of an) email *email*. For this purpose, the user may need to enter the corresponding passphrases. Note that **reply**(eab, *email*) is a special case of **replyall**(eab, *email*).
* The algorithm **receive**(eab) allows the user to receive each incoming email *email*. If there is a record in eab corresponding to the sender of *email*, the email address is substituted with the corresponding icon. Otherwise, the user may be asked to add a new record into eab. Note that whether the email corresponds to a record in eab is determined by comparing *email.username* appearing in the email and the plaintext *username* appearing in eab. (In the rare case that *email.username* = NULL, the user may be asked to browse the icon's in eab.)
* The algorithm **deleteaddress**(eab, new.folders, icon) allows the user to delete a record from eab. However, special care is taken to ensure that there is no email involving the user associated with the record. If this property is not guaranteed, there would be some emails whose addresses cannot be recovered (even by the legitimate user).
* The algorithm **compose**(eab) allows the user to compose an email. It allows the user to insert an address in eab. Similarly, the algorithm **forward**(eab, *email*) allows the user to forward the email *email*.

Finally, there are two ways for one to **initialize** our system. The first is a fresh bootstrapping with an empty email address book and empty email boxes. The second is to appropriately process an existing email address book and its associated email boxes. Since the first scenario can be seen as a special case of the second, we will focus on the second scenario. The algorithm **initialize**(ces.ab, ces.folders) first calls eab.setup(ces.ab) to transform an existing address book ces.ab into an encrypted address book eab, and then substitutes every email address in every email box with the corresponding icon.

4.2 Implementation and Evaluation of Our Prototype System

We implemented two prototype systems — one for the PC platform, the other for use on a cell phone (whose camera may naturally provide photos of the users appearing in an email address book). The desktop version is called Enhanced Pooka — an enhancement of the original Pooka email client [10]. This system was written in Java 1.4.2. The cell phone version is called MiniPooka and acts as a full email system. The hardware chosen was the Palm Treo 650 for multiple reasons. First, the widespread prevalence of smartphones in the business world caused us to consider phones with their functionality. Second, there is a wide variety of simulators that run the Palm OS operating system, allowing strong testing in the design phase of the project. Third, the widespread usage of the Palm OS naturally led to a wide variety of tools for designing a system quickly. Further, the authors' access to a Treo 650 allowed testing in real world simulations and experiments, valuable to determine the viability of MiniPooka. MiniPooka also has the capability to capture images for use with the Enhanced Pooka system, as described below.

Performance. Our solution is a user-end one, meaning that it does not incur any communication delay, even with the email server. Furthermore, our prototype system showed that the performance in terms of delay imposed on the relevant procedures (e.g., sending emails) is not noticeable by a human being, except of course that the users may need to enter the passphrases that are embedded onto picture images.

Preliminary usability analysis. Our prototype system for the PC platform was preliminarily tested by a small group of volunteers. Some were from computer science professions while others used email regularly but were in other fields. These volunteers were surveyed to determine if our prototype system was an effective replacement for their current email system and by doing so, determine if our prototype system would be a deployable one. A questionnaire using the Likert scale for providing a level of measurement was applied. The questionnaire listed a series of statements and requested the respondent to answer with "strongly disagree", "strongly agree", "neither agree nor disagree", "agree", and "strongly agree". For example, the question "easy as CES?" asks whether our prototype system is as easy as their current email system to use, and the question "can read RTT?" asks the easiness in dealing with the reverse Turing test (i.e., CAPTCHA in our experiment). Their answers were then mapped to a score from one to five and averaged across those respondents. These results are shown in Figure 5.

While the results of our preliminary usability tests were quite encouraging, we read it with caution. When asked which part of the process would be most time-consuming or difficult, an overwhelming number of responses suggested that that task would be obtaining pictures for a contact. Fortunately, a user only once needs to obtain a picture for a person whose email address appears in the user's email address book; i.e., this cost of "bootstrapping" the scheme is done once-and-for-all. Moreover, our systems were designed for incremental deployment, meaning not only that partial deployment

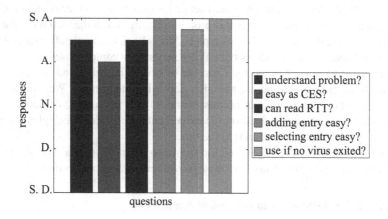

Fig. 5. Questionnaire results

could already be effective, but also that one can selectively protect the email addresses the user cares most (i.e., only those email addresses in the email address book and email boxes are encrypted using our method).

5   Effectiveness Analysis

In this section we analyze the effectiveness of our approach to protecting email addresses in the address books and email boxes.

5.1   Methodology and Metric

To examine effectiveness, we conduct a simulation study based on the real-life email network of [4]. This data set is based on email traffic during the period of sixteen weeks (or nearly 10^7 seconds). This dataset contained 41,991 anonymized senders and recipients and 406,600 emails. This email network can be modeled as an "email graph" $G(V, E)$, where each email sender or recipient (i.e., an email address) is a vertex or node $v \in V$ and an edge $e \in E$ connects v_1 and v_2 if v_1 sent an email to or received an email from v_2. In particular, each node has an address book based on the email graph G, and may or may not deploy our mechanism.

To accommodate the worst case scenario, we make the following assumptions. First, we assume that the email virus is crafty in that it does not simply spread itself in a straightfoward fashion (otherwise, simple countermeasures such as virus throttling [20] can easily detect and block it). Instead, it intends to be as stealthy as possible. To this end, the email virus tries to mimic the behavior of the victim users. For simplicity, this is captured by substituting every email sent by a compromised user with one that is sent by the email virus. Second, we assume that at system initialization the email address books at the nodes corresponding to the graph G are already formed (by "system initialization" we mean that when our mechanism is deployed). Third, if a user is compromised at system initialization, then the email address book is completely compromised at that time. Fourth, any email sent by a compromised user is malicious, and the recipient immediately becomes compromised or infected. If the victim recipient has not deployed our mechanism, then its email address book is completely exposed to the virus; otherwise, its email address book is not necessarily compromised.

The metric of interest is the total number of nodes (i.e., email addresses) that are exposed to an email virus, before and after deploying our method. We consider three factors that may have an impact on this metric: (1) the percentage of nodes that are compromised at system initialization, (2) the percentage of nodes that deploy our mechanism at system initialization, and (3) the time.

In what follows we explore the metric from two perspectives: the *overall effectiveness at the end of the simulation* and the *effectiveness with respect to time*.

5.2   Overall Effectiveness at the End of Simulation

Figure 6 shows the percentage of email addresses that have been exposed to the attacker at the end of the simulation. This metric depends on two factors: the percentage of compromised nodes (denoted by "initially compromised %" for short) at system initialization (i.e., 0%, 20%, 40%, 60%, 80%, and 100%), and the percentage of nodes deploying our mechanism (denoted by "eab deployment %" for short) at system initialization (i.e., 0%, 20%, 40%, 60%, 80%, and 100%). In any case where only some nodes are compromised or deploy our mechanism, we assume that these nodes are randomly selected from the population V.

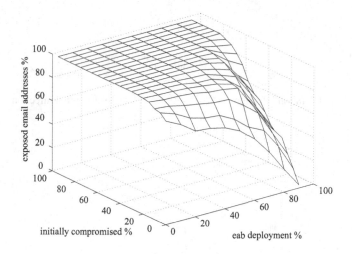

Fig. 6. Percentage of exposed email addresses at the end of the simulation

From Figure 6 we draw the following observations. First, if many nodes are compromised at initialization, then our solution's success is limited. Specifically, if more than 70% of the nodes are initially compromised, after all emails are sent the number of exposed addresses still reaches 100%. This is inevitable because the address books of the compromised nodes already cover a significant portion of the email address population. However, it is more likely that a small percentage (e.g., 1%) of nodes would be initially compromised. In this case, our solution is quite effective even if only portions of the nodes deploy our mechanism (see below for details). Second, for any fixed percentage of initially compromised nodes, the number of exposed email addresses decreases as the percentage of eab deployment grows. Third, for any fixed percentage of eab deployment, the number of exposed email addresses decreases as the percentage of initially compromised nodes drops.

5.3   Effectiveness with Respect to Time

We explore the evolution of the number of exposed email addresses with respect to time. Figure 7 shows the effect of the number of initially infected nodes on the average number of exposed email addresses as the simulation proceeds. The average is taken over 10 runs. Figure 7.(a) corresponds to the case that 1% of nodes are initially compromised and 25%, 50%, 75%, and 100% nodes deploy our mechanism, respectively.

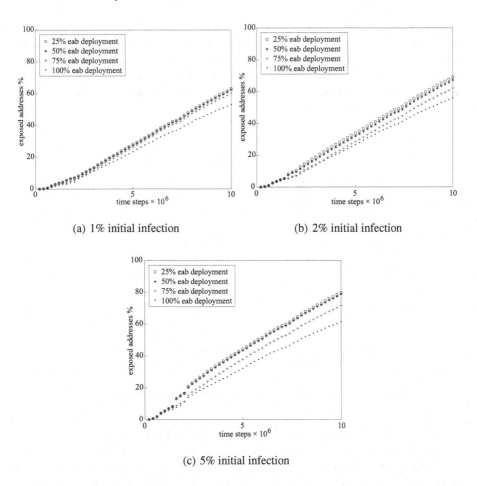

(a) 1% initial infection   (b) 2% initial infection

(c) 5% initial infection

Fig. 7. Exposed email addresses vs. initial infection

Figure 7.(b) corresponds to the case that 2% of nodes are initially compromised and 25%, 50%, 75%, and 100% nodes deploy our mechanism, respectively. Figure 7.(c) corresponds to the case that 5% of nodes are initially compromised and 25%, 50%, 75%, and 100% nodes deploy our mechanism, respectively.

Figure 7 allows us to draw the following observations. First, the more nodes that deploy our mechanism, the fewer email addresses will be exposed. The more initially compromised nodes there are, the more significant the above tendency. For example, we can see significant differences between the numbers of eventually exposed email addresses in the case of 50% eab deployment and in the case of 75% eab deployment. In the case of 1% initially compromised nodes, the difference is 3%; in the case of 2% initially compromised nodes, the difference is 6%; in the case of 5% initially compromised nodes, the difference is 9%. Second, the number of exposed email addresses increases almost linearly with respect to time t. This perhaps means that, on average, emails are sent to new email addresses as time proceeds.

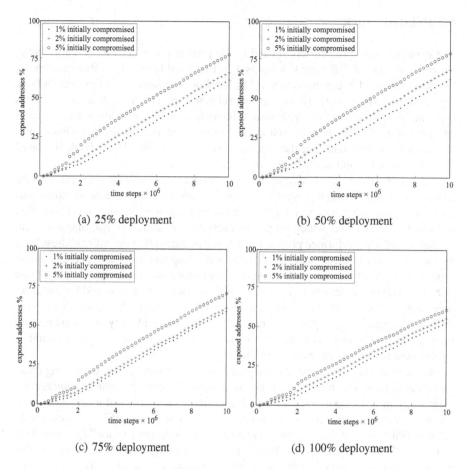

Fig. 8. Exposed email addresses vs. new mechanism deployment

Figure 8 plots the same simulation results (i.e., the one shown in Figure 7) from a different perspective. First, it clearly shows that, for any fixed percentage of eab deployment, the number of exposed email addresses increases as the number of initially compromised nodes grows. Second, the differences between the numbers of exposed email addresses in the case of 2% initially compromised nodes and in the case of 5% initially compromised nodes decreases as the percentage of eab deployment increases. Third, our mechanism is effective even if only portions of the nodes deploy our mechanisms. For example, suppose that 50% of the nodes deploy our mechanism. Then, about 40% of the nodes will not be exposed to the attacker at the end of the simulation in the case of there being 1% initially compromised nodes, about 35% of the nodes will not be exposed to the attacker at the end of the simulation in the case of there being 2% initially compromised nodes, and about 22% of the nodes will not be exposed to the attacker at the end of the simulation in the case of there being 5% initially compromised nodes. This is of practical value because it is unlikely that all nodes (or users) will deploy our mechanism (for whatever reason).

6   Related Work

The existing work most closely related to the present paper is actually some implemented commercial software. Courier is a full-featured email client that runs on the Windows family of operating systems [11]. ViraLock is another for Microsoft Outlook and Outlook Express [18]. However, both schemes encrypt the address book entries using the same key, and thus are bound to be ineffective against address harvesting as analyzed in the Introduction. In contrast, our methods encrypt each address book entry with a *different* key, meaning that compromise of the whole address book is slowed down by a factor proportional to the size of the address book.

It should be noted that our scheme does not necessarily obviate encryption of the address book with a single key; this is complementary to our scheme for some purposes. For example, users may wish to ensure privacy of nicknames (A_1) and other address book details, for which single-key encryption is ideally suited. Single-key encryption should be performed prior to our scheme by encrypting the entire address book file, which is much simpler than individually decrypting addresses after performing our scheme, particularly as the latter would also necessitate any file encryption passphrase to be retained in memory or re-entered each time. Moreover, this would be useful for preventing attacks which are beyond the scope of this work, such as a worm transmitting an eab to another computer, where a human user would identify the passphrases in the images in order to decrypt the addresses. Note we believe such a scheme would be far too expensive for most email worms to employ in practice.

Our solution can be seamlessly integrated with other solutions to countering email viruses to provide a more comprehensive protection. For example, our solution is complementary to virus throttling [20], which rate-limits the number of a user's outgoing emails to distinct recipients. As a follow-up to [20], Twining et al [17] proposed a technique called "using sending history to predict future mailing behavior." However, both [20] and [17] may not be able to block or slow down outgoing malicious emails that can mimic the behavior of legitimate emails as well as their senders. This is certainly possible because the attacker has compromised the victim machines.

Our idea of embedding a "twisted" passphrase onto a background picture is somewhat inspired by the CMU CAPTCHA project [3,1] (indeed, the Gimpy instances are based on their implementation). However, it is worthwhile to note that our usage of challenging the users with some "twisted" characters has two utilities: (1) It can tell a computer program from a human being. Even if this is similar to the utility of CAPTCHA, there is a crucial difference in the system model. In their model, the verifier is a remote server (i.e., computer program) that knows the correct answer. Whereas, in our model there is no concept of verifier in the sense of checking the correctness of the answer (i.e., there is no computer program that serves as a verifier). This is because the correctness is checked by a human being based on the decryption result. (2) It can relieve the users from the burden of memorizing the passphrases; this usage may be of independent value.

There are also some loosely related works. [12] proposed a mechanism to prevent the harvesting of addresses by an SSH worm. This differs from our approach because while their solution involves protecting specific files in a manner reminiscent of password files (which use random salts and hash functions to hide the identities of known hosts), our system encrypts each valid address within any number of files and folders. Finally, we should mention that Wong et al. [19] analyzed network traffic traces collected from a college campus and presented an in-depth study on the effects of two mass-mailing worms, SoBig and MyDoom, on outgoing traffic.

7   Conclusion

We systematically explored how to encrypt (user-selected) email addresses in the address books and email boxes. Our solution is a user-end one, meaning that it affects only the email client software and is completely transparent to the email server. An entry in an address book is encrypted using a unique key, and hard AI problems are utilized to relieve the users of memorizing passwords while defeating offline dictionary attacks. Simulation shows that our solution is effective, even if only a portion of users deployed it (i.e., it can be incrementally deployed). We implemented two prototype systems. The result of our preliminary usability test is positive, and encourages us to conduct a more thorough test. We also plan to enhance the functionalities of our prototype systems so that one can change the pictures and/or passphrases of the users appearing in the address book and email boxes.

References

1. von Ahn, L., Blum, M., Hopper, N., Langford, J.: CAPTCHA: Using Hard AI Problems for Security, Eurocrypt (2003)
2. Bellare, M., Rogaway, P.: Random Oracles are Practical: A Paradigm for Designing Efficient Protocols. In: ACM Conference on Computer and Communications Security, pp. 62–73 (1993)
3. http://www.captcha.net/
4. Ebel, H., Mielsch, L.-I., Bornholdt, S.: The Data of the Email Network, http://www.theo-physik.uni-kiel.de/ ebel/email-net/email_net.html
5. Goldreich, O., Goldwasser, S., Mical, S.: How to construct random functions. J. ACM 33(4), 792–807 (1986)
6. Katz, J., Yung, M.: Complete characterization of security notions for probabilistic private-key encryption. ACM STOC, 245–254 (2000)
7. W32/Mydoom.ag@MM, http://vil.nai.com/vil/content/v_129630.htm
8. Mironov, I.: (Not So) Random Shuffles of RC4. In: The proceedings of Crypto 2002, pp. 304–319 (2002)
9. Palm OS Developer Suite, http://www.palmos.com/dev/tools/dev_suite.html
10. Petersen, A.: Pooka: A Java Email Client, http://suberic.net/pooka
11. http://www.rosecitysoftware.com/courier/
12. Schechter, S., Jung, J., Stockwekk, W., McLain, C.: Inoculating SSH Against Address Harvesting. In: The 13th Annual Network and Distributed System Security Symposium (2006)
13. SHA256, http://csrc.nist.gov/CryptoToolkit/tkhash.html
14. Win32/SirCam Worm, http://www.pspl.com/virus_info/worms/sircam.htm
15. W32.Klez.gen@mm, http://securityresponse.symantec.com/avcenter/venc/data/w32.klez.gen@mm.html

16. https://www.trustedcomputinggroup.org
17. Twining, D., Williamson, M., Mowbray, M., Rahmouni, M.: Email prioritization: Reducing delays on legitimate mail caused by junk mail. In: Usenix Annual Technology Conference (2004)
18. http://www.soft14.com/Utilities_and_Hardware/Antivirus/ ViraLock_5641_Review.html
19. Wong, C., Bielski, S., McCune, J., Wang, C.: A Study of Mass-Mailing Worms. In: Proceedings of ACM Worm (2004)
20. Williamson, M.: Design, Implementation and Test of an Email Virus Throttle. In: Omondi, A.R., Sedukhin, S. (eds.) ACSAC 2003. LNCS, vol. 2823, Springer, Heidelberg (2003)

Toward Non-parallelizable Client Puzzles

Suratose Tritilanunt, Colin Boyd,
Ernest Foo, and Juan Manuel González Nieto

Information Security Institute
Queensland University of Technology
GPO Box 2434, Brisbane, QLD 4001, Australia
s.tritilanunt@student.qut.edu.au,
{c.boyd,e.foo,j.gonzaleznieto}@qut.edu.au

Abstract. Client puzzles have been proposed as a useful mechanism for mitigating denial of service attacks on network protocols. Several different puzzles have been proposed in recent years. This paper reviews the desirable properties of client puzzles, pointing out that there is currently no puzzle which satisfies all such properties. We investigate how to provide the property of non-parallelizability in a practical puzzle. After showing that obvious ideas based on hash chains have significant problems, we propose a new puzzle based on the subset sum problem. Despite some practical implementation issues, this is the first example that satisfies all the desirable properties for a client puzzle.

Keywords: Denial of Service Attacks, Client Puzzles, Non-Parallelizable Cryptographic Puzzles.

1 Introduction

Cryptographic puzzles, or *client puzzles*, have been proposed as a mechanism to defeat resource exhaustion denial of service (DoS) attacks in network protocols, particularly in key exchange protocols. Client puzzles counterbalance computational usage between client and server machines. By forcing the client to solve a computational puzzle before attending to a request, the server ensures that the client spends sufficient resources before committing its own. In particular, an adversary who wishes to flood a server with connection requests will have to solve a huge number of puzzles. The idea of using cryptographic puzzles in computer networks was first introduced by Dwork and Naor [5] for combating junk emails. Juels and Brainard [10] extended the concept of puzzles to thwart Denial-of-Service (DoS) attacks in network protocols. Recently, Moskowitz developed the host identity protocol (HIP) [16], which employs a client puzzle mechanism for protecting the server against resource exhaustion attacks.

Although a variety of client puzzles have been proposed to solve DoS attacks, limited analysis of these proposals has appeared in the literature. An exception is the work of Price [17], who introduces a generic attack against hash-based client puzzles. Another investigation of hash-based client puzzles has been carried out by Feng et al. [7]. They examine client puzzles based on six parameters: unit

F. Bao et al. (Eds.): CANS 2007, LNCS 4856, pp. 247–264, 2007.
© Springer-Verlag Berlin Heidelberg 2007

work, range, mean granularity, maximum granularity, exact control and parallel computation.

A client puzzle is *non-parallelizable* if the solution to the puzzle cannot be computed in parallel. Non-parallelizable client puzzles can be used to defend against distributed denial-of-service (DDoS) attacks, where a single adversary can control a large group of compromised machines and launch attacks to the targeted server from those machines. If the client puzzle is parallelizable, such an adversary could distribute puzzles to other compromised machines to obtain puzzle solutions faster than the time expected by the server. A client puzzle is said to provide *fine granularity* if it allows servers to adjust the solution time precisely. Both non-parallelizability and fine granularity are important properties of good puzzles. A survey of existing client puzzles reveals that only time lock puzzles [19] are able to provide both non-parallelizability and fine-grained control. However, these puzzles suffer from being computationally expensive in puzzle construction and verification.

In this paper we propose a new puzzle construction based on the subset sum problem. The primary strengths of this puzzle over others are the simple and cheap construction and verification for the server, as well as non-parallelizability. The main contributions of this work are:

- to provide a summary and analysis of client puzzles for DoS-resistance;
- to compare strengths and weaknesses of existing client puzzles;
- to propose a new construction, called *Subset Sum Client Puzzles*.

In the next section we will summarise existing proposals for client puzzles and review their properties. Section 3 examines possible ways to use hash chains as non-parallelizable puzzles and then Section 4 introduces and analyses our new puzzle.

2   Survey and Analysis of Client Puzzles Approaches

Client puzzles functioning as proofs of work can be constructed from a number of underlying problems. Although many puzzles have been proposed using different techniques, all of them should satisfy seven important properties described by Aura et al. [2]; for instance puzzles should be easy and cheap to construct and verify for the server, but lead to a significant computational effort for adversaries who attempt to flood a large number of bogus requests to the server.

Feng et al. [7] proposed some additional criteria for evaluating *efficiency* and *resolution* of cryptographic puzzles. As defined by Feng et al. [7], the puzzle efficiency represents speed of puzzle generation and verification on the server's machine compared to the puzzle solving on the client's machine. Meanwhile, the resolution or *puzzle granularity* represents the ability of the server to finely control the amount of work done by calibrating the puzzle difficulty to the client. The following list represents the properties that we examine in this paper.

Server's Cost identifies the computational effort on the server's machine. This factor is divided into three subcategories consisting of pre-computation cost, construction cost, and verification cost.

Client's Cost represents the amount of computational effort on the client's machine. We assume that the server and the client have similar resources regarding both CPU and memory units to process these puzzles. We note that this may not be realistic in some applications; for example, some legitimate clients may have restricted resources.

Non-parallelizability describes whether the client puzzles can be distributed and solved in parallel computation. In some circumstances, non-parallelizable puzzles can prevent coordinated adversaries from distributing puzzles to a group of high performance machines to obtain solutions quicker than the specified period assigned by the server. Consequently, the server becomes overloaded by a huge amount of attack traffic and unable to process any upcoming legitimate messages.

Granularity represents the ability of the server to finely adjust puzzle difficulty to different levels. Indirectly, this parameter also affects the traffic flow of arriving packets to the connection queue within a certain time. Three different types of granularity; *linear*, *polynomial*, and *exponential* are compared. Linear granularity is the best that we hope to deal with, while an exponential one is the worst case.

We now conduct a short survey and comparison in term of strengths and weaknesses of existing proposals for client puzzles.

Hash-based Reversal Puzzles: In 1999, Juels and Brainard [10] introduced the construction of client puzzles using a hash function; clients need to calculate a reverse one-way hash value of a puzzle generated by the server. In this technique, the server is able to adjust the difficulty level of the client puzzle by increasing or decreasing the number of hidden bits of the pre-image sent to clients in the puzzle. The client performs a brute-force search to find missing bits of pre-image whose output is given by hashing each pattern until matching the answer. To verify the solution, the server needs to perform only a single hash operation.

An alternative construction was proposed by Aura et al. [2]. Different from Juels and Brainard's construction, the puzzle generation requires only a single hash instead of two hash operations as in Juels and Brainard's scheme. Given part of the pre-image and the length (k) of zero bits at the beginning of the hashed output, clients need to perform a brute-force search to find a matching solution.

In summary, the major strength of these two hash-based reversal schemes is the simple and fast construction and verification. On the other hand, the weaknesses are that they are parallelizable and their granularity is exponential which brings a difficult task to the server to control and adjust the incoming rate of requests.

Hint-Based Hash Reversal Puzzles: As the granularity of hash-based reversal schemes is too coarse, Feng et al. [6] proposed the idea of hint-based hash reversal puzzles to allow the granularity to be linear. The technique of this mechanism is that the server provides extra information called *hints* attached to the puzzle. Instead of checking every possible solution, the client searches for a solution within a range of a given hint. Apart from this action, all remaining processes are similar to the original work from Juels and Brainard [10]. Hence, the simple puzzle generation and verification as well as the linear granularity for fine grained control are the strengths of this construction. However, it is still susceptible to distribution and parallel processing attacks, as is the original hash-based reversal scheme.

Repeated-Squaring or Time-Lock Puzzles: Time-lock puzzles were developed by Rivest et al. [19] in 1996. The major goal of this technique is to defeat the high-end adversaries who attempt to solve puzzles more quickly by using parallel computers. Time-lock puzzles rely on the notion that a client has to spend a pre-determined amount of computation time performing repeated squaring to search for a solution. To achieve this goal, the server estimates the performance of a client by the number of squaring operations a client can perform in a certain period, and determines the amount of time it expects a client to spend solving the puzzle.

To solve the puzzle, the client is required to compute a modular squaring operation repeatedly. This computation must be calculated sequentially so it cannot be distributed and solved in parallel. Since the period of solving the puzzle is easily controlled and determined by the server at puzzle generation time, we can conclude that the time-lock puzzles have a linear granularity. Another strength of this scheme is its non-parallelizable characteristic because it requires an inherently sequential operation to solve a puzzle. In the original paper, the major purpose of this scheme is the long term protection of secret information, for example, in the application of the on-line auction. However, the primary concern of this scheme in DoS mitigation applications is the high-computation in the construction and verification because the underlying technique requires the server to perform a costly modular exponentiation.

DH-based Puzzles: Diffie-Hellman based puzzles were proposed by Waters et al. [25] in 2004. The construction requires an expensive Diffie-Hellman operation, while the verification could be simply done via table lookup, which is considered a cheap operation, because the server has already generated puzzle solutions at the construction and stores them in the memory. Therefore, the expensive construction would be a drawback, while the cheap verification would be the major positive characteristic.

Given the range of a solution as in hint-based schemes, the client searches for a solution by testing each candidate value in the range until it finds a correct solution. Similar to other hint-based puzzles, this scheme then provides a linear-grained control to the server. Considering the non-parallelizability, because clients require a specific range of attempts to find a correct solution, the puzzle can be distributed and computed in parallel to obtain a correct solution. As a result, this scheme does not support non-parallelizability.

Trapdoor RSA-based and DH-based Puzzles: Gao [8] developed two puzzle mechanisms based on trapdoor functions to overcome weaknesses over the hash-based construction. By pre-computing some parameters and expensive operations before starting the protocol, Gao's implementation can reduce the overhead of puzzle construction. However, this pre-computation workload is a disadvantage to these types of puzzles.

On the positive side, the protocol computes and stores the solutions at puzzle generation time to save workload at verification. As a result, the server requires only a single comparison in order to check validity of the solution from the client. In the puzzle solving, the client is given a range of candidates to run a brute-force search for a correct solution. Hence, the granularity of these two constructions is linear-grained.

On the negative side, both trapdoor-function based schemes can be distributed and solved in parallel by a group of adversaries as for other hint-based puzzles. Moreover, these schemes involve modular arithmetical operations which are more expensive than hash functions. Although Gao [8] suggested to perform pre-computations to avoid CPU burden at construction time, puzzle generation still requires a number of modular exponentiations.

Table 1 compares seven cryptographic puzzle constructions based on the analysis criteria previously discussed. For purposes of comparison, we include our new subset sum puzzles in the table. Details will be discussed in Section 4.1. The highlighted field (displayed as the **bold and italic style**) in individual columns represents the best candidate for each analysis criterion. In the server's and client's cost entry, we use the number of operations as a measurement for comparison. More precisely, the hash-based cryptographic puzzles require a number of hash function computations displayed as *hash* in the table, while the arithmetic-based puzzles require a number of modular exponentiations represented by *mod exp* and modular multiplications represented by *mod mul*. Modular arithmetic consumes much greater resources than hash functions. Hence, the preference for this entry would be the technique which expends a small number of hash operations. We can conclude that the puzzle construction based on hash-based reversal would be the most effective technique.

The non-parallelizability characteristic plays an important role for defending against coordinated adversaries who attempt to distribute puzzles to other users

Table 1. Comparison of existing Client Puzzles for DoS Resistance

Puzzle Type	Server's Cost			Client's Cost	Non Parallel	Granularity
	Pre-Compute	Construction	Verification			
Hash-based Reversal	-	*1 hash*	1 hash	$\mathcal{O}(2^k)$ hash	No	Exponential
Hint-Based Hash Reversal	-	*1 hash*	1 hash	$\mathcal{O}(k)$ *hash*	No	*Linear*
Repeated-Squaring	-	2 mod mul	2 mod mul	$\mathcal{O}(k)$ mod mul	*Yes*	*Linear*
DH-based	-	1 mod exp	*1 comparison*	$\mathcal{O}(k)$ mod exp	No	*Linear*
Trapdoor RSA	1 mod exp 1 mod mul	3 mod mul 2 additions	*1 comparison*	$\mathcal{O}(k)$ mod exp	No	*Linear*
Trapdoor DLP	1 mod exp	2 mod mul 3 additions	*1 comparison*	$\mathcal{O}(k)$ mod exp	No	*Linear*
Subset Sum	n hash	*1 hash*	*1 comparison*	L^3 reduction	*Yes*	Polynomial

or high-performance machines in order to obtain puzzle solutions quicker than the specified time without wasting their own resources. Since non-parallelizability has not been defined as a primary requirement in the original work [10, 2], most existing techniques lack this characteristic. From the evaluation shown in Table 1 only repeated-squaring puzzles can thwart this type of attack strategy. Unfortunately, high computation of the puzzle construction causes this technique to be susceptible to flooding attacks. As a result, this gap becomes the most interesting point for our work to develop new schemes which achieve non-parallelizability, while the puzzle construction and verification are also simple and cheap.

3   Hash Chain Puzzles

We have seen in the previous section that currently only time-lock puzzles can provide the characteristic of non-parallelizability but they suffer from an expensive set up operation for the server. One promising method to prevent adversaries from distributing and computing a puzzle in parallel would be a *chaining* technique. Because the characteristic of chaining requires the previous value for constructing the next consecutive items, it will defeat those coordinated adversaries who attempt to solve puzzles by parallel computing. Recently, there are two constructions using the chaining technique based on hash functions proposed by Ma [14] in 2005 and by Groza and Petrica [9] a year later. The aim of these constructions is slightly different from what we have in mind, since they are interested in partial solving of the chained puzzles. Nevertheless it is interesting to examine whether they will be useful as stand-alone puzzles. Following are short descriptions of these two puzzles and an analysis of their suitability.

Ma's Hash Chain Reversal Puzzles: The concept of hash chain puzzles was introduced by Ma [14] in 2005 as password puzzles for use in the IP layer. The construction begins with a random number chosen as an initial value h_0. Then the server applies a one-way function to h_0 repeatedly to generate a hash chain $h_0, h_1, \ldots, h_k$ where $h_{i+1} = \text{hash}(h_i)$ and k is the desired length of the chain. According to Ma, this computation would lead to an advantage for the server by storing the entire hash chain for future use. Because the server knows a corresponding solution in advance, the server saves computation and time when verifying the puzzle solution by reducing the cost of verification to a single table lookup.

For puzzle solving, given a puzzle challenge containing the last value of a hash chain (h_k) along with an index value k, a client is required to compute a hash reversal starting from index k back to the beginning point h_0 to obtain the entire hash chain. A characteristic of hash chain operation is that an output from the former state is required to be fed to the next state as an input, similar to a recursion in programming. We conclude that this scheme is a non-parallelizable technique, and the cost of the verification requires k hash operations similar to the construction.

This is a simple and intuitive construction, but there are a number of practical problems. First, it requires the server to store every value of the entire hash chain in order to be able to verify the solution. Although this has an advantage in verification effort, this scheme is susceptible to memory exhaustion attacks. Second, when used with a typical cryptographic hash function the scheme will be too difficult to invert for even one hash value, let alone a chain of many values. Therefore some mechanism must be chosen to make the individual steps in the chain invertible with reasonable effort. Ma [14] suggested that a hash function be used which has 16-bit outputs, but this does not seem to be an acceptable requirement since such a function can be easily stored completely in a look-up table which makes solving the puzzle as easy as constructing it. A more plausible mechanism is used in the next construction that we consider.

Groza and Petrica's Hash Chain Puzzles: This puzzle scheme [9] was constructed from a hash chain of random numbers. Generally, the idea is similar to the puzzle auction proposed by Wang and Reiter [24]; i.e. the more links of the chain computed on a client's machine, the more services from a server a client obtains. At the beginning, the server generates the first element by choosing two state-dependent random numbers, ρ and r, and concatenating them to obtain a value σ. The first output, P_0, is constructed by double hashing σ_0. Hence, the parameter σ_0 serves as an input to the next state of the chain. The rest of the puzzle will be created by XORing two new state-dependent values with hashed output of σ from the previous state. Thus, the puzzle elements challenged to the client would be a series of pairs $[(P_0, r_0), (P_1, r_1), \ldots, (P_n, r_n)]$, where $n \geq 1$ is the length of the hash chain. Meanwhile, the client is required to perform a forward process of reconstructing the hash chain by searching for ρ_i values, with $\sigma_i = \rho_i \parallel r_i$.

Unfortunately, this scheme has a major drawback which risks resource exhaustion attacks on the server because it requires three hash operations per state for producing a series of hashes chained either in the construction or verification phase. This action requires a similar amount of computational effort as the solving task on the client's machine. This circumstance violates the fundamental requirement; i.e. client puzzles should be easy to generate and verify by the server but hard to solve by the client. Furthermore, the high-bandwidth consumption required to transmit a puzzle challenge is another drawback of this scheme.

In summary, we have seen that the hash chain puzzle has a major strength in non-parallelizability and linear-grained control because of its structure. Lightweight verification by one comparison is another interesting potential property. However, the proposals so far using this technique require high computation in the construction, high-bandwidth connection for communication, and huge storage to cache an entire chain for avoiding CPU burden at the verification. Therefore, currently it seems impractical to use hash chains as client puzzles and we look for an alternative.

4 Subset Sum Puzzles

Hash based puzzles are the most prevalent due to their simple construction and cheap verification. As shown in Section 2, such puzzles are susceptible to coordinated attacks because they do not provide the non-parallelizability property. In this section, we propose a technique called *subset sum puzzles*. The predominant characteristic of this new approach is not only a simple construction and verification as cheap as hash based puzzles, but also a non-parallelizable characteristic.

A subset sum (or knapsack) system associates a given set of items which have specified weight, with a knapsack which can carry the number of items no more than a certain weight. The solver is required to search for a maximum value by picking as many items as the knapsack can carry in terms of weight. To find whether a solution exists for a specified weight, this becomes a decision problem and the knapsack falls into the NP-completeness category which means no polynomial algorithm can break the knapsack problem within polynomial time as long as P $\neq$ NP. This is why the knapsack problem was long considered a promising underlying technique for constructing a public-key based cryptosystem.

A famous tool used to successfully break subset sum cryptosystems is the *lattice reduction*. There are several lattice reduction algorithms but the best method so far for breaking the subset sum problems is the *LLL* or L^3 algorithm (details are provided in Appendix A) developed by Lenstra et al. [13] in 1982. The interesting characteristic of the LLL scheme is that it is a polynomial time and non-parallelizable algorithm because it requires highly sequential computation on an iterative function. We remark that practical application of our construction requires clients to implement the LLL algorithm. While this is not a major problem on PC platforms it may be undesirable, particularly on low-powered platforms. Therefore we regard our construction as more a proof-of-concept that non-parallelizable puzzles are feasible, rather than as an ideal solution.

4.1   A New Proposal – Subset Sum Puzzles

We first introduce the notation used in the puzzle challenge-response protocol. I represents a client and R represents a server of the protocol. Communicating messages used in the protocol execution will carry the subscript I or R representing whose these messages are; for instance, ID_I represents the identity of the client and N_R represents a nonce generated by the server. A secret parameter is denoted as s and puzzle difficulty by k. The desired weight of the subset sum problem is W, while the set of candidate weights is $w_1, w_2, \ldots, w_n$. Finally, $H(\cdot)$ represents a hash operation on arbitrary length input messages, and $LSB(\cdot, k)_2$ obtains the k least significant bits from the output of the hash function.

Puzzle Construction
To establish a secure connection to a server, I sends a request containing an identity (ID_I) along with a random nonce (N_I) to R. The server chooses a secret parameter s randomly in order to make the output unique for each communication, and decides a puzzle difficulty k depending on the workload condition. The value of k[1] should be selected to be at least 25 (refer to Table 2 for a

---

[1] For the definition of subset sum puzzles, the number of items n is used as the puzzle difficulty k.

	I	R
		Precomputed parameters
		set of random weight w_n
		$w_n = H(w_{n-1})$
		choose *secret* $s \in_R \mathcal{Z}_n$
		....
1) send *request*	$\xrightarrow{\quad ID_I, N_I \quad}$	choose *puzzle difficulty* k
		$25 \leq k \leq 100$
		$C = LSB(H(ID_I, N_I, ID_R, N_R, s)), k)_2$
		$W = \sum_{i=1}^{k} C_i \cdot w_i$
2) verify ID_I, N_I	$ID_I, N_I,$	$puzzle = (w_1, W, k)$
generate $w_k = H(w_{k-1})$	$\xleftarrow{ID_R, N_R, puzzle}$	
form a Basis Set $\boldsymbol{B}$		
run *LLL Reduction* $\rightarrow$ get C'		
check $W \stackrel{?}{=} \sum_{i=1}^{k} C'_i \cdot w_i$		
3) return C'	$ID_I, N_I, ID_R,$	check $C' \stackrel{?}{=} C$
	$\xrightarrow{N_R, puzzle, C'}$	

Fig. 1. Subset Sum Puzzles

comparison of the experimental result) to guarantee that the coordinated adversaries approximately requires over a thousand compromised machines to brute-force search or over a hundred compromised machines to run the branch & bound algorithm on the subset sum puzzles at the equivalent proportion to the legitimate user performing LLL lattice reduction. As a practical choice we suggest to take a value of k between 25 and 100 and then if weights are chosen to be of length 200 bits we can ensure that the generated knapsack has density at most 0.5. Practical experimental tests are shown in Section 4.2 which support our proposal.

To construct a puzzle, R computes a hash operation $(H(\cdot))$, and computes $(LSB((\cdot), k)_2)$ to obtain k bits from the output of hash function. In practice H could be implemented by truncating the output of SHA-256. Finally, R forms a *puzzle* by computing a desired weight (W) that it wants a client to solve from a pre-computed set of random weight (w_n). To save on protocol bandwidth, the weights can be generated given the initial random weight w_1 by iterative hashing. Hence, a puzzle contains an initial value of weight of the first item (w_1), a desired weight (W), and puzzle difficulty (k). The construction of the subset sum puzzle requires only one hash operation and addition. Figure 1 demonstrates the puzzle challenge-response protocol.

Puzzle Solving

To ensure that the client follows our requirement, we have to configure the puzzle difficulty so that the efficient LLL method of solving is more efficient than brute-force searching, even when the latter is divided amongst many parallel attacking machines. As mentioned above in the description of puzzle construction, when k is in the range between 25 to 100 we can expect that a puzzle would not be solved faster by brute-force technique. Moreover, when k is around 50 or larger the LLL method is more efficient than brute-force search even when the latter is divided amongst 10000 parallel machines in approximation.

By using the LLL algorithm, users can simply treat the subset sum schemes as a lattice problem. In 1985, Lagarias and Odlyzko [11] announced the first successful attack on low density[2] subset sum cryptosystems; i.e. a density below 0.6464 approximately. A few years later, Coster et al. [4] proposed the improved version of the Lagarias and Odlyzko technique. They claimed that their method was able to break *almost all* subset sum problems having density below 0.9408 in polynomial time. This result guarantees that our subset sum puzzle would be solvable in polynomial time by using LLL algorithm.

Consider the client's job when receiving a puzzle challenge from a server. It begins to generate a series of random weights, $(w_1, w_2, \ldots, w_k)$, by computing a hash chain on an initial value w_1. Then, the client constructs a basis reduction set B as follows.

$$b_1 = (1, 0, \ldots, 0, w_1); \quad b_2 = (0, 1, \ldots, 0, w_2)$$

$$\vdots$$

$$b_k = (0, 0, \ldots, 1, w_k); b_{k+1} = (0, 0, \ldots, 0, -W)$$

Finally, the client runs a L^3 lattice reduction [13] which is known from the community to be the most effective method to find moderately short lattice vectors in polynomial time. The algorithm guarantees to return a set of outputs in which one is a solution of the puzzle. To the best of our knowledge, *almost all* subset sum problems having density below 0.9408 can be effectively solved by the improved LLL version of Coster et al. [4]. In addition, this improved version is a highly sequential process because the underlying algorithm requires recursive computation as explained in Appendix A, so the puzzle cannot be distributed for parallel computation.

In terms of the puzzle granularity, there are two possible options for the server to adjust the puzzle difficult; 1) adjusting the item size (n), or 2) adjusting the density (which will cause a change in B because the density relates to the maximum weight of the items). Both modifications affect the running time by a factor $(n^\alpha \cdot \log^\beta B)$, where α and β are real numbers dependent on the version of LLL basis reduction. Since the complexity of LLL basis reduction is a polynomial function, we conclude that our subset sum puzzles provide a polynomial granularity.

---

[2] The density is defined as $\frac{n}{\log(max\ a_n)}$, where n is a number of items and $max\ a_n$ is the maximum item value.

Puzzle Verification

Puzzle verification is a simple and cheap task for a server which eliminates the risk of puzzle solution flooding attacks. Generally, there are two options for the verification process;

1. *avoiding CPU usage*: this case minimizes CPU usage at verification time. By storing the value of C and W corresponding to the client's identity (ID_I, N_I), the verification requires only a table lookup for comparing the claimed solution from a client to the stored solution.

2. *avoiding memory usage*: this option eliminates memory usage prior to verification. The server uses a stateless connection in which no information is stored until the puzzle is solved. Once the server receives a solution, it is required to re-generate C and W from the arriving message. In order to protect against replay attacks, implementation of the timestamp should be used in the computation of the parameter C. The re-constructing process is a very cheap and fast computation that costs little more than a single hash computation, which is the typical cost of verification for hash-reversal puzzles.

We conclude that the upper bound of computational complexity in the former case is $\mathcal{O}(1)$ for the table lookup, whereas the upper bound for computational complexity in the latter case is $\mathcal{O}(k)$ additions which is similar to the construction of the first state. The evaluation and comparison of the subset sum puzzles is previously shown in Table 1.

4.2 Experimental Results

To demonstrate how LLL lattice reduction and the subset sum problems work in practice on client machines, we set up an experiment to create a random set of subset sum problems based on different criteria including density and a number of chosen items. In terms of hardware, we simulated the LLL reduction algorithm using a Sun Enterprise 420R computer operating with four UltraSPARC-II 450 MHz CPUs with 4096 MB of RAM running on Sun Solaris 9 (Sparc). We created MATLAB source code for generating random subset sum problems which have different densities between 0.3 and 0.8 for a range of instance sizes between 20 and 100. To solve these problems we wrote a subset sum solving function for testing the LLL implementation provided in MAGMA. The version of MAGMA installed on our testing machine was a full version patch number V2.13-11 released on April 5, 2007 (details at http://magma.maths.usyd.edu.au). The LLL version provided in MAGMA is based on the floating point arithmetic version (*FP-LLL*) proposed by Schnorr and Euchner [21].

The following briefly provides the methods that we used to evaluate our new scheme. Two different searching methods, a backtracking and a branch & bound algorithm [15], are taken into account for comparing with the LLL lattice reduction method.

Backtracking or Brute Force Searching: This is the simplest method which is also known as exhaustive search because it gathers all possible solutions and then checks for one satisfying the solution. This guarantees that it will always return an optimal solution. However, this technique consumes more CPU power as well as running time.

Branch & Bound Technique: To reduce the time of the brute force searching, *pruning techniques* can be used for avoiding some unnecessary nodes during the searching process. By storing and traveling only to states whose total weight does not exceed the limit, it can generate a specified solution faster than brute force. The branch & bound technique is one of those pruning methods. It specifies an upper bound on the output, so any descendant tracks having value above or not below their ascendant node will be eliminated from the possible solution. This can reduce running time and storage space.

LLL Lattice Reduction: This advanced tool, explained in Appendix A, can efficiently solve subset sum problems. This method can solve the subset sum puzzle within polynomial time rather than exponential time as the two previous techniques do. Recently, there have been many implementations for accelerating the running time of LLL reduction. In our experiment, we use two techniques: the first one, Int-LLL, is the original developed in 1982 by Lenstra et al. [13] provided in Mathematica, while the second one, FP-LLL, developed by Schnorr and Euchner [21], is a modified version using floating point arithmetic and provided in MAGMA.

Table 2 shows the experimental result compared among the brute force searching, branch & bound technique, and LLL Lattice Reduction examining puzzles having small size between 5 and 30.

Table 2. Average Running Time of The Subset Sum Puzzle on the specified methods

Number of Items (n)	Average Running Time (seconds)								
	Backtracking			Branch & Bound			LLL		
	Data 1	Data 2	Data 3	Data 1	Data 2	Data 3	Data 1	Data 2	Data 3
5	0.034	0.034	0.025	0.049	0.049	0.053	0	0	0
10	0.086	0.083	0.083	0.06	0.064	0.082	0	0	0
15	1.70	1.69	1.67	0.134	0.40	0.137	0	0	0
20	51.85	52.74	53.74	2.633	3.691	1.43	0	0	0.01
25	2320.70	2262.80	2428.60	315.743	456.97	602.81	0.01	0.01	0.01
30	–	–	–	1437.758	1865.001	1647.246	0.01	0.01	0.01

By evaluating the results from Table 2, we summarize that the reasonable range of puzzle difficulty would be at least 25 for preventing coordinated adversaries who can control a number of compromised machines to obtain puzzle solutions at the same capacity to the legitimate user performing LLL lattice reduction.

Table 3. The Experimental Result of The Subset Sum Puzzle

Number of Items (n)	Average Running Time (seconds)																	
	Random Set 1						Random Set 2						Random Set 3					
	Density						Density						Density					
	0.3	0.4	0.5	0.6	0.7	0.8	0.3	0.4	0.5	0.6	0.7	0.8	0.3	0.4	0.5	0.6	0.7	0.8
60	0.10	0.12	0.23	1.02	2.42	77.11	0.16	0.28	0.19	0.31	3.64	3.70	0.14	0.22	0.21	0.61	0.64	3.21
65	0.14	0.14	0.29	1.59	4.09	190.68	0.18	0.29	0.23	0.57	6.53	6.86	0.17	0.23	0.26	1.70	2.19	18.94
70	0.15	0.15	0.32	2.94	7.33	342.53	0.18	0.29	0.28	1.34	12.97	26.30	0.21	0.25	0.27	2.29	2.29	41.72
75	0.20	0.14	0.78	5.23	13.47	663.24	0.24	0.31	0.38	1.95	27.23	35.65	0.23	0.25	0.34	3.49	4.37	92.37
80	0.27	0.22	0.89	9.63	26.17	1745.97	0.25	0.33	0.52	2.75	58.70	87.12	0.26	0.29	0.45	5.66	8.82	226.76
85	0.37	0.25	1.24	17.38	49.22	4158.73	0.29	0.37	0.72	4.44	120.44	208.86	0.28	0.32	0.62	9.40	18.15	1315.29
90	0.50	0.29	1.63	31.44	96.39	9435.02	0.39	0.40	1.17	7.58	250.52	509.60	0.30	0.37	0.89	16.42	37.75	1344.35
95	0.59	0.34	2.34	55.68	173.30	21351.72	0.43	0.43	1.75	12.78	504.88	1158.45	0.36	0.43	1.28	28.14	79.36	3160.86
100	0.70	0.40	3.43	98.39	317.27	51124.86	0.46	0.47	2.87	21.45	1008.23	2737.79	0.41	0.50	2.03	46.63	168.72	7451.26

Before illustrating the second experimental result, we need to briefly explain the reasoning behind our configuration. By investigating the primary result comparing between FP-LLL and Int-LLL, we have found that Int-LLL works well for low density problems with data size below 100. Once the density grows, the Int-LLL performance drops gradually and becomes ineffective when we run it on high density examples. This behaviour was also observed by LaMacchia [12] as well as by Schnorr and Euchner [21]. Due to this degradation of Int-LLL with large instance and high density problems, we suggest to use FP-LLL in the puzzle solving to avoid the situation that legitimate users are unable to solve their puzzles. The reason is that a floating point arithmetic returns the Gram-Schmidt coefficient in the reduction process more precisely than integer arithmetic. As a result, the FP-LLL reduction provides a more correct output.

Table 3 shows the result of puzzles having size between 60 and 100. We restrict to this range because we are only interested in the values where the LLL performs faster than brute force searching, otherwise the protocol would be vulnerable to parallel attacks if the adversaries are able to run a brute force searching. The table shows that there is a good range of puzzle times suitable for practical use.

5   Discussion and Open Problem

As our main objective has been to design non-parallelizable puzzles, subset sum problems with the LLL lattice reduction bring us this characteristic and fulfill our requirement. However, simplicity and performance of the existing LLL schemes are a concern for deploying them in general applications. As several experiments have shown the failure of original LLL in dealing with large instances and high density problems, recently several attempts have been made to scale down the computation time of the size reduction process as well as increase the accuracy for dealing with the large instances. One example was using dynamic approximation and heuristic technique [3] to speed up the reduction process. To our knowledge, the fastest LLL reduction scheme for solving subset sum problems is the segmentation FP-LLL proposed by Schnorr [20] that minimizes the running time to be $\mathcal{O}(n^3 \log n)$.

Parallelization of the LLL lattice reduction was discussed and proposed by Villard [23]. The idea of that paper is to select non-overlapping parameters and separate them into two independent phases in order to speed up the exchange of parameters during the size reduction of the lattice basis. Thus, these outputs might be able to be computed in parallel by using $n \cdot m$ processors, and dividing them into n columns of m processors. Villard claimed that the running time complexity of this technique may be reduced to $\mathcal{O}(n^5 \log^3 B)$ binary arithmetic steps and $\mathcal{O}(n^4 \log^2 B)$ binary communication steps by using $\mathcal{O}(n)$ processors. This running time complexity could be improved by the factor of n by increasing the number of processors to $\mathcal{O}(n^2)$ units. However, the unclear practical efficiency of the algorithm and the requirement for the larger size of parameters than in the original LLL algorithm [13] mean that future investigation and development are required.

Another disadvantage of the subset sum puzzle is the memory requirement. By investigating instances when the item size n exceeds 100, we found that the memory resource is exhausted in some trials. That is because the LLL reduction constructs a $n \times n$ lattice matrix and allocates it into reserved memory. As a result, the practical range of puzzle difficulty would be up to $n = 100$ for avoiding memory exhaustion. In addition, the running time within this range would be reasonable and acceptable for most users. When we compare this bound with the hash-based reversal puzzles, the reasonable puzzle difficulty for hash-based reversal schemes would have k between 0 and 40 which results in a smaller length puzzle than our construction.

Since we are concerned with the problem of puzzle distribution and parallelizability, we focus on resolving the parallelizable characteristic rather than implementing linear granularity. However, even though our new scheme has coarser granularity than other hint-based schemes, it does offer polynomial granularity which is better than exponential granularity found in hash-based reversal puzzles recently used in some client puzzle protocols. As a result, our new design can be easier to control than many existing ones.

Comparing our construction with repeated squaring (Table 1) we find that, although repeated squaring offers non-parallelism and linear-grained control to the user, it suffers from high computation at construction time which means that a server using these puzzles would be susceptible to flooding attacks. As a result, an interesting open problem for the research community is to explore techniques to find new puzzles providing both non-parallelization and linear granularity.

References

1. Adleman, L M.: On Breaking Generalized Knapsack Public Key Cryptosystems. In: the 15th Annual ACM Symposium on Theory of Computing, pp. 402–412 (1983)
2. Aura, T., Nikander, P., Leiwo, J.: DoS-resistant authentication with client puzzles. In: Security Protocols Workshop 2000, Cambridge, pp. 170–181 (April 2000)

3. Backes, W., Wetzel, S.: Heuristics on Lattice Basis Reduction in Practice. Journal of Experimental Algorithmics (JEA) 7, 1–21 (2002)
4. Coster, M.J., Joux, A., LaMacchia, B.A., Odlyzko, A.M., Schnorr, C., Stern, J.: Improved low-density subset sum algorithms. Computational Complexity 2(2), 111–128 (1992)
5. Dwork, C., Naor, M.: Pricing via Processing or Combatting Junk Mail. In: Brickell, E.F. (ed.) CRYPTO 1992. LNCS, vol. 740, pp. 139–147. Springer, Heidelberg (1992)
6. Feng, W., Kaiser, E., Feng, W., Luu, A.: The Design and Implementation of Network Layer Puzzles. In: Proceedings of IEEE Infocom 2005 (March 13-17, 2005)
7. Feng, W., Luu, A., Feng, W.: Scalable, Fine-grained Control of Network Puzzles. Technical report 03-015, OGI CSE (2003)
8. Gao, Y.: Efficient Trapdoor-Based Client Puzzle System against DoS Attacks. In: Master of Computer Science by Research, School of Information Technology and Computer Science, University of Wollongong, Wollongong, Australia (2005)
9. Groza, B., Petrica, D.: On Chained Cryptographic Puzzles. In: 3rd Romanian-Hungarian Joint Symposium on Applied Computational Intelligence (SACI), Timisoara, Romania, pp. 25–26 (May 2006)
10. Juels, A., Brainard, J.: Client Puzzles: A Cryptographic Defense Against Connection Depletion Attacks. In: NDSS 1999. The 1999 Network and Distributed System Security Symposium, San Diego, California, USA, pp. 151–165. Internet Society Press, Reston (1999)
11. Lagarias, J.C., Odlyzko, A.M.: Solving low-density subset sum problems. Journal of the ACM (JACM) 32(1), 229–246 (1985)
12. LaMacchia, B.A.: Basis Reduction Algorithms and Subset Sum Problems. Master Thesis, Department of Electrical Engineering and Computer Science, Massachusetts Institute of Technology (1991)
13. Lenstra, A.K., Lenstra Jr., H.W., Lovász, L.: Factoring Polynomials with Rational Coefficients. Mathematische Annalen 261(4), 515–534 (1982)
14. Ma, M.: Mitigating denial of service attacks with password puzzles. In: ITCC 2005. International Conference on Information Technology: Coding and Computing, 2nd edn., pp. 621–626 (2005)
15. Martello, S., Toth, P.: Knapsack Problems: Algorithms and Computer Implementations. John Wiley & Sons, Inc., Chichester (1990)
16. Moskowitz, R.: The Host Identity Protocol (HIP). Internet Draft, Internet Engineering Task Force (October 2007), http://www.ietf.org/internet-drafts/draft-ietf-hip-base-09.txt
17. Price, G.: A General Attack Model on Hash-Based Client Puzzles. In: 9th IMA International Conference on Cryptography and Coding, Cirencester, UK, pp. 16–18. Springer, Heidelberg (2003)
18. Radziszowski, S., Kreher, D.: Solving subset sum problems with the L^3 algorithm. Journal of Combinatorial Mathematics and Combinatorial Computing 3, 49–63 (1988)
19. Rivest, R.L., Shamir, A., Wagner, D.A.: Time-lock Puzzles and Timed-release Crypto. Technical Report TR-684, Massachusetts Institute of Technology, Cambridge, MA, USA (March 10, 1996)
20. Schnorr, C.P.: Fast LLL-type Lattice Reduction. Information and Computation 204(1), 1–25 (2006)
21. Schnorr, C.P., Euchner, M.: Lattice Basis Reduction: Improved Practical Algorithms and Solving Subset Sum Problems. In: Budach, L. (ed.) FCT 1991. LNCS, vol. 529, pp. 68–85. Springer, Heidelberg (1991)

22. Smart, N.: Cryptography: An Introduction, 2nd edn. McGraw-Hill, New York (2006)
23. Villard, G.: Parallel Lattice Basis Reduction. In: ISSAC 1992. The International Symposium on Symbolic and Algebraic Computation, pp. 269–277. ACM Press, New York (1992)
24. Wang, X., Reiter, M.K.: Defending Against Denial-of-Service Attacks with Puzzle Auctions (Extended Abstract). In: SP 2003. The 2003 IEEE Symposium on Security and Privacy, Berkeley, CA, USA, pp. 78–92 (May 11-13, 2003)
25. Waters, B., Juels, A., Halderman, J.A., Felten, E.W.: New Client Puzzle Outsourcing Techniques for DoS Resistance. In: CCS 2004. The 11th ACM Conference on Computer and Communications Security, pp. 246–256. ACM Press, Washington DC (2004)

Appendix

A   A Brief Overview of Lattice Reduction

LLL lattice basis reduction is a polynomial time algorithm developed by Lenstra et al. [13] in 1982. The concept was originally used to solve the shortest vector problem (SVP) and closet vector problem (CVP) of a lattice. Adleman [1] seems to have been the first researcher to apply LLL lattice basis reduction as a cryptanalysis tool to successfully break the subset sum problem. By using the LLL, users simply treat the subset sum schemes as a lattice problem. Since its original use, many researchers have improved not only the performance of the algorithm, but also its accuracy when dealing with large instances of the lattice dimension.

LLL lattice basis reduction algorithm has been widely used in breaking subset sum cryptosystems because the algorithm is able to terminate in polynomial time. Moreover, it is highly sequential because an underlying program requires recursive computation. From this perspective, LLL is a promising technique to fulfill our requirement in terms of non-parallelizability and thwart coordinated adversaries from distributing the client puzzle to calculate the solution in a parallel manner. To explain the LLL lattice basis reduction, we refer to materials provided in Smart's book: *Cryptography: An Introduction (2nd edition)* [22].

Definition 1. *Let $\{b_1, b_2, \ldots, b_n\}$ be a set of vectors in $\mathcal{Z}^n$ that are linearly independent over $\mathcal{R}$. Then the set of all integer linear combinations of $\{b_1, b_2, \ldots, b_n\}$ is called an integer lattice. In a formula:*

$$B = \left\{ \sum_{i=1}^{n} a_i \cdot b_i \mid a_i \in \mathcal{Z}, 1 \leq i \leq n \right\} \tag{1}$$

Definition 2. *The **Gram-Schmidt** algorithm transforms a given basis $\{b_1, b_2, \ldots, b_n\}$ into a basis $\{b_1^*, b_2^*, \ldots, b_m^*\}$ which is pairwise orthogonal. The algorithm uses equations*

$$\mu_{i,j} = \frac{\langle b_i, b_j^* \rangle}{\langle b_j^*, b_j^* \rangle} \quad for \quad 1 \leq j < i \leq n \tag{2}$$

where $\mu_{i,j}$ is called a Gram-Schmidt coefficient.

$$b_i^* = b_i - \sum_{j=1}^{i-1} \mu_{i,j} \, b_j^* \tag{3}$$

Definition 3. *A basis* $\{b_1, b_2, \ldots, b_m\}$ *is called LLL reduced if the associated Gram-Schmidt basis* $\{b_1^*, b_2^*, \ldots, b_m^*\}$ *satisfies*

$$|\mu_{i,j}| \leq \frac{1}{2} \quad for \quad 1 \leq j < i \leq m \tag{4}$$

$$\|b_i^*\|^2 \geq \left(\frac{3}{4} - \mu_{i,i-1}^2\right) \|b_{i-1}^*\|^2 \quad for \quad 1 < i \leq m \tag{5}$$

Equation (4), so called *size reduction*, ensures that we obtain a basis in which the vectors are short in length, while equation (5), the so called *Nearly Orthogonal Condition*, guarantees that the obtained vectors are nearly orthogonal. The LLL algorithm works as follows (also in Fig. 2);

1. We examine a fixed column k in which k starts at $k = 2$;
2. If equation (4) does not hold, we need to perform *size reduction* by modifying the basis B;
3. If equation (5) does not hold for column k and $k - 1$ (it means the obtained vectors are non-orthogonal), we have to swap those columns and decrease a value of k by one (unless k is already equal to two). Otherwise, we increase k by one;
4. Once k reaches to m, the algorithm stops.

Since attacks on the subset sum problem using LLL reduction were proposed, there have been several experiments set up to compare the practical performance with the theoretical limits. The first such experiment was published by Radziszowski and Kreher [18] in 1988 to run a performance test of LLL on subset sum problems that have an item size (n) between 26 and 98 with different densities. The experimental result showed that when n grows up to 98, their implementation succeeded at density below 0.3 which is lower than the theoretical value proposed by Lagarias and Odlyzko [11]. Later, LaMacchia [12] set up an empirical test on problem sizes between 26 and 106. The result showed that the original LLL worked well for all problems with $n \leq 26$ and density ≤ 0.6408, but the accuracy degraded quickly when n grows above 50. By running on the improved version, the performance was improved up to $n = 106$ with density 0.3. In the meantime, Schnorr and Euchner [21] proposed a way to speed up the reduction step by using floating point instead of integer arithmetic as in the original LLL, plus adding the deep insertion technique to their scheme. In comparison with

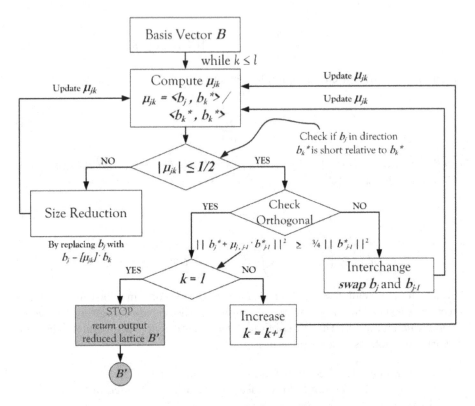

Fig. 2. LLL Lattice Reduction Process

LaMacchia [12], they claimed that their experimental result had higher success rate at the same data range. In this paper, our experiment was set up and tested using the implementation of the Schnorr and Euchner [21] version provided in MAGMA (http://magma.maths.usyd.edu.au).

Anonymity 2.0 – X.509 Extensions Supporting Privacy-Friendly Authentication

Vicente Benjumea[1], Seung G. Choi[2], Javier Lopez[1], and Moti Yung[3]

[1] Computer Science Dept., University of Malaga, Spain
{benjumea,jlm}@lcc.uma.es
[2] Computer Science Dept., Columbia University, USA
sgchoi@cs.columbia.edu
[3] Google & Computer Science Dept., Columbia University, USA
moti@cs.columbia.edu

Abstract. We present a semantic extension to X.509 certificates that allows incorporating new anonymity signature schemes into the X.509 framework. This fact entails advantages to both components. On the one hand, anonymous signature schemes benefit from all the protocols and infrastructure that the X.509 framework provides. On the other hand, the X.509 framework incorporates anonymity as a very interesting new feature. This semantic extension is part of a system that provides user's controlled anonymous authorization under the X.509 framework. Additionally, the proposal directly fits the much active Identity 2.0 effort, where anonymity is a major supplementary feature that increases the self-control of one's identity and privacy which is at the center of the activity.

Keywords: Anonymous authentication, X.509 certificates, group signatures, ring signatures, traceable signatures.

1 Introduction

As the number of remote Internet transactions grows, the amount of personal information that organizations collect also increases. In the near future, the majority of transactions that a user can perform in her daily life will be done remotely via the Internet (e-government, e-bank, e-commerce, e-library, e-services, etc.). This, together with the fact that information systems are able to collect, store and cross reference big amounts of data, implies that the Internet will become the largest surveillance system ever devised.

Anonymity can be seen as a cornerstone in individual privacy protection in environments like the Internet. Recently, new signature schemes oriented towards providing support for anonymity have been designed from a pure cryptographic point of view. These signature schemes focus on anonymity from different point of views with many interesting features. Group signatures [10,1,14], ring signatures [30,14], traceable signatures [24,27,12], are among them. However, though they exhibit very interesting features, they have not been transferred to practical open systems yet, and no one has even studied in what available systems framework they can be well supported.

F. Bao et al. (Eds.): CANS 2007, LNCS 4856, pp. 265–281, 2007.

X.509 public key and attribute certificates [23] conform a standard and secure mean to convey users' identity and authorization information respectively. They are widely used means to convey user's information in open systems. However, they were designed to support identities and anonymity was not considered in their design, let alone the available recent new anonymous signatures.

Motivated by the above two issues, this paper presents a semantic extension to X.509 certificates aimed at incorporating the aforementioned new signature schemes. Compatibility, simplicity yet high level of applicability to many various existing anonymous schemes is at the core of the work.

This semantic extension entails that a standard framework can be applied to new scenarios where anonymity is an issue, featuring the interoperability that the standard provides. On the other hand, it allows adapting the framework to new anonymity requirements with no need to alter the standard. In a sense, its importance is in showing the robustness of the X.509 framework to basic semantical changes in its operating environment and its ability to support credentials in a much wider range than originally intended.

Moreover, we note that this semantic extension can also be applied in a similar way to other frameworks, such as SPKI [15,16] and others.

The present work is part of a broader ongoing work and a system that attempts to use these extended X.509 certificates to create a user centric system where the user is able to access system resources while controlling how and which kind of information is disclosed.

Anonymity is at the core of the system, and users are entitled to anonymously prove that they have enough privileges as for being authorized to perform a given transaction.

This process is ruled by authorization policies specified for each resource. The system fits in the X.509 framework and mixes with existing systems, supporting both identified and anonymous authorization.

In the current Identity 2.0 [21] effort the user is the center of the system, and decides what information to disclose in order to be authorized to perform a remote transaction. Under this approach, the user controls her identity and how it is used, as opposed to Identity 1.0 where service providers hold personal information in order to identify the users and make them accountable for their actions.

Anonymity is perhaps the cornerstone in a user centric point of view, since allows the user to access resources but avoids disclosing user's sensitive information. Therefore, if anonymity is joined with the user controlled disclosure of information, we find that the system fits and is one step beyond the Identity 2.0 effort.

The paper is organized as follows. Section 2 presents some related work and overviews the fundamentals which our work is built on. Then, Sect. 3 describes the main idea behind the proposed extension. Section 4 shows how the above mentioned signature schemes can be integrated into the proposed extension and describes their main properties. Section 5 describes how the X.509 public key certificate can be extended to incorporate this extension in a controlled way and how the extension also applies to X.509 attribute certificates. Section 6 presents some performance results for our implementation of traceable signatures (which is part of the overall broad system design and demonstrates its feasibility). Sect. 7 concludes the paper. Finally, the appendices give the ASN.1 specification of the certificate semantic extension.

2   Background

2.1   Related Work

Anonymity has been largely studied since D. Chaum introduced the problem in [7,8], yielding many privacy aware interactive systems [9,11,25,5,6,34,29]. Some studies have been oriented towards providing support for anonymous authentication in different contexts [32,33,28,3,4], and, as far as we know, only a few of them [28,3,4] have been focussed to some extend on interoperating with standard frameworks, however they are not perfectly integrated and require dedicated protocols to fulfill their aim. Moreover they only provide a fixed flavor for anonymity. In the presented proposal, many different flavors of anonymity are gently introduced into X.509 certificates, which are then transparently supported by the underlying infrastructure, with no need of dedicated extra protocols. It also provides a suitable way to incorporate new forthcoming signature schemes for anonymity into the standard framework.

2.2   X.509 Certificates

X.509 public key certificates (PKC) [22,20] have been designed to bind a public key to a subject, under the consideration that such a subject is the only one that knows the associated private key (Fig. 1). In these certificates, the certification authority, i.e. the entity that certifies the binding, is equally important. Any entity using the public key certificate will trust the binding of the subject and the public key if it trusts the entity that issued the certificate. The relationship between the subject and the public key holds as long as the associated private key is known only to the entity that the certificate subject field refers to.

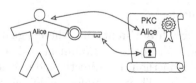

Fig. 1. Relationship between user and public key certificate

X.509 public key certificates have been proved as a very useful tool for providing authentication in many different contexts, such as electronic mail, the World Wide Web, user authentication and IPsec. Particularly, the TLS [13] (and

SSL [19]) transport layer protocol uses X.509 public key certificates to provide an authenticated secure communication channel to application layers.

X.509 attribute certificates (ATC) [23,17] bind a holder with a set of attributes, and at the same time can be linked with a X.509 public key certificate (Fig. 2). The attribute authority is the entity that certifies such bindings. The attributes can be used for authorization purposes in many different ways, providing a flexible authorization approach. The holder of the attribute certificate will be authenticated by means of the linked public key certificate to enjoy the privileges associated with the specified attribute. Here again, the authorization verifier needs to trust the certificates issuers in order to trust the bindings that they state.

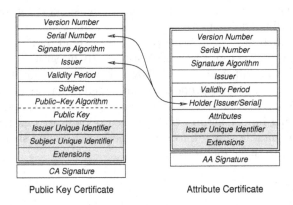

Fig. 2. Relationship between public key and attribute certificates

X.509 certificates are valid for a limited period of time that is specified in the certificates. However, under certain circumstances, the binding can be revoked, e.g. if the private key is compromised, or if the specified attribute no longer relates with the holder. If a certificate is revoked, the fact is made public by means of a *certificate revocation list* (CRL). Additionally, OCSP [26] provides an interactive way to check if a given certificate has been revoked.

2.3   Digital Signatures

Signature Schemes for Identification. These signature schemes are those ones that, when used in an adequate environment such as the X.509 framework, provide an authentication method that directly and uniquely identifies the entity that is being authenticated. They are unforgeable and provide authentication and non-repudiation features. In these schemes, one public key corresponds to a unique private key, and an adequate environment provides a correlation between the public key and the identity . Such correlation is based on the fact that only the one who knows the private key is the entity that performs the authentication. Examples of these kind of signature schemes can be DSA [18], RSA [31], and others.

Signature Schemes for Anonymity. We mean here those ones that allow the breaking of the correlation between a public key and the identity of the entity that owns an associated private key. With the work of D. Chaum and E. van Heyst [10], a new kind of signature schemes have been developed, where many different private keys correspond with one public key in a *one to many* relationship, and even in some schemes different private keys correspond with different public keys in a *many to many* relationship. These signature schemes allow to focus the anonymity from different point of views with many interesting features.

In *group signatures* [10,1], a group public key defines a group. A designated *group manager*, who owns the group private key, is responsible for joining new members. Whenever a new member is added, she gets her own private membership key that allows to sign on behalf of the group. The signature issued can be verified with the group public key and it is neither possible to distinguish which member of the group issued the signature, nor even to link the signature with any other one issued by any member. However, the group manager has the special capability to identify which member issued a given signature, providing in this way with *reversible anonymity* in the sense that if a member abuses of her anonymity, the group manager can *open* the signature and disclose the identity of its issuer.

In *ring signatures* [30,14], a ring is made up of the public keys of the entities that compose the ring. These entities do not need to be aware of the existence of the ring, since their public keys are freely available. Any entity in a ring is able to produce a signature that can be verified with the ring public key, but no one is able to distinguish which entity issued the signature, or even to link it with any other signature produced by any entity in the ring. They offer similar features as group signatures, but ring signatures can not be *opened* to disclose the identity of its issuer. Thus, they provide *irreversible anonymity*.

Traceable signature schemes [24,27,12] are group signature schemes with additional tracing capabilities, what makes them very suitable for real-world applications. In addition to group signature properties such as indistinguishability, unlinkability, and the ability of the group manager to open a signature issued by any member of the group, a user is able to claim that a given signature has been issued by herself. Additionally, it is possible, with the help of the group manager that provides a member trapdoor, to identify which signatures within a set were issued by a given member with no other disclosure of information. These additional capabilities make this scheme very suitable for real world applications, since the tracing capability is necessary in many real situations. Some performance results are described in section 6.

3   Extending the Semantic of X.509 Certificates

Though not explicitly stated, X.509 public key certificates were originally designed for public key algorithms where one public key corresponds with one private key and where the public key is bound to the identity of that one who knows the corresponding private key.

With the advent of new signature schemes, such as group signatures, ring signatures, traceable signatures and others, the aforementioned semantic becomes too restrictive to allow the integration of these signature schemes with X.509 public key certificates, thus avoiding the X.509 framework to enjoy the numerous advantages that the new schemes offer.

3.1   Semantic Extension

While keeping the same structure, we can extend the semantic of X.509 certificates to additionally allow the use, as public key algorithms, of aforementioned signature schemes in those environments where their use could be appropriate.

Because in some of the new signature schemes, one public key can correspond with several different private keys (each one owned by different entities), we can define a *X.509 public key certificate with extended semantic* as a X.509 public key certificate where *the public key is not bound to a single entity but it is bound to a concept*. In the traditional semantic, the concept relates to a single entity, such as a system or a person, that owns the unique private key corresponding with the public key in the certificate (and the public key algorithm is a one-to-one scheme). However, in the extended semantic, the concept can be a more abstract definition where all entities that own a private key that can be verified with the certificate public key share the concept stated in the certificate. Each private key must be unforgeable, unique and not shared with other entities. Note that the extended semantic is a superset of the traditional one. In other words, an extended X.509 public key certificate binds a public key with a concept and, therefore, binds the concept with every entity that owns a private key that is publicly verifiable with the public key in the certificate (Fig. 3), which also specifies the public key algorithm to be used for such verification.

This extended semantic entails the use of standard extension fields defined for that purpose in the X.509 specification. Additionally, by means of these standard extension fields it is possible to control and restrict the usage of X.509 public key certificates in those scenarios where this is required (Sect. 5).

This broader semantic for public key certificates directly affects to X.509 attribute certificates. Since an attribute certificate binds a set of attributes with

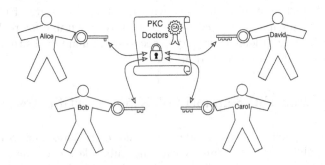

Fig. 3. X.509 public key certificate with extended semantic

a public key certificate, the represented concept in the public key certificate and related entities are able to enjoy the privileges associated with the bound attributes.

3.2 Entity Authentication – Identification and Anonymous Authentication

Up to now, *entity authentication* was usually considered equivalent to *identification*. However, in the context of this extended semantic, identification is a special kind of entity authentication where the concept in the public key certificate identifies a single entity. Entity authentication has now a broader semantic, since now the entity being authenticated by means of a public key certificate might not be directly related with his real identity, as in the case of these new signature schemes. Therefore, we can define the concept of *anonymous authentication* as a special kind of entity authentication where an anonymous entity becomes authenticated as a valid subject of the concept stated in the certificate. This authentication can be performed as usual by proving knowledge of a private key verifiable with the public key in the certificate.

4 Integrating New Signature Schemes into Extended X.509 Public Key Certificates

This section overviews how the new signature schemes can be added to the X.509 public key certificates. Though we only overview group, ring and traceable signature schemes, the semantic extension is not only restricted to those ones, but it is also open to others, even future ones. A summary of the properties of the aforementioned signature schemes is depicted in table. 1.

Table 1. Properties of some signature schemes

	Anon	One2Many	Unlink	Reversible	Traceable	MRevoc	SRevoc	Fair	NRep	MultiG	DShar
Ring sign.	•	•	•		•						
Group sign.	•	•	•	•						•	
Traceable sign.	•	•	•	•	•	•	•				

4.1 Ring Signatures

A ring can be made public and available by issuing a public key certificate with the ring public key being linked to the concept that such a ring represents. As rings do not need managers, a certification authority can create the ring public key from the sequence of the public keys of the members.[1] Of course it is up to the certification authority to decide in advance which members compose the ring. Members of the ring are able to be authenticated as holding such certificate

---

[1] In [30] the ring public key is the sequence of the public keys of the members, however in [14] the ring public key is created from the public keys of the members.

and to enjoy the associated privileges. In this case, the ring signature does not need to convey the public keys of the members of the ring, as specified in [30], since such information is held in the ring public key certificate. In [30] the size of both, the ring public key as well as the ring signature, are proportional to the number of members that compose the ring, however in [14] the size of the ring public key is proportional to the number of members, but the size of the signature is constant.

When a member of a public ring is authenticated by using her private key, her real identity becomes concealed. Thus, the member authentication is unlinkable and anonymous among the set of members of the ring. This scheme provides *irreversible anonymity* to the X.509 framework since no entity is able to correlate the authentication (a ring signature) with the real identity of the involved user. The ring public key certificate may be revoked as any other certificate, yielding in this way with the revocation of the whole ring and all its members. The certification authority can add and remove members to/from a concept represented by a ring by means of revoking the ring public key certificate and re-issuing a new one with the public keys of the members that now compose the concept represented by the ring. Note that users do not need to be aware of this fact except for using a fresh certificate that has not been revoked. However, the scheme seems more suitable for static rings with occasional modifications during its lifetime.

4.2   Group Signatures and Traceable Signatures

As with ring signatures, a public key certificate can define a group by binding the group public key to the concept that the group represents. The certification authority must verify that the group manager is suitable to manage such a public group and that the policy for joining new members to the group is suitable with respect to the aim of the certificate. New members can be joined to the group at any time, and as result they get their private membership keys. These members can be authenticated as holders of the group public key certificate and are able to enjoy its associated privileges. In these schemes, the size of both, the group public key and signatures, are constant.

When a member of a public group is authenticated by means of her private membership key, her real identity becomes concealed. Thus, the member authentication is unlinkable and anonymous among the set of members of the group. However, under certain circumstances, the group manager may consent to open a given authentication (a signature) and to disclose the real identity of the user involved. Additionally, as traceable signatures offer some extra features, the group manager can disclose a trapdoor for a given member, and some designated entities are able to identify, from within a set of anonymous authentications, which ones were performed by such member of the group. Moreover, a member of the group is able to claim that a given anonymous authentication was performed by herself.

The whole group can be revoked by revoking the public key certificate. Additionally, in case of traceable signatures, by means of the member trapdoor, it is possible to revoke individual members of a traceable group. There should be a trusted entity that holds a record with the private trapdoors of revoked members. Whenever a member is authenticated, in addition to check if the whole group has been revoked, the signature issued for authentication is sent to this trusted entity to be checked against the list of revoked member trapdoors.

These signature schemes provide *reversible anonymity* and *reversible, traceable and revocable anonymity* to the X.509 framework respectively.

5   The X.509 Public Key Certificate Extension

System security, authentication and authorization protocols make use of X.509 public key and attribute certificates to convey authentication and authorization information. Though the X.509 semantic extension explained in Sect. 3 uses the standard fields to convey the main information (issuer, subject, public key algorithm and public key), it also entails (for a proper usage), new semantic information to be added to the extension fields of the X.509 public key certificate (see appendix A for the specification in ASN.1).

The extensions field allows addition of new fields to the certificate without modification to the definition. An extension field consists of an extension identifier, a criticality flag, and an encoding of a data value of a type associated with the identified extension. If an extension is marked as *critical*, then any processing entity that does not recognize the extension will reject the certificate. On the contrary, if an extension is marked as *non–critical*, then any processing entity that does not recognize the extension will simply ignore it.

The X.509 standard has already defined some extension fields, though many others may be added. Among the extension fields defined by the standard, we highlight: *key usage* indicates the purpose of the key contained in the certificate; *certificate policies* indicates the policy under which the certificate has been issued and the purposes for which the certificate may be used; and *authority information access* indicates how to access certificate information and services for the issuer of the certificate.

Our proposed semantic extension entails the use of aforementioned extension fields, and define a new extension field that states the features of certificates with extended semantic.

The main important contribution to public key certificates is the support of the new signature schemes as public key algorithms (new OIDs should identify them). Then, new semantic information should be added to standard fields:

– A new extension field, *certificateFeatures*, should be added to X.509 public key certificates, stating some features of the certificate. These features depend on the public key algorithm properties and on the certificate issuing method. This new extension field must be marked as *critical* if present. It is a bit string defining flags for different properties. The following flags should be considered, though new flags can be added as required by other signature schemes.

Extended: The certificate is defined with extended semantic. This flag should be activated if any of the following flags is activated.

One2Many: The public key in the certificate corresponds to many different private keys.

Anonymous: There is no a direct way to know the identity of the entity being authenticated with the certificate.

Unlinkable: It is not possible to link different signatures as being performed by the same entity.

Reversible: There is an indirect way to know the identity of the entity being authenticated with the certificate.

Traceable: It is indirectly possible to identify, within a set, which signatures were issued by a given entity.

MemberRevocable: It is possible to revoke a specific entity, even if the public key algorithm is a *one2many* scheme.

AuthRevocable: If it is possible to revoke the entity that was involved in a given authentication process, even if the public key algorithm is a *one2many* scheme.

Fairness: There exists a *trusted third party* that guarantees that special disclosure actions are performed when it is appropriate to do so.

MultiGroup: There exists a mechanism that guarantees that the same real user actually belongs to several groups.

DeterSharing: There exists a mechanism that dissuades anonymous users from sharing the certificate private key.

OneLevelAnon: The identity of the user can be disclosed in just one anonymity backtracking, i.e. if the policy requires an identified user to be joined to the group.

Note that these properties are somehow inherited from the public key algorithm, however they depend on the way they are managed by the environment. For example, if the public key algorithm is a group signature scheme which provides reversibility, and the member joined the group either being identified or by means of a reversible anonymous authentication, then the certificate property should specify that the anonymity is reversible. However, if it was allowed that the member joined the group by using a irreversible authentication, then the certificate property should reflect that the anonymity is irreversible.

- The subject field of the certificate should contain the concept description, which in the case of group signatures or ring signatures specifies either the ring or group identification, which is composed by either the ring or group name and the identification (distinguished name) of the ring or group manager. New OIDs for both *ring name* and *group name* have to be added as attribute type to distinguished names.

- In the key usage extension field the *digitalSignature* flag should be asserted. In this case, such flag state that entity authentication is allowed. If the user joined the group by means of a non-repudiable authentication and the certificate public key algorithm provides non-repudiation, then the *nonRepudiation* flag should also be asserted because it is possible, under certain

circumstances, to identify the member that issued a given signature and that the member can not deny such action.
- The certificate policies extension field indicates the policy under which the certificate has been issued, its meaning, the conditions required to create the ring, or to join the group, the conditions required to be threw out of the group, and the conditions under which a member's identity would be disclosed, etc.
- Regarding public key certificate revocation, the same support as for normal public key certificates is required, that is, the *CRL distribution points* extension can be used. Additionally, if OCSP is used as a mean to access revocation information, then the *authority information access* extension should be used.
- If it is possible to revoke individual members of a given group, this is done by storing in a private database the group public key certificate together with a list containing the member trapdoors for every member that has been revoked from the group. By using an OCSP-like protocol, the client queries if a given member has been revoked (providing the group and signature used for authentication). The identification of this member revocation manager is specified in the *authority information access* extension field. A new accessMethod OID should be defined for this case.
- If some fairness authorities guarantee that the disclosure of restricted information is performed when it is appropriate to do so, then the identification of these entities are specified in the *authority information access* extension field. A new accessMethod OID should be defined for this case.

Note that this semantic extension provides new features to applications willing to use them, however it is harmless to unaware applications since public key certificates with unrecognized critical extensions are kindly rejected. Additionally, if an application does not support the public key algorithm then it also rejects the certificate.

5.1 Attribute Certificates

When issuing an attribute certificate to be bound to a public key certificate with extended semantic, it means that any entity able to be authenticated with such a public key certificate can enjoy the specified privilege. Therefore, the policy to get an attribute certificate must be tightly linked with the policy required to join the associated group or ring.

If unlinkability is a property exhibited by a public key certificate, then all entities being authenticated with such a PKC must share the same certificate and the same attribute certificates bound to it. That is, for a given attribute and public key certificate, the same certificates are shared among all the entities. The figure 4 shows how several entities, that can be authenticated with a public key certificate, all share the same attribute certificates.

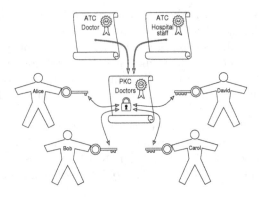

Fig. 4. Extended X.509 public key and attribute certificates

6   Traceable Signatures Performance Results

This section briefly shows some statistical results for the *traceable signature scheme*, but they can also be taken as a reference point for group signatures and alike ones. However, there is still room for optimization, since the implementation is based on [24], where some other proposals, such as [27,12] based on *bilinear pairings*, claim better efficiency.

Table 2 shows performance statistics for the basic *traceable signature* primitives. They are taken in an off-line environment where the host machine was an Intel Pentium Centrino running at 2.00GHz the Debian GNU/Linux Operating System and Sun's J2SDK 1.4.2 as Java runtime. The performance results, in milliseconds, show the arithmetic mean after several executions. A security parameter of 1024 bits was defined for Traceable Signatures and SHA-1 has been used as secure hash function.

Note that group creation and group joining depend on the search of suitable random primes, therefore their timings may vary. Group creation is an expensive operation, but it is usually performed off-line, so its cost has minor influence in system performance. The joining procedure may be speeded up by using precomputed values for suitable random primes at group manager side. The reveal primitive just take a stored value and does not need any extra computation.

Table 2. Traceable Signature Primitives

	millisec
Create-Group	23680.2
Join-to-Group	1764.2
Sign	460.6
Verify	548.1
Open	55.8
Reveal	0.0
Trace	23.4
Claim	35.4
VerifyClaim	39.3

7   Conclusions

A new semantic extension have been proposed for X.509 certificates which provides enhanced features to both X.509 public key and attribute certificates. It has been explained how new signature schemes can be incorporated into the X.509 certificates with new extended semantic. In this way, the X.509 framework can benefit their very interesting features. As result, new anonymity features can to be added to the X.509 framework.

This semantic extension entails a new concept for entity authentication: identification and anonymous authentication. One very important advantage that this extended semantic provides is the fact that both identification and anonymous authentication coexist under a common entity authentication and, where allowed, the same protocols, data structures, etc. are valid for both. That is, there is no need to separate both authentication modes, a simple policy may discriminate between them if discrimination is required, or both can be accepted under the common entity authentication. This simple fact simplifies very much architecture and system design.

The presented work is part of a system that provides support for a user centric authorization model, where identified as well as anonymous authorization are supported. The system fits into the X.509 framework and into the Identity 2.0 initiative, being the user the core of the system. Additionally, anonymity increases the strength of the user in this approach.

Finally, some performance results for a prototype of a traceable signature scheme have been presented, which can be taken as a reference point for group signatures and derived ones, and in some way show their feasibility.

7.1   Future Work

Though ring, group and traceable signatures provide very interesting properties with respect to anonymity, there are some real world scenarios where they are not completely suitable for supporting anonymity. These signature schemes seem suitable to support anonymity in real world applications, since in these kind of scenarios, it is usually covenient that the user is accountable for her actions, and it is also very interesting the capability to trace anonymous transactions performed by a given user under suspicion. However, some real world scenarios motivate us for searching for new digital signatures.

(i) Though the group manager may be trusted with respect to joining new members to the group, in some scenarios, the group manager is not usually trusted with respect to safeguard the anonymity of the members, since in many cases the group manager is an interested party. Therefore it is necessary to split the duties of joining new members on the one hand, and disclosing sensitive information such as open/reveal/trace on the other hand. This capability of breaking anonymity should be as distributed as possible.

(ii) Additionally, it is common to prove that a user simultaneously belongs to several groups in order to be authorized to carry out some transaction. Then it is interesting to incorporate multi–group [2] features that enable the user to prove that the same real user does indeed simultaneously belongs to the required groups. This feature guarantees the verification entity that the proof has not been collected from different anonymous users.

(iii) Public key authentication systems are based on the fact that private keys are only known by just one entity, however an anonymous scenario may increase the temptation to share the private keys that allow to prove membership to groups, a case that would subvert the basis on which the whole system security relies. Therefore, it is also desirable to incorporate some mechanisms to dissuade users from sharing her private keys.

A signature scheme that enjoys all the aforementioned features, as well as those ones from group and traceable signatures would be very convenient for supporting a wide range of anonymous transactions in real world open systems.

References

1. Ateniese, G., Camenish, J., Joye, M., Tsudik, G.: A practical and provably secure coalition-resistant group signature scheme. In: Bellare, M. (ed.) CRYPTO 2000. LNCS, vol. 1880, pp. 255–270. Springer, Heidelberg (2000)
2. Ateniese, G., Tsudik, G.: Some open issues and new directions in group signatures. In: Franklin, M.K. (ed.) FC 1999. LNCS, vol. 1648, pp. 196–211. Springer, Heidelberg (1999)
3. Benjumea, V., Lopez, J., Montenegro, J.A., Troya, J.M.: A first approach to provide anonymity in attribute certificates. In: Bao, F., Deng, R., Zhou, J. (eds.) PKC 2004. LNCS, vol. 2947, pp. 402–415. Springer, Heidelberg (2004)
4. Benjumea, V., Lopez, J., Troya, J.M.: Anonymous attribute certificates based on traceable signatures. Internet Research 16(2), 120–139 (2006)
5. Brands, S.A.: Rethinking Public Key Infrastructures and Digital Certificates Building in Privacy, The MIT Press, Cambridge (August 2000)
6. Camenisch, J., Lysyanskaya, A.: Efficient non-transferable anonymous multi-show credential system with optional anonymity revocation. In: Pfitzmann, B. (ed.) EUROCRYPT 2001. LNCS, vol. 2045, pp. 93–118. Springer, Heidelberg (2001)
7. Chaum, D.: Blind signatures for untraceable payments. In: Chaum, D., Rivest, R., Sherman, A. (eds.) CRYPTO 1982: Advances in Cryptology, pp. 199–203. Plenum Press, Santa Barbara, CA (August 1983)
8. Chaum, D.: Security without identification: Transaction systems to make big brother obsolete. Communications of the ACM 28(10), 1030–1044 (1985)
9. Chaum, D., Evertse, J.H.: A secure and privacy-protecting protocol for transmitting personal information between organizations. In: Odlyzko, A.M. (ed.) CRYPTO 1986. LNCS, vol. 263, pp. 118–170. Springer, Heidelberg (1987)
10. Chaum, D., van Heyst, E.: Group signatures. In: Davies, D.W. (ed.) EUROCRYPT 1991. LNCS, vol. 547, pp. 257–265. Springer, Heidelberg (1991)
11. Chen, L.: Access with pseudonyms. In: Dawson, E.P., Golić, J.D. (eds.) Cryptography: Policy and Algorithms. LNCS, vol. 1029, pp. 232–243. Springer, Heidelberg (1996)
12. Choi, S.G., Park, K., Yung, M.: Short traceable signatures based on bilinear pairings. In: Yoshiura, H., Sakurai, K., Rannenberg, K., Murayama, Y., Kawamura, S. (eds.) IWSEC 2006. LNCS, vol. 4266, pp. 88–103. Springer, Heidelberg (2006)
13. Dierks, T., Rescorla, E.: RFC-4346. The Transport Layer Security (TLS) Protocol. The Internet Society (April 2006)

14. Dodis, Y., Kiayias, A., Nicolosi, A., Shoup, V.: Anonymous identification in Ad Hoc groups. In: Cachin, C., Camenisch, J.L. (eds.) EUROCRYPT 2004. LNCS, vol. 3027, pp. 609–626. Springer, Heidelberg (2004)
15. Ellison, C.: RFC-2692. SPKI requirements. IETF SPKI Working Group (September 1999)
16. Ellison, C., Frantz, B., Lampson, B., Rivest, R., Thomas, B., Ylonen, T.: RFC-2693. SPKI certificate theory. IETF SPKI Working Group (September 1999)
17. Farrel, S., Housley, R.: RFC-3281. An Internet Attribute Certificate Profile for Authorization. The Internet Society (April 2002)
18. FIPS 186. Digital Signature Standard. U.S. Department of Commerce/N.I.S.T., National Technical Information Service, Springfield, Virginia (1994)
19. Freier, A., Karlton, P., Kocher, P.: The SSL Protocol. Netscape (November 1996)
20. Housley, R., Polk, W., Ford, W., Solo, D.: RFC-3280. Internet X.509 Public Key Infrastructure Certificate and Certificate Revocation List (CRL) Profile. The Internet Society (April 2002)
21. Identity 2.0, http://www.identity20.com/
22. ITU-T Recommendation X.509. Information Technology - Open systems interconnection - The Directory: Authentication Framework (June 1997)
23. ITU-T Recommendation X.509. Information Technology - Open systems interconnection - The Directory: Public-key and attribute certificate frameworks (March 2000)
24. Kiayias, A., Tsiounis, Y., Yung, M.: Traceable signatures. In: Cachin, C., Camenisch, J.L. (eds.) EUROCRYPT 2004. LNCS, vol. 3027, pp. 571–589. Springer, Heidelberg (2004)
25. Lysyanskaya, A., Rivest, R., Sahai, A., Wolf, S.: Pseudonym systems. In: Heys, H.M., Adams, C.M. (eds.) SAC 1999. LNCS, vol. 1758, Springer, Heidelberg (2000)
26. Myers, M., Ankney, R., Malpani, A., Galperin, S., Adams, C.: RFC-2560. X.509 Internet Public Key Infrastructure Online Certificate Status Protocol - OCSP. The Internet Society (June 1999)
27. Nguyen, L., Safavi-Naini, R.: Efficient and provably secure trapdoor-free group signature schemes from bilinear pairings. In: Lee, P.J. (ed.) ASIACRYPT 2004. LNCS, vol. 3329, pp. 372–386. Springer, Heidelberg (2004)
28. Persiano, P., Visconti, I.: A secure and private system for subscription-based remote services. ACM Trans. on Information and System Security 6(4), 472–500 (2003)
29. Persiano, P., Visconti, I.: An efficient and usable multi-show non-transferable anonymous credential system. In: Juels, A. (ed.) FC 2004. LNCS, vol. 3110, pp. 196–211. Springer, Heidelberg (2004)
30. Rivest, R., Shamir, A., Tauman, Y.: How to leak a secret. In: Boyd, C. (ed.) ASIACRYPT 2001. LNCS, vol. 2248, pp. 552–565. Springer, Heidelberg (2001)
31. Rivest, R.L., Shamir, A., Adleman, L.: A method for obtaining digital signatures and public key cryptosystems. Communications of the ACM 21(2), 120–126 (1978)
32. Schechter, S., Parnell, T., Hartemink, A.: Anonymous authentication of membership in dynamic groups. In: Franklin, M.K. (ed.) FC 1999. LNCS, vol. 1648, pp. 184–195. Springer, Heidelberg (1999)
33. Stubblebine, S.G., Syverson, P.F., Goldschlag, D.M.: Unlinkable serial transactions: Protocols and applications. ACM Trans. on Information and System Security 2(4), 354–389 (1999)
34. Verheul, E.R.: Self-blindable credential certificates from the weil pairing. In: Boyd, C. (ed.) ASIACRYPT 2001. LNCS, vol. 2248, pp. 533–551. Springer, Heidelberg (2001)

A   ASN.1 Specification of Anonymity Extensions for X.509v3 Certificates

This appendix describes the ASN.1 specification of the proposed extensions for X.509v3 certificates. The following OIDs and structures should be incorporated to the extensions of X.509v3 certificates. The new OIDs are members of the anonymity extensions arc, `id-ae`[2], that is under the standard private extensions arc `id-pe`.

```
id-ae    OBJECT IDENTIFIER ::= { id-pe 32 }
```

New OIDs should be defined for ring, group and traceable signature schemes.

The subject field in standard X509v3 certificates is a sequence of distinguished names, which is a set of attribute type and value pairs. New OIDs are defined to identify ring, group, traceable–group and fair–traceable–group names for attribute types:

```
id-ae-at    OBJECT IDENTIFIER ::= { id-ae 2 }

id-ae-at-ringName     AttributeType ::= { id-ae-at 1 }
id-ae-at-groupName    AttributeType ::= { id-ae-at 2 }
id-ae-at-tGroupName   AttributeType ::= { id-ae-at 3 }
```

and the syntax for the respective values:

```
RingName      ::= X520name
GroupName     ::= X520name
TGroupName    ::= X520name
```

The *certificateFeatures* extension MUST be marked critical, with the following OID and value syntax:

```
id-ae-ef    OBJECT IDENTIFIER ::= { id-ae 3 }

id-ae-ef-certificateFeatures  OBJECT IDENTIFIER ::= { id-ae-ef 1 }

CertificateFeatures ::= BIT STRING {
      extended        (0),
      one2Many        (1),
      anonymous       (2),
      unlinkable      (3),
      reversible      (4),
      traceable       (5),
      memberRevocable (6),
      authRevocable   (7),
```

---

[2] Note that the number of this arc is a suggestion, and should be defined to avoid conflicts.

```
fairness        (8),
multiGroup      (9),
deterSharing    (10),
oneLevelAnon    (11)
}
```

The authority information access extension in standard X509v3 certificates is defined as a sequence of access description, which is composed of an access method identifier and access location that specifies the URI for the corresponding method. The new OIDs for the new *member revocation access* and *fairness authorities* access methods are as follows:

```
id-ae-aia    OBJECT IDENTIFIER ::= { id-ae 4 }

id-ae-aia-am    OBJECT IDENTIFIER ::= { is-ae-aia 1 }

id-ae-aia-am-memberRevAccess       OBJECT IDENTIFIER ::= { is-ae-aia-am 1 }
id-ae-aia-am-fairnessAuthority     OBJECT IDENTIFIER ::= { is-ae-aia-am 2 }
```

Author Index

Lecture Notes in Computer Science

Sublibrary 4: Security and Cryptology

Vol. 4249: L. Goubin, M. Matsui (Eds.), Cryptographic Hardware and Embedded Systems - CHES 2006. XII, 462 pages. 2006.

Vol. 4237: H. Leitold, E.P. Markatos (Eds.), Communications and Multimedia Security. XII, 253 pages. 2006.

Vol. 4236: L. Breveglieri, I. Koren, D. Naccache, J.-P. Seifert (Eds.), Fault Diagnosis and Tolerance in Cryptography. XIII, 253 pages. 2006.

Vol. 4219: D. Zamboni, C. Krügel (Eds.), Recent Advances in Intrusion Detection. XII, 331 pages. 2006.

Vol. 4189: D. Gollmann, J. Meier, A. Sabelfeld (Eds.), Computer Security – ESORICS 2006. XI, 548 pages. 2006.

Vol. 4176: S.K. Katsikas, J. López, M. Backes, S. Gritzalis, B. Preneel (Eds.), Information Security. XIV, 548 pages. 2006.

Vol. 4117: C. Dwork (Ed.), Advances in Cryptology - CRYPTO 2006. XIII, 621 pages. 2006.

Vol. 4116: R. De Prisco, M. Yung (Eds.), Security and Cryptography for Networks. XI, 366 pages. 2006.

Vol. 4107: G. Di Crescenzo, A. Rubin (Eds.), Financial Cryptography and Data Security. XI, 327 pages. 2006.

Vol. 4083: S. Fischer-Hübner, S. Furnell, C. Lambrinoudakis (Eds.), Trust and Privacy in Digital Business. XIII, 243 pages. 2006.

Vol. 4064: R. Büschkes, P. Laskov (Eds.), Detection of Intrusions and Malware & Vulnerability Assessment. X, 195 pages. 2006.

Vol. 4058: L.M. Batten, R. Safavi-Naini (Eds.), Information Security and Privacy. XII, 446 pages. 2006.

Vol. 4047: M.J.B. Robshaw (Ed.), Fast Software Encryption. XI, 434 pages. 2006.

Vol. 4043: A.S. Atzeni, A. Lioy (Eds.), Public Key Infrastructure. XI, 261 pages. 2006.

Vol. 4004: S. Vaudenay (Ed.), Advances in Cryptology - EUROCRYPT 2006. XIV, 613 pages. 2006.

Vol. 3995: G. Müller (Ed.), Emerging Trends in Information and Communication Security. XX, 524 pages. 2006.

Vol. 3989: J. Zhou, M. Yung, F. Bao (Eds.), Applied Cryptography and Network Security. XIV, 488 pages. 2006.

Vol. 3969: Ø. Ytrehus (Ed.), Coding and Cryptography. XI, 443 pages. 2006.

Vol. 3958: M. Yung, Y. Dodis, A. Kiayias, T.G. Malkin (Eds.), Public Key Cryptography - PKC 2006. XIV, 543 pages. 2006.

Vol. 3957: B. Christianson, B. Crispo, J.A. Malcolm, M. Roe (Eds.), Security Protocols. IX, 325 pages. 2006.

Vol. 3956: G. Barthe, B. Grégoire, M. Huisman, J.-L. Lanet (Eds.), Construction and Analysis of Safe, Secure, and Interoperable Smart Devices. IX, 175 pages. 2006.

Vol. 3935: D.H. Won, S. Kim (Eds.), Information Security and Cryptology - ICISC 2005. XIV, 458 pages. 2006.

Vol. 3934: J.A. Clark, R.F. Paige, F.A.C. Polack, P.J. Brooke (Eds.), Security in Pervasive Computing. X, 243 pages. 2006.

Vol. 3928: J. Domingo-Ferrer, J. Posegga, D. Schreckling (Eds.), Smart Card Research and Advanced Applications. XI, 359 pages. 2006.

Vol. 3919: R. Safavi-Naini, M. Yung (Eds.), Digital Rights Management. XI, 357 pages. 2006.

Vol. 3903: K. Chen, R. Deng, X. Lai, J. Zhou (Eds.), Information Security Practice and Experience. XIV, 392 pages. 2006.

Vol. 3897: B. Preneel, S. Tavares (Eds.), Selected Areas in Cryptography. XI, 371 pages. 2006.

Vol. 3876: S. Halevi, T. Rabin (Eds.), Theory of Cryptography. XI, 617 pages. 2006.

Vol. 3866: T. Dimitrakos, F. Martinelli, P.Y.A. Ryan, S. Schneider (Eds.), Formal Aspects in Security and Trust. X, 259 pages. 2006.

Vol. 3860: D. Pointcheval (Ed.), Topics in Cryptology – CT-RSA 2006. XI, 365 pages. 2006.

Vol. 3858: A. Valdes, D. Zamboni (Eds.), Recent Advances in Intrusion Detection. X, 351 pages. 2006.

Vol. 3856: G. Danezis, D. Martin (Eds.), Privacy Enhancing Technologies. VIII, 273 pages. 2006.

Vol. 3786: J.-S. Song, T. Kwon, M. Yung (Eds.), Information Security Applications. XI, 378 pages. 2006.

Vol. 3108: H. Wang, J. Pieprzyk, V. Varadharajan (Eds.), Information Security and Privacy. XII, 494 pages. 2004.

Vol. 2951: M. Naor (Ed.), Theory of Cryptography. XI, 523 pages. 2004.

Vol. 2742: R.N. Wright (Ed.), Financial Cryptography. VIII, 321 pages. 2003.